"A Light of Guidance"

"To make a contribution to the welfare of mankind through an invention is certainly a commendable deed. However, to teach the next generation about how to patent and from an invention is an even greater accomplishment. The author of this book, Bob DeMatteis, is a brilliant inventor. His achievement of making this knowledge available to the public deserves recognition. It will shine a light of guidance on all of them, so that they too can contribute to the future welfare of mankind."

Yujiro Yamamoto, PhD
Internationally renowned inventor
Creator of the cordless telephone, telephone answering machines,
and holder of more than 45 patents.

"A Must Read"

"The information in this book is rock solid and the best foundation that an inventor can get anywhere in one book. It's absolutely a must read for inventors, innovators or anyone in the intellectual property field. *From Patent to Profit* is destined to become the handbook and bible for inventors."

Stephen Gnass
Founder of the Invention Convention™
and chairman of the NCIO

"Knows How To Teach!"

"*From Patent to Profit* is a book written by a successful inventor who not only knows how to invent and take products to market, but also knows how to teach!"

George Margolin
Inventor and nationally known inventor advocate
Holder of 25+ patents

from
Patent
to
Profit

Secrets & Strategies For The Successful Inventor

Bob DeMatteis

Best Wishes,
Bob DMatteis

A PERIGEE BOOK

Every reasonable effort has been made to provide reliable information and data, but the authors, editors, and publisher do not assume responsibility for the validity of any or all materials contained herein or the consequences of their use. The authors are inventors and not attorneys, and the content of this book is not to be considered legal advice.
If you require legal advice, seek the services of an attorney.

A Perigee Book
Published by The Berkley Publishing Group
A division of Penguin Putnam Inc.
375 Hudson Street
New York, New York 10014

Copyright © 1997, 1998 Inventions, Patents & Trademarks Co.

Cover design by Doug Brooks and Oscar Maldonado

All rights reserved. This book, or parts thereof,
may not be reproduced in any form without permission.

Avery edition: August 1999
First Perigee edition: July 2001
Perigee ISBN: 0-399-52738-9

Published simultaneously in Canada.

Visit our website at www.penguinputnam.com

The Library of Congress has catalogued the Avery edition as follows:

DeMatteis, Bob.
From patent to profit / Bob DeMatteis.—1st ed.
p.   cm.
Includes index.
ISBN: 0-89529-879-1

1. Inventions. 2. Patents. 3. New products.
I. Title.

T339.D46 1999   608.773
QBI99-789

Printed in the United States of America

10 9 8 7 6 5 4 3 2 1

CONTENTS

4. INVENTING AND PROBLEM SOLVING, 70

PART TWO
PATENTING

5. ALL ABOUT PATENTS, 79

6. YOUR PATENTING STRATEGY, 103

This book is dedicated to my most favorite invention …
my 5-year-old daughter, Lindsey Ellen …
who is also an inventor!

ACKNOWLEDGMENTS

I would like to thank the numerous people who have helped me during the writing of this book. My publisher, Rudy Shur, has made it all possible with his invaluable insights into the organization and structure of the book. I am also grateful for the support and patience of my wife, Dilcia, who has endured many long hours at night while I was writing and editing. Many thanks go to my sweet, inventive daughter, Lindsey, whose fearless birth gave me the incentive to strike out on my own, to teach and write. Thanks to my Dad for passing on his natural problem-solving genes that has helped make me a successful inventor.

Special thanks go to two family members who passed away last year. First to my mother, who gave me the spirit and creativity to be able to write this book in the first place and second to my brother, Paul, from whom I learned all about marketing and relationships. He was one of the smartest marketing experts I have ever known.

I also have to give many thanks to all the From Patent to Profit workshop participants over the years. Without their timely input and questions, this book would never have been organized effectively.

Many thanks to the expert inventors--Yujiro Yamamoto, George Margolin and even Jerome Lemelson via the Lemelson Foundation-- whose invaluable input and confirmations helped shape the content of the book. Many thanks to the manufacturing and marketing experts-- Joe Bowers, Joe Justin, Don Pansier, Ken Robbins, Joan Lefkowitz-- whose input helps prove to the readers that the concepts work.

Last, there is a very special expert who worked many hours behind the scenes helping me organize my thoughts and write them down in an effective, personable and yet instructive manner. Gerry Kaskell is that most exceptional expert. Thanks Gerry for making me look good!

PREFACE

THERE'S AN INVENTION REVOLUTION IN AMERICA!

I never would have thought that after pursuing my first idea in autumn, 1986, that today I would have fourteen U.S. Patents, seven others pending and a 100% success rate in developing and marketing them. According to the U.S. Patent Office this is unusual since it claims that only 3% of all patents ever earn any money for the inventor.

I also never would have believed the wonderful direction my life took in pursuit of that first idea and all the others that followed. My first opportunity landed employment as a product developer, working for the president of a major packaging manufacturer. We began by developing the plastic grocery sacks you see in supermarkets today and some of the merchandise bags used by major retailers.

During this employment I had the opportunity to teach Quality Management techniques and teamwork concepts. Being trained by Tennessee Associates--the same group responsible for the turnaround at Harley Davidson and Ford Motors in the 1980's--I held seminars to train 300 employees at our three facilities. It was some of the most fun I have ever had!

After four years directing new product development and one year teaching TQM, I partnered a new venture in plastics R&D for about two years. But I discovered this was not the type of partnership I wanted. I decided to leave this partnership on the day my daughter, Lindsey, was born--March 23, 1994.

Just watching her come into the world spurred me on to create my own future as well. I decided to start working for myself and develop my own licenses--at the time I owned about 5 of my patents and had several others pending. I had a few licensees of the patents and patents pending that I owned. I also decided to do something that I loved tremendously--teach!

During the next year and a half, I worked to develop my own licensees and to develop a curriculum to give workshops on the subject that I enjoyed best, inventing. I contacted some colleges and universities to confirm that they wanted to offer the courses. The response was excellent.

As I developed the curriculum, I came across a stumbling block that was not going to be easy to resolve. I wanted to have a book and training materials that taught what I knew how to do best. That is, to develop ideas into marketable products--not just get a costly patent and hope that it will be a success. I could not find a single book anywhere!

Thus, I realized I had no other choice. I begin writing my own materials. The first outcome was three small books, *The Art of Patenting, The Art of Innovating,* and *The Art of Licensing and Marketing.* For two years they served as the textbooks in the workshops.

Meanwhile, my licensing efforts were flourishing. I was having a great time developing new products and locating marketing experts. We introduced a new plastic grocery sack, some new retail bag styles, bakery and deli bags, and even some new produce bags.

Then in late 1997, the first publication of *From Patent to Profit* was released. It was the product of two years of workshop experience, my most recent licensing efforts, and reflected the teamwork concepts that I had previously taught. It also includes the wisdom of several successful inventors I have had the fortunate experience of meeting and befriending in the past few years.

For the first time ever, a book was written that teaches inventors how to develop an idea and know that it is going to be a success…that it would make money. From Patent to Profit shows inventors--first time or experienced--how to develop their ideas in a timely manner, get them patented and get them earning income, at little expense to the inventor. This is exactly what I have done. After all, good ideas don't need your money. As you will find out, there are plenty of people and companies willing to invest theirs!

INTRODUCTION

Welcome to the world of inventing and patenting! You are about to embark on one of the most exciting journeys in your life!

This manual will provide you with a "road map" to guide you on your journey. It will help you make the choices that are right for you. Whether you plan to go into business or license your invention, *From Patent to Profit* will teach you how to be successful.

Both first-time and experienced inventors will find the invention development system used in this manual invaluable. It is based upon my eleven years of inventing and patenting experience and also incorporates the advice and strategies of many other experts.

About This Manual

This manual reveals the secrets of successful inventing and patenting. It reveals for the very first time that successful inventing consists of four, overlapping, inter-related processes, that together form the *From Patent to Profit*™ system. *From Patent to Profit* divides the four processes into several easy-to-follow steps. Each step is outlined in the *From Patent to Profit* ***Strategic Guide*™**.

How to Use This Manual

This manual is both a training aid and a reference guide. When used as a training aid, it will teach you how to turn your ideas into patents and make money from them. When used as a reference guide, it becomes a handy information source of invention management options to refer to again and again.

If you are a first-time inventor with an idea you want to develop, read the manual from beginning to end to learn how to protect it, evaluate it, patent it and get it producing profit for you. If you are an experienced inventor, you too would be wise to start at the beginning-- to learn many new and exciting strategies to help propel your current efforts. Experienced inventors may find that the *From Patent to Profit* system saves them months, even years, of development time.

The *From Patent to Profit* system shows you how to be the team leader who guides the four invention related processes. They are:

1. Inventing
2. Patenting
3. Manufacturing
4. Marketing

To lead you in these four processes, this manual is divided into four main sections. The first two sections relate directly to the first two processes (Inventing and Patenting); the third section relates to the last two processes (Manufacturing and Marketing). Because licensing is a key to your success, it requires a separate section.

The Table of Contents includes a heading for each section followed by headings for all chapters and topics. It should be a handy way for you to locate material about the various issues you may want to review.

The Appendix is an inventing, patenting and marketing resource containing valuable, qualified information.

Part I: Inventing

This section will set your invention journey in motion. You will learn about the *From Patent to Profit* system and how to track your invention development progress. You can use it to position and evaluate your invention as early as possible, before you invest a lot of money. You will also learn how to apply the winning concepts used by successful inventors and innovators worldwide. Finally, you will learn how to solve key problems. Problems are opportunities. If you can overcome them, you might just find an exciting breakthrough opportunity!

Part II: Patenting

As you learn about patents, you will discover that there are more ways to get protection than you realized. This section reveals how to get a patent without spending a lot of money. You will learn that an inventor should play a key role in the patenting and patent writing process. You will learn how to do so and why it is so important that patent writing and product development occur simultaneously.

You will also learn about trademarks, copyrights and other means of intellectual property protection. You will understand when and when not to patent and how this decision can impact your future.

Part III: Marketing and Manufacturing

This section will help you create your manufacturing and marketing strategy. You will learn how to locate and evaluate potential manufacturing partners and marketing experts.

Most inventors fail in the marketing segment of the invention process, but you will learn to excel! This is the most exciting and enlightening part of the *From Patent to Profit* Manual. You will learn that marketing is key to success and profit.

Part IV: Licensing

You will learn about licenses and licensing a producer that fits your needs. You will also learn some creative approaches to licensing that can even entice others into entering into an agreement with you.

Now you are ready to start inventing! "Rev up" your mind… get those creative juices going and start dreaming. Then, take the next step…turn the page and turn your patent into profit!

PART ONE
INVENTING

1

ALL ABOUT INVENTING

A lot of work, a lot to learn and a lot of fun…
and it can be very rewarding as well!

GOT A GOOD IDEA?

That is what America is all about: good ideas, innovations, entrepreneurs and dreams that come true! If you're one of those innovative people and you've got a good idea and want to act on it…this manual is for you. While Americans unquestionably lead the world in innovating and inventing, there are still a surprisingly large number of good ideas that never get to market. The chief reason is really quite basic. It is that first time innovators and inventors simply do not know how to develop an idea and then get it patented, mass-produced and sold, producing profit.

Successful entrepreneurs-inventors-innovators know that the world of invention and innovation is a lot of hard work. But they also know it can be a lot of fun and very rewarding. Those who take action and follow all the right steps will be successful.

If you have a good idea, that is the first step and the easiest part of the process. Next comes the more difficult part, which is learning how

We live in a country essentially created by inventors. America's economic strength and global competitiveness depend more than ever upon the successful harvesting of the great ideas of this gifted group of people.
…Donald Grant Kelly, Director, U.S. Patent Office

7

to turn your idea into a reality. Then you can enjoy the benefits and rewards of your creative ability.

DO YOU WANT TO PURSUE YOUR IDEA?

Remember, successful inventors take action, they don't sit on their ideas. They invest time, money and energy to get the proverbial ball rolling. That's the process. It's a journey. Remember what Goethe said, "Whatever you can do, or dream you can, begin it. Boldness has genius, power and magic in it."

...Stephen Paul Gnass

Before you decide to pursue your idea, there is an important point to consider. Success is based on commitment. To be successful with the launch of a new invention requires your commitment to invest the time and effort to see it through. In other words, you must take action and be determined to follow through until you have attained the outcome you want. Invariably, this will also require a significant amount of patience.

Are you willing to set out on an exciting journey that requires your total commitment, determination and patience to learn all you can and weather the storm through all obstacles? If you are willing to make a commitment and make all the right moves, chances are you *can* turn your good idea into profit. And you will have a whole lot of fun doing it!

The best news, which is a little-known secret, *is that it does not have to cost a lot of money* to do it! That is what this manual explains. You are about to learn how you can do--in a fraction of the time and at a fraction of the cost--what it takes corporate giants several years to do. You are also going to learn how to protect your ideas before filing for patents and to secure patents in a timely manner. You will learn how to evaluate your invention's potential, how to find manufacturing and marketing partners and how to master the art of inventing and patenting.

TODAY'S BUSINESS CLIMATE IS PERFECT

Inventors and beginning entrepreneurs are individuals who, knowingly or not, are participating in one of this country's myths. I do not use this term pejoratively; a myth is a fictional story that reveals a great truth or strong value of a society.

The belief that the inventor exhibits is that if you have a good idea, work hard to make it viable, you can be successful and in the process of benefiting yourself, you benefit the community in which you live.

July 10, 1997

...Norris Bell, Director of the former National Innovation Workshops (NIW)

Not only does it not have to cost you a lot of money, but your timing may never have been better. We are living in one of the most creative, inventive, opportunistic times in American history. Recently, creative Americans have been developing ideas and inventions into new patents and products at a record rate. In 1996, over 215,000 patents were filed at the U.S. Patent Office and just over 115,000 patents were granted. Consistent with America's entrepreneurial spirit, about 25% of these patents are from independent inventors and small companies.

The Department of Commerce reports that in 1997, there were over 14 million home-based businesses. Of these, over 4 million earned in excess of $100,000 a year. By the year 2000, over 50% of all U.S. households will operate a home-based business. Entrepreneurs with new innovations and inventions represent one of the growing groups of home-based businesses. Much of America's current creativity is a result of corporate downsizing, job elimination due to robotics and computers and elimination of entire industries that have moved overseas. This incredible shift in just the past 10-15 years has caused an unprecedented number of people to become "re-employed" in entrepreneurial home-based businesses and new, start-up companies.

What has been the result of this enormous shift of talented individuals? A comment recently reported in the *Wall Street Journal* sums it up:

"The U.S. economy is the envy of the world..."

After the trials and tribulations of the 1900's, we are about to enter the 20th century just as we began the 18th century, but with even greater force. A country filled with new ideas and inventions will once again shape the future of the world.

Today's business climate is excellent for another reason. Small- and medium-sized businesses need proprietary products to compete against their large, generic competitors. The best way to create such products is though invention, innovation and patented technologies. Since many of these businesses do not have R&D departments, they are interested in partnering those new ideas and new technologies--high tech or low tech--that are conceived by creative individuals like you.

If your intention is to start a business, you will find your customers will pay more for well-thought-out, high performance, patented products. If you are an independent inventor who wants to license your ideas and inventions, you can find quality businesses willing to pay for your good ideas and inventions. There is more opportunity than ever before to find special partners who are willing to listen to your good ideas and license them.

The factor that differentiates this manual from all other invention books is its focus on making money on your inventions, without spending a lot. You will learn about the various options available, and the sound principles you can apply to turn your idea into a reality and make money from it!

LAWS, COURT CASES AND NEW LEGISLATION

There are four legal factors that are having a positive impact on innovators and inventors. First, new patent laws as of June 1995 allow independent inventors and small companies to file a "provisional patent application" for only $75. A provisional patent application allows an inventor to post "Patent Pending" on a new product for an entire year, while he/she tries to run up sales or secures a licensee. If sales are poor, the inventor can save a lot of money before filing the more expensive, regular patent application.

Second, the Doctrine of Equivalence, struck in 1952, states that if a product functions "essentially the same as that which is claimed in a patent", it infringes. This Doctrine was tested recently in the U.S.

A few years ago the U.S. Gross National Product (GNP) was reported as being about 26% of the world's GNP. With the recent Asian difficulties coupled with the persistently prosperous U.S. economy, the American GNP is now reported to be as much as 33%. The U.S. is the largest single marketplace in the world. This is why virtually everyone and every company--regardless of their country of origin--wants to sell their products in the United States.
...Bob DeMatteis

America's fourth most prolific inventor, Jerome Lemelson, was an independent inventor with over 500 patents. From the early 1950's until his recent demise, he took advantage of a ripe business climate and created many products that affect us today. Some of his most notable inventions include key components of the VCR and audio cassettes, Laser-guided robots used in modern manufacturing, and many popular toys and components including the flexible car track popularly known as "Hot Wheels".

Inventors are learning that, if they are to wield influence with respect to policy development, they'll have to remain mindful of a new "set of needs" shared by their constituency in the quest for global patent protection and marketing opportunities.
...Donald Grant Kelly, Director, U.S. Patent Office

Numerous record judgments have been awarded to patent holders in the past few years. From his famous intermittent windshield-wiper patent, Bob Kearns has been awarded tens of millions for patent infringement by Ford and several other automakers. More recently, Ron Chasteen, an Arizona inventor, was granted a $57- million award from Polaris Industries and Fuji Heavy Industries of Tokyo for stealing his electronic fuel injection system for two-stroke engines.

Sound business practices tell us that before we invest a lot of money on developing a new idea (patents, trademarks, etc.), we should investigate the field we have selected!

Doesn't that make sense to you? If you were going to open a pizza shop, wouldn't you want to first learn all you could about pizzas, how to make them, how much they cost to make, what profits you could expect and even if there was a demand?

You would be wise to do the same with inventing.

The most disheartening thing about inventors who have been taken advantage of by scam companies is not that they've lost money, but that they've lost something much more valuable... their spirit of inventing.
...Stephen Paul Gnass

Appeals Court with the Hilton Davis case. In March 1996, the case went to the U.S. Supreme Court and on March 3, 1997, Supreme Court Justice Clarence Thomas handed down a decision. In essence, his ruling upheld the impact of the Doctrine and further clarified its meaning, in favor of the patent holder.

Third, pending legislation originally slated to help large corporations (and consequently have a negative effect on independent inventors) has been stopped...and amended in favor of independent inventors and small companies. The bills, HR 400 and S 507, have been subject to substantial resistance from concerned Americans throughout the U.S. Now that the bills have passed through write-up and the Judiciary Committees, most experts anticipate favorable outcomes.

Fourth, hundreds of recent court decisions have been ruled in favor of patent holders. It is commonly understood in the world of intellectual property, that 80% of all court cases on patent infringement are being ruled in favor of the patent holders.

In Part Two of this manual, you will learn about patents and patent strategy and more about these four legal topics and how they can positively affect you and your efforts.

The real benefit of these recent developments is that patent protection is better than ever. Patent values have soared because of it. Most experts say the values have increased 20-50 fold or more.

THE BEST AND WORST FIRST STEPS...

The "first step" in inventing is exactly what you are doing, right now: learning what it is all about and what to expect. When many first-time inventors get an idea, the first thing they frequently do is run out and hire a patent attorney. Some others respond to TV and radio ads and hire an invention assistance company and waste thousands of dollars with them.

It is always recommended to use patent attorneys in a timely manner and they are usually a pleasure to deal with, but they are not usually the best "first step" an inventor can take.

As for invention assistance companies, almost all provide little help. In fact, they can do harm to the inventor by prematurely disclosing an invention. In most cases, the supposed "invention research" work they do is "boilerplate", with the same words and sentences lauding an invention, regardless of whether it is a simple hair styling implement or a high-tech electronic device. Almost all invention assistance companies have extremely low success rates. Read their literature and you will see that their success is infinitesimal.

THE FIRST SECRET TO SUCCESSFUL INVENTING

The first secret to successfully bringing your idea to fruition is that you, the inventor, must pilot your own invention. You have to be in charge of your own dream. You can't turn your dream over to someone else and expect results. You will have help and will team up with experts along the way, but you must always maintain control of your invention's destiny.

As you pilot your invention to success, you will be learning all about it--how you can turn it into a desirable invention, get it patented, mass-produced and sold, thus producing income. Like a navigator, you, the inventor, will pilot your invention on a journey to success. When you have achieved your dream, you will feel a sense of accomplishment you've never felt before and will capture a little piece of history in the process.

THE SECOND SECRET IS THE *FROM PATENT TO PROFIT*™ *SYSTEM*... FOUR KEY PROCESSES, NOT ONE

Once your idea, your dream, begins to unfold, and you have made a commitment to take control of your invention's development, the second secret to success is to master the processes required to be an expert pilot-inventor. The *From Patent to Profit* system will teach you how to accomplish your objectives.

To help you on your journey to success, a guidance system, a chart referred to as the *Strategic Guide,* is included on the last two pages of the manual. You can use it to track your progress on a daily, weekly or monthly basis. You can literally check off each small step you take on your journey.

You see, inventing is not a single, linear, step-by-step procedure whereby you start at step one, end at step ten, and presto you are rich. Success in inventing and patenting is based on your piloting of four processes. They are expressed in the *Strategic Guide* by four overlapping, continuous and flexible timelines. The four processes you will pilot are:

1. **Inventing.** This process refers specifically to activities relevant to your invention. It includes your initial evaluation of sales potential, prototyping and the development of the idea into a real invention and ultimately, a salable product. Along the way, it will include several improvements that will overcome potential objections and will also give it "sex appeal".

2. **Patenting.** This process starts with learning the basics about patenting, protecting your idea with an invention disclosure, conducting a patent search, creating the best possible patent strategy and then

Don't abdicate your power. Be accountable and responsible for your own success and you'll never have to worry about unscrupulous scam operators. Education is the key. Be a smart consumer and don't become an invention scam statistic.
...Stephen Paul Gnass

If you are a parent, you know best how to raise your child. You can't pay someone else to do it for you. Inventions are like children; you want to raise them properly so they will become mature, desirable products.

The difference between inventions and children is that inventions can make money, while children cost money!

This manual is best used as a reference guide throughout your invention development process. You may find yourself going from one section to the other; that is exactly what the invention process is about. Since you are coordinating four simultaneous, overlapping processes, expect to focus on one process at a time.
...Bob DeMatteis

writing a patent application. In most cases, the first application will be a provisional patent application, followed by a regular application a year later. Once filed, the regular application is prosecuted and hopefully granted. Last, you may have to prepare for others infringing your patent, which usually results in good news!

3. Manufacturing. A new invention must be cost-effectively manufactured with the right quality, at the right price and must be accompanied by great service and timely delivery. Reaching those goals is not quite as easy as it sounds. To generate sufficient sales and garner sufficient profit or royalty income, you must find the very best "fit" between your invention and a manufacturer.

4. Marketing. Far too many inventors fail miserably here. They think that having a good idea and getting it protected with a patent is enough. But it's not. If the invention doesn't get sold, it will not earn any money. *From Patent to Profit* focuses on this perspective--your invention's ability to earn money.

In your invention-related activities, you will be piloting and developing all four processes concurrently. The overlapping timelines for the four processes are flexible and approximate. Your ultimate success depends on the interrelationship between the processes and the successful completion of each one. While it may appear overwhelming at first, relax; it gets a lot easier as you move forward!

In the *Strategic Guide*, your journey starts in the upper left-hand corner with "you have an idea". From there, you will take many small steps to protect your idea, evaluate it and go out and make things happen. The four parts of this manual correspond with these four processes. All the possible alternatives you may encounter along the way are discussed right here.

THE THIRD SECRET TO SUCCESS: IT'S A TEAM EFFORT

An invention invariably starts as a single idea from a single inventor. But sooner or later, it will require a team effort to make it happen. Bringing a new product to market requires a tremendous amount of effort. If nothing else, you simply will not have enough time to do it all.

In addition, ask yourself if you are an expert in all facets of your invention. Of course you're not. The *From Patent to Profit* system is about building your team, so you can pursue and enjoy the fruits of your success.

Your team will consist of four primary team members: a patent attorney, your manufacturing partner, a sales and marketing expert and you. These four will work together as a committed team to do whatever

---

I was asked recently at one of my seminars about what would be the smartest first step to take in the invention process. I thought about it and one thought jumped into my mind. I waited for awhile before I committed to this one thought, but realized that it was the key to all invention success. The answer is, get a strong marketing expert on your team as soon as you can!
...Bob DeMatteis

Making sound business decisions in a timely manner is what the Strategic Guide is all about. This is right at the heart of making money on your inventions. If you are uncertain about what your next step might be, the Strategic Guide will always be there to help and direct you.

it takes to get the project launched. You will learn how to find and evaluate these partners later in the manual.

The team members you select are crucial to your success. You want a manufacturer who can give you the quality, service and price you expect. You want a sales and marketing expert who can get your new invention sold and producing income. A smart marketing expert can get orders before the product is manufactured. You will find out later exactly how to accomplish this.

With an expert, committed team, you will be able to shorten the development time frame significantly and thereby save a lot of money! Think about it. It might take six months to get an appointment with the decision-maker of a key retailer, and then you might have the expense of flying to a faraway corporate office. A marketing expert who has all the right contacts can do this in a matter of days or weeks and without any cost to you. You will learn more about this in Part Three.

YOUR INVENTION – INNOVATION OBJECTIVES

Some may think that getting a patent is your main objective, but that is misleading. Patenting is only one aspect of the big picture that will bring about ultimate success. Others might think that making a big hit quickly is your main objective. They are wrong.

Each invention, innovation and inventor is different, but the objectives are basically the same for all. They are to:

1. **Make money.** You have to evaluate your inventions and their ability to produce the monetary rewards you expect. After all, that will be your true measure of success.

2. **Gain security.** You want to protect your ideas and inventions in a timely manner with patents and trademarks, without incurring large patenting expenses. This also helps ensure long-term income, not just short-term profit.

3. **Gain knowledge.** Learn the patenting process and the industry around your invention, so you can do it all over again! Through knowledge, you can extend the life of your invention and earnings.

4. **Have fun.** Yes, you must have fun, because if it isn't fun, you won't maintain the necessary interest and drive to be successful.

EVALUATING AN IDEA… KNOWING IT IS WORTH PURSUING

You will be evaluating your invention's worth, based on its potential to fulfill your four objectives. This is so important, and one of

Inventors should spend their time working on what they do best—inventing. They can partner with others to do everything else.
...Joan Lefkowitz, Accessory Brainstorms, NYC

Staying Focused

When you kick-off your invention career, you want to make sure it is in a field you enjoy tremendously.

Once you have developed some special relationships with your manufacturing and marketing partners, you will find it will be a lot easier to launch additional inventions /creations in the future.

Thus, from the perspective of having fun and developing solid relationships with your team members, you will want to stay focused in one single industry. You will not want to jump around from one industry to another continually seeking new manufacturing and marketing experts.

Years after you have had some success, then you might consider branching out into new fields.

Good News…No Business Plan Required!

Of the dozens of inventions I have licensed, I have never written a business plan. I consider this to be a waste of time. Drafting business plans is what those companies that license your invention should do. Your goal should be to do a preliminary, unbiased evaluation, which you can then present to your potential licensees. The more thorough this evaluation, the better off you will be. Your evaluation can be a simple one-page summary, like that on page 192 or it can be an in-depth prospectus, like that on page 204. Regardless of how thorough your evaluation and prospectus might be, a potential licensee/partner will still want to show due diligence and get their own facts for themselves.

…Bob DeMatteis

Getting the patent has to be part of their plan. Inventors have to look down the road and see they're going to actually make some return on the investment in a patent application.

…Donald Grant Kelly, Director, U.S. Patent Office

the first things you will do in the invention development process. In fact, I suggest that you do it on the earliest possible date.

You must be able to evaluate your invention honestly and accurately. You do not want to chase a dream that is going to cost you a lot of time and money. Sometimes, the emotion surrounding a new idea can cloud reality. You must be realistic. You cannot expect to capture even 20%-30% of an existing market, unless you already own a substantial percentage. Established competitors are not going to let you run over them and then close their doors and go out of business. It just doesn't happen very often; in fact, it happens almost never.

If you are active in the field of the invention, you probably already know its potential. For instance, if yours is an established business, you may already know that your idea will help you protect current sales and allow you to capture additional markets in the future. Obviously, pursuing and patenting a new improvement will help secure your future.

But if you plan to start a new business or license your invention, you will want to evaluate it before spending your resources. This is particularly important if you are not familiar with the field. Be sure to do some solid research.

You may already have a company in mind that will want to buy or use your new invention. As an independent inventor, you possibly have some firms targeted to license, manufacture and sell products. Be conservative and realistic in your evaluations. An inadequate, invalid evaluation can cost you a lot of money and a lot of time.

Usually an invention begins because your intuition or instincts tell you that your idea is a good one. If you know the field well, you can count on your intuition or instincts to be more accurate than an 82-page business plan accompanied by an expensive marketing research study!

Besides, writing business plans on new inventions is difficult, because you are dealing with the unknown. How can you project sales on something that has never before existed? Frequently you can't. In their unimaginative world, bankers want a track record. The only way you might be able to provide a bank with a track record is to use some of your past invention successes.

Nevertheless, there are ways of evaluating new ideas. The following topics will help you do just that.

The First, Most Important Evaluation Criteria: Money

Your first and most important objective is determining the moneymaking potential of your invention. Sales generate money, which equates to profits or royalties for you. In contrast, patents do not necessarily generate money. Neither does the manufacture of a product generate money. It must be sold before profits and royalties are generated.

So use sales potential as your guide. Don't make the common mistake of assuming that your ability to get a patent is a guide to how much money you are going to make. And don't make the mistake of defining a manufacturer willing to make the product as any measure of sales potential.

Sales will be generated based on these three basic economic principles:

1. Is the product needed or desired? Need usually results in higher sales than desire. We take care of our needs first.

2. What price can you charge? Can you sell it for more than the current generic products on the market? Most new inventions are sold at higher prices than those of current products are and then sometime later, their prices tend to decline when volume is much higher. If the type of invention you have created is in an industry that has little price elasticity, you may not be able to get a premium price, which will result in low profits. For instance, slightly more expensive, attractively printed, designer trash bags were a flop because users would just not pay more for pretty flowers printed on them. Would you? You will need to determine a fair market price right away.

3. How big is the market? Is it wise to proceed if the fully developed sales will be only $250,000 a year? Probably not.

How can you answer these three most important questions? If you are an expert in the field of the invention, you can probably get the information by networking with potential customers and sales associates. Or, like many large corporations, you can have an inconclusive, and relatively expensive, beta test conducted. Beta tests frequently result in inaccurate, misleading reports.

The best, and most inexpensive way to determine marketability, is to locate a sales-marketing expert who wants to sell your invention. Through his/her experience, you can get a good idea of the sales potential. Sales potential determines earnings potential, which is the first objective you will want clarified as soon as possible. You can read more about how to use sales-marketing experts while protecting your invention in Chapter 2.

The Second Evaluation Criteria: Security

In addition to having an idea about how much your invention will sell for and what sales can be anticipated, you must consider whether you can hold onto the business. You have to carefully consider the following factors and competitive responses:

When evaluating the potential sell price of a new product, keep in mind that you are dealing with the consumer's perceptions--not the product's cost plus mark-up.

If you cannot zero-in on this accurately, it will be difficult to sell your idea to anyone. Once you have a general understanding of what the market will bear, then your objective becomes figuring out how to get it made for the right price.

How to Make Small Market Penetration Profitable

If your invention evaluation shows that the market for your new innovation is fairly limited, but it can be made with fairly high profit margins, then go into business yourself and put up a Web site. For only a few thousands dollars a year, you can establish and maintain a small, home-based business, which can become fairly profitable.

Licensees will be reluctant to enter into a product development relationship, which does not have reasonably good patent protection. As an inventor, it is wise not to waste your valuable time pursuing products that will not provide adequate patent protection.

What you might consider instead is to try to imagine the next generation and see what patent protection it provides instead.

One of the toughest barriers to entry to overcome is in markets that are dominated by several giant competitors. An example is the automobile manufacturing or oil industry. If your invention were in this kind of arena, it would be wise to pursue the aftermarket instead of OEM (original equipment manufacturer).

1. Will you be able to get a patent (better yet, more than one patent) to help protect your long-term security? Will the patent give you broad enough protection to keep others out of the marketplace? You will learn more about this in Part Two, Chapters 5 and 6.

2. Is the invention worth patenting? At the beginning, it can be relatively inexpensive. However, to secure a patent with adequate coverage and protection will eventually require the input of an expert patent attorney and usually costs several thousand dollars. Will sales be sufficient to justify the costs? Without patent protection, entry into the market may be easy for competitors.

3. How will competitors respond? If you capture a noticeable portion of the market, are they going to stand still? Are they going to lower prices, trying to drive your prices down? Will they try to develop a new competitive version of what you are doing? Will the competitors take a chance on infringing on your patent? You will learn more about competitive responses in Chapter 2.

4. Is your invention a fad or is it a long-term trend? If your invention is a short-term fad, is it worth pursuing? Is it worth patenting? If your new invention is based on having "instant" success, it can also fade away just as quickly. If your invention is a short-term fad--the Pet Rock™ is probably the most classic example--do you really want to spend a lot of time and money on product development and patenting? No, it is a waste of your precious resources. You want long-term trends that represent long-term security for your efforts.

5. Are there any other barriers to entry, such as the inability to purchase raw materials and components, attain or license other technologies, or overcome environmental or safety hazards?

The Third Evaluation Criteria: Knowledge

Knowledge in the field of the invention will allow you to make good decisions and to make all the right contacts much faster. Don't be scared if you don't have a lot of knowledge in the field; just be willing to learn.

The theory that "knowledge is power" is true when it comes to inventing. Once you have the knowledge, you will be able to pilot inventions and innovations to success faster.

You should always be in a "learning mode" as you carry out your invention activities. After all, inventing and innovating represent a process of learning and discovery. The world of patenting is also based upon discovery and learning. Answer the following questions:

1. Do I have adequate knowledge in its field to make my invention successful?

2. If not, am I willing to invest the time and expense to get the knowledge I need? Will I be able to learn from the resources that are available to me? The resources include people, schools, books and magazines, Internet, etc.

3. Are any barriers blocking me from learning all that I need to learn and know?

You must be willing to learn all you can and do all the right things as you go on your journey. You must be inquisitive and constantly aware of what is happening in the invention development process. Be flexible in your approach and always consider, even create, new options along the way.

The Fourth Evaluation Criteria: Fun

You must enjoy what you are doing. If you don't, you will lose interest or end up doing something you hate. Both will result in poor performance and not much financial success.

Here are two key questions:

1. Is the field of your invention an area that is enjoyable to you? Would you like to spend most of today, and the next ten years, creating new ideas in this field?

2. Are you really going to have fun talking to the people in this industry? Will you enjoy working with them and on the processes?

Earning enough money can make just about anything fun, but you must enjoy the day-to-day process as well. If not, your profits will probably be short lived.

THINKING LIKE A SUCCESSFUL INNOVATOR-INVENTOR-ENTREPRENEUR

Innovators and inventors are essentially the same. The dictionary definition of an innovator is "someone who begins or introduces something new". For an inventor, it is "someone who contrives a previously unknown device". In other words, inventors lean more toward creating new things and innovators lean more toward introducing them.

Successful inventors tend to be good at innovating and successful innovators tend to be good at inventing. Both are naturally creative, intuitive, flexible, problem-solving people. Fortunately for you, whether you call yourself an innovator or inventor, you will be using all

Knowledge Can Be Acquired

Learning is right at the heart of developing new, exciting inventions that consumers want to buy. Learning is also right at the heart of being a successful inventor and making smart business decisions. The result of learning all you can and acquiring the knowledge you need, is companies willing to license your innovations.

The two best traits an inventor can develop are tenaciousness and patience. Work on some aspect of your invention every day and temper yourself for delays, setbacks and disappointments along the road to success.
...Joan Lefkowitz, Accessory Brainstorms, NYC

I have to write over 1000 rejection letters annually. I am ever aware of the fact that the annals of business are filled with inventors who are laughed at, kicked out, sent home and beaten up by companies only to eventually become multimillionaires from their idea. That tells me that the one quality an inventor must have is tenacity!
...Ken Robbins, Product Development Agent, Dirt Devil

The success gained by the inventor will be in direct proportion to his/her commitment, ability, preparation and most importantly, his action and tenacity.
...Stephen Paul Gnass

If you want to be a successful inventor, you'd first better define what success means specifically to you.
...Stephen Paul Gnass

What comes first, an "understanding" of your invention or a "commitment" to making it a success? While it seems to make sense that a good understanding would come before commitment, it doesn't. If this were so no one would ever get married, because we would never truly understand our spouses.
It is similar with inventing. Smart inventors know that if they make a commitment to learn all they can during the invention development process, and make their decisions based upon what is best for the customer, that the end result is going to be a good one.

Did you notice that one of the attributes of being a top inventor/innovator is that you do not need to have good marketing skills? Some inventors think that they must be like Ron Poppiel in order to have any success. This doesn't hurt, but it is certainly not necessary. Get the right marketing expert on your team and that void will be instantly filled.

New inventions create jobs, stimulate the economy, and make significant contributions to the social well-being of our country.
...Donald Grant Kelly, Director, U.S. Patent Office

your natural characteristics as you travel on your day-by-day journey to success. Learn how to develop them well and you will achieve the outcomes you want.

Here are some of the valuable traits of successful innovators and inventors that you should model:

1. Commitment, persistence, a sense of urgency
2. Decisions based on intuition and instincts (Lee Iacocca)
3. Always learning and thinking ahead, anticipating
4. Thinking in terms of customer benefits
5. Fast, flexible and focused
6. Enthusiastic and positive
7. Continually improving

The more you think and act like an innovator-inventor, the sooner you will become a successful one.

ONE MORE THOUGHT ON POSITIONING YOURSELF

Once you establish yourself as an innovative leader in your field, your customers' and licensees' doors will be open for future improvements and ideas. Best of all, when you are ready to introduce new innovations and new products, you will have a built-in customer base, ready to help test and market.

Do you need all seven of the above attributes to be a successful inventor? Yes. Sooner or later, you will find your efforts hindered because one or more of the attributes has not been fulfilled.

You can change and improve your attitude, your position, just like you change and improve products and systems. After all, you are an inventor who is bringing change to the world. So why not bring change to yourself as well? Just remember...

The weak indulge in resolutions, but the strong *act!*

THINKING AHEAD...WHAT TO DO WITH YOUR INVENTIONS AND PATENTS

When your invention is fully developed and patents are granted, you have some alternatives to consider. If your patents are being developed specifically for your business, you probably already know your intentions. If you are an independent inventor, you may also have some good ideas about what you want to do. As an independent inventor, you have four choices to consider:

1. **Outright sale.** Any reasonably good patent should be worth at least $100,000 to the patent holder. But values are difficult to determine. To determine a value, you can consider your sales pro forma for 20 years and then capitalize it as you would real estate. But purchasers of patents generally assign higher risk to patents than they do to real estate.

As an example, you may project sales of your patent for the next 17 years as $51,000,000 (averaging $3 million per year). With a typical royalty rate of 3%, your total income would be $1,530,000. However, it may take a few years to establish annual sales of $3 million. And besides, would a purchaser have the same sales and profit projections as you have?

2. **Create a job.** One of the best outcomes for an inventor is to create a job with an established firm. Together, you can commercially develop the patent. There are many alternatives regarding your compensation for the value of the patent. Royalties can be exchanged for stock (or stock options) and of course, steady income. The income from the job should be enough to live comfortably while you pilot the development and ultimate success of your invention.

The chief advantage to this approach is that you have the invention know-how to make it happen and the firm has the money to develop it correctly. With almost any new idea or invention, a company expecting to market it with a high degree of success will have to hire a product development manager. Why not you? With the promise of the marketing success of your product, you can have a secure future with new invention opportunities as well.

3. **Go into business.** This approach is only for those who have financial resources to tap. You will be building a business based on your inventions and patents. While this approach can be extremely profitable, it is also the most time consuming. You will need lots of energy and stamina, since building a business and developing new inventions and patents is like having two full-time jobs!

4. **License it.** Since trying to arrive at a value for a sale is difficult, licensing is generally more acceptable to manufacturers and marketers. Excluding the many companies that develop their own patents for internal use, licensing is the most popular method of earning profits from patents. It is similar to a leasing plan. Through leases, a business can conserve cash while investing money on equipment, raw materials, inventory, etc. Through licensing, you can typically earn from 1%-5% on sales, which can be more profitable than an outright sale.

It is very difficult to find a willing buyer for an unproven patent. There are too many variables that can affect its value. Besides, if you sell your patents, you are probably selling out for a lot less than if you licensed them.

Working at a department store during holidays in 1903, 22 year-old Joshua Cohen was asked by his boss to create an attractive window display with a toy train to help attract customers.

Joshua took a metal, pull-string toy train, installed a small electric motor and sent it round and round in the window display.

It attracted customers...most of whom wanted to buy the electric toy train!

After the holidays, Joshua started his own company, named after his middle name--Lionel.

Many highly successful inventors found out early on that they should keep doing what they do best... that is, invent and create.

One of the most prolific inventors in U.S. history, Jerome H. Lemelson, licensed his 500-plus patents after a bad attempt at going into the manufacturing business.

Yujiro Yamamoto, inventor of the cordless telephone, the telephone answering machine, the air purification system used by General Motors, and many other inventions, licensed his as well.

Both Lemelson and Yamamoto knew very well to do what they do best...invent...and leave the marketing up to the experts!

ARE YOU READY TO TAKE ACTION?

If you are ready to take action now, keep in mind that invention success can happen quickly or take years. There are many determining factors, such as the amount of time you have to invest, the timing of your invention's release and the chance meeting of key team members.

If you are a first time inventor, don't quit your job. It is going to take you a while to develop various contacts and build a successful team. You will want to start out part time and hopefully you can catapult your successes into a full-time occupation. As you learn the system of successful inventing, the time frame for new introductions will decrease each time. If your invention is in your field, it will be easier for you to take action and start building a team while working at your current job. But before you take any action, read the next chapter, so you will understand the basic strategy of the *From Patent to Profit* system and how to develop your ideas and inventions into a moneymaking enterprise.

Don't Be Paranoid!

Many new inventors become paranoid that someone will steal their idea. This paranoia almost always hinders their ability to take action.

You must overcome your paranoia in order to be successful. You can do this by following the guidelines in this manual.

2

YOUR INVENTION STRATEGY

Don't start out by spending a lot of money…
With good ideas, others will finance your efforts.

THE SEVEN STRATEGIC STEPS TO PROFIT

If you feel your idea is good enough to pursue, here are the steps to take. They are not in a step-by-step sequence, but in order as they relate to the four *Strategic Guide* processes. They are presented in the approximate order of transforming your idea into an invention, a patent, and ultimately into profit (with estimates of your total time investment in parenthesis).

1. **Protect it.** This is traditionally thought of as establishing your "date of original conception", since the U.S. is a "first-to-invent" country, not first to file. Another criteria that is of equal importance is "reduction to practice" or following through and making it. With a well-written disclosure, you can establish an official date of original conception. By maintaining logs and other records as you "reduce to practice" the development of your invention, you will validate your position. (.05%)

The seven steps to profiting from an invention dovetail with your manufacturing and marketing strategy.

21

One of the biggest advantages of having qualified experts evaluate your invention early on is not getting stuck developing an idea that is going to be a loser.

Pouring a lot of money into patenting and prototyping before properly evaluating its money-earning potential usually results in an un-sellable product. The outcome instead is an emotional attachment after years of expounding a huge effort and substantial expense.

One older traditional approach to inventing talks about five steps to success. They are: 1) protect it, 2) do a patent search, 3) file a patent application; 4) make a prototype and 5) try to market it.

This 5-step approach will usually guarantee three outcomes. They are: 1) You will spend a lot of money on a patent in which you have absolutely no idea how much money you will make; 2) You will probably design around your patent by the time you have finished the prototyping, and; 3) You will have wasted a lot of time and emotion on pouring money into a dry hole, and may never invent again.

2. **Evaluate its marketability.** You can do an evaluation. It can be done via a beta test or by others who are experts in the industry. You would be wise to have at least one marketing expert assist you in any evaluation. (1%-2%)

3. **Conduct and evaluate an accurate patent search.** This may occur before or after you have done some initial development. Regardless, you will want to do it with a reputable company and before you get too far down the road. You do not want to talk seriously about licensing until a thorough search has been conducted. (.05%)

4. **Develop the invention to a functional state.** Your idea will go through various prototyping phases that will include testing and lead to customer trials. Your manufacturer and sales partners can help you do this. (5%-30%)

5. **Write and file patent applications.** You will want to start writing your first provisional application sometime during the development process, after you have made sufficient progress to portray your discoveries and their unique attributes. Then, file the provisional application in a timely manner. Later, you will file the permanent patent application. (1.5%)

6. **Follow through with your marketing and manufacturing experts, pilot your invention and get it *SOLD!*** New inventions are invariably fine-tuned along the way. Your marketing and manufacturing experts will help you do this. (68%-93%)

7. **Improve it.** It is common for breakthrough ideas to occur in later stages. It is a rare first invention that is a smash hit. It is usually sometime later that an improvement will really propel sales upward. (Percentage-wise, improvements take far less time to develop.)

Based on these seven steps, it may be more appropriate to describe the process as "how to turn your ideas into profits and then into patents." And frankly, that is one of the keys to the *From Patent to Profit* system. You will find that as you master the four processes in the *Strategic Guide*, you can begin earning money before you incur any expenses. In fact, properly done, you can avoid almost all costs--certainly the major ones--you might otherwise have to bear! This includes costs to patent, prototype, license, test market, etc.

STRATEGIC STEP #1: PROTECT YOUR IDEA

You will begin the invention protection process by first preparing an appropriate disclosure document describing your invention. Since this is directly related to your patenting potential, it should be as accurate as possible. Be sure to follow the detailed instructions on writing an invention disclosure as illustrated in Part Two, Chapter 6. When the disclosure document is completed, check the appropriate box on the *Strategic Guide* chart.

Your invention disclosure will start the paper trail you will create as you reduce your invention to practice. You will learn the importance of reducing your invention to practice to protect your first-to-invent status in Part Two, Chapters 5 and 6.

MAINTAIN LOGS AND OTHER RECORDS

The next step in your paper trail is to start a log and begin recording your invention-related activities. Your invention records will consist of logs (usually in notebook form), sketches and drawings, letters, diskettes, prototypes, samples and any other materials related to your invention. You can keep these records in envelopes, file folders or cardboard cartons. Give your invention a nickname (if you haven't already) and write it on the notebooks, sketches, files and containers you use.

Logs are first used as a means to establish the fact that you are reducing your invention to practice, hence securing your first-to-invent status. If substantiation is ever needed to prove that you are the original inventor, or to prove the date on which you conceived of the idea, logs can represent an indisputable paper trail. Without logs and records, you could lose your first-to-invent status and your claim to an invention.

Another positive aspect of maintaining logs is that as you record your day-to-day activities and discoveries, you are also developing a quick reference guide that you can use to quickly review what you have learned. Inventing takes time; over the weeks and months you may forget key elements of discovery. With a well-maintained log, you will have a great resource when you need it. It can save you hours and will assuredly help speed along your invention activities.

You can maintain a dedicated log for your invention-related activities or you can keep the records in a daily log that includes your other daily activities. Try using a glue-bound notebook of standard lined or graphed paper with a defined left column. If you use the typical commercially available notebook as your dedicated log, try dating the pages along the left column as you record your entries to the right. (See Fig. 2-1.)

If you use a log that is also used for other daily activities, try dating each page in the upper left-hand corner. (See Fig 2-1a.) Use a new sheet each day. As you record your daily checklist of things to do, you can also record your invention activities, identified by a special mark (perhaps an abbreviation or the nickname), on the left. If you need more

*Inventors should be aware that, along their journey to the marketplace, they are likely to encounter some ruthless highwaymen--**Invention Marketing Firms**. In all fairness, some of these companies offering services to help boost an idea out of the garage and onto the marketplace are competent and reliable. But too many others are simply and accurately characterized as scams. Stay awake. These scoundrels have become more innovative than the innovators themselves.*
...Donald Grant Kelly, Director, U.S. Patent Office

A Totally Absurd Patent

A U.S. Patent on a "boat-ball" will change your way of looking at everyday objects. The inventor had a unique vision of how boats can look and operate. Unlike everyday boats that create drag through the water, this motorized ball floats/rolls over the surface. The result is greater speed with lower fuel consumption. The airplane-like passenger cabins mounted on the sides of the monstrous ball remain horizontal as the boat-ball rolls ahead. In the event of a Titanic-like mishap, the watertight cabins can be released from the rotund mother ship and sail on their merry way.
...totallyabsurd.com

space for a sketch, you can use the back of the page. Be sure to indicate on the front that a sketch is on the other side.

| **Dedicated Log** | **Daily Notebook** |

Dedicated Log

6-15	Adhesive reorder with high melt
	Try to apply to both sides:
	A. Open end panel:
	B. Back panel 1.1
	C. Bottom panel .0
	1. Why so low tack?
	2. How can we improve it?
	3. Is it even serious?
6-16	Call Sam S. for stress tests
	Sam's comments:
	....Yes! serious ... must resolve.
	this is a design issue.
6-17	locate raw material suppliers with built in adhesives...

Fig. 2-1

Daily Notebook

6-15	
	Call Tom Smith 505-5112
	Do the summary report for GVD.
	Test the new adhesive.
ZpE	Cost per pound is too low
	Pick up accounting report
ZpE	What about heat treating instead of glue?
	Pay bills
ZpE	1. Ask Caloric about heat temp.
	2. Ask Dow about temps.
	Pick up roses for Lindsey
ZpE	illustration on back of possible heat seal config.

Fig. 2-1a

To help ensure continuity in your log records, some say it is best to have a notebook that is a glued tablet. This will help prevent someone from fraudulently trying to insert pages at a later date. But security can also be accomplished with other types of binders, if each page is sequentially numbered. The best method is to sign and date each page daily and have someone who understands the subject matter review, sign and date it.

The main topics to include in a log are:

- Those to whom you have talked and what was discussed
- Discoveries about your invention
- Solutions to manufacturing problems
- Simple sketches
- Test results from experiments
- Ideas for new inventions...related or unrelated
- Ideas on how to use or market your invention
- Problems that may be anticipated

Try to keep the log with you at all times. You never know when the creative juices might flow. Sometimes the "video in the brain" plays something important that you want to remember when you are driving in the car. You may want to pull over and make a quick sketch. If you do not have your log, use whatever is available to sketch your ideas, even the placemat in a restaurant.

If you want a dedicated log, the Inventor's Journal, published by IPT, has complete instructions telling you how to use and maintain your records.

The Inventor's Journal includes a special grid pattern that also helps you do more accurate sketches.

To obtain an Inventor's Journal, look for IPT in the Appendix under Inventor Education and Resources.

Maintain sketches, drawings and notes.

Beginning on the first day of conception, date all sketches, drawings and handwritten notes. You should sign some sketches and most drawings (engineering or otherwise), especially if you think they may be used later with a sub-contractor, supplier or potential licensee.

If a sketch is later corrected, maintain both the correction and the original. If you are ever challenged, a paper trail with serially dated sketches showing the metamorphosis of your invention will help substantiate that you are the inventor.

Keep file folders specifically for INVENTION-related activities.

In file folders that you can keep in your filing cabinet, write your invention's nickname on the tabs and keep the following data:

- Incidental sketches and notes, even if they contain errors
- Correspondence to suppliers or others involved in the project
- Technical data from suppliers

Keep separate file folders specifically for your PATENT-related activities.

In these folders, maintain the following data:

- Your invention disclosure
- Several patent application drafts (By maintaining sequential application drafts, the paper trail improves.)
- All correspondence to potential licensees, attorneys, the Patent Office, etc.

It is not uncommon to create three or four file folders on a single invention in a short time period.

Store items in cardboard cartons.

When your file folders become full, you can consider storing part of them in cardboard cartons. Make sure to keep the cartons in a place where they will not get wet or damaged. In addition to the overflow from file folders, use cardboard cartons to keep the first prototypes of your original invention, regardless of how crude. These original prototypes can be important in proving reduction to practice. Write the invention's nickname on the outside of the boxes.

STRATEGIC STEP #2:
EVALUATE THE MARKETABILITY OF YOUR IDEA

In concert with the *Strategic Guide,* which allows you to track your progress, Fig. 2-2 is a simple flow chart showing how the initial

You will learn throughout this manual that there are many ways to protect your rights and your intellectual property...not only via patenting.

The first-to-invent laws of the United States are unique and are an exemplary example illustrating how our patent system helps independent inventors. In contrast, most countries are first-to-file countries which favor large corporations.

Some say that only stitched journals should be used and that a line or page should never be skipped. But sometimes this is difficult to do.

I found early on that an inventor's journal is only one of many items that will become part of a paper trail. Thus, what may be written in a log will almost always be corroborated in other materials.

While a stitched or well-glued journal may be best...it is not essential. What is more important is that you take action, move forward, and "reduce your invention to practice". That is, prove your invention works the way that you say it does.

If you can do this with sketches and diagrams in your log, you are helping to preserve your patent rights. There is more about "reduction to practice" in Chapter 6.

invention evaluation process dovetails with your patent protection process. You have three alternatives to secure and maintain protection of an idea while you are evaluating it. First and best is to evaluate its merits and sales potential with a marketing expert you know and trust. Second, if you do not know a trusted expert, you can use confidentiality agreements. You will read about how to use confidentiality agreements in Chapter 10, and how to find and evaluate marketing experts in Chapter 12.

Many companies I have dealt with will not even consider an outside idea unless it is patented or a patent is applied for. As one corporate attorney told me, patenting an idea shows that the inventor is serious enough to invest in his own idea.
...Robert Platt Bell, Esq.

Third, if you want to spend the extra money and gamble on having your invention ready for production and producing income in a year, you can file a provisional patent application for as little as $75. As a matter of policy, many larger companies will not sign confidentiality agreements. If you feel you must discuss the potential licensing with a large firm, filing a provisional patent application can replace the need for a confidentiality agreement and serves to protect your invention's priority date.

If you file a provisional application, you can more openly negotiate with your potential manufacturing or marketing partners. The downside of filing a provisional application at an early stage is that you will incur the higher costs of patenting a year later. One year is not a lot of time to build your team and fully develop your invention. But sometimes it is more than ample. You'll read more about the exciting ways to use provisional patent applications in Part Two, Chapters 5 and 6.

Following are the three primary alternatives to determine the merits of your invention:

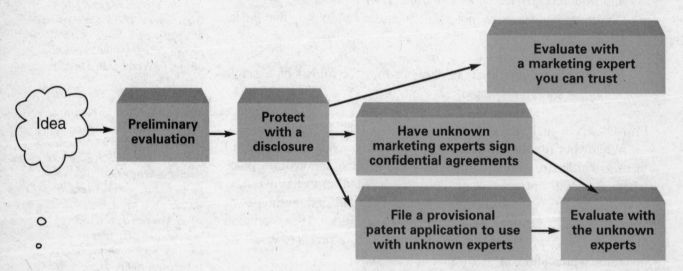

Figure 2-2 Invention Evaluation--Patent Protection Flow Chart

DOING A QUICK PRELIMINARY EVALUATION YOURSELF

If you have the time to conduct a preliminary evaluation, here are two approaches you can use:

1. If your product is to be sold in a retail store, talk to a store manager or department supervisor. Tell him/her that you are looking for a certain type of product and ask if they carry it. For instance, ask, "Do you have a multi-purpose solvent that is biodegradable?" If he/she responds affirmatively, you know it has already been developed. If the answer is "no", ask if he/she thinks that it could be sold in that store. A "yes" is good news. If the answer is "no", don't be concerned. Ask other supervisors in other stores.

2. If your invention is for industrial or commercial use, you can contact the appropriate management individual in a plant and qualify his/her interest level. Generally speaking, you should talk with someone in operations and not with someone who does the buying. For instance, ask the Vice President of Operations in a manufacturing facility, "Would you be interested in a new electronic device that automatically monitors hydraulic press safety hazards?" If the answer is "yes", you know your invention might have some potential. If the answer is "no", find out why. There may be little demand as a result of few hydraulic-related problems in the industry. Always talk to more than one person and contact more than one company to do your research.

Frankly, by talking to several candidates who will either use or sell your products at retail, you are building a network of potential customers who can help in the start-up stage. As you will see, they can also become valuable aids in helping you find manufacturing and marketing partners.

If you receive a lukewarm response from your survey or with the marketing contacts you meet, don't give up right away. Try to field as many objections as possible to better understand them. In Chapter 3, you will learn about some of the secrets to making your inventions more desirable and more salable to end users. In fact, what you will learn in Chapter 3 will become a central focus in all your invention-related developments.

A GOOD GUIDING PRINCIPLE TO EVALUATE INNOVATIONS

The best innovations are those which create a long-term trend. If your invention is only a fad, you may waste a lot of time and effort. Use your intuition, instincts and just plain common sense to determine if your idea is a fad or trend.

The method of asking a department supervisor for information about a new product is a method taught by Phil Henry, President of Gray Electronics. Phil has several successful electronics-related inventions. Phil also uses this method of screening as what he calls a "Poor Man's Patent Search." In other words, if the expert working for the retail outlet says that a product is not available and Phil wants to pursue the invention, he feels that is reason enough to have a thorough patent search done.

A Totally Absurd Patent

U.S. Patent 4,605,000, Greenhouse Helmet, creates your own personal biosphere! This invention consists of a sealed plastic dome with plants living on tiny internal shelves near your ears. The dome also has speakers and a microphone for communication with the outside world. The mini greenhouse is designed to allow the user to breathe the oxygen given off by the plants. It's uncertain how we might be able to survive with the measly amount of oxygen from a couple of cacti...unless, of course, we plan to be permanently comatose.

Do you suppose a preliminary market evaluation was done on this invention?
...totallyabsurd.com

Corporate America often looks for short-term successes, short-term profits. This is similar to a president asking, "Why don't you sales-marketing people go out and look for new gimmicks and fads for us to sell?" This is in direct contradiction to the philosophy of the same corporate head that says, "All we want to make are long-run, generic products." Gaining short-term profit is usually not compatible with long run, generic products.

Also remember that if your innovation-invention is based on having "instant" success, it can fade away just as instantly. As an inventor, don't waste time and money on short-term fads. Look for the long-term trends that will slowly develop and give you the long-term security and income you deserve for your efforts.

BREAKTHROUGH OPPORTUNITIES USUALLY TAKE TIME TO BE ACCEPTED

If you know your innovation-invention is a good one, but it is not being readily received, be patient. If you have carefully thought out all the attributes and you know that sooner or later it will have a broader acceptance, a *trend* will ultimately develop. You are probably just a little ahead of your time.

It is ironic but true that it sometimes takes years for a trend to develop, even with the best of ideas. But when a trend does take hold, it sticks around for the long term. Some excellent examples are Ziploc® bags, Sony Walkman and even small cars! Always try to innovate with future trends in mind.

Another important factor in spotting and developing trends is to continually improve your inventions. Rarely does a first invention become a smash hit. Invariably, you will find some improvement later on representing a breakthrough opportunity that propels sales dramatically.

COMPETITIVE RESPONSES

Another key element in the introduction of inventions is to make certain your competitors will not respond by trying to drive you out of business. This can happen regardless of how wonderful your new innovation may be. If your invention is a threat to their existing technology and your sales are soaring, they will most likely be determined to fight.

Competitors that are "vertically integrated" can also create problems. Vertically integrated means they also supply some of the raw materials or key components required in the product. For instance, a vertically integrated cardboard box manufacturer owns its own paper

---

If your idea is not a long-term trend, but a short-term fad and you want to try to market it, then forget patenting and just go out and try to sell as much of it as you can, as fast as you can! Just go for it before others start copying you.

Design trends in vacuums in the 20th century tended to follow scientific developments in transportation. The first ones with the little headlight resembled a locomotive, then when the jet age arrived, the new canister versions resembled jets and rockets.

When Inventing, Keep in Mind the Competitor's Strengths and Weaknesses

Just as you have considered competitive responses to your ability to enter the marketplace, you will want to carefully consider competitive responses to each unique attribute of your invention. As one of the keys to inventing and innovating, you must declare your niche and be prepared to move forward and take it! You want to make sure it is a niche you can protect.

When evaluating each potential Customer-Driven Innovation, consider how your competitors will respond. The more difficult their response, the better your opportunity.

Even if you erred and did not anticipate their response, being first to market can give you the competitive edge to maintain your newly found niche. Just keep inventing and stay ahead of them!

and recycling mill. A plastic bag producer may be a division of a plastic resin company that supplies raw material to make the bags.

If you are a threat to any of these companies, you may not be able to secure a consistent supply. This can be particularly distressing in a market that is being "run up", as supply tends to fall short of demand anyway. On the other hand, when old-fashioned industries are being replaced by new technologies, there may be little challenge to your inventive efforts. There is much to learn in new industries with great opportunities for new products and innovations. A few examples of new industries replacing old are:

- PC's and their software replacing business machines and large computer rooms
- Plastic bags replacing paper bags
- Plastic bottles replacing glass bottles
- Lasers replacing surgical scalpels
- Robotics replacing people
- Small cars replacing large cars

While you will find that creating new ideas may not elicit much of a competitive response, you will also find that trying to sell your innovative ideas to old-fashioned corporate management is just as difficult. You will learn in Part Three, Chapter 9 that old-fashioned industries that think in terms of high-volume, generic products and protecting their existing market share find it difficult to embrace invention and innovation.

COMPARE YOUR INVENTION TO THE PRESENT STATE OF THE ART AND THE INDUSTRY

You can rate your invention relative to the present state-of-the-art and the existing suppliers in the industry. First, you want to evaluate the present state-of-the-art in your industry. To give you an example, when plastic grocery sacks began replacing paper sacks in supermarkets, it was fairly easy to see that the current state-of-the-art consisted of a number of large, inflexible, paper bag manufacturing conglomerates. These mega-corporations had little desire to do anything but protect their market share.

The plastic sack that would ultimately cost far less than paper was clearly an opportunity for an innovative company. Using the chart in Fig. 2-3, the large paper bag producers and the state of the art of their product line would be rated between 1 and 4. The innovative plastic bag producers would be rated between 5 and 10.

An Invention Assistance Company Blunder

I recently encountered a fellow who spent tens of thousand of dollars with an invention assistance company to develop a product for use in the lottery.

The assistance company failed to take the most basic step of all--qualifying with the state the inventor's ability to use the magnetic strip on the lottery tickets. A year later a friend pointed out that the magnetic strips were intricately coded and that it was illegal for anyone other than an authorized lottery vender to use them.

The assistance company refused to refund his several thousand dollars, but evidently he is pursuing relief through the Federal Trade Commission's recent fraud complaints against seven of the largest companies.

As a reminder, the rate of success in which an inventor has earned more money than he/she has invested with these companies, is generally less than $1/100^{th}$ of 1%! That's right--1 success out of 10,000 clients.

You can use this same guideline to get an idea of where your new invention is positioned.

- In Fig. 2-3, mark the appropriate location of the state-of-the-art in your industry.
- Next, mark the positioning of certain key competitors.
- Last, mark your invention's posture.

Figure 2-3 Invention Positioning

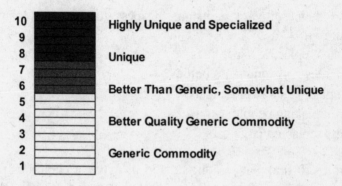

LOOKING FOR THOSE UNIQUE ATTRIBUTES THAT SELL!

Make sure that the attributes that will make your invention a big success are features and benefits that consumers want...not attributes that you, personally, or your family, would like to have.

Is your invention a major innovative improvement with unique attributes or is it just a minor variation on the same old-fashioned theme? You need a decided advantage to entice customers to buy your invention. If you or your marketing expert feels your invention does not have an advantage, don't worry just yet. In Chapter 3, you will learn about several different attributes and methods to improve your invention's salability.

If your invention is related to unique attributes of existing products, you will probably find it difficult to sell to an existing manufacturer that dominates the old-fashioned industry. But you will learn in Part Three that there are ways to get around that barrier. Your marketing expert can help tremendously.

STRATEGIC STEP #3:
CONDUCT AND EVALUATE AN ACCURATE PATENT SEARCH

While your patent search has great impact on the patentability of your invention, it can play a part in its future development as well. A patent search usually occurs sometime after you have done some initial development. When you get it back and analyze it, you might find you are not infringing any other patents. While this is good news, you might want to also check into the related art and ask yourself if any of them has been successful. If not, why? Try to use this to your advantage. Perhaps the industry is dominated by just a few and the barriers to entry are too great. Most often, new inventions fall flat because of poor marketing plans.

In contrast, if it appears that the inventive matter in your invention is already patented, can you or do you want to proceed? You may have some serious development decisions to make. If a patent exists and is still in force, it is illegal to sell anything under the scope of its claims without its owners' permission. This is infringement. You then have three development alternatives to consider:

1. Do you want to try to license it from the owner?
2. Do you want to drop the project altogether?
3. Do you want to try to design around it?

From the perspectives of pure creative inventing and brainstorming, designing around an existing patent can be challenging and fun. Read carefully the section on how to read patents in Chapter 6. From it you can get your creative juices flowing and try to figure out a "design-around" that can make money.

In any design-around activity, try to imagine the next generation. Ask yourself what the next generation of this type of invention is likely to be. If you can answer that question, you will be taking a major step forward in your career as an inventor.

STRATEGIC STEP #4: DEVELOP THE INVENTION TO A FUNCTIONAL STATE

Developing your idea into a functional state means that you have also "reduced it to practice". This is the second key to preserving the potential of your patent rights.

Your idea will go through various prototyping phases that will include in-house testing, customer trials and eventually larger, expanded test markets. Your manufacturing and marketing partners can help you tremendously during this phase. You would be wise to get them involved as early as possible.

THE FIVE PHASES OF PROTOTYPING

A prototype is usually necessary for you to properly develop your invention with all the right Customer-Driven Innovation (CDI™) attributes. (See Chapter 3 for more on CDI.) It is not a simple one- or two-step process. But as you will see, it can be done quickly and inexpensively if you take all the right steps.

In the field of plastic packaging, there are about 30 patents for square bottom plastic bags. But none of them have ever been commercialized. The reason is that they add from 30% to 300% onto the cost of making a plastic bag. Thus paper continues to be used in fast food applications.

Only recently was a process invented that makes square bottom plastic bags cost effective.

When considering a design - around remember…

It's not what it is, but what it can be.
…George Morgan, Esq.

A prototype invariably begins as a crude model and then transforms itself, little by little, into a cost-effective, working model with the proper marketing attributes. It is from this perspective that your prototyping will probably not be entirely completed until you have assembled your manufacturing and marketing team members. Your final prototype must be what your marketing expert says is "salable" and your manufacturing expert says, "can be cost-effectively manufactured."

What follows are the prototype phases that a typical, simple invention follows. You may only do a few before you get one that can be presented in sales presentations. Subsequently, the final working model will be manufactured and put through final testing before being released to the public.

*Phase 1

The first prototype is for size, shape and basic design. (It may be non-functional or function crudely.) It may not be made in the desired material. For instance, it may be carved in balsa wood or molded from clay, instead of being injection-molded plastic.

*Phase 2

The second prototype can be used for testing functionality and may be in the (perceived) desired material. Do as much testing as possible, regardless of redundancy. As early as possible, get a marketing expert involved in determining the best attributes.

*Phase 3

This prototype has improvements as a result of your testing. Hopefully, you will be able to put some "dazzle" or "sex appeal" into it at this stage. This prototype stage can be tested by you, but it is more important to have it tested by select end users in a test environment. When you test and observe, be super observational and hyper-aware. Try to "crawl inside" your invention and see what is really going on. Always listen to the comments you hear, positive and negative. All negative comments are good news and represent great opportunities.

Phase 4

This is a first article, a true working prototype. It is tested in actual working conditions by real end users who do not know that they are "guinea pigs". Don't call them that. Remind the "testers" that they are the lucky ones who are the first to use the innovation. You are present during the test. You listen to all the "ooooo's" and "ahhhhh's". You learn all you can about the testers' opinions regarding size, shape, style, etc. You casually ask what they do like and what they don't like--never assume. Watch the actions and movements of the testers carefully.

"The Prototype"

*When introducing new inventions, I have frequently been asked if I have made "the prototype". This question insinuates that there is "**only one prototype**" and that after it is made, "the **prototype**" can be used to make sales. This is rarely the case.*

A prototype tends to go through several phases...literally a transformation. Once it is well developed with all the CDI benefits, it can be used to effectively secure sales.

...Bob DeMatteis

Sourcing materials and parts for the construction of your prototypes can be a large part of the prototyping job. If you would like to save money and time on prototype development, consider offering to do the sourcing yourself.

...Paul Berman T2Design Corporation

It is much easier to excite the imagination of a potential licensee with a working prototype. In addition, a prototype proves the concept will work.

...Robert Platt Bell, Esq.

After extensive observation and listening to their feedback, you will advise on the final improvements.

Phase 5

The final prototype phase represents the production models that are used in a substantial test market. Instead of a single application, use several; instead of one store, use an entire district. Unlike the previous prototypes, these are usually sold to the customer (the end user).

* At times, these prototype phases might be shortened by a series of drawings and sketches that show the invention's attributes and allow the team members and end users to evaluate them.

CREATIVE PROTOTYPING METHODS

Inventors are inherently creative. You can use your creative ability to create and make your first stage prototypes. Here are several suggestions:

- Can you get a similar product and modify and adapt it?
- Can you use wood and paint it with chrome paint to resemble steel?
- Can you use only graphics to illustrate the invention? Salespeople don't typically carry around products as large as computers anyway. If you can, sell off the sheet with some great graphics.
- Can you give your initial sales presentation at a distance, so no one will see how crude your prototypes are?
- In your sales presentation, can you smile at the VP with whom you are meeting and then laugh at your prototype and tell him/her how the real working model with the attractive graphics wasn't made in time… or that it had an unexpected delay? (Almost always true!)

HOW TO GET PROTOTYPES MADE AT LITTLE OR NO COST TO YOU

Being a successful inventor requires fast, economical prototyping and testing, while also making sure that the prototypes have all the attributes you want. The best way to do this is through a team effort. With the right team players, you can create prototypes with the attributes you want and with little out-of-pocket expense. Here is how.

Industrial and Commercial Applications

Inventions dealing with industrial applications are usually directly related to problem solving and result in saving customers money, time or space. So it is not difficult to get an audience with a potential

---

Licensees are notorious for losing or destroying prototypes while reviewing them. Try to protect your prototype investment by requiring that a Prototype Review Agreement *is signed which states that the manufacturer accepts full responsibility for repair or replacement of the prototype if it is lost or damaged while in the manufacturer's possession.*
…Paul Berman, T2Designs

Prototyping Tips From an Expert

Paul Berman of T2Designs gives these suggestions:
- *Scavenge around at a local toy store for a plastic mechanism or an electronic circuit that would otherwise cost $1000's to replicate.*
- *Bondo is a plastic resin used for filling in car dents, but can be used to fabricate almost any shape to fill in unwanted holes and gaps.*
- *Molding can be purchased at any number of plastic stores or home centers in order to replicate complex curvatures.*
- *Paint the finish in order to create the "off the shelf" look. Take care in doing some finish sanding beforehand.*
- *The Thomas Register can be used to locate obscure parts. Find it at most libraries.*

Expensive Prototyping Alternative

If your invention is one that will require highly technical, expensive components and research and development, look for a special relationship with a potential licensee. This relationship may even include being on his/her payroll during the initial design phase.

For instance, instead of spending $100,000 of your money on an electronic telephone alarm paging system, seek out a partner that will confidentially work with you to develop the desired results. He/she can pay you a contract salary until the product is launched. Then royalties thereafter.

Remember, with this kind of relationship, you will need to have some expertise in the workings of the invention...you can't just "take an idea to them" and claim inventorship. You have to show them how it works to be the real inventor.

You'll read more on inventorship in Chapter 5 and about licensing in Chapters 9-12.

Number One Key to Free Prototyping

Your sales expert can get an audience with a customer that can result in an order or commitment. The other great benefit to having a sales expert on your team in the early phase is that he/she will most likely know the attributes that will make the invention more salable, such as color, size, which bells and whistles to include, etc.

Finding a sales expert for your team early on can quickly propel your efforts!

customer if your idea or invention falls in this category. You are in an excellent position to get an order or at least a commitment to buy before large sums are spent on physical prototypes. When dealing with industrial and commercial applications, develop a working partnership. This partnership will be a team effort focused on problem solving within a customer's and manufacturer's operation.

The four team members who will contribute to and benefit from this prototyping partnership will interact as follows:

1. You. You will contribute your time and know-how (you invented the product or system in the first place) and will work directly with the customer as he/she tests your invention. Remember that you are the pilot in control of the ship.

2. Your Sales-Marketing Expert(s). He/she contributes his/her time to set up initial customer presentations. He/she will either get an initial order or get a commitment from the customer to test your idea. Depending on the nature of your product, the salesperson's relationship with each company and the willingness of the customer, you can use crude (even handmade) prototypes at initial presentations.

3. A manufacturer of the invention. The manufacturer will not necessarily play a part in the initial customer presentation. But once you and your sales expert have an order or commitment in place, you can present it to a willing manufacturer. To get this business--ship the initial order--the manufacturer must simply prove its worth!

The manufacturer will need to prove that it can make the product with the quality and performance you and the customer expect. Thus, the manufacturer must commit to *make or pay for the prototypes* that will be used in testing. After all, it is the manufacturer that will be warranting the performance of the product.

In many cases, the prototypes will ultimately be sold and billed to the customer by the manufacturer. It is easy for a manufacturer to justify the costs of prototyping in such an event. In fact, it is not uncommon for a manufacturer to spend a lot more to retrofit equipment than it will realize from the initial order. Why? It must be able to cost effectively make the new product. In the long run the manufacturer obviously benefits from having the new business. In fact, it will most likely want to arrange an exclusive manufacturing agreement with you.

4. A customer. A willing customer must contribute the time necessary for you to complete your in-house testing. With new industrial products and innovations, you will typically begin with one unit, "get the bugs out" and then expand your sales within the same customer's business to several units as required. The benefit to your customer is obvious.

Retail Applications

Retail applications are not as simple as industrial or commercial applications, since a relatively fine-tuned prototype (including representative packaging) may be needed. But retail applications are not impossible.

The format here is essentially the same as with an industrial-commercial application, but more work by you is required. With retail applications, you will also need an additional expert to get your prototype prepared for market. Here is the scenario:

1. **You.** It starts with you piloting the invention and working with the other team members.

2. **A sales expert.** This person has excellent ties with a retailer of sufficient clout to make a commitment. For instance, if your invention is electronic, the retailer might be Radio Shack; if it is paint related, Sherman Williams; or if kitchen related, Target Stores. The sales expert schedules an appointment with his/her good connections and gets a commitment from the retailer to carry the product (or at least test market it in a given district--usually 20-50 stores).

3. **A manufacturer.** In receipt of an order or commitment, the manufacturer will be ecstatic to have a new customer of this magnitude. Most likely, the manufacturer will go out of its way to get the final prototyping done and get the packaging finished as well.

4. **A customer.** A willing customer who trusts your sales expert will be helpful in striking a purchase order conditioned by (or contingent upon) hitting a certain price range and delivery. It is even more appealing to this first customer if he/she can have an exclusive for a certain start-up period! This is how Direct-TV started. RCA was first and others, including Sony, were added later. It depended on who came up with the cash to "buy position". Similarly, because retail is so competitive, a good salesperson can secure an order "on the come", if the products represent possible profits to a retail outlet. For instance, could you imagine if only Toys 'R' Us had "Tickle Me Elmo" dolls available during the first year?

5. **A packaging expert.** You may want a packaging specialist on the team. He/she can quickly make up prototype packaging with great graphics. The artist can do the job for free, based on receiving the contract, or the manufacturer can pay for it. Prototype packaging that looks awfully close to the final printed version can even be generated on a computer.

If you plan to construct a sophisticated all-electronic prototype with the intention of licensing the rights to a company, consider creating a photo-realistic rendering of the product instead, for initial presentations. You may find that no one is interested enough in your product to ask to see the prototype.
...Paul Berman T2Design Corporation

Whether you use a dedicated prototyping company or are working with a manufacturer, communication is key.
...Paul Berman T2Design Corporation

Prototyping expert Ken Tarlow recommends that if at all possible, the inventor should build his/her own prototype. If you have someone else make it for you, then they should sign a "Work for Hire" agreement. This agreement says that you are paying them and that you own 100% of the results. It also says that if any improvements they make are patentable, they must assign the rights to you. The confidentiality agreement in Chapter 10 of this book is an example of this kind of form.

The Key to Free Prototyping

As you have discovered, the key to free (or virtually free) prototyping is to get an order or a commitment first. With an order in hand, it is not difficult to convince a manufacturer to pay for at least the final working prototypes you need to finalize testing, prior to the shipment of the initial product.

MAKING SUCCESSFUL PRESENTATIONS WITH PROTOTYPES

When using prototypes for presentations, there are several important considerations. You, if you have good sales-marketing skills and connections, or your sales-marketing expert, will arrange this call. Here are some of the key ingredients for a successful first sales call.

- **If the invention falls within an industrial or commercial category, meet with a Vice President of Operations, *not a buyer!*** Buyers are rarely authorized to make changes and test new ideas and systems. Think about it. In an industrial application, will buyers understand labor savings, productivity or timesavings? Usually not. Even if they do, they're usually not in a position to authorize change.

- **If the invention falls within a retail category, contact the Vice President of Merchandising or the Purchasing Director, *not a buyer!*** New products can be introduced quickly with the support of a VP of Merchandising, who usually directs the allocation of shelf space, oversees advertising, arranges district meetings and determines how store managers merchandise new products. All of this is not the buyer's job. Speak to the person who can authorize change or who can approve new product purchases. Since most inventors are not salespeople, get a sales expert on your team who can do this naturally! It is what they do best. Even if he/she refers you to the Buyer at least it comes from the boss.

- **Focus on and speak in terms of "benefits".** Not to you, but to the other team members. For the commercial or industrial customer, identify the problems, and then focus on the CDI benefits and how your invention is going to solve them. In retail, can you give a customer an exclusive sales arrangement for the start-up period? Some free publicity? The benefits to your salesperson should be an exclusive sales agreement (or perhaps a license) in his/her area, as long as he/she continues to get the job done. The manufacturer should be guaranteed a supply contract for a certain term, in return for the initial start-up expense.

- **Use a "partnering" approach.** Get everyone on the team to be a partner in the launching of the new product. The industrial-

---

Zero Cost Prototyping

I have never paid for prototyping and making working models. With my first invention I brought orders to my licensee worth $20,000 a month. They spent a about $25,000 retrofitting their machines to make the new style of plastic bag.
    ...Bob DeMatteis

Making Presentations with Crude Prototypes

It's funny, but true. The decision-maker with a customer will frequently not even want to touch your prototype or even try to use it. It probably has to do with fear of not knowing how to use it.

You can frequently make presentations from a far enough distance that the customer will not notice that it is not a polished production prototype, but a crude, handmade one. Just focus on the benefits to your customer and you will do fine.
    ...Bob DeMatteis

commercial customer gives you the ability to test, monitor and help them. The retail customer allows you to go into stores and help merchandise and set up counters. The sales partner can also help by following up on the shipments, out-of-the-area store managers, etc. The manufacturer also partners by being ready to make any necessary changes and improvements required to successfully build the needed prototypes and then ship the product.

- **Always ask for an order…even if it is conditional.** Remember that you are developing a partnership with the customer. Guarantee him/her success by saying, "We will do whatever it takes to make this a success for you". Then *do whatever it takes!*

You don't need a huge first order. Manufacturers take in a lot of money and part of their budget is based on new dies, molds, etc. It is easier for them to justify prototyping costs than it is for you. Most manufacturers would rather gamble thousands of dollars on prototyping a new product than blow it at a Las Vegas casino, especially if they have an order!

Finding the Right Partners

Look for the right team members. Not all sales people and manufacturers understand the importance of "getting in on the ground floor," or being first to market. Keep networking until you find those who can help you get your inventions launched.

WHAT IF YOU CAN'T GET A COMMITMENT?

Sometimes prototypes must be thoroughly developed, before you can secure an order. But what if the cost for a prototype is more than you can afford? You still have some alternatives to consider.

Alternative #1

Once you have added a marketing expert to your team, he/she can confirm or even provide some estimate of sales. Next, with your marketing expert, meet with a manufacturer (perhaps one the marketing expert knows, represents or works with) and ask the manufacturer to do the prototyping, based on being the dedicated supplier. Your marketing expert should be able to persuade the manufacturer to move forward and pay for prototyping.

Alternative #2

Seek a strong, marketing-oriented company (it will be your marketing expert) instead of a manufacturer and license the company. In exchange for the marketing company paying for prototypes (or reimbursing you), it will have exclusive sales rights. You can also consider passing up the initial deposit (usually applied against royalties) in lieu of the prototyping expense. This is simply a different type of partnership, but it works.

Alternative #3

Maybe you are not getting the interest you want, which could mean that your invention is not a significant enough improvement. In this

If you are having a difficult time getting a commitment from marketers and manufacturers, don't give up. I recall an instance when two large corporations passed up the opportunity to enter into a manufacturing agreement on one of my new packaging innovations, but a third was eager to do so.

As it turned out, the first two could not justify the return on investment (ROI). The third was a fully integrated plastics producer and saw the potential to add a substantial volume to not only its packaging plants, but to its new resin facility. It asked for an exclusive agreement!

...Bob DeMatteis

case, ask yourself, "What is the next generation to this invention? Can I invent that instead?" For instance, the next generation to a button on a key chain that disarms a car alarm and unlocks the door is a voice-activated mechanism. As you approach the car, you simply say, "Open, please". The device identifies your voice, disarms the alarm and unlocks the doors. An alternative would be to make it sensitive to your fingerprints. As your hand grasps the door handle, it recognizes your prints and unlocks the door.

Alternative #4

You may want to consider abandoning the project altogether. Your inability to get interested parties may mean that the benefits you perceive in your invention are not being well accepted. Use your creativity for other inventions and opportunities.

STRATEGIC STEP #5:
WRITE AND FILE PATENT APPLICATIONS

Most Experienced Inventors Don't Rush to File

Over the years, virtually all the experienced inventors I have met use the same process to develop their inventions.

That process is to wait until the last possible moment before public disclosure to file a patent application, thereby preserving cash flow and preserving worldwide patent filing rights.

This is particularly advantageous now with provisional patent applications.

...Bob DeMatteis

You will want to start writing your first application--it will most likely be a provisional application--sometime during the development process. Based on pure strategy, initially writing a regular application makes little sense, unless at least one of the following factors prevails:

1. **Infringement is imminent**. In this case, you will want to secure your patent protection as soon as possible, so you can plan your patent infringement strategy.

2. **The sales window is short.** If your product has a very short window of opportunity and you want patent protection, it makes no sense to file a provisional application first.

3. **You have money to burn.** If so, don't waste time on filing provisional applications.

FILING FOR PATENTS AND YOUR INVENTION
DEVELOPMENT STRATEGY

*The U.S. patent system has worked well for more than two centuries and is often referred to in the context of the **American Dream.***

...Donald Grant Kelly, Director, U.S. Patent Office

Since ours is a "first-to-invent" country and the recording of the date of conception followed by your reduction to practice activities has protected you, it is not necessary to rush to file patent applications.

Smart inventors will write their patent applications while they are developing their inventions. There are very good reasons for this. First, they are protected by the first-to-invent laws of this country. Second, this is particularly true if a thorough patent search was conducted and shows no conflict, recent or otherwise.

By developing your idea more thoroughly and then writing your application at a later date, you will have made sufficient progress to portray your discoveries and their unique attributes. Filing too soon may require you to file an additional patent application on new inventive matter, to broaden your original claims.

Based on the new laws, you can easily file a provisional patent application in a timely manner for only $75. The tremendous savings over the cost of filing a regular application (at $2500 or more to write and file) can be used on your invention development. Later, within one year of the provisional filing, you should have some sales generated on your invention, which will make the cost much more affordable. Your objective is to file provisional patent applications based on the correct inventive matter with a broad enough scope to ensure adequate patent protection.

In any event, an inventor should not think that he/she can wait forever while the invention is being developed. If someone across the country is developing the same idea, and reduces it to practice and files for patents before you do, you may be out of luck. The patent laws say that you cannot claim your first-to-invent rights if you wait more than one year after the granting of an identical invention to another party. After one year, any request for an interference will be denied. You can read more about this subject in Part Two, Chapter 6.

A Common Mistake, Rushing to File

All to often inventors who have rushed to file regular patent applications have found that by the time the invention was developed to a marketable state, they have "designed around" the original subject matter in the patent application!
...Bob DeMatteis

STRATEGIC STEP #6: FOLLOW THROUGH ON YOUR MARKETING AND MANUFACTURING PLAN

This step is by far the most time consuming of all your activities. Once your invention is well developed, you will soon be on your way to a product launch. You have made a few crude prototypes and tested them to your satisfaction. Now you will want to refine them so they can be tested more thoroughly.

The testing of your invention starts in-house with you and a few associates and eventually will move outside your sphere to end-user customers. Invariably, your inventions will be fine-tuned along the way. It is best to refer to testing in-house as "tests". But once you start using real customers, call them "trials".

During testing, you and close associates, hopefully your manufacturing and marketing partners, strive to get the desired results. If there are minor problems, make sure you correct them, because end users will be dissatisfied otherwise.

During this phase, you will want to make certain that your packaging is correct. Confirm that the manufacturer has secured UPC codes, the selected colors are just right and your marketing expert agrees with all the decisions. Remember that he/she is the one who will be selling the product. You will find an in-depth discussion of invention marketing in Part Three.

While working with your manufacturing and marketing partners at this crucial start-up point, you are actually turning over the reigns that frees up your time.

Don't take things for granted at this point. Your manufacturing and marketing experts need your input and your assistance to complete the fine-tuning of the product.

STRATEGIC STEP #7: IMPROVE YOUR INVENTION

Pez was a German peppermint candy dispenser introduced in the 1950's to give smokers an alternative to cigarettes.

The persistent marketing effort was a failure until the company changed its target market to youngsters. It improved upon the design by adding little cartoon heads (Mickey Mouse, Batman and so on) and changing the candies to fruit flavors. Sales soared and continue today.

In any phase of business or life, there is one common element that leads to success. This single principle will almost guarantee your success. This principle is to *"continuously improve"* all that you do. Breakthrough ideas are rarely a first invention, but are usually some improvement on the initial concept. Thus, it is important to continue to develop your invention and look for opportunities to improve it.

In terms of innovating and inventing, improvements are usually small in comparison to the original idea. They are usually easier to incorporate into the product's design and to launch as well. You already have the manufacturing and marketing team in place. You will follow the *Strategic Guide* one more time. From this perspective, the successful inventing process is a circular, continual process. Figure 2-4 shows how the on-going invention development process becomes your team's modus operandi.

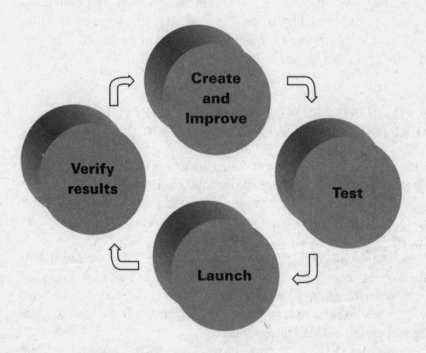

Figure 2-4 Continuous Improvement

In a 1994 interview, world renowned inventor, Jerome Lemelson said, "I am always looking for problems to solve. I cannot look at a technology without asking: How can it be improved?"

By continually improving your invention, you are reinforcing its ability to be a continued success. New patents will evolve, giving you added protection against competitors and sales will continually climb, providing more profit.

What may be more important is that you are becoming the expert in your particular niche. As you continue to develop your niche, taking it further into the future, you are distancing yourself from the other "me-too" products.

Apple Computer became a hit quickly, but sales did not really take off until certain improvements were made. New software additions suddenly made the PC more usable in everyday business applications. The addition of the mouse sent Apple Computer to the next level altogether. Once it became the industry giant and the creators sold their interests, Apple stopped developing new innovations. Today, it is no longer the leader. In fact, it has a bit of an identity crisis that hopefully the company will resolve soon.

To every inventor, I always say, "Don't give up, ever." But I also say to inventors, "Hug your families every day. The invention process is a long road and you need those people behind you. On every balance sheet you should list **family** *as an asset."*

...Donald Grant Kelly, Director, U.S. Patent Office

3

DEVELOPING YOUR INVENTION

The fun begins…discoveries are made…
insurmountable problems solved, a creation forms.

WHAT MAKES A GOOD INVENTION ANYWAY?

It goes without saying that inventions people want to buy will make money. What are some of the attributes of moneymaking inventions? How can you incorporate them into your invention?

Before you consider any one attribute, let's first focus on the state of mind that can help you determine which ones are best. This is referred to as a "Customer-Driven Innovation". It will become the central theme of all your invention-related activities.

A great invention is one that solves an existing problem and saves the customer money.

By solving an existing problem, it makes it fairly easy to get an audience with a potential customer.

By saving the customer money as well, it is then fairly easy to get purchase orders.

…Joe Justin, Pinnacle Group

THE CUSTOMER-DRIVEN PHILOSOPHY

Manufacturing has changed dramatically since the beginning of the twentieth century. The beginning of this century marked the end of the era in which *individual efforts* of a single person or a small group resulted in individual products. In the early 1900's, Henry Ford ushered in the production line. The U.S., followed by other first-world

42

countries, became a *production-driven* country. By the 1950's, the emphasis in manufacturing had changed to a *sales-driven* philosophy-- one in which sales promotions became the driving force. In the U.S., we did not begin thinking in terms of the customer's satisfaction until the 1980's.

History of Manufacturing

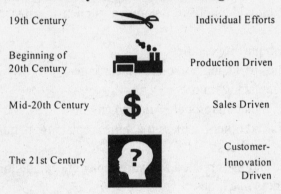

19th Century		Individual Efforts
Beginning of 20th Century		Production Driven
Mid-20th Century		Sales Driven
The 21st Century		Customer-Innovation Driven

Customer satisfaction is a key component in the Quality Management systems (sometimes referred to as QM, TQM, or Total Quality Management) used by many of the world's leading corporations. Unfortunately, in the U.S., the Quality Management transformation began decades after the systems had been adopted, and proven highly successful, in Japan. Going into the 21st century, customer satisfaction is more important than ever to the survival and future success of any company.

Take it to a Higher Level...*Customer-Driven Innovation*

Today, highly successful entrepreneurial companies of any size know that if there is one underlying key to success and future security, it is their *customer-driven* philosophy. Yet most companies confine the evidence of their customer-driven philosophy to better service and faster customer response. Few firms really consider a customer-driven philosophy when designing, manufacturing or developing their products. A focus on *products that customers want to buy* should be the key element of any company's philosophy.

Emphasizing product innovations and inventions that appeal to your customers' *real needs* and *desires* is a winning theme for finding new customers and keeping old ones. This theme defines *"Customer-Driven Innovation"*.

As an inventor, always remember that CDI (Customer-Driven Innovation) is your innovation-design focus. It will make or break your invention's success.

Invention in America in the 19th and 20th century brought the modern era in which we live today to the entire world. This was principally done with inventions that saved time for women in their daily chores at home and in the kitchen. All Mondays used to be "wash days", then all Tuesdays were "ironing days" and so on.

These inventions that changed the world forever include washing machines (Maytag), vacuums (Hoover), sewing machines (Howe and Singer), refrigerators (General Electric), stoves and ovens that could be regulated and many other devices such as electric irons, toasters, mixers, juicers and coffee percolators. What about tomorrow? Are the PC and the myriad of electronics and satellite communications bringing in an entirely new era?

During WWII, innovative toy companies went to work for the war effort. Marx toys started making bazookas, Fisher Price began making bomb crates.

Before WWII metal was the preferred toy material. But since it was in scarce supply, the outbreak of war spurred on the use of plastic in toy making, which it has dominated since.

How to Make All the Right Decisions

If you make your invention, marketing and manufacturing decisions based upon what is best for the customer, you will almost always be making the right decisions. It is a foolproof approach to decision making! Use CDI when making decisions and you can't make a wrong one.

...Bob DeMatteis

FOCUS ON NICHE PRODUCTS

Any inventor or business can use the CDI principles and create niche products that can be protected long-term. Meanwhile, many high-volume competitors will want to continue promoting and expanding market share of their generic product lines.

Virtually every entrepreneurial start-up effort begins as a niche. In time, some of these niches became high-volume, generic products. Even major worldwide industries started as niches. For instance:

Even commodities can be niched. Any discovery that improves the performance or yield of a commodity is valuable. Users of commodities are always looking for ways to improve their output and profits. A small manufacturer discovering an innovative way to produce a commodity product that improves customer productivity and output, will undoubtedly be able to attract and retain many customers.

- Electricity replacing candles
- Automobiles replacing horse-drawn carriages
- Airplanes replacing trains
- Jet engines replacing propeller-driven engines
- Calculators and other business machines replacing manual accounting practices
- Computers and their related software replacing calculators and other business machines

Once a niche has grown into a dominant market, it is typically split into many new niches. For instance:

- Neon lights replacing some incandescent lights
- Small cars and multiple styles replacing the basic family sedan
- Airplanes in all sizes and types, including helicopters
- PC computers replacing the mini- and micro-computers and even some super computers
- Ziploc® bags replacing plastic bags, plastic wrap, waxed paper and aluminum foil

The Greatest Niche Ever?

In the mid-70's Jobs and Wozniak invented/created the first mass-marketed PC that used software...the Apple computer.

What they really created was an entirely new industry...an entirely new way of life.

In 1997, computers outsold TVs. And when you think about it, how many jobs today are directly related to PC computers, software and their offshoot, the Internet?

What they started just a few years ago, may become one of the greatest innovations affecting the history of the world.

And it all started out as a small niche...

Apple Computer, Honda and Hewlett Packard are just a few examples of companies that were able to create innovative, customer-driven products and niches in existing high-volume markets. Even though all these companies had become competitors, they beat out their competitors to huge, new niche markets! Apple beat out IBM, Honda beat out Ford and GM, and HP beat out Xerox.

Today, there are many small, inventive and entrepreneurial companies that are destined to be tomorrow's giants by introducing customer-driven innovations and carving out new, even smaller niches. As an inventor, just focus on a new niche. If sometime later, it grows into a marketing monstrosity, you will have surpassed your dream.

GENERIC VS. VALUE ADDED

Successful innovators know the advantage of differentiating by selling value-added, customer-driven products. Value-added is usually synonymous with better profit margins too. If you focus on value-added benefits for your customers, you will discover the secrets to products they will want to buy!

The "Total Product Concept" flower (Fig. 3-1) developed by Ted Levitt at Harvard, helps us to better understand product focus. Most manufacturing firms concentrate their efforts on the two inner rings. It is here that products can become overly engineered and more and more generic. Most manufacturers (especially larger ones) concentrate their efforts on making products cheaper, instead of better. They focus solely

Figure 3-1

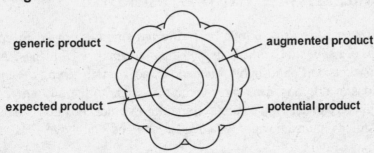

on cutting sizes, gauges, raw material requirements and scrap rates and reducing downtime, to compete in a generic marketplace. Instead, they should be inventing and creating value-added products that can garner higher prices, profits and customer satisfaction.

Innovators often focus their efforts on the two outer rings. Innovative companies such as Apple, Intel, Hewlett Packard and Compaq have become industry giants by doing so. They focused on the augmented and potential benefits to their customers.

To expand on this concept, the long-term strategy of traditional, large U.S. manufacturing companies focuses on generic products and looks like the flower in Fig. 3-2. In contrast, the long-term strategy of innovative companies looks like the flower in Fig. 3-3, with the focus on the augmented and potential product.

Keep in mind that it is difficult for large, cumbersome, established companies to change their production philosophy. It usually takes years and sometimes never happens! From the examples in Fig. 3-2 and 3-3, it is easy to see that there are excellent opportunities for small, flexible manufacturing and marketing companies to cash in through innovation.

Do You Want to See Sure Death?

Any company with a generic product that ignores future trends and fails to grasp the need for customer-driven products will be wiped out by those firms that do.

During the past two decades, many U.S. companies and entire industries that could not adapt to the new trends disappeared. In the paper business, there was Crown Zellerbach and Diamond International. In retail stores, there was Woolworth's and Newberry's. There are entire industries...U.S. steel, large automobiles and electronics that were eliminated. Company after company and industry after industry have stood by and watched their generic market shrink, while smaller, flexible entities beat them to market with superior Customer-Driven Innovations!

Figure 3-2

Figure 3-3

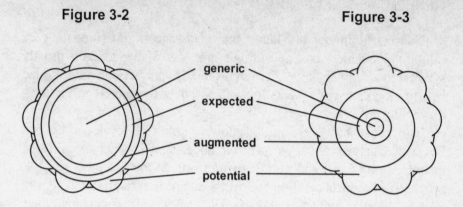

WHERE IS YOUR MINDSET
AND WHERE IS YOUR INVENTION POSITIONED?

When I review a new product, I evaluate its potential to replace an existing product. In particular, I like to replace existing products that are production or sales driven with new innovations that improve quality and economics. Invariably, the existing production or sales driven suppliers will have a poor retort to the new innovation.
...Marketing wizard, Joe "Truckload" Bowers

Have your inventive efforts been directed simply to make cheaper products or have you been focusing on creating small, CDI niches? Are your concepts and philosophy founded in "not-very-different, me-too" inventions or do your ideas carry some real value to the customer? In Fig. 3-4, you can determine your current philosophical position. To be a successful inventor-innovator, you need a rating of 8 or above.

Figure 3-4 Philosophy

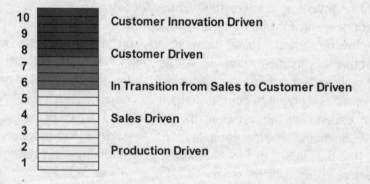

Your challenge is to seek out and create niches you can protect. The niches which are the most profitable, with long-term security, are those created by unique and highly specialized ***Customer-Driven Innovations***.

EIGHT WAYS TO MAKE CDI WORK FOR YOU

Think of Your Invention in Terms of Customer Benefits

Start thinking of your invention in terms of its CDI potential and how it directly benefits your customers. To get an idea of where you are now, answer these questions:

- What features and benefits do customers expect from the existing products? Are they getting them now?
- Do you know the real needs of customers? Do they want improved productivity? Lower labor costs? Better convenience of use?
- Is your innovation/invention presented only to buyers or do you know the all-important operations and merchandising people and end users?
- Do you know the problems that customers are experiencing with existing products?

Make Your Personal Philosophy "Flexible"

In the process of developing and fine tuning your invention, be flexible in your approach. Don't be so fixed on your ultimate objective that you ignore possible changes that might improve sales or the ease of manufacturing.

Adapting your innovation to existing manufacturing processes may be a challenge. You want it to be easily manufactured, so it can be sold at a reasonable price. But it must also have as much pizzazz as possible.

Through your newly found flexibility, you may also discover opportunities and related inventions, including a new production process that may be patentable. All this will give your new invention further security. If you are contracting all or part of the production, persuade your sub-contractors to adopt your CDI approach and be flexible, open-minded partners. They have as much to gain as you do!

Get Everyone Involved and Communicating

Once you have established your team, get everyone involved in the CDI commitment. If you have an innovation that is going to benefit your customers (which in turn benefits your team and all employees), everyone must know what is going on. You will not be successful if everyone in the communication stream--from top management to manufacturing to sales to the customer--is not actively involved.

Good communication starts with you and goes down to supervisors and workers who will make the product. It is your responsibility to make certain that communication is flowing down to the very last employee who will be making your invention. Through open communication, the importance of the customer-driven innovation

A Totally Absurd Patent

Look, up in the sky, it's a bird! It's a plane! No, it's Bat Boy! Able to leap tall speed bumps in a single bound, our superhero with his helmet-like hair and Leonardo DaVinci-like mechanical wings is one of the goofiest looking outfits we've seen in ages. All kidding aside, a recently granted U.S. Patent supposedly helps neophytes learn to roller blade by simply flapping the mechanical wings in the wind.

How would you view this invention in terms of customer benefits?

...totallyabsurd.com

In-house Training

In my invention efforts, I have frequently trained employees at the manufacturer on how to make the new innovation. Teaching various shifts about the quality the customer expects and showing them why they expect it is of great value. How else are they going to learn?

I have even gone so far as to post quality standards in both English and Spanish. How was I able to do this? Simple. I asked the top management, which is usually most willing, since training costs money and I was doing it for free!

...Bob DeMatteis

Inducing the birth of a new product can be agonizing. It is too easy to just "assume that it will be made correctly". We usually communicate only with management, but we must make sure that the expected quality is communicated to everyone...down to the very last detail. We must remember that many production workers are being paid minimum wages and are not experts in your new innovation.

How will you make sure they know it is being made correctly with all the right attributes?

(your invention) will be conveyed and more easily maintained. Every employee can (and must) take part in ensuring that improvements and innovations take place on schedule and with the desired outcome.

Think about it...without total communication to the very last person, making changes in products is difficult. There will always be employees who will revert to the old way of doing things. It happens all the time and can be one of the most frustrating experiences in product improvement and innovation an inventor-innovator can have.

Fig. 3-5 shows the areas of responsibility for a successful, innovative firm. Most of the responsibility for product innovation rests in the hands of top management. However, the shaded area containing the responsibility to "make [things] happen" is more important. The "make happen" arena is where supervisors and workers become more involved in the effort. As you can see, it is everyone's responsibility to "make [it] happen." Frequently, it is in this "make happen" arena where the lack of communication delays and thwarts innovative efforts.

Figure 3-5

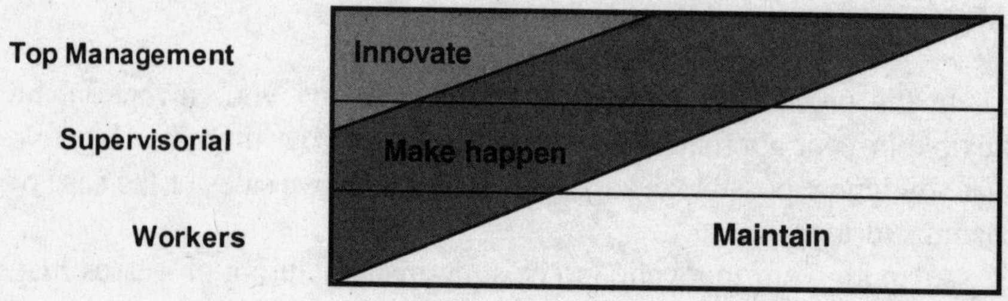

For innovative efforts to be successful:

***All communication barriers must be eliminated to allow immediate feedback** from one person to another...from management to supervisors, from one production process to another and from one shift to another.*

Excellence in Management

In a study conducted by Tom Peters and Robert H. Waterman on the qualities of 43 "excellently managed" U.S. companies, including IBM, Eastman Kodak, 3M, Boeing, Bechtel, Proctor & Gamble and McDonald's, they found several common traits, in addition to consistent profitability. At the top of the list is the fact they are "unusually successful in responding to their customers' needs."

Get Super Close to Your Customers

Start by taking the time to get to know your customers well, from the top level right down to the all-important end users. One of the best ways to locate innovation opportunities is to be super-sensitive to problems your customers have with existing products, the lack of an existing product or in their industrial/commercial operations. Your customers' problems are your greatest opportunity!

Buyers, operations people and managers do not always have the answers. This is why you must gain as much access as possible to a customer's entire operation. Remember that ***you are more likely to be the expert on your invention and product line and are in a better*** *position to discover new innovations they will want...and perhaps* cannot live without! If you understand your customers' needs and problems, you will have the opportunity to create some brilliant inventions and improvements to existing products.

Remember that decisions to change are made at upper management levels. Presentations of new CDI inventions and improvements to existing products to top management are usually well received. Upper management can provide valuable input and pave the way to innovation trials. It is usually easy to get appointments with top executives to introduce new innovations...if you just ask.

Your innovative solutions to customer and end-user problems can quickly propel sales of your invention. Supplying continual improvements focused on customer benefits is a sure-fire way to secure long-term, profitable relationships with customers.

Think Small

Too often in America we think in terms of large volumes, big dollars and huge markets. Even in terms of innovation, we have a tendency to think in terms of major changes.

To be a successful, continually innovative firm, it is far better to think small. The Japanese have learned this lesson well, and at the expense of many American companies. Thinking small means not only thinking in terms of smaller (niche) markets, but of smaller innovations. You don't need to recreate the wheel overnight. It is best to recreate it one spoke at a time.

It is unlikely that your first invention will be a smashing success. With a little experience, you will be in a position to introduce future innovations that will become breakthrough opportunities. It is usually invention four or five that is an improvement on the first product that really propels sales. With a series of small innovations, you will either reinforce your current market niche or be able to capture new ones. Either way, you are warding off competitors, expanding your sales volume and profits, and securing your future via more and more high-quality patents.

Without question, once you become experienced in developing inventions, the time it takes to bring them to market will be reduced. You will be able to bring innovations and products to market with lightning speed that dazzles your competitors. Of course, your competitors will be continually struggling to keep pace with your last dazzling innovation!

Use Intuition (or Instincts) to Guide Your Innovations

This is what experienced innovators do. The more you use your intuition or instincts, the smarter you become. However, there is a difference between the two. "Intuition" is defined by *The American*

Having marketing experts on your team who are well connected with the customer will dramatically reduce the amount of time it takes to get your innovation to market. If they are good, they are already "close to the customer". They will have relationships with potential customers that would take you years to develop.

When I think about launching the sales of a new packaging product, I like to start out with a small test run. I can usually get the manufacturer to make these at no cost to the customer.

This is an easy way to get a new product tested. It behooves the manufacturer too, as it will help overcome any final glitches.

Then, working closely with the customer, when I see it is working out as anticipated, I ask for blanket, truckload orders to cover an entire year and keep the competitors out.

...Marketing wizard, Joe "Truckload" Bowers

There are several views about which nationalities make the best inventors, but inventors appear to be from all over the world and in all nationalities.

For the most part, it seems that inventors run along genetic lines. If your parents or grandparents were creative people, artists or problem-solving engineers, chances are you will follow in their footsteps.

What may be more important than having a creative ability, is being in a position to use it. This is one of the wonderful aspects of inventing in America!

I was working with General Motors on a project and was having difficulty trying to keep it on track. I was having to fly to Michigan far too often and it was wearing me down.

On one of my visits to Detroit, I decided to apply this one bit of advice--"Find a champion to my cause and let him lead".

It worked! It not only helped my effort and saved me immeasurable weeks of travel and a lot of money--but it greatly enhanced General Motors' ability to quickly conclude the project for an immediate launch.

...Yujiro Yamamoto, world renowned inventor

Heritage Dictionary as "the act or faculty of knowing something without the use of rational processes." *American Heritage* defines "instinct" as "the innate aspect of behavior that is unlearned, complex, and normally adaptive." Which one fits you best?

Myers-Briggs differentiates between two personality types. "N" types generally prefer to use their intuition. "S" types prefer to use their instincts. Inventors are more likely to be "N" types, but "S" types can be dynamic innovators as well. Leonardo Da Vinci, Benjamin Franklin and Thomas Edison were certainly "N" types. Lee Iacocca and George Patton are perhaps two of the most famous "S" types. Either skill--intuition or instincts--will serve you well in the invention development process.

Use them to:

1. Determine the merit of your existing products or new ones you want to release.
2. Determine the changes or improvements your innovations need to be successful.
3. Help identify the underlying *causes* of problems hindering the success of your inventions.
4. Locate and evaluate solutions.
5. Pilot your on-going invention developmental processes.
6. Direct your future innovations.
7. Evaluate relevant financial matters.

If you are inexperienced in invention development and innovation, be well aware of your decision-making preferences. Take the time to develop this important facet of your personality. An undeveloped intuition that is out of touch with reality can result in products too far advanced for the current market or impossible to manufacture at competitive prices. Likewise, using your instincts without seasoned experience and a clear understanding of the future can result in ineffective, misdirected efforts.

Find the Champions to Your Cause and Let Them Lead!

In every innovative effort, there will be leaders who rise to the top to help move your CDI efforts forward. Look for those who take charge in your various projects and give them the leeway, encouragement and power to make things happen fast. You send powerful messages to the work force when the champions are given the power to push forward (and occasionally ramrod) an innovative effort. They may ruffle some feathers and cause some problems and disagreements, but they must be supported and rewarded. The message must be crystal clear: nothing stands in the way of your invention and improvement efforts!

Zero in on Your Target Market

Your invention-innovation attributes should target a specific target market that you can identify and keep in focus. Once you have done this, continually ask yourself what your target market wants. What is the next invention or improvement they need or would like? Think about this:

> *If you make all your decisions based on the needs of and benefits to your target market, you will make only excellent decisions.*

Your target market is your niche. It is where you will become the premier expert in your field. You will become well known in this field over the years. Don't lose sight of your target market and it will never let you down. The field of opportunity is yours to create.

FOCUSING YOUR EFFORTS ON CDI

What are some of the attributes your customers are seeking? Which of their problems can you solve? Frankly, your customers do not always know their problems. In fact, they frequently don't! It is often difficult for customers and end users to articulate their true needs.

Your chief task as an inventor is to uncover their problems. It is not an easy task. But if you think of your inventions in terms of potential CDI benefits to your customers and how your inventions might help them, you will discover several good opportunities. These opportunities can include the creation of new products as well as many future improvements.

While you are developing your innovations, keep in mind this simple, but important concept that will influence which attributes your innovations will have:

> **Cleverness can create innovations,**
> **but *character* sells them!**

This should be your underlying theme as you strive to find Customer-Driven Innovation opportunities. You will learn more about this concept at the end of this section.

RATING YOUR INVENTION

Keep in mind that developing CDI benefits represents the potential, not the actual. Inventions must have solid, customer-benefit attributes or they will have little success. There is no substitute for the evaluation

Keep in Mind the Competitor's Strengths and Weaknesses

Just as you have considered competitive responses to your ability to enter the marketplace, you will also want to carefully consider competitive responses to each unique attribute your invention will have. You must declare your niche and be prepared to move forward and take it! You want to make sure it is a niche you can protect.

When evaluating each potential Customer-Driven Innovation, you will always want to weigh them against how your competitors will respond. The more difficult their response, the better opportunity you have.

Even if you erred and did not expect their response, being first to market will still give you the competitive edge to help maintain your newly found niche. Just keep inventing and stay ahead of them!

of an invention based on input from your marketing experts and potential customers. This is covered in depth in Chapter 2.

The balance of this chapter is dedicated to the discussion of Customer-Driver Innovation aspects you can use to develop and evaluate your innovations/inventions.

CDI BENEFIT #1:
INVENTIONS SHOULD BE GOOD FOR MANKIND

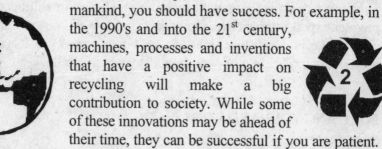

It might sound a little corny, but it is true. If you can develop inventions and innovations that improve the health and welfare of mankind, you should have success. For example, in the 1990's and into the 21st century, machines, processes and inventions that have a positive impact on recycling will make a big contribution to society. While some of these innovations may be ahead of their time, they can be successful if you are patient. For instance if you develop a process that eliminates or neutralizes certain types of contaminants, expensive toxic waste dumping charges could be avoided by the users...but you may have to wait until the legislation is in place.

A good example of creating a niche with an environmentally sound innovation is the new biodegradable detergent on the market. The soap-making giants just can't adapt their huge processing systems to make these small runs. It has become an attractive niche for companies like Planet® Brand and EarthCare® to capture and protect, based on the inability of the larger detergent companies to effectively respond. Besides, environmentally sound products are not normally associated with corporate giants.

Making products better for mankind applies both to inventions and the many ways to improve existing products. When you improve the environmental qualities of an existing product you may be manufacturing, or have licensed, you also improve your ability to maintain the current sales position. Here are some questions to consider in your invention activities:

- Can you alter existing formulas to reduce or eliminate contaminants?
- Can you lower the amount of raw material used, hence reducing waste?
- Can you use a material that will double the life of the product (thus reducing trash)?
- Can you incorporate a secondary use of the product?

A Totally Absurd Patent

With U.S. Patent 4,276, 033, "Windmill Boat", the lack of wind will never put a damper on your sailing again. Since wind is unpredictable, most sailboats carry gas-powered motors. But fuel is not cheap and causes pollution. The politically correct Skipper can turn to the amazing Windmill Boat. Its umbrella-shaped sail slowly rotates to propel the boat while also generating electricity. The electricity is stored in batteries for later use or can be used to power cabin appliances. This boat eliminates air and water pollution at the same time!

...totallyabsurd.com

- Can you redesign it to improve capacity, hence reducing the number of units used?

   By monitoring proposed legislation for laws mandating environmental changes, you can improve your timing for a market release. But why wait? Take a leadership position and do it now and this can be your declared niche!

CDI BENEFIT #2: SAVING TIME, MONEY AND SPACE

   Everyone looks for savings, which can come in many forms. The three most powerful savings you can provide your customer are:

   1. **Saving time**. Time *is* money. In the current madness, everyone is looking for ways to manage their time better. If you can save your customers valuable time, you will find plenty of followers.

   2. **Saving money**. There are several ways to save money for your customers. Be wise and look for innovations that have a ***total*** cost-cutting impact. Cost-cutting means lower expenditures on the bottom line, not necessarily a lower price per unit. Anyone can create a lower price per unit by cutting quality. Per unit costs can be very deceiving.

   3. **Saving space**. Here is where thinking small can really pay off. Americans tend to do this poorly while the Japanese understand this concept well. With the high cost of real estate today, space is at a premium. Large "anythings" that you can replace with small, efficacious "anythings" are in demand. Computers and cars are prime examples, but there are opportunities in virtually every field.

   A good example of savings is the reduction of raw material by using one that is stronger. As stated in CDI Benefit #1, we know it makes a strong environmental statement, but it can also save your customer space and time. For instance, you could pack 24 items per case instead of 12. These savings can indirectly improve an industrial or commercial customer's bottom line, regardless of the unit cost.

Saving my customers money is the central theme of every purchase. Try to make sure all your innovations save money and they should be well received.
   ...Marketing wizard, Joe "Truckload" Bowers

New, *Improved!*

Your inventions and innovations can be in the form of improvements on existing products or completely new concepts. Sometimes we see them in supermarkets with labels reading "new, improved formula". You can use the many CDI benefits for both original ideas and improvements to existing ones.

You can also look for other areas in industrial, commercial and retail applications, in which your innovations can be "improvements." For instance, look for ways to improve down-time, change-over time, handling, shelf life, strength attributes, durability, assembly, ease of operation, speed, defect reduction, etc., etc.

A Totally Absurd Patent?

Riding a motorcycle gives you the feel of wind like you're flying. But if you crash while cruising down the highway, the bike stops and you are unfortunately catapulted through the air. Newton's Law of Gravity says, "What goes up, must come down", which is translated into "You will come to a crashing, painful halt."

But not if you had strapped on "Crash Wings" (U.S. Patent 5,593,111). When ejected from a motorcycle, a set of para-wings pops open and lifts you away from the crash site and floats you back down to earth safely.

...totallyabsurd.com

Convenience

There is no end to innovations that strive to improve a product's convenience. Improvements can be made continually until the product works automatically...which will be your ultimate innovation!

A Totally Absurd Patent

U.S. Patent 4,888,836 is for lighter-than-air furniture that can be levitated with helium gas and stored on your ceiling when not in use! Floating furniture saves space and allows you to freely roam about your home during the day, and sleep comfortably at night! To take a nap, just grab the tether and pull the bed down from the ceiling. Imagine! You'll never again have to make your bed or clear off the dinner table. Simply inflate the unmade bed and untidy table and they're out of site!

...totallyabsurd.com

CDI BENEFIT #3: SAFETY

Several companies have had tremendous success by being the safety experts. Mercedes Benz, Volvo, and the originators of seat belts and airbags come to mind. In industry, safer equipment is now mandated by OSHA (Occupational Safety Hazard Act). Why not exceed OSHA requirements? Why not apply safety facets in every product, regardless of whether they are mandated by law?

Every producer has a challenge to design products that are inherently safe to use and safe around children. If you are waiting for the government to require you to improve safety, you could be losing a competitive advantage. Strive to make all your products safe to use. By designing innovations that exceed safety standards, you can consider safety the focus of your niche. Every field can support a niche supplier that focuses on being the safety leader.

CDI BENEFIT #4: CONVENIENCE

How convenient is "convenient"? Developing your ideas into products that customers find convenient is a never-ending opportunity. You will not exhaust the search for innovations that make your products convenient to use until you have made them totally automatic in every way imaginable. In fact, that is your goal! When your customers tell you that they like your products because they are convenient to use, you will know your innovations are right on track. A few examples of convenient-to-use products are:

- One-at-a-time Kleenex® dispensers
- Remote control devices such as TV and stereo controls, electric garage door openers, key chain car door locks and alarms
- Automatic dialing for phones and fax machines
- Computer Internet services for banking, travel plans, etc.
- Automatic ice makers and water dispensers in refrigerators

Think about the future generations of items listed above…there is really no end to the possibilities.

CDI BENEFIT #5: COMFORT

In many respects, we take comfort for granted. Yet, if we think about it, our homes have been comfortable for only the last several decades. As recently as 100 years ago, most people had few of the comforts we enjoy today. These comforts include chairs, sofas, beds, plush carpeting, hot water heaters, baths and showers. The list goes on and on. Comfort also includes other aspects of life such as clothes, cosmetics and personal items.

There are still exceptional opportunities to improve the level of comfort in our lives, such as:

- Comfortable airplane seats
- Bicycle handlebars, handle grips and seats
- Air conditioning that does not extract all the moisture but does extract pollen and dust
- Telephone systems (Isn't it ironic that we still hold phones up to our ears most of the time?)
- Clothing

Adding comfort to an innovation may make the difference you need for success. For instance:

- Luggage and other portable devices with carrying handles and over-the-shoulder straps can still use a lot of improvement. At least we can design larger, easier-rolling wheels.
- Why not design backpacks that physiologically adapt to an individual's shape? It is amazing that backpacks today resemble those of centuries ago.
- How about a tennis racket with a form-fitting handgrip that adapts to--literally molds to--the player's hand. Automatically, the player's hand grasps the racket in the perfect location every time. Would that improve a player's game?

Look for "comfort" opportunities in your innovations, because most manufacturers will not!

CDI BENEFIT #6: ENTERTAINMENT

Americans like to be entertained, but in their work places, they rarely are. While computers satisfy this need in some respects, there are also many other options. With the many Internet and virtual reality concepts available, there are limitless opportunities to make work activities more entertaining.

Can you imagine creating new and entertaining machinery and processes for business? For instance, why can't gauges be both entertaining and informative? What about attaching a standard thermometer that reflects 0-250 degrees to a display that shows a thermometer with a little head. The face on the head smiles at you and a little arm reaches out and gives the OK sign when the proper temperature is maintained. But when it moves out of the designated safety range, and needs some attention, it starts frowning, then waves

"The ultimate objective for inventing tomorrow's kitchen would be to have "no kitchen at all"...a fully automatic kitchen that can prepare food, cook it, set the table and clean up afterwards." This comment is from a home economist of the 1940's.

Product safety is relatively new. Some of Disney's first toys in the early 1930s--figures of Donald Duck and Mickey Mouse --were made of eggshell thin celluloid, which is highly flammable.

Some children bought the toys only to set them on fire. When touched by a match, they would explode into a brilliant display of colored flames.

Disney became concerned and changed the material, leading the way for all manufacturers to make safe toys for children.

A Totally Absurd Patent

"Summer Sled" may not be so "totally absurd" after all. As seen on NBC Today, this sled provides summer fun for a traditional winter sport. As reported by Mental Engineering, the creators of Summer Sled, their objective is to give birth to a whole new line of ride-on vehicles that never existed before now.

Doesn't this sound like a good idea to you?

...totallyabsurd.com

As a product scout, I always have my eyes open for products in the latest hot areas. The ones I look for are: 1) Aging/geriatrics/ convalescence; 2) Self-reward; 3) Gardening; 4) DIY home repair/improvement; 5) Personal fitness; 6) Cleaning water; 7) Millennium; 8) Security against crime; 9) Pets; 10) Convenience; 11) Saving money.

...Ken Robbins, Product Development Agent, Dirt Devil

Is It Our Problem or Is It a Design Error?

We frequently point fingers at operators when production equipment is working poorly or the products are defective. It is important to keep in mind that if operators are continually having the same problems with a machine, there is something inherently wrong with the machine's design.

The most inexperienced operators should "naturally" understand how production equipment works. Don't blame the equipment--fix its design!

Software Manuals

While not exactly an invention, I find most software manuals somewhat humorous.

I don't know if others agree, but I find them difficult to understand, although they appear to be so simply written.

...Bob DeMatteis

its hands, then finally whistles at you. At high temperatures, steam shoots out of its ears! As it cools, it begins to turn blue, shivers and then icicles form on its ears.

In the years to come, industrial machines should take on transformations that make them entertaining. Just as teenagers are entertained as they skillfully manipulate Nintendo's Mario Brothers, workers can skillfully manipulate "The Production Brothers".

Only your imagination can limit the possibilities. It might sound funny, but providing entertainment can boost morale in boring jobs. The result would be improved productivity, less waste and fewer defects. If you can make your innovations and products entertaining and fun to use, you will find many followers.

CDI BENEFIT #7: EASY TO LEARN

Learning is something that people either like or dislike. However, one thing is for certain--learning is at the heart of getting ahead in life. Innovations that make learning easy, whether for adults or children, will be in demand.

Some of the new computer programs are tremendous aids to learning. There is no reason that learning about electronic or machine innovations cannot be directly tied into a computerized format that makes them easy to learn.

Production processes can become not only entertaining, but can, and should, become dynamic learning experiences as well. A user should be able to check his/her performance against the established standards and learn from other operators' experiences too. Statistical Process Controls should be an inherent part of any computer-controlled machine or system. The immediate and continual feedback from the computer should quickly enable the user to identify what can be done to improve performance.

There are other, simpler learning opportunities as well. One example involves the resetting of clocks and other electronic devices. Some are getting easier by talking to you when you press the button. Why can't all be that easy? Perhaps the instructions for many other things can be accomplished by talking.

How about the assembly (or re-assembly) of rarely used apparatuses by using coded or sequentially numbered parts to help teach a user how to assemble them quickly. This would give the user the comfort of knowing that if he/she forgets the method of assembly, he/she will not be intimidated the next time. Camping tents are an example of an article that can be either very easy or very difficult to learn how to use.

For children, there are many untapped learning opportunities. Toys can and should become learning experiences. Books do not have to be solely pages with words and pictures. Why not jazz them up with bells, whistles, snaps, fragrances and textures? For that matter, why can't books listen and then talk back to teach our children how to read?

CDI BENEFIT #8: APPEAL TO THE SENSES

This is one way you can give your inventions some character. Appealing to the senses of your target market can be an important advantage. We can appeal to the senses of children through toys, videos, tapes, games and books, but there are many more opportunities with adults.

When household machines are operating, do they have to be so noisy? Can't we find motors and systems that are quiet? Do conventional stoves and ovens have to be so archaic looking? Can't they be more visually attractive? Why can't dentists' drills make a soothing hum instead of the intimidating "whir"? Can you imagine a drill that has a euphoric effect? Patients would be knocking down the dentists' doors to get their teeth drilled!

In industrial applications, can the mixing of two ingredients impart a sweet odor when they are thoroughly mixed? Do all industrial cleansers have to smell like ammonia or lemon? Can the design of a new mechanical device be aesthetically pleasing instead of so square and *mechanical*? Of course we can do all this--if more inventors and innovators take the initiative.

CDI BENEFIT #9: APPEAL TO VANITY

Can your innovation outwardly or subtly appeal to one's vanity? For instance, if a new or improved product can improve the softness of one's hands, it should be a hit. If women are the most common users of this product, it will have a strong following. A good example of this is the introduction of plastic grocery sacks. The use of paper sacks by baggers and checkers frequently resulted in dry hands and even paper cuts. Because plastic sacks cause none of this, many users were encouraged to use more plastic sacks and fewer paper bags. Could this concept be applied to reams of paper? Could a paper manufacturer develop a process of cutting that eliminates paper cuts when users handle the paper? That quality should be worth an extra twenty-five cents per ream or perhaps more.

CDI BENEFIT #10: IMPROVED PRODUCTIVITY

One of the greatest industrial and commercial invention opportunities in the world today reflects *improved productivity*. With high labor costs, virtually every manufacturer is striving to improve

---

Product Don'ts for Infomercials

- *The product is not attractive to look at*
- *The product is not trendy enough*
- *The product is **too** trendy*
- *The product is uncomfortable to use*
- *The product makes the user feel clumsy*

   ...Joan Lefkowitz, Accessory Brainstorms, NYC

Some great moneymakers, especially great TV products, appeal to one of three variations on the seven deadly sins...vanity, greed and sloth. Fitness and beauty products (vanity) make up 34% of infomercials. "How to make money" type tapes (greed) were the top three infomercials of the last year. They were tied overall with household devices designed to ease our burden (sloth) at 17% of the infomercial products. Keep this in mind when trying to figure out why your product might be desirable.
   ...Ken Robbins, Product Development Agent, Dirt Devil

A Totally Absurd Patent

*U.S. Patent 4,825,469 is a motorcycle airbag that resembles a Martian body suit. But it's really **fashionable, inflatable, motorcycle wear**. Doubling as a protective airbag, it cushions the rider's fall during an accident.*
   When forcefully ejected from a bike, the suit fills with compressed gas until it covers head, arms, torso, and legs but not, apparently, the fingertips. Oh well, stubbing a finger or two is not so bad. It still keeps your vanity intact.
   ...totallyabsurd.com

output or throughput. The basic economic principle that *productivity produces income* is a vital consideration in a manufacturing company's operations and purchases. Smart presidents, vice presidents, operations people, buyers and managers know this economic principle.

Yet it will always remain a wonder to some salespeople who offer a product at a 20% lower price and do not get the order. Lower per unit costs with even a small decline in productivity can be disastrous to many companies. Consider the situation of a $25-million a year manufacturing firm that can save $20,000 per year on a cheaper packaging film. But the cheaper film slows productivity (output) by 3%. Is there really a savings? Of course not! The 3% loss in output equals $750,000 in lost output, which can be converted to lost sales! This far exceeds the measly $20,000 savings on the packaging film.

Look at the situation in reverse. A similar-sized manufacturing company presently using the cheaper film could switch to the new invention, the more expensive film, and expand its sales by 3%. They will most likely not have to hire additional personnel. Innovations that improve productivity are big hits.

There is no question about it--it is important to remember that:

Companies pursuing niche markets by providing improved productivity to their customers should have great successes!

CDI BENEFIT #11: THE SYSTEMS APPROACH

Instead of thinking of your inventions in terms of individual components, try thinking of them in terms of "systems". By thinking of your products as systems, you may find many excellent ways to improve productivity. Some examples of individual components that have been effectively converted into dynamic systems are:

- A plastic bag—plastic sacks and holders like those used in supermarkets
- A can of stain—a stripping and staining kit with disposable tools for furniture refinishing
- A chipboard box—an automatic filling system for the box
- A sprinkler—an automatic watering system
- An industrial flashlight—an emergency back-up lighting system

In the first example, trying to sell simple plastic bags to a supermarket would be fruitless. They would simply be too difficult and time consuming to use. But when a producer creates a bag holder, suddenly the combination becomes a viable system. It becomes a smashing success and almost completely replaces the use of paper

If your invention does not improve productivity, but reduces it instead, what should you do?

Do what every smart inventor does, solve the problem and turn it into a product that does improve productivity.

...Bob DeMatteis

Systems Represent Great Patenting Opportunities

As you will discover in the Patenting section, if you combine two or more prior art components into a new system, you may be able to secure a patent. Systems patents such as these can afford tremendous patent protection, at times even greater than the actual product or apparatus itself.

sacks in a matter of a few years! This supermarket system significantly improves productivity over old-fashioned paper bags. And today, plastic bags sell for half the cost of paper bags as well!

The systems approach automatically changes a producer's image with the customer. For instance, no longer is the producer just another company selling plastic bags. The producer becomes a packaging-systems specialist with the objective of improving productivity and lowering overall packaging costs. This is music to the ears of the economically minded corporations in the U.S. and other first-world countries.

Systems also represent excellent opportunities for patenting and expanding a product line. Once your system is in place, it becomes a lot easier to add peripheral products and new components or introduce new systems in other facets of your field.

CDI BENEFIT #12: PEOPLE FRIENDLY–THE GREATEST INNOVATION OPPORTUNITY OF ALL

The computer and electronics industries brought us several new feats of engineering and science in the last few decades. For laymen, many of these new products were too difficult to understand and operate. You can see this phenomenon in far too many products and machines in both industrial and residential settings. To make matters worse, complicated manuals frequently make these products even more difficult to use.

Look at your present or anticipated inventions and ask yourself, "Are they people friendly?" While they may be a feat of science or engineering, it is *more* important to remember that people must use them. Customers and end users simply prefer products that are convenient, easy to use and people friendly.

If yours is not, you need to make some innovative changes, or it might be more appropriate to say that you have great opportunity for some innovative improvements. Making your products "people friendly" is also the best way to build brand loyalty.

HOW TO MAKE YOUR INVENTIONS "PEOPLE FRIENDLY"

The following five concepts relate to making products "people friendly". The secret to doing this is to keep the end user in sharp focus. Remember, the end user is not some middleman, like a distributor or boss, nor is it necessarily your marketing expert. The end user is the individual who actually uses your innovation and will determine its success. In focusing on the end user, you will want to be hyper-aware and super observational as you determine the best approach to making your invention "people friendly".

Adapt to or Replace the "Old System"?

There are two distinctly different approaches to replacing existing systems. You can use some of the existing components and adapt your invention to them or your can replace only key components of the old system. Both have their advantages.

When developing product improvements and expanding or improving upon existing systems, it might be quick and easy to incorporate some existing components. For instance, what if your new invention is a long-lasting gear that will fit on the existing bearings?

Your customer might have a large investment in time, money and lost production if all the bearings have to be retrofitted as the new gears are being replaced. Who pays for this? This approach leads right into the CDI concept of "thinking small" and taking small innovative steps, one at a time.

In contrast, if you do have the financial ability and the people power to retrofit customers with proprietary gears and new bearings, do it! This will protect your niche much better in the long run.

People Friendly--a Personal Favorite

Most of my innovations and patents are directly related to making plastic bagging systems easy to use. While many scientists strive to improve the strength and processing characteristics of plastics, I have found success in designing people-friendly plastic packaging systems.

It never ceases to amaze me how many opportunities there are to make other products in additional fields, people friendly as well!

...Bob DeMatteis

How to Develop Superior Ergonomics

In striving to create step-saving innovations, you usually improve the ergonomics of an invention. While some view ergonomics as an engineering process, there is a much better way to look at it.

Try looking at ergonomics from the viewpoint of what would be ideal. Attempt to visualize the most natural way for someone to use your product. By doing this, you are applying some basic ergonomics to your design. Then have your invention engineered with these facets.

By visualizing the ideal, you can take giant steps forward. You may have to break these giant steps down into smaller ones, but this is a good problem to create!

Your goal is to strive to make your new innovations a "no brainer" to use. If you can do this, you will greatly improve your chances of success. When users ask, "Why didn't they make it like this in the first place" or say, "You're not going to take my new ZYZYX away from me," you know you have made your invention very people friendly. Making products easy to use almost always causes a positive emotion and most frequently improves productivity in industrial and commercial applications.

Capitalize on the Users' Natural Tendencies

With any new or improved innovation or system, what are the natural tendencies of the end user? You can capitalize on making your new innovation people friendly by incorporating these natural tendencies into your design. That way, they will instinctively know what to do.

Step inside an automobile and you can see several good examples and perhaps recall a few bad or confusing ones. If you were to improve the design in one of the following automobile components, what changes would you consider?

1. **Steering.** Would you want to use anything other than a round steering wheel?

2. **Brake pedal.** Can you imagine pressing on anything other than a foot pedal to stop?

3. **Transmission gearshift.** Placing it on the column or console is probably best. In the early 1960's, Chrysler's "superior engineering" came up with the modern push-button version. Dodge and Plymouth had buttons in the dash and Chrysler's were placed where the horn button used to be. Can you see it now? You are driving along in your new Chrysler and someone cuts you off. You retaliate by blasting them with your horn. Instead, you screech to a halt as your transmission explodes and metal shrapnel is strewn all over the freeway! How about that new Plymouth? Your 4-year-old daughter reaches up to change radio channels, just like she used to. Whoops! Of course Chrysler abandoned the push button system after just a couple of years.

4. **Headlight switch.** At first they were only push-pull switches located on the left side of the dashboard. Then some switches became push button, some moved to the right side, others were incorporated on the turn indicator and yet others had a separate turn indicator-type switch on the steering column.

Have you ever rented a car at night in a strange airport? After walking out to the dark parking lot, you climb inside, half-frozen, and try to turn on the headlights so you can see where the heck to insert the key to start the engine. Not only can you not find the headlight switch, you cannot read the little names or tiny logos on them either. In frustration, you reach for the...

5. **Dome light.** But of course, no luck here either. The dome light switch is either part of the "mystery" headlight switch, button or turn indicator post. Or is it a separate switch somewhere on the dash or on the console? Who knows? The most obvious solution is to have the switch near the dome light where drivers will naturally look or reach. Many automakers are doing this now.

Several car manufacturers have discovered an even better people-friendly solution to this problem. Simply put, the overhead dome lights remain lit for several seconds after entry into the automobile. Now, back to looking for the headlight switch or button or is it this thing on the column? Whoops, there go the wipers!

Perhaps the best example of designing based on the natural tendencies of human beings is a computer keyboard. The original keyboard was developed so that the operator's most dexterous fingers would be used for the most frequently used letters. While there are many new, ergonomic designs being introduced, it is still best to use one that incorporates the natural typing motions so ingrained in the populace. Most of the new, super-easy, super-fast keyboard systems emulate these natural "QWERTY" typing motions. Could you imagine having to start all over with a different format?

In your invention-related matters, try to incorporate the natural tendencies of the users into the design, or else you may be forcing them to do something they consider unnatural or that will require a lot of retraining. Using natural tendencies in industrial and commercial applications can also contribute to improved productivity and the reduction of errors.

Instant Recognition

Make the functions of your new innovations easy to recognize, so the user will know how to use them. It is surprising how often new improvements are not improvements at all...after you try to use them.

The icons used in computer software programs give an instant explanation of their use. For instance, the trash bin icon is commonly known as the place to delete files, folders and even entire programs. Other icons make file identification easy.

Some other good and bad examples are:

I use this concept in almost all of my invention activities in order to make them people friendly.

For instance, in developing a new plastic bagging system, I always consider the following: 1) the method in which plastic bags are dispensed; 2)the method in which they are opened; 3) the method in which they are packed; 4) the method in which they are carried by the consumer, and; 5) the method in which the loaded bags are transported home.

...Bob DeMatteis

A Totally Absurd Patent

U.S. Patent No. 4,827,666 is a fruit and vegetable mold that shapes fruits and vegetables into a wide variety of fanciful shapes, including the human head! Even the details of hair, eyebrows, nose and mouth are reproduced with amazing accuracy. No special growing conditions are required. Place a growing fruit or vegetable inside the transparent mold and it will expand and fill the entire mold cavity. Imagine the comments when you serve Sylvester Stallone squash, David Hasselhoff zucchini, or a Clark Gable gourd head.

...totallyabsurd.com

- A good example is emergency shut-off switches. They should be large, red and in the areas they are most likely to be needed.

- A bad example is the alien shower-bath-hot-water, cold-water pressure-control knob, commonly seen in hotels on the East Coast. Are you ever sure if you are turning the shower on or off? Or the hot water on or off? At the very least, these shower knobs should be separated into two or more distinct functions, with each function made easier to recognize and understand.

- A bad example is the push rod style bar on a door that makes it difficult to know whether the door opens to the left or the right.

Natural Mapping

Natural mapping means using or emulating existing natural shapes and forms. One of the best examples of this concept is the seat adjustment buttons used on Mercedes, Jeep and several others. There are two buttons in the shape of the seat; one forms the seat itself and the other the back support. The user simply moves each button to put the seat at the desired height and the back support at the desired angle.

Figure 3-6

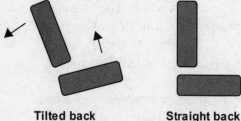

Tilted back
support
Tilted seat

Straight back
support
Level seat

In general, computer software companies strive to incorporate a form of natural mapping in their schemes, but they often fall short. In fact, the incredibly large "help folders" and user manuals are evidence of the problem. One example of successful natural mapping is Hewlett Packard's touch screen, which makes it easy for the user to follow. There is no need to understand computers; simply having a finger is all the user needs.

One of the best opportunities to use natural mapping exists in remote control devices, but it is rarely used. Think about this... Remote control devices usually have a whole series of little buttons with lots of little words printed on them. Of course, everyone who uses them has 20/20 vision and can easily read them, even with the lights out. Remote control fanatics consume a lot of vitamin E to improve their night vision.

OK, all jokes aside. Why can't at least some of these buttons be ones that the user can touch and intuitively recognize their uses? Here are some possibilities for a VCR:

A Totally Absurd Patent

If your tiny tyke likes to ride on your shoulders but you find it hard to hang on to fidgety feet, you need the Shoulder Saddle, U.S. Patent 3,698,608. Mount the saddle's plastic yoke over your head and the saddle's breast plate and back plate evenly distributes the load. The breastplate also makes an effective kick guard. However, it leaves the ears exposed, and your petite passenger can still slap your ears repeatedly to get you to go faster!

Does this patent use natural mapping?

...totallyabsurd.com

- Obvious, raised (and opposing) arrows on the rewind and fast forward buttons
- An oval or round play button between the rewind and fast forward buttons
- An octagonal stop button apart from the above three buttons
- A volume control button in a rocker switch with the "up" volume at the top and the "down" volume at the bottom
- The top of the volume button has a raised knob and the bottom has a simple round dimple
- Some knobs might have knurled edges so they can be easily identified and not be mistaken for other knobs
- The eject button can be eliminated; the same result would occur when the stop button was pressed twice

Natural mapping techniques can be used in many types of control (knob and button) applications in every industry. Natural mapping inherently reduces errors and improves performance and productivity.

Save Steps, Save Time, Reduce Confusion

You can capitalize on the basic economic principle of "productivity produces income" by reducing the number of steps required to use a device or perform a function. It goes without saying that if you can reduce the number of steps required to use your innovation, productivity will improve and your customer's profit potential will increase. Operations managers (who are usually powerful decision-makers) make their living trying to cut labor costs through timesavings. You will greatly appeal to these decision-makers if you can eliminate entire steps in their operations.

Step-saving products are also at the heart of the computer industry. Have you noticed that new versions of software programs tend to require fewer steps to execute commands? Even macros are easier to make than ever before.

Another example of eliminating the steps required to perform a function is in the supermarket. The customer checkout is faster than ever, due to laser scanners and plastic bagging systems. With laser scanners, the checker saves time in handling the purchases. In concert with the scanning, a fast, step-saving, "self-opening" plastic bagging system keeps pace. Compared to paper sacks, plastic sacks save about 4-6 seconds to open and load. The combined result is that you save minutes in the checkout line.

Here are some other step-saving innovation opportunities:

- The elimination of mixing two-part epoxy glue
- Preset settings to start a machine after a long shutdown

A Totally Absurd Patent

It's a bird! It's a plane! No, it's...it's...your neighbor with a trash bag strapped to his back? That's right...Super Trash Man! U.S. Patent 4,854,003 scoops up trash as you walk, collecting garbage with every stride. Complete with shoulder and feet harnesses, this working class superhero's weapon gathers leaves and grass clippings with a single bound.

How's this for a step-saving invention?

...totallyabsurd.com

Cash Registers

The next generation of Americans will not know what a cash register is. They will also not know that older folks learned to type on typewriters before there were computer keyboards. Even noisy dot matrix printers will be antiquated in a matter of years.

What's next? How about printing presses and cloth dying machines? Get ready, because these industries will be converting to the new ink jet technology. Yes, even the clothing industry will soon change!

Jerome Lemelson was a master at developing products and systems that reduced labor. His first invention was a universal robot, which was transformed into a "flexible manufacturing system", which ultimately become the automated machine shop of today. It is one of his most far-reaching inventions forever changing the ways of improving manufacturing processes.

A Totally Absurd Patent

U.S. Patent 4,681,332, "Western Skater", combines a hobbyhorse with roller skates. For beginners, this invention provides needed support. As the inventor puts it, "The vehicle permits a beginning skater to train in a relatively uninhibited manner..." This is quite true as you would have to be pretty uninhibited to get on this hobbyhorse in public.

...totallyabsurd.com

A commonly used concept in sales/marketing today is, "don't sell the steak, sell the sizzle". You should think in terms of what "sizzle" your invention generates with its users.

- A machine's ability to remember settings the next time the same job lot is run
- Automatic emergency shut-off devices that detect human error (or presence)
- Totally automatic drip coffee makers that measure the amount of coffee and water according to a pre-determined strength
- Better uses for the right click button on a computer mouse

A key approach to step saving is to strive to make your product or system totally automatic, with no potential for error, human or otherwise. This simple approach can result in a lifelong series of projects and innovations for a smart team.

Monkey See, Monkey Do—Minimum Training Required

Invariably, new products require some training. If you can reduce it dramatically, you have done your job of inventing quite well! Keep in mind that although your new product may be the eighth wonder of the world, if it requires extensive training, you have a tough, expensive time ahead.

If you can make your industrial and commercial innovations easy enough to use, so that very little instruction and training is required, you will also have instant blessings from management. Training is expensive, so if you can honestly characterize it in your sales presentations as monkey see, monkey do, the expense of training becomes a moot issue. Management will usually give quick OK's to innovative changes if the aspect of training is covered.

AN INSIDE SECRET TO DEVELOPING GREAT INVENTIONS

We know that inventions are based on having some new, unique function that ultimately gives it its patentability. We also know about being focused on CDI benefits so that the unique functions will be ones that customers want to buy. But perhaps the most important aspect of the buying decision is what we talked about at the beginning of this chapter. That is, it's the "character" that sells products.

Almost all of us have heard that "form follows function". While this may have been true in the past, it is no longer true today. It is one of those old adages that never seems to die.

Great innovators, inventors and designers (many artists too) know there is a higher truth to follow to success. It is *"form follows emotion"*. Don't kid yourself. People usually buy because the purchase raises a positive emotion. It may be the speed, the super silence, the ease of operation or the power potential. It could be simply the appeal of the color or the softness that raises an emotion that elicits a favorable response from the buyer. It could even be the zippy trademarked name.

A good example of form following emotion is the design of Apple Computer's original Macintosh PC's. They were compact, futuristic, exceptionally easy to operate and had the software to back them up. In short, they were carefully designed to elicit a positive emotion from their users. The result was that Apple created and quickly dominated a new niche market with weak competition from IBM and Digital, the industry giants. Today, Apple is differentiating less and losing market share as a result.

Another example was when Kawasaki Motorcycles took on the three motorcycle leaders—Honda, Yamaha and Harley Davidson—with some dazzling new cycle designs. The emotion the designs elicited from their buyers was a sense of speed and power. Kawasaki stole the power position from the others because of the emotions their cycles elicited in customers.

Look for ways to elicit emotions that will drive your products to success. Then design the products accordingly. Don't let function dictate your ultimate design; let the emotion that will be elicited drive the design instead.

Here are possibilities and the emotions they might elicit:

1. Racy design: "I feel upbeat, modern, sexy."
2. High-speed performance: "I can feel the power, the exhilaration."
3. Easy to use: "Wow, it's automatic. I can sit back, relax and watch."
4. Long lasting: "It's the last one I'll ever buy. I feel so secure."
5. Smaller design: "It fits in my vest pocket, so I feel confident that it won't be seen."
6. Totally enclosed: "No parts are exposed; I feel safe."
7. Sharp print copy: "Quality is exactly what I am all about!"
8. Easy to fix: "I feel confident and safe, now that my wife can quickly fix it."
9. Self-adjusting: "Wow, even my 10-year-old can do this. All I have to do is enjoy it."
10. Great color choice: "It matches my boat...it's sexy and makes me feel that way too."
11. Patriotic: "It's made in the U.S.A. and I want to do my part."
12. Comfortable: "A seat that actually feels good. I feel like a king."
13. Classic curves: "Do I ever feel beautiful; it's the perfect image for me."
14. Free 24-hour service: "Now I can feel safe, no matter where I am."

There are many other emotional responses you can look for in your innovations. For certain, developing character in your innovations that creates a positive emotional response in the end user is at the heart of a Customer-Driven Innovation.

When Was the Last Time You Bought Something Because of its Function?

In its television ads a few years ago, Chrysler Corporation indicated that "form follows function," with an inference that Chrysler's cars were somehow better made.

When was the last time you bought something and afterward said, "Wow, I really dig how this thing functions?" The reality is that you bought it because something about the product and sale made you feel good.

People buy Chrysler automobiles not because they are the best functioning cars, but because they create a positive emotion within them. Why did you buy your last car?

Any great consumer invention should invoke in the user, "now why didn't I think of that!"

...Joan Lefkowitz, Accessory Brainstorms, NYC

Henry Dreyfus was one of the first creators of "beautiful, modern devices" that tried to appeal to "form" instead of "function". One of his first "beautiful creations" was the hand crank washing machine of the 1920's. A later creation was the Princess telephone of the 1960's that forever changed the way we used and purchased telephones.

Two Reasons to Buy

An old adage in sales says that you need two good reasons to buy something. If you can create a laundry list of positive attributes, your potential customers will have many good reasons to buy. Hopefully, two of them will make them get their wallets out.

Catalogs, home shopping channels and infomercial marketers have a similar vision of the "perfect product." The perfect product is a mass consumer product, produces miraculous results, is protectable from copies, and has a USP--unique selling proposition. It's the miracle results and uniqueness that make a successful product irresistible.

...Ken Robbins, Product Development Agent, Dirt Devil

An important consideration with new innovations is to make certain performance attributes are not sacrificed in areas such as strength, capacity, safety, maintenance, etc.

A new innovation may be able to replace the old product, and it may save a lot of time with its improved operation, but if it cannot maintain the same quality expectations it will become a great idea doomed to failure.

DESIGNING TO ELICIT EMOTION

How do you design for emotion? It's not difficult to do. When you discover something unique, some emotion will automatically be there. But you can take it one step further and add a little pizzazz, pop and sex appeal that will make your invention even more desirable. Try this:

Close your eyes and imagine the desirable end result and the emotion you want to elicit. What are the end users doing, saying and feeling?

Now make a list of all the little things you can incorporate into your invention that will elicit the emotion. Then design as many of them into the invention as possible and figure out how to manufacture it. Insist that your manufacturer go the extra mile to accommodate your design. Don't allow the manufacturer to dictate how the design should look.

An important facet of designs that elicit emotion is the need for manufacturing processes that can produce them. Part of the problem is that typical, old-fashioned manufacturing companies tend to have "square", functional-thinking managers and employees. Likewise, their equipment frequently follows suit and makes only "square" products.

Be determined to solve any manufacturing problems associated with the design. You will learn in Part Three that your manufacturer must be a part of the team that can get this done. Regardless of how your new invention is going to be produced, you cannot kowtow to the mediocrity of everyday mass-manufacturing processes. You must maintain your vision and insist that it be fulfilled.

OTHER ATTRIBUTES AND SECRETS

The preceding CDI benefits are not all the possibilities. They just serve to help get your imagination going and to create innovations that will be well received. Focusing on CDI benefits to the customer is key to evaluating the potential of innovative ideas. Determining exactly what benefits an end user may want is somewhat subjective. Nevertheless, solid, creative, innovative ideas that last long-term are invariably found in attributes that reflect truth, beauty and goodness. While this may sound somewhat idealistic, it is true. Those who seek innovations and products that appeal to the ideals of humanity are unquestionably on the road to success! Sooner or later, they will have the success they desire.

ABOUT CDI AND QM

Customer-Driven Innovation and Quality Management principles and philosophies go hand in hand. In most respects, CDI is a QM system for monitoring and controlling your products and innovations. In certain respects, where continuous improvement (QM) leaves off, Customer-Driven Innovation (CDI) takes over. The illustration in Fig. 3-7 shows the continuity between the two concepts and where responsibilities lie for innovation, continuous improvement and on-going maintenance.

Figure 3-7 QM and Innovation

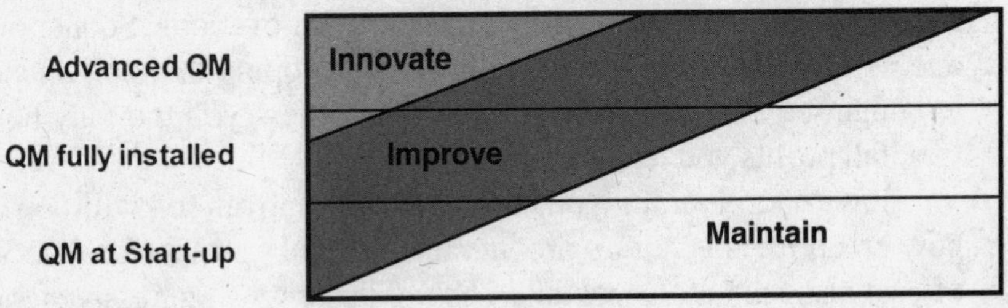

CDI AND PATENTING

Any invention that has the usefulness to solve customer problems should be patentable. Patents can help steer your invention activities and protect them as well. As you will read in Part Two on patenting, the owner of a patent has the right to exclude others from making, using or selling his/her products. So, as you invent and improve on your innovations, you can also secure more patents, which will protect your interests further.

Patents also give you and your innovation experts a chance to be a little part of history. Some of them may contribute in the future and have their names on patents as well. Whether being a manufacturer, a sales specialist or one of the engineers on your new improvement, everyone on an invention-development team works harder when they receive recognition for their contributions.

Becoming patent-wise as you invent will give you a sound basis to design around a competitor's patents. You will be better able to determine a competitor's future direction. As a result, you will be able to adapt your future developments accordingly. Don't be surprised that your CDI knowledge allows you to "out-fox" them in the marketplace altogether! It is very possible that the nature of your patenting thrust will be quite different from theirs. Large companies tend to develop an invention along the lines of engineering, whereas yours is a more successful, *customer-driven approach*.

A few schools of Quality Management tend to treat patents negatively. The two chief reasons for this are: 1) QM generally teaches to take "small steps" forward and patents tend to refer to taking "giant steps" forward, and; 2) QM is heavily embraced by Japanese companies, which tend to dislike the American patent system and instead, tend to think in terms of very small improvements.

CDI AS A MODUS OPERANDI

The goal of Thomas Edison, one of the premier innovators-inventors on this planet was "a minor invention every ten days and a big thing every six months or so." However, Thomas Edison was in the business of inventing and had a full-time staff of engineers and scientists assisting him. Their aggressive pace would be unreasonable for an innovative entity to maintain with any given product line, except perhaps for more complex products, such as computers and automobiles.

Depending on the nature of your invention, CDI should be your modus operandi. Just as continual improvement is a key to success, you should regularly release improvements and innovations. Sooner or later, one will become a "big thing". Edison was hoping that only one out of ten might be a winner. If you hit one out of ten, you too may be in for windfall profits you never thought possible.

How often you and your team release innovations will depend on how broad the invention's product line becomes and the product's level of sophistication. Depending on philosophy, aggressiveness and product life, some guidelines you can follow are:

- For entities with a few (3-10) moderately sophisticated products in its line (for instance, 5-6 types of industrial water pumps)--Minor CDI improvements should be on-going, probably 1 to 3 per year for each individual product. At least once a year, one major innovation should be released. It may be the complete revamping of an existing product or an entirely new invention altogether. Over time, at least one of these new releases should result in an exceptional, long-term, breakthrough opportunity. Remember that minor improvements can also bring about breakthrough opportunities. Even if a new release doesn't make a big hit, it should still have a positive impact on your overall developments.

- Entities that produce a small number of sophisticated products (such as 1 or 2 types of machines)--Because of the investment, it is best to continually and aggressively develop a series of minor innovative improvements every few weeks or months, perhaps 10 to 20 per year per machine. Each department responsible for various aspects of the machine's components can spearhead its own improvements at a much faster pace. Chances are that one or more of these continual improvements will lead to some major breakthrough discoveries. Then, once every 5 to 10 years, you can consider developing a totally new CDI machine.

- Entities that produce a large number of unsophisticated products (for instance, 120 different novelty greeting cards addressing 10 different seasonal markets)--These entities might want to use a shotgun approach. They should release a relatively large number of

One thing is for certain...if a QM production company does not file for patents on their new improvements, inventions and discoveries, they may find themselves always trying to stay ahead of copycats.

Jerome Lemelson averaged a patent a month for more than 40 years, all of which he accomplished independently. An optimistic and vibrant man, he amassed the fourth largest portfolio in American History.
...National Collegiate Inventors and Innovators Association (NCIIA)

innovations and see which "stick". This approach is usually the least innovative and probably the least likely to succeed without some experience. But in time, the efforts might pay off. If your team can become adept at a rapid turnaround time for new releases, you can stay one step ahead of competitors.

Inventions with very small markets and those being made in start-up companies with limited funds will need to determine innovation timeframes that best suit their needs. As a baby does, start with baby steps and later, take some giant steps forward. But, unlike a baby, small start-ups with good financing have every opportunity to be relentlessly innovative and aggressive!

All major innovations will need both thorough in-house testing and customer trials. The exception may be the shotgun approach used when there are several simple (but potentially major) releases. Nevertheless, stay close to the customer to track your success.

THE BEST NEWS ABOUT CONTINUAL CDI AND INVENTING

It is apparent that after a first innovation is completed, you have only one thing to do. Invent, innovate and do it again. Each time you seek to introduce a new Customer-Driven Innovation to the trade, it gets easier. You will already have your manufacturing and sales experts in place and ready to go. After two or three innovations, you will find inventing and innovating so natural that you can't stop!

Staying ahead of the competition with innovative individuality is like building a retirement fund for you and your invention business. No one else can have it, because no one else is *you*. You will become the all-knowing expert in your field with a strengthening of your position each and every year. Perpetuating your invention efforts becomes natural and rewarding, not only financially, but because it is a whole lot of fun!

Being creative is a gift only a few people have. There is nothing better than living your life today as you imagine and create the future. Never have truer words been said:

Your destiny is determined, moment by moment, by the achievements of your day-to-day creative efforts. Your actions today determine tomorrow's destiny!

Money-Making Breakthroughs

Inventors should continue to develop their innovations once they have been patented. It is rarely the first idea or patent which results in making an inventor a lot of money.

Usually by patent 4 or 5 an inventor will develop some improvement on the original invention that will result in a breakthrough opportunity and good income.

…Yujiro Yamamoto, internationally known inventor

Keep on Inventing!

The most successful inventors rarely made all of their money from one idea, but rather had a panoply of ideas and inventions. Some make money, some do not. Inventors who put all of their efforts into one invention or idea are seldom successful and typically end up in protracted, bitter, patent litigation.

…Robert Platt Bell, Esq.

4

INVENTING AND PROBLEM SOLVING

You are the expert. They will look to you
to fulfill their needs and solve their problems.

INVENTION-INNOVATION USUALLY BEGINS
AS THE CREATIVE PROCESS OF A SINGLE PERSON

Finding innovative solutions to problems usually begins as a creative, inventive process by a single individual, you. If it were anything else--something simple and obvious--it probably would have already been discovered and available. Sometimes just identifying a problem (opportunity) immediately reveals a solution. Other times it can be far more complex and time consuming. Most likely, your innovation discovery process will fall somewhere in between.

The invention process usually consists of extensive trial and error testing. As the inventor, you will be hyper-aware of all that is happening. Indeed, innovating is an on-going learning and discovery process. All the while, you will become more and more aware and curious about what is taking place. Innovative solutions and opportunities are usually found as a result of the discovery process. As

In the middle of difficulty lies opportunity...
...Albert Einstein

70

an innovator-inventor developing an invention, you will try to manipulate the various phenomena to attain the CDI innovation you seek. You do not know exactly how that outcome will occur.

By using creativity and imagination and following your intuition and instincts, you will invariably find solutions to, and the direction of, your CDI initiatives. Always keep in mind that

Successful innovators are successful not because of what they do, but because of what they _strive_ to do.

It is in the process of striving for better solutions to problems (and adding character to your innovations) that your discoveries will be made. You will also find that discovering something unique frequently reveals a principle in physics...after the fact. But an innovator-inventor does not need to understand why the invention works. Nor is it necessary to understand the physics or the engineering processes of your innovations.

After you have made an innovative discovery, engineers can take it, understand the physics involved, and engineer excellent products from it. For innovating engineers, or those on innovation teams, it is best to let go of any preconceived notions and see what happens in the developmental process. There are always surprises along the way that seem to defy the physics that should be involved.

THE IMPORTANCE OF TEAMWORK IN INVENTING AND INNOVATING

Sooner or later, you will establish a dedicated team to help you attain your goal. Your team can give valuable input into the CDI attributes you desire and can quickly solve the problems associated with new product development. They can help propel your project far faster than you could by working alone. With a committed innovation team, it is amazing what you can accomplish and how dramatically you can reduce the development time frame.

Your invention development team will have at least one creative inventor type (most likely you), plus your manufacturing expert (the president, GM, etc.) who has access to engineers who can help solve problems. Included is the important sales expert who will act as a liaison with customers and will be sensitive to their needs. Here is a synopsis of how some of your team elements may work together:

- **Creative inventor:** You should be free to imagine, create and invent. To better understand problems and turn them into opportunities, you should be able to visit a customer's facility (if commercial or industrial) or observe end users (if retail). Through

---

A Totally Absurd Patent

U.S. Patent 5,713,081 is for inventrixes. Actually, this invention is a three-legged pantyhose, which is an arguably practical, yet goofy-looking solution to an age-old problem. You know--the dilemma of unsightly runs. The aptly named, "Pantyhose x 3" eliminates the need to carry spare hose. With this ingenious design you simply (and discretely) rotate your leg into the third, unblemished pantyhose appendage. The damaged hosiery leg is then tucked into a pocket in the crotch.
...totallyabsurd.com

Exponential Increases

Adding one person to your team does not double a team's potential performance. It is more like a 4-fold improvement. Adding the third team member is more like a 9-fold advantage.

For instance, if you try to do the entire project alone, it might take you 4 years. With one key team member, the two of you (2 times 2 = 4) could reduce the time to 1 year. With a third team member, it could be reduced to 5-6 months (3 times 3 = 9).

these observations, you can discover, explore and question as much as possible and discover needed solutions.

- **Manufacturing and Production:** With the stamp of approval from the president or general manager, you will have a commitment to manufacturing the innovation quickly and effectively. The participation of this key member in the invention process allows production to begin in a timely manner.
- **Engineers:** Under the direction of the president or general manager, they can be used to fine tune the inventions and innovations and make the necessary adaptations and modifications to the manufacturing processes.
- **Sales experts:** Will be used to validate the various CDI attributes and will act as the on-going liaison with the customers and end users. They will keep them informed of activities and progress, and will provide the invention development team with timely feedback.

In your team efforts, remember that knowledge and information must be shared among all members. Otherwise, the process is worthless. One last important aspect to remember about invention development teamwork is:

Innovative progress demands individuality; mediocrity is perpetuated by standardization.

TESTING AN INNOVATION

Most inventions will be thoroughly tested. Always start testing in-house (your facility) before commencing customer trials. Every possible scenario of use should be tried before trials begin outside your plant, in the real world, with your customer and their end users.

Not all innovations are created with a specific customer in mind. Regardless, you must completely test and be thoroughly satisfied with your in-house model. You cannot overdo testing. There always seem to be a myriad of problems--mostly minor--to resolve. Even if the innovation performs well from the onset, there is still much you can learn from continued, even redundant, testing. Hopefully, after your innovation team signs off on the in-house test models, the innovation will be ready for your customer's trials.

It is best to not send the first model(s) to the customer for his/her initial trials, but to deliver it personally, if possible. It is best that the members of your expert innovation team set up, prepare and train at the initial kick-off. During this initial trial at the customer's facility, it is critical to remain as close as possible to the customer and end users. Trials can (and invariably will) uncover new problems, which can also

Tests vs. Trials

Your in-house testing activities are best called "tests". However, when the product goes out to the customer, it is best to call your activities "trials". Your customers (or end users) should not think they are guinea pigs, testing unproven products.

It is best to let them know that the "tests" have been concluded, and now you are taking it to the customers to see if there is any fine-tuning needed. This approach is more positive.

lead to new solutions. Keep everyone involved in his/her support role, until you know for certain that the trial is a whopping success!

During the initial in-house testing and customer trials, *be patient.* As the saying goes, "Rome was not built in a day". Invariably, the initial testing, product refinement and customer start-up trials will take more time than expected. If you are new at innovating and new product releases, it can be a frustrating process. Just keep your cool. Remember to start small with a trial at only one of your customer's facilities (or machines), then expand to other facilities. Later, you can take your innovation into other customers' facilities.

PROBLEM-SOLVING BASICS

Problems with the performance of your new invention will likely arise. Most of them will surface during in-house testing. Some will surface later in the field with your customers. Overcoming these problems can make or break your innovation's success. Be extremely sensitive to problems, try to identify the underlying causes and solve them. The solutions will become your key to success.

Once you have identified problems that must be addressed in the production process, convey them to your manufacturing expert. It will either be something that is quick and easy to change or some unknown design change may be required.

Here is a basic, step-by-step approach to innovation-production-related problem solving:

1. **Assemble a meeting with your innovation team.** Announce the meeting with an agenda describing the problem. Let the team members know the meeting is about solving the problem and ask them to bring their ideas for resolving it. Allow sufficient time on the agenda to thoroughly address the problem.

2. **Together, break the innovation or the product down into pieces.** Identify all the pieces as to how and why the innovation (or the innovative phenomenon) does what it does. This should include having a thorough understanding of A) **materials** and their characteristics; B) the **machinery** being used in the manufacturing process; C) the **people** using them; D) the product's design; E) the manufacturing **process**; F) the manufacturing **environment,** and; G) the means of **measurement**. Use the "fishbone" chart in Fig. 4-1 as an aid to listing the various influences. Discuss, identify and then draw a circle around potentially problematic areas.

3. **Examine each piece.** Draw a flow chart with all the components (pieces). Try to understand and identify what is happening or not happening. Can you verify that each component is performing

A Totally Absurd Patent

The All Terrain Stroller (ATS), U.S. Patent 4,422,452, is for those urban parents who want to get out of crowded cities. Stick your little bambino in this torpedo-shaped baby carriage with tank tracks and glide over virtually any terrain, no matter how rough. There's even a convenient hand brake on the ATS for descending steep mountainsides.
...totallyabsurd.com

Ask yourself, "Why did they do that the way they did? There is clearly a better way."
...George Margolin

Figure 4-1 Fishbone Chart

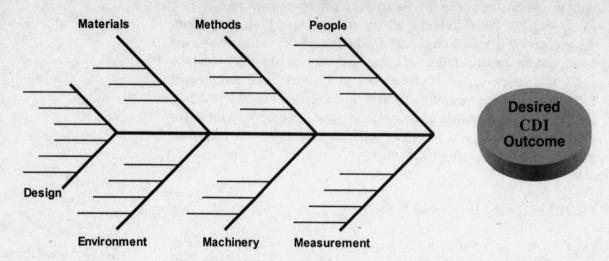

the way it is expected to perform? If not, why? At your meeting, use the flow chart to help identify alternative processes or means. The flow chart in Fig. 4-2 is representative of manufacturing stackable storage cubes for an industrial application.

Figure 4-2 Flow Chart

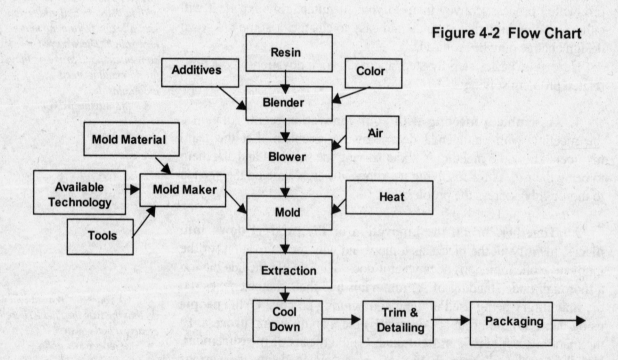

4. **Identify the dominant idea and crucial factor.** *Dominant ideas* are *the ideas that dominate the issue and cannot be challenged. Crucial factors* are *those factors that are holding you up and keeping you to the old approach.* You must identify the dominant idea and crucial factor to weigh viable alternatives. For example, you want to

manufacture strong, plastic toy blocks that can be easily stacked. We identify the *dominant idea* as using inexpensive, strong, high-density plastic material in a standard mold. The *crucial factor* is that this high-density material is naturally quite slippery. Our task is to find a means to mold stackable toy blocks so they are not overly slippery when stacked up.

5. **Brainstorming.** The team can now brainstorm about the many possible ways to give the blocks a non-slip outer surface. Solutions to this problem may include:

- Applying a special tackifier coating to the surface
- Application of heat to roughen up (or remove the "slip" from) the surfaces
- Modifying the die's surface in the desirable areas to include non-skid ridges
- Putting a no-slip additive in the resin
- Putting interlocking male-female components in the corners of each block

Fig. 4-3 shows the previous flow chart with alternative possibilities in the shaded boxes. If desirable, any one of the components in the flow chart can be broken down into another, more detailed flow chart.

Brainstorming

Everyone should participate in the problem-solving process. In meetings, and in particular when brainstorming, never criticize team members for their thoughts and ideas, no matter how outrageous. List all of them.

Criticism stymies innovation. As the brainstorming process unfolds, only those parts pertinent to the solution will emerge and be tackled anyway.

Figure 4-3 Flow Chart

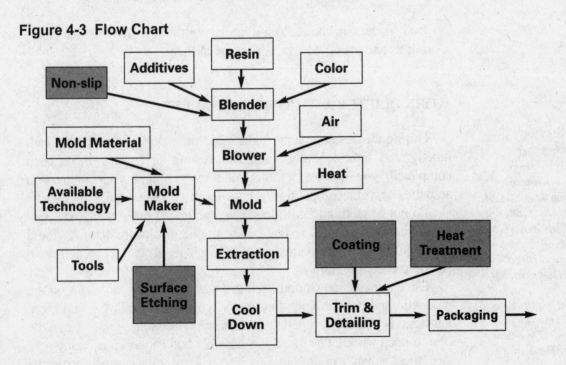

If for some reason, your team cannot find good solutions to the problems you encounter, you can always seek outside experts. You could also consider more creative (drastic?) approaches. This may mean a major change in the product's design and its processes. For instance, the stackable blocks may be best suited to a different molding process that uses a stickier, low-density resin.

Be determined to not give up until every possible solution has been tested. Before shelving the project, do the testing again to see if there was an error or something was overlooked. The worse case scenario is to put the innovation on the back burner for a while, but don't trash it. Frequently, solutions to the problems will surface later, when you are not expecting them.

BE SENSITIVE TO RED FLAGS

Quit looking at all the problems as obstacles and start looking at all of them as opportunities. Problems when converted become your best opportunities.
...Stephen Paul Gnass

Red flags are warning signals that something is wrong. They usually appear during manufacturing, in-house product testing or customer trials at a plant or in the field. As you stay close to your customers, turn on your intuition and learn to spot these red flags. When you spot them, you will realize that they are actually masked opportunities. You are really uncovering problems that will enable you to improve your product through creative innovation. Always keep in mind that…

Red flags invariably represent good news!

Red flags can be outstanding opportunities, if you have the awareness and insight to take advantage of them.

WORK QUIETLY AND CONFIDENTIALLY

When inventing and developing with your team members, think in terms of "stealth" and remember all those innovations that just sprang onto the market and captured a niche. For instance, Stealth bombers, the Personal Computer, Direct TV, Celestial Seasonings Teas and Hot Wheels.
The element of surprise is a powerful ally in launching "marketing warfare" in a new market segment. That's why it is called "marketing warfare".

During the developmental stage of an innovation, it is best to work quietly and confidentially. Until all testing and trials have been completed, you do not want anyone telegraphing your innovation activities to your competition. This means that your team of experts should not be talking to outsiders. Even your first customers, who may be helping with product testing before public disclosure occurs, should sign confidentiality agreements. You want to protect your ability to patent in every possible way.

Once a major innovation becomes a success, you can tell it on the mountain and get publicity, but only if you think it will get you more business. If you are competing against some sleeping giants, it may be best to keep working as quietly as possible and round up as many new customers as you can. It is usually best to keep your competitors in the dark for as long as possible and let them be surprised later, after you have captured the new business and established your niche.

PART TWO
PATENTING

5

ALL ABOUT PATENTS

Patents can provide security and a sense of accomplishment, and are a whole lot of fun.

YOUR PATENT MAY BECOME YOUR MOST VALUABLE ASSET

We frequently think of assets in the form of real estate, cars and investments, such as stocks and bonds. But a well-written, carefully prosecuted patent application can result in another form of valuable asset--a United States Patent. Collect several U.S. Patents and you may be reinforcing your or your company's financial security for many years to come.

Commonly referred to as a form of intellectual property, patents today have more respect than ever before. In the past fifteen years, record judgments have been awarded to patent holders against patent infringement. In the world of patents, it is well known that patent values have increased 20-50 fold in just the past several years.

More and more new products and new, high-performance variations on old products are coming to market. Yesterday's high-volume generic product is being splintered into many new innovative niches. And the best means of protection for these new niches is in the form of patent protection.

*Don Kelly, Director of the U.S. Patent Office says that only 3% of all patents make money for an inventor. However, if you follow the teachings of this book, 100% of your patents can make you money! Keep in mind that patents cost money and sales make money. Patents will only afford protection to these sales long-term. The key element this book teaches is only develop those ideas and invention that **can** make you money and become your most valuable asset!*

For this reason, many domestic and foreign entities want to develop new innovative niches to secure their futures. And, many of these manufacturing companies are small- to medium-sized companies that do not have built-in research and development departments. Some may try to develop new products by simply copying existing products. But more and more companies are looking for an advantage over their competition by licensing new ideas and technologies.

Simply put, developing and licensing new patented ideas can be a fast, economical way for these companies to launch new niche products, gain new profits and protect their futures. If you are an independent inventor or have a small business, this can be good news for you.

The best way for you to ensure your future as an inventor-innovator and possibly as a licensor or partner of such a company is to have a sound patenting strategy. This strategy includes careful development of your invention and testing of prototypes while you write and develop your patent application. It also includes timely marketing feedback to ensure that your invention will be effectively sold. In this manner, your patent can become a valuable asset…a United States Patent.

WHAT IS A PATENT?

A patent is a document declaring that a novel, unobvious, useful discovery or invention is being credited to an individual or group of individuals. When granted, the patent covering a new discovery or invention is given a number, filed with the U.S. Patent Office and publicly disclosed when issued. Once issued, it gives the inventor the exclusive rights to sell, manufacture and use the invention. It can be thought of as a grant of property rights by the United States government to the inventor(s).

In broad terms, there are three types of patents.

Utility Patents

These refer to the usefulness of an invention. They are by far the most common types of patents. As of June 8, 1995, they are enforceable for a span of 20 years from the date of filing an application. Prior to this date they were enforceable for up to 17 years from the date they were granted. Patents on drugs, food additives and medical devices are considered utility patents but under special circumstances may be extended for an additional 5 years (25 years total). An extension is generally granted due to the amount of additional time that is required to test and subsequently pass FDA scrutiny.

In the 19th and 20th century there were 1673 patents on washing machines…few of which made the inventor any money. It wasn't until Maytag invented the rotary washing machine that the lives of women in the home were changed forever.

A Totally Absurd Patent

Have you ever wondered exactly how much energy cow burps emit? Satisfy your curiosity with U.S. Patent 5,265,618, a "System for Measuring Metabolic Gas Emissions From Animals"! The device is a tube that is fed to the animal and acts as an internal tracer to measure how much energy free-roaming livestock actually burp up. Knowing this, the most effective diet can be formulated. Reportedly, a prominent university in Great Britain is interested in acquiring this patented device. Do you think this falls under the category of being unique and useful?
…totallyabsurd.com

Utility patents generally give an inventor the most protection and hence have the most value. Utility patent protection is the chief focus of this manual and is what every inventor should seek.
…Bob DeMatteis

Plant Patents

These refer to new plant varieties that have been asexually reproduced, which includes mutants, hybrids and newly founded seedlings. These patents are also valid for 20 years from the date an inventor files.

Design Patents

These refer to any new, original ornamental design for an article to be manufactured. Thus, only the appearance of the article is protected. They are good for 14 years from date of actual issue, not from the date of filing.

After the expiration of a patent's term, either 14, 20 or 25 years, the patentee loses the exclusive rights to the invention. It becomes part of the public domain and anyone may practice its teachings.

WHAT RIGHTS DO PATENTS GIVE YOU?

Patents can represent powerful property rights. These rights can be powerful tools if used effectively. Patent rights can bring substantial income through the manufacture or licensing of the patent's claimed invention and represent long-term security as well. According to the U.S. Patent Office…

A U.S. patent "gives the owner the right to exclude others from making, using or selling the invention."

However, if your patent application is not well thought out and thoroughly researched, you may have absolutely no rights or a weak patent position at best. Leave no margin of error in your patenting activities. To have a genuinely effective patent, you must wisely plan and develop your invention, execute your plan and file an application with the most advantageous timing.

To secure the most effective patent claim coverage, you will want to use an expert patent attorney. In this manual, you will learn how to do this without spending a lot of money up front, thus delaying your costs until later when your invention is producing income.

WHO CAN FILE A U.S. PATENT APPLICATION?

Any person who is the original (first) inventor may file for a United States patent. Upon submitting your permanent patent application to the U.S. Patent Office, you will sign an "Oath of Inventorship". This oath

The U.S. Patent system serves to motivate innovators to create new technology and affords security to investors in exchange for financial support of invention development and marketing. Patent holders are provided with potential powers that pose barriers to market entry, thus limiting competition.
…Donald Grant Kelly, Director, U.S. Patent Office

It is generally understood that 95% of all patents don't earn the inventor any substantial income. The 2 most common reasons are they are too easy to design around or the initial marketing was poorly researched.
…Bob DeMatteis

On June 4, 1992, Robert W. Patch got his first patent-- U.S. Patent No. 3,091,888--on a toy truck. Robert was 6 years old at the time!
…DewRay Calendars, June 1992

One significant success story is the development of "Liquid Paper", which is used on written documents and to "clean up" typing errors and artwork.

Liquid Paper was invented by a 17-year-old woman who was a high school dropout! It quickly became a multi-million dollar product!

Bette Nesmith Graham originally marketed the product as "Mistake Out" and made it in her kitchen. When demand skyrocketed, she changed the name to Liquid Paper and applied for a patent and a trademark.

In 1975 she sold the company to Gillette Corporation for $47.5 million!

is a declaration stating that you are the first and sole (or joint) inventor(s).

If someone other than the original (or first) inventor received a patent, it would be invalid. If there is more than one inventor, they should file jointly for the patent. It is important to list everyone who contributed to the novelty of the invention. To clarify this point, it is not necessary to list any participant in the invention process who was only "following your instructions".

Confine your invention activities to a tight group of people. It can be especially dangerous to include outsiders as part of the process. They may try to claim some ownership of the patent, even though you already knew what they contributed or suggested. The last thing you want is litigation from an outsider claiming you stole his/her invention. Look at the application's claims you will be filing (Chapter 7 talks in detail about claims). If a participant has not created or at least influenced one of the claims, he/she should not be a co-inventor.

Only when a person dies or becomes insane may another file for him/her. If an inventor refuses to file for a patent (or cannot be found) and the company for which he/she works stands to profit, a co-inventor or proprietor may file on his/her behalf.

IS IT DIFFICULT TO GET A PATENT?

Don't undertake a project unless it is manifestly important and nearly impossible to achieve. ...Edwin Land, Polaroid Land Camera inventor.

If you have a genuinely unique discovery or invention, you will most likely receive a patent. To give you an idea of recent activity at the U.S. Patent Office, in 1997 over 220,000 applications will be filed and about 115,000 patents will be granted. Of these patents granted, about 25% will be from independent inventors!

The chances of receiving a patent are better than 50% and probably closer to 80% or 90%. The chief reasons the Patent Office will not grant a patent are (1) due to the unforeseen discovery of prior art in a patent search or (2) the invention is deemed "anticipated", which would make the invention "obvious" in the eyes of a patent examiner.

Prior art refers to any form of subject matter previously or currently known. If prior art exists on the inventive matter in your patent application, a patent will not be granted.

There is one additional factor that contributes to a fair percentage of applications not resulting in patents--the inventors decide to abandon them. This generally happens because (1) they are unable to get broad enough patent protection, (2) sales of the invention are inadequate during the patent pending stage or (3) they lose interest.

WHAT IS NEEDED TO HAVE AN INVENTION PATENTED?

The U.S. Patent Office has rules and laws that apply to the granting of patents. In filing for a patent on your invention, you must meet these three important criteria:

1. The invention must be *useful*. Remember Eli Whitney's cotton gin and Edison's light bulb? How about the invention of the paper clip or the now common, spring-loaded mousetrap? More recent inventions are Velcro™, ZipLoc™ bags and the process of reading DNA in genes. If the product or process in a patent application is not considered useful, the Patent Office will reject it. For instance, square tires will probably not be considered useful…nor would a vaccine that would cause a disease such as AIDS.

2. The patented invention must be *operative*. In other words it must work according to the claims in the application. For instance, square tires would be considered neither useful nor operative. A patent on a plastic material whose claims are based upon improved strength, but does not perform as indicated, is not valid.

3. The invention must be *new* or *novel*. An invention cannot be patented if:

- The invention was known in any part of the world at any given time before you came up with the idea.
- It was previously described in an article and published anywhere in the world.
- It was previously patented anywhere.
- The difference between your invention and a previous patent (or publicly known product, process, etc.) is such that it would have been obvious to any person skilled in the art. For instance, simply changing size or color will not be acceptable.
- Your invention was put into use more than one year prior to filing for a patent in this country.

WHAT CANNOT BE PATENTED?

There are three areas to avoid. They are:

1. **Perpetual motion machines.** The U.S. Patent Office says they are not patentable. The U.S. Patent Office does not accept this concept as being possible. So if you think you have developed one, call it something else such as an "improved power system".

2. **Methods of doing business.** Methods of doing business and related printed matter may not be accepted as being patentable. You may ask, "If a company's method of doing business includes a special packaging means, would this be considered a method of doing business?" The answer is "no", provided that the special packaging has a specific utility or design value in and of itself. If so, it would fall

There is no area of the law in which, for those not trained and practicing in it, there is more confusion among the public--often including general lawyers-- than what is called "Intellectual Property Law". This confusion arises as to the types of available protection and for what subject matter. Thus, there are patents (utility, plant and design), trademarks and service marks, (both registered and common law), copyrights (both registered and unregistered and domain names). There is also "trade dress" and "trade secret" protection. These subjects are addressed in this book, but a clear understanding of them comes only with repetitive work and a great deal of exposure in the intellectual property field.
...Bill Pavitt, Esq.

Today, we are learning that America's independent inventors have arrived. They effectively hold a seat at the table with other intellectual property policy makers. And, as they slide their chairs up to the table, they are finding that with their newly gained influence comes a heavy responsibility.
...Donald Grant Kelly, Director, U.S. Patent Office

under a utility patent, based upon its utilitarian merits or a design patent, based upon its unique appearance.

3. **"I have an idea about a product that would be super..."** Merely having an idea cannot be patented. Nor can you get a patent on the "suggestion" of a "new, unique invention". A patent is granted based upon a specific design for an apparatus, a product, process, etc., which works in at least one form, as stated in the patent application.

If you employ a patent attorney, he/she will almost always ask you if you have a sample prototype. If you do not, you will need to show due diligence and in the near future prove your invention works. This is called "reduction to practice". It can be accomplished by building a working prototype or supplying detailed drawings illustrating the utilitarian function. If you are filing for a process or systems patent, you will sooner or later need to show some illustrations or perhaps a video about how it works. "Pie in the sky" ideas cannot be patented. You must show how the idea can be implemented into an invention and how it functions.

To expand on this, if you suggested an idea for an invention to a friend, without indicating how it could be made to work, and your friend subsequently figured out (discovered) a novel way to implement your idea, you will probably not be considered the inventor. At best, you may be considered a co-inventor. If your friend receives a patent for his efforts in implementing your idea, you may be out of luck, even though the original idea was yours. You cannot claim rights to any invention or discovery by merely thinking something would be a good idea.

On the other hand, if you suggested an idea to someone and showed the person in a relatively detailed drawing how it could be made to work, and he/she made a working model *based upon your drawing,* that person would not qualify as the inventor. If you saved the drawing and could prove that the concept was yours, you would be the one to whom any patent should be issued. Patents are serious business and stealing "original ideas" and claiming "original ownership" is fraud.

WHAT IS NOT A PATENT?

There are five types of intellectual properties that are not subject to patenting, some of which are also processed at the United States Patent and Trademark Office (also referred to as the "USPTO" or the "PTO") or its related branches. They are trademarks, service marks (the two are sometimes referred to solely as "marks"), trade dress copyrights and domain names.

In the last several years I have frequently heard from people with good ideas who want to give them to someone else "for half of the royalties". How generous!

Obviously they are unaware of the work and effort that lie ahead. That work and effort is worth 99% of the royalties, not 50%!

A good example...suppose one hundred years ago, a person had the idea of making a vehicle that could fly. He would not get a patent on that idea, but the Wright Brothers, who made a flying machine, would and did get a patent on their flying vehicle.
...Bill Pavitt, Esq.

What's More Valuable: a Trademark or Patent?

Initially, a patent is more valuable because it keeps others from making the same product. However, in time, brand loyalty to a trademark can cause its value to surpass that of a patent. Patents tend to decrease in value over the years, whereas trademarks increase in value the more they are used.
...Bob DeMatteis

Trademarks

Trademarks relate to any word, symbol or device used to describe the origin of goods or services and to distinguish them from others. For instance, McDonald's and its golden arches, Shell Oil's shell, or the numerous insignias used by Coca-Cola. Trademarks legally begin the first time they are used in public. Registered trademarks are those filed with the U.S. Patent and Trademark Office, reviewed by the PTO and granted as "unique". They qualify as unique if they are not in conflict with any other trademarks.

Commonly used words cannot be trademarked; they must be unique by their very nature. An exception to this rule applies to common words that have been used exclusively to describe an article and have not been contested as a mark for a period of five years. The owner may file for and be granted a trademark registration. Dual-tab® and Big Red® are examples of registered trademarks.

Service Marks

Service marks are similar to trademarks but refer to a manner in which goods are offered for sale. In other words, they refer to the service, not the product. Burger King's "Have it your way", Wal-Mart's "We sell for less…always" and Sears "You Can Count On Me" are examples of service marks.

Unlike patents and copyrights, trademarks and service marks last indefinitely, if the owner continues to use them. Between the 5th and 6th year after the initial registration of the mark, a registrant must file an affidavit verifying its use to keep the registration alive. Thereafter, the mark may be renewed every ten years, into the indefinite future.

To secure a registered trademark, a user files for either a "use" application, meaning that it has already been used in commerce or an "intent-to-use" application. The use of a mark within one state does not constitute commerce use. In other words, marks may be registered only when they are used in interstate commerce.

The owner of a mark is usually an individual, a corporation or partnership. If the owner is an overseas entity, the owner must have a representative in the U.S. process all paperwork with the U.S. Patent Office. Either the owner of a mark or the representative may file for a registered trademark or service mark.

Before a trademark is submitted to the Patent Office, the owner may consider doing a search for conflicting marks. However, the PTO does not require it. A search can be conducted at the U.S. Patent Office, a trademark-searching company or at any of the Patent and Trademark Depository Libraries. (See Appendix)

From the first date of use, the owner may use a "TM" or an "SM" after the mark to alert the public to the claim. The owner may use the

In establishing the fact of whether or not there is a likelihood of confusion between two trademarks, there is an excellent summary posted on the Internet that explains it in detail. Go to (yes…this is only one URL!):

weber.u.washington.edu/~engli b/ptdl/trademarks/tmloc.html

Doing a Trademark or Service Mark Search

As of December 29, 1998, inventors can do a trademark or service mark search at the U.S. Patent Office's Web site on the Internet. The URL is: www.uspto.gov/tmdh/index.html.

Try using the Boolean search method and search for marks that are either registered or pending.

You can also search for non-registered trademarks and service marks on the Internet. By searching the words or word string on the many search engines, you should have a reasonable idea of its use. Also, search it as a URL. You can also do a trademark search at thomasregister.com.

If you are not on the Internet, you can conduct a search at any of the U.S. Patent and Trademark Depository Libraries.

When searching, be careful to search for similar words and phrases, which may be in conflict.
…Bob DeMatteis

"circle r" registration symbol (®), only after a mark is registered and issued by the U.S. Patent and Trademark Office.

For complete information, instructions and forms for filing a registered trademark, call the U.S. Patent Office at 800-786-9199 and ask for the free pamphlet, "Basic Facts about Registering a Trademark".

Some examples of marks are:

Trademarks: **BIGmouth™**

Registered trademark: **Jeep**®

Service mark: **Have it Your Way!**ˢᴹ

Trade Dress

Trade dress is a newer concept that applies primarily to product and package configurations. These configurations can be protected against unfair competition if they meet three basic criteria: (1) non-functionality, (2) proof of secondary meaning or (3) likelihood of confusion. The common law tort of unfair competition has given protection against copying nonfunctional aspects of consumer products.

A few examples that have been cited in common law actions include the configuration of a cereal biscuit, a loaf of bread, a medicinal tablet, a root beer bottle, a cologne bottle, a crescent wrench, a washing machine, a clock and a padlock.

Trade dress is technically a trademark and can be registered at the USPTO using the same forms as a trademark. You, the inventor, should consider the registration of the trade dress of your new invention if at all possible. Like a trademark, trade dress does not expire. After years of use it can result in a form of intellectual property much more valuable than a patent.

Copyrights

Copyrights protect the writings of an author or artist/designer. They protect the form of expression, not the subject matter or content. Neither names nor titles are copyrighted. Examples of copyrights are:

- Books, magazine or newspaper articles, maps
- Artwork, patterns and designs, sculptures
- Songs, sound recordings, motion pictures
- Notes written on a piece of paper

On the Internet, the U.S. Patent and Trademark Office has forms for filing trademarks. You can download the form (prinTEAS), fill it out and mail it, or you can file electronically (e-TEAS).

The Internet URL is: uspto.gov/teas/print/welcome.htm

*In the **From Patent to Profit** workshops, we teach inventors and innovators to develop a trademark strategy right along with a patent strategy. Try to develop a catchy trademark, register it in due course and use it as part of a licensing agreement. Licenses on patents usually expire on the last expiration date of the licensed patents, but trademarks last indefinitely. Upon the expiration of the last of the patents, a new license for the use of the trademark can be struck.*

...Bob DeMatteis

A copyright arises the moment the work is completed and no copyright notice is required. However, when the work is published it is wise to include a notice. Being published only makes a copyright publicly known. A notice strengthens protection by warning others and can help the owner get damages in the event of infringement. Damages can be granted if others copy your mark and use it for personal profit or if the commercial value is harmed--regardless of whether they tried to profit from the use of the copyrighted material. The correct form of copyright notice and an example are:

Copyright [date(s)] by [author/owner]

Copyright © 1999 by IPT, Grass Valley, CA

The circle "c" (©) may be used instead of the word "copyright". The phrase "All Rights Reserved" was a requirement in some countries, but it is no longer needed. Materials that were copyrighted after January 1, 1978 last the lifetime of the author plus 50 years.

The posting of your copyrighted material to the Internet, Usenet or a Web page does not constitute putting it in the public domain. Public domain means that anyone can use it. This can only occur when the owner/author has explicitly said so, using language such as, "I hereby grant this writing to the public domain."

"Fair use" of a copyright is not infringement. Fair use refers to the use of a copyright without the author's consent in commentary, news reports, research articles, education, etc. It is not intended to damage the commercial value of the copyrighted material.

Free ads promoting an owner's copyrighted material are not considered "fair use". It is up to the owner to determine if it is OK. It is interesting to note that government publications and notices are not protected by copyright laws. They can be freely copied and disseminated by anyone.

Copyrights can be registered with the Copyright Office of the Library of Congress in Washington D.C. Send an application, a copy of the copyrighted work plus a registration fee of $20. See the Appendix for more information.

Domain Names

Domain names represent a newer field of intellectual property used on the Internet and have become a major part of the business. They can be seen as the "trademarks of the Internet". A domain name represents your "address" on the Internet. A "top level" domain specifies the broad category and ends with **.com** (company), **.net** (network infrastructure), **.org** (non-profit organization) and **.edu** (4-year degree-granting institution). A second-level domain name represents an individual as in **YOURNAME.com**.

Since copyrights include artwork, designs and patterns, I have occasionally heard from inventors who feel they do not need a patent because the design or the production blueprints (patterns) for manufacturing of their invention is copyrighted.

In part this might be true. But keep in mind that copyrights on a particular design are limited to only those aspects of its artistic "printed" appearance. Blueprints, or patterns, can be modified and changed and be easily designed-around.

In contrast, a utility patent tends to cover the entire functionality--utility--of the invention.

When you're seeking a Sovereign Granted Monopoly (i.e. a patent) to market an invention, in exchange for disclosing your idea to the public for the benefit of Society as a whole, keep an open perspective to entertain having several "picket fences" around you invention concept: e.g. utility patent, design patent, trademark, trade dress, copyright, trade secret and even a license.

Doug English, Patent Attorney

Good domain names are getting harder and harder to find. If you can zero-in on one that meets your criteria...get it as soon as you can. It may eventually become very valuable.

You Don't Have to Be a Scientist, but It Doesn't Hurt!

On April 30, 1897, (Sir) J.J. Thompson announced before scientists at the Royal Institution of Britain, his discovery of a "corpuscle" of electrically charged matter--the electron. As a result, one hundred years later, electronics industries and their dependents generate $10 trillion in annual sales.

...Greg Aharonian, PATNEWS

NCIIA - A Leader in Invention Education

The National Collegiate Inventors and Innovators Alliance or NCIIA is a unique interdisciplinary educational program started at Hampshire College in November 1995 with the generous support of the Jerome and Dorothy Lemelson Foundation. The mission of the Alliance is to foster and promote the teaching of invention, innovation, and entrepreneurship at colleges and universities around the country.

The Alliance provides support in the form of grants to faculty and students, services and information for members, and meetings workshops and so on.

Domain names are used much like trademarks, logos and brand names. They are entered into the computer of your Internet service provider (ISP), and are referred to as Domain Name Servers. The DNS (your domain name) represents your business identity. Once registered, others are prevented from using it, provided you are not infringing a trademark or company/corporate name. Domain names are also portable. No matter what server or ISP you may use, your domain name goes with you.

Registering a domain name is relatively easy. You conduct a quick Internet search and the name is recorded with InterNIC. InterNIC is the Network Information Center--the Internet's administrative registration agency. Your current ISP or other companies on the Internet can conduct this registration process for you. They charge a one-time fee of $50-75 to register and establish a DNS. InterNIC subsequently charges $100 for the first two years and $50 per year thereafter.

MISCONCEPTIONS ABOUT PATENTS

There are many misconceptions about patents. Let's dispel some of the more common ones:

1. **You have to be a scientific genius to successfully invent and patent your ideas.** Patents are not necessarily of a scientific nature. There are many considerations for the granting of useful patents, most of which are not scientific. You will find that even with a little education you can invent and develop a unique product, system, or an improvement on an existing product, and get a patent.

Frequently, patents are granted because they are useful to mankind, not because they are scientific marvels. For instance, an innovation that saves time, reduces scrap or makes a machine, product or system easier to use should be patentable and quite valuable. Sometimes you are better off not having a degree in the sciences with pre-set rules and regulations to follow. The chances are that you are creative and intelligent enough without a scientific education.

2. **A university or college can teach you how to create, patent and develop your ideas.** Colleges and universities that teach how to invent and patent are hard to find. So don't count on signing up for some classes at the local college. However, there is a growing trend with educational institutions that do specialize--even encourage-- dreaming up ideas that can improve our lives.

3. **Inventors are well trained in engineering.** While some inventors are excellent engineers, most are not. Frequently, inventors "create" or "discover" new concepts from which engineers then engineer new products. The focus in engineering is on dealing with

something already known. In inventing, the focus is on dealing with something yet to be discovered. Engineering schools train engineers based upon what is already known. They rarely teach how to think creatively or outside given norms and standards.

4. **It cannot be patentable because the idea is too simple or the change is obvious.** This is frequently not true. For instance, what if a product has been made of leather for 40 years and an inventor has just discovered how to make it from a new plastic material that has several benefits over leather. At first glance, you might say that the change is obvious because it is the same product with just a change of material. This usually means it would not be patentable.

But wait a minute. No one has introduced this product in plastic for 40 years! There must be a reason. The reason usually represents the bona fide patentable concept. For instance, it may be that the process of making the product in plastic was not previously feasible.

Perhaps the smart inventor who discovered how to hand-make the prototype in plastic can also discover how to mass manufacture it as well. This is where new, patentable concepts and means may be found. It is not the product, previously made in leather and now made in plastic, that is patentable. It is the manner in which the new plastic product is being made.

5. **Why even get a patent? By changing a product 10%-15% someone can design around it anyway.** There is no such thing as changing a product by a certain percentage that validates a "design-around". We know that merely changing color or size will not change the power behind a patent. Changes must be "substantial" to not infringe upon an existing patent.

This concept is substantiated by the Doctrine of Equivalence, which was established in a 1952 court case. In summary, the Doctrine of Equivalence states:

If it operates in substantially the same manner, by substantially the same means, and produces substantially the same result, it infringes.

On March 3, 1997, in the Hilton-Davis case, the Supreme Court upheld the Doctrine of Equivalence and further clarified its interpretation. In summary, the Court's decision states that:

A. We will continue to adhere to the Doctrine of Equivalence.
B. The determination of equivalence should be applied objectively on an element-by-element basis.

About 15%-20% of our workshop participants are engineers, 40% are women, many already have patents. A few are scientists and we have an occasional attorney. All seek the same information about how to take ideas and inventions From Patent to Profit.
...Bob DeMatteis

Square Bottom Bags

Margaret Knight of Boston is credited with being the inventor who created the square bottom bags that are still used in grocery stores today. Her patents were from 1870 to 1879.

She also had 90 other inventions and 22 patents covering textiles, shoe-making machinery, domestic devices and even a "sleeve-valve" automobile engine.

...Invention Dimension, Lemelson-MIT

Obtaining a patent is like anything else in life...it requires a lot of hard work, hours of frustration solving problems and always hoping for new discoveries that will make your job easier.

If anyone thinks that Edison, Lemelson, Land, Yamamoto and the many brilliant inventors who have contributed so much to our American way of life had a gravy train waiting for them, think again.

The monetary rewards to inventing and patenting inherently come from the process of problem solving and enjoying what it is you are doing. It almost never comes from casually inventing something and selling the patent for millions of dollars.

People often tell me they don't have the money to pursue their ideas. I tell them that "if the idea is good enough, the money is in the ideas."
...Stephen Paul Gnass

How About $4-$5 For a Patent?

On April 10, 1790, George Washington signed into law the first U.S. Patent bill. The cost was $4-$5!

...DewRay Calendars, April 1992

C. If a patent holder can demonstrate that an amendment required during prosecution had a purpose unrelated to patentability, then it should not affect the scope of the patent's claim.

The Doctrine of Equivalence works in your favor most of the time. For a more in-depth understanding of how to apply it in reading patents, see Chapter 7, pages 119 and 120.

6. **Once you have a patent, you can sit back and "cash in" on the royalties.** Unfortunately, this is not normally the case. But you certainly can realize significant financial gain. Developing an idea into a patent and then into a product requires a lot of hard work. The amount of time it takes to dream up the idea plus the time spent on patenting is only 5% of your total time investment. The balance consists of developing, manufacturing and marketing. But don't be discouraged; the process is a lot of fun and very exciting. The result can be a piece of intellectual property with real value.

7. **It costs a lot of money to get a patent.** While some companies may spend a lot of money, it's not necessary. You can do much of the work yourself and are usually better off when you do. By doing your own patent writing you will have more control over the outcome of the inventing-patenting process and the resultant patent itself. If you follow the guidelines in this manual, you can defray a substantial amount of the cost of patenting.

In addition, this manual will teach you how to successfully bring in manufacturing partners, develop sales in a timely manner and get a patent with little up-front money. You should be able to generate a positive cash flow during the developmental process before you incur any major patenting costs.

HOW MUCH DOES IT COST TO GET A PATENT?

Hopefully, until the time for filing, it will cost you nothing! Nevertheless, there will be some patenting expenses you need to consider. Very few inventors can write an acceptable patent application with legal claims. Any write up an inventor does should be reviewed by a patent attorney. The Patent Office also charges a patent application filing fee and when the patent is granted, a patent issuing fee. There are also maintenance fees at 3-1/2 years, 7 years and 11-1/2 years after the patent issue date.

Filing fees for small entities are half that of those for large entities. A small entity is one with a maximum of 500 employees; a large entity has over 500 employees. Non-profit organizations are considered small entities. When counting the number of employees, include all of the company's divisions, plus *all* those employed by the owner's affiliates, sister companies and subsidiaries. Both full- and part-time employees are counted. If the size of your entity changes anytime in the future, you will adjust your payment status accordingly.

In addition, you will incur other expenses, such as fees for an attorney or patent agent. Legal expenses are generally $200-$300 per hour for an attorney and $100-$150 per hour for a patent agent. The writing and filing of a relatively simple patent application by an attorney should cost a total of $1500-$2500, aside from the filing fees. You can save a lot of money by writing your own application and having an attorney prepare the final draft for you. This subject is covered in detail in Chapter 7.

If you hire a draftsperson to do the drawings, he/she will charge from $25-$50 per hour. The total cost to have professional drawings done is usually about $250-$400. You can save money by hiring college and university engineering students, who can produce excellent work for as little as $10-$18 per hour.

Patent costs can also vary depending upon the number of claims. The costs increase if you have more than 3 "independent claims". These are the written claims at the end of the patent that are thought of as claims that "stand alone". Multiple dependent claims also incur an additional cost, as they add to the complexity of studying the inventive material. Usually these types of claims can be avoided with a well-written application. You can learn more about independent and dependent claims in Chapter 7. After your patent application is reviewed at the PTO, you will incur patent prosecution costs, charged by your attorney for an additional $1000-$2000.

Also keep in mind that the Patent Office fees are published every year in October. But don't let patent costs and fees discourage you. Well-conceived patents will earn far more money than the cost of patenting. Your patent will help to preserve your rights to make money, not spend it.

The cost estimate in Chart 5-1 is a high-low cost summary of writing a patent and having it filed, prosecuted and granted. It is based upon filing a simple invention and having an attorney write at least the final draft to a regular application, add the claims and then file and prosecute it. It assumes no major prosecution problems and a small entity status.

These costs are spread out over a period of several months to a few years. With the right development strategy and aggressive marketing in the early stages, you should have sufficient cash flow before you need to pay the legal costs. You can read more about hiring a patent attorney and how to pursue an economical patent writing strategy in Chapters 6 and 7.

The Key Word Is "Commitment"

*If you have been negotiating a license with a large entity, but have not made a **commitment**, you can still file as a small entity. The key word is "commitment". But be careful. An error in identifying the size of your "entity" may invalidate your patent. If you have any doubts use your attorney to accurately assess the situation.*

Chart 5-1 Patent Cost Estimate

Low Cost	Comments	Event	Comments	High Cost
$ 0	You write	Disclosure		
$ 0	You write	Provisional	Attorney writes	$1200 - $2000
$ 90	You file (Fed/Ex)	Provisional	Attorney files	$90 - $120
$ 500	Attorney does final draft	Regular	Same as Provisional	$0
$1000	Attorney writes	Claims	Attorney writes	$1500
$ 0	You do	Drawings	Out-sourced	$400
$ 385	Attorney files	Filing Fee	Attorney files	$500
$1000	Attorney prosecutes	Prosecution	Attorney files	$2000
$ 770	Attorney files	Issuing Fee	Attorney files	$900

$3745 = Total low estimate   Total high estimate = $6590 - $7420

WHAT EXACTLY DOES "PATENT PENDING" MEAN?

It means that the U.S. Patent Office has received a patent application covering an invention. Only on or after the date the PTO has received your application can the words "patent pending" (some businesses prefer "patent applied for") be used.

It is illegal to post "patent pending" notices on any material or product if the U.S. Patent Office has not received your application. It constitutes fraud and makes you subject to fines. You can make sure your application has been received by using either certified mail or Federal Express. You can call Federal Express to verify that the package was received. They will also give you the name of the patent office employee who signed for it.

Patent pending is a warning notice to others. During the patent pending time span, an inventor does not have any rights to cause a competitor to cease and desist. But it would be unwise of a firm to pursue the manufacture of an invention, knowing it could be potentially liable for patent infringement after the patent issues.

FILING A PATENT APPLICATION

There are two kinds of patent applications. One is referred to as the regular patent application, which will become the permanent, numbered patent. The other is the temporary, provisional patent application. The provisional application is covered in greater detail in the next section.

The regular, non-provisional patent application is a complete specification in compliance under 35 USC #112 in United States patent law. It will include the actual, legal claims of the novelty of the invention, which should be written by a qualified patent attorney or patent agent. Once granted, your patent rights will be defined by the claims. They will ultimately be the determining factor as to whether

The Post Office Is an Agent of the USPTO

It has been reported that since the U.S. Post Office is an agent of the Federal Government and that the Patent Office is a department of the same government, that your parcels are considered delivered to the Patent Office once you have delivered them to a U.S. Post Office. Thus, you can have a patent pending status the same day.

If you do this, make sure you send it via a means that will provide a receipt that will properly identify the contents such as: registered, certified or express mail. Then, make sure you keep your receipt!

there is infringement by others who are making products similar to yours. This application should be as tightly written and professionally prosecuted as possible, to give you adequate patent protection. You should leave no margin for error. The next 20 years may depend upon the integrity of this document.

In summary, a regular patent application includes:

- Complete specification of the invention
- Drawings representing the invention (if needed)
- Claims
- Abstract summary of the invention
- Oath of inventorship
- Small entity status declaration
- Power of attorney (If you use an attorney, he/she will act on your behalf to file and prosecute the application.)

After your application is received by the USPTO, they will mail you or your attorney or agent a confirmation of receipt.

PROVISIONAL PATENT APPLICATIONS...
A GREAT OPPORTUNITY

On June 8, 1995, Congress put into effect a new law referring to what is called "a provisional patent application". This greatly simplified patent application allows an inventor to file at the U.S. Patent Office "a detailed specification" of the invention accompanied by the necessary drawings. Upon receipt of the provisional patent application at the USPTO, an invention officially has a "patent pending" status.

In summary, the provisional patent application has the following elements:

- Complete specifications of the invention
- Drawings representing the invention (if needed)
- Cover sheet (a simple form from the USPTO)
- Small entity status declaration
- A $75 filing fee

That's all! The simplified format greatly reduces the time and expense required to file an application. The claims, abstract and oath of inventorship are not required in provisional applications. The toughest, most costly part of filing a patent application is usually the claims. For this reason, provisional applications are a lot easier to write and far less expensive to file.

Here are a few other key elements of a provisional patent application:

Patent Law Changes

Changes in U.S. patent law can present a leveling effect on inventors' rights. In some respects, the new provisional patent application places U.S. inventors on an equal footing with their foreign counterparts. Foreigners have long relied upon the powerful legal effects of their own national filing (priority) dates abroad, and those dates can be as much as a year before the U.S. filing. With the provisional patent application, U.S. inventors enjoy the same basic advantage of being able to claim benefit of their "domestic priority" filing, while gaining that one-year decision window.

...Donald Grant Kelly, Director, U.S. Patent Office

Provisional Patents and Broadening the Scope

In a recent project, I have filed 7 provisional patent applications blanketing every possible aspect of the invention. We still have two more to file.

This new invention is already licensed. Part of the agreement is that the licensee is paying for the cost to patent.

The wisdom behind filing several provisional patent applications is based upon protecting our national and international rights to the new development and preserving cash flow during the costly start-up phase.

Thus, the licensee is spending its money now on marketing and generating sales and income. In a timely manner, the permanent, non-provisional patents will be filed.

...Bob DeMatteis

Testing Provisional Applications

Since the laws regarding the filing of provisional patent applications are so new, they have not been tested in court. Certainly they are legal documents, but how close the regular patent application must read on the provisional has not been tested. It goes without saying that the closer the language of the two documents matches, the better off you will be.

Provisional Patent Tip

Some patent attorneys say that a provisional patent application should include claims to make absolutely sure it covers what it says it covers.

I disagree. I think this is premature and could even be dangerous...potentially limit the scope of the final non-provisional.

As an inventor, I know how difficult it is to identify exactly what the inventive matter is. In fact, frequently inventors and attorneys do not truly understand the inventive matter until well after a patent application has been filed and after the product has been more fully tested and used. This is one reason there are so many patent applications that become a CIP--Continuation in Part.

As I draft my provisional patent applications, I make sure they are as broadly written as possible. I do not include any legal claims, but I do include a "List of Claims", which in extremely broad terms covers all the inventive matter in the application--and probably a lot more-- in simple layperson terms.

By doing this, the application stands a better chance of enduring the scrutiny of its scope.

...Bob DeMatteis

- "Patent Pending" can be posted on your products.
- It is not reviewed by the Patent Office.
- The PTO discards it after one year.
- A regular, non-provisional application must be filed within one year and reference the provisional application.
- The filing cost is only $75 for small entities and $150 for all others!
- It can preserve your worldwide filing rights for one year.

To establish a priority date, it is most important to file a provisional application in a timely manner. To preserve the priority date, an inventor must file the regular, permanent patent application within one year of filing the provisional. When the regular patent application is filed, the provisional is referenced, hence preserving the original filing date. The permanent U.S. patent will have a 20-year life, beginning on the original filing date of the referenced provisional.

The priority date becomes important if two or more inventors have filed for the same inventive matter. See page 95 to learn more about the importance of having an early priority date.

Filing a provisional patent application can give an inventor one entire year to test the marketing of his/her invention without incurring the high cost of filing and prosecuting a regular, permanent patent application. With careful planing, by the end of the one-year period, an inventor may be earning sufficient income from his invention to afford the higher cost of filing for the regular patent application.

Provisional applications should not be construed as a substitute for an "invention disclosure". You will read about protecting your ideas with invention disclosures in Chapter 6. Provisionals should be well-written documents and clearly understood so that the disclosure supports the claims that will be made in the regular, non-provisional application. If they are not, the subject matter in the provisional may be deemed irrelevant to the content of the regular application and the priority date may be lost. The best way to write a provisional application is to use the same guidelines as are used for a regular, non-provisional patent application, excluding the claims and abstract. This subject is discussed in great detail in Chapter 7.

While provisional patent applications offer a great opportunity, they also require words of caution to an inventor. Provisional applications do not give an inventor rights to exclude others from making, using or selling the invention. A provisional can only serve as an interim step before filing a permanent, non-provisional application. Only the granting of the regular, permanent patent application implies any rights.

A caution about filing a provisional patent application involves the "one-year rule". That is, once your invention has been publicly disclosed, you have one year to file an application. You can file a provisional application within one year after public disclosure, but you will lose your rights to file internationally (except for Canada and Mexico). This is discussed in more detail on the following pages.

FIRST TO INVENT

Because the U.S. is a "first to invent" country--not "first to file"--only the first, true inventor(s) will be acknowledged as the patent grantee(s). Any invention or discovery an inventor is working on that has not been abandoned has precedence over subsequent discoveries which are the same or similar in scope.

If two persons are granted patents on the same subject matter, the inventor who can prove his/her discovery has precedence over the other will have the valid patent. This is regardless of who filed first or which patent was granted first.

However, some say that it is important to file a patent application as soon as possible after the initial conception to protect the first-to-invent status, because the inventor who files first is more likely to be proven to be the one with the valid patent. The "first to file" is considered to be in the senior position. The inventor who files his application second is considered to be in a junior position. This is an uncommon occurrence and is referred to as interference.

INTERFERENCE

Since a valid patent can only be granted to the applicant who was first to invent, a proceeding referred to as "interference" is initiated by the PTO to determine who is the first inventor. An interference proceeding may also be initiated between an application and an already granted patent, providing the granted patent was not issued more than one year before the filing of the new application.

Interference occurs in less than 1/10 of 1 percent of the regular patent applications received by the U.S. Patent Office. In other words, about one out of every 1500 applications is involved in a dispute over who was the first to invent. According to Ian Calvert, an administrative patent judge at the USPTO, in 1995 there were only 147 interference proceedings. Of those, 52.5% were in favor of the senior party, 31.7% were in favor of the junior party, about 9.4% resulted in no patents being issued, 5.8% involved no interference in fact, and 0.7% resulted in a split reward. This indicates that the "first to invent" laws truly work. With 200,000 plus applications being filed every year, it is easy to see that there is only a marginal advantage over being first-to-file…if any at all.

In interference proceedings, each party submits facts proving when the invention was made. With no log or supporting facts, the filing date

"First to invent" favors the true inventor who pursues his/her ideas in a timely manner. A "first to file" patent system, like Japan's, is best for large companies with a lot of R&D money to spend on patents.

A prospect that every inventor must bear in mind is that she or he was probably not the first, nor the only inventor to recognize the problem being solved by her or his invention. Don't forget, after all, there are nearly 6 billion people across our planet struggling against the forces of nature, facing and overcoming barriers with the one tool that defines us from all other creatures: inventive thinking.
…Donald Grant Kelly, Director, U.S. Patent Office

There has been much misinformation about the importance of being in the "senior position". It is apparent that the "first to invent" laws in the U.S. work and that there is no significant advantage to being the first to file. More important is good documentation and reducing your invention to practice in a timely manner.
…Bob DeMatteis

Patent Office Facts

Information from the Patent Office reveals that interference annually affects about 35-40 patents filed by small companies and independent inventors. Of these, only about 8 more inventors in the senior position will retain the first to invent status over those in the junior position, which is about what one would expect. Because interference occurs in less than one of every 1500 patents filed, it is not worth any worry.

A One-Year Rule Strategy

Some inventors like to use the one-year rule as part of their marketing/development strategy. They like to stretch out their budget and delay patent filing for as long as they possibly can.

Since most of the expense does not come until the filing of the permanent application (two years later) and its subsequent prosecution (three years later), the method can be a smart approach for inventions that may not produce substantial income, but are still worthy of development.

is considered the earliest date. A board of three Examiners-in-Chief will then determine which inventor has the priority date based upon the evidence they have received.

Two factors are considered in the determination of priority. The first is the "date of conception of the invention", which refers to the first, original date the inventor conceived the idea or the inventive subject matter. The second is when the invention was "reduced to practice", which refers to illustrating how the invention works or the actual construction of the invention in its physical form. The filing of a regular application that completely discloses the invention is treated as the equivalent of reduction to practice.

The inventor who proves to be the first to conceive and the first to reduce the invention to practice will be seen as having the priority over the other inventor. More complicated situations are not so easy for the examiners to determine.

THE ALL-IMPORTANT ONE-YEAR RULE

In the United States, once an inventor ***publicly discloses*** an invention or offers an invention for sale, he/she must file a provisional patent application or a regular, non-provisional patent application within one year or he/she will forever lose the right to file. You can use this one-year rule to your advantage if you are unsure of the marketability of your invention. One year should give you plenty of time to test the marketing of the product.

If you elect, you can extend this one-year further by filing a provisional patent application and then within one year of the provisional filing, you file the permanent application. This can give you a total of almost two years before incurring the higher costs of patenting. If sales are marginal, you may ultimately decide not to file the more expensive permanent application or you may abandon your sales effort altogether.

Careful development of your product and timely filing of your patent application can be key to having a highly successful, effective patent. By waiting until the end of the developmental period when sales have begun, you will have most of the development problems solved. You will be filing a patent application on the preferred embodiments of the invention and will be making your claims stronger, more accurate and less vulnerable to scrutiny and potential invalidation.

PROTECTING YOUR RIGHTS TO FILE WORLDWIDE

You can preserve your ability to file worldwide by making sure that you file a provisional or the regular, non-provisional application before your invention is publicly disclosed or is offered for sale. The exceptions to this rule are Canada and Mexico. They will concur with our guidelines that follow the one-year rule.

Foreign filing must occur within one year of the filing of a regular or provisional application. See page 122 to read about a worldwide patent filing strategy.

PROSECUTING AN APPLICATION AND HOW LONG IT TAKES TO ISSUE

Once a utility patent application has been filed, it will be assigned to a designated patent examiner for his/her review. It generally takes about one year before the review begins. You will receive an office action based upon the examiner's review.

Almost all patents are rejected in the first office action! You should take some time to review the objections and rejections the patent examiner cites. You have 90 days to do this. There can be three or more office actions before a patent is granted, finally and formally rejected by the PTO or abandoned by the inventor. Each office action typically takes another 2-4 months, sometimes longer.

Don't be discouraged during these office action delays. The examiner is trying to evaluate the claims based upon the subject matter in the application. You will have the opportunity to file an amendment and revise the claims or correct other subject matter in the text to clarify your inventive matter. Following through to correct them only benefits you in the long run.

Sometimes the examiner may cite that what you are claiming is not related to the inventive material in the text. In other words, the examiner may bring up the objection of "unrelated subject matter". This is not the end of the world.

You may still file a Continuation In Part (CIP). A CIP is treated much like a new application and allows you to carefully rewrite parts of the original application to more specifically address and clarify the inventive subject matter. It is not an uncommon occurrence. Filing a CIP might prolong the application's issuance by as long as 6-9 months or more. Your original date of filing will not be lost.

It can easily take 12 to 36 months for a patent to issue. Some patent attorneys believe that the longer the wait, the better, because it indicates that the examiner is having a difficult time finding any prior art. If you wish, you can also include a petition with your application that will expedite the review of your application. This can be particularly important to a company that is relying on the patent's issuance to secure financing or combat a serious patent infringement problem. The petition costs about $150.

"Haste Makes Waste"...but "Lethargy Loses Rights"...

Don't rush to get a patent on your invention until you first ascertain a real market therefor. However, once conceived, one must with due diligence obtain at least a constructive reduction to practice by filing for letters patent, or one may be estopped from filing at all, market notwithstanding...

...Doug English, Patent Attorney

It is rare that a patent is accepted in its entirety at full value in the first office action. Of all my patents, the only one I ever received on a first office action was the least valuable one.

...Bob DeMatteis

On Sunday, December 15, 1836, the U.S. Patent Office was destroyed by fire. Thousands of models, drawings and applications were lost. Hopefully, delays of this sort will not occur with your application!

...DewRay Calendar, December 1996

WHEN A PATENT IS GRANTED

When you have overcome the objections and rejections of the patent examiner, you will receive a notice of allowance. In other words, you will receive your patent! You then have 90 days to pay the issuing fee. When your check is received, your patent will be officially granted and issued in about 3 to 4 months.

Your legal rights begin on the date of issuance. From this point on, you have the right to stop all others from making, selling or using your patented material. Fig. 5-1 is a flow chart of the patenting process from beginning to end.

Figure 5-1 Patenting Process

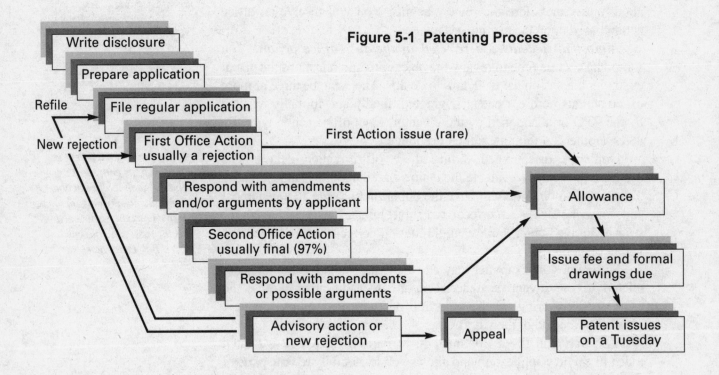

Copyright © 1995 Robert Platt Bell, Esq. & IPT 1997

WHEN A PATENT APPLICATION IS FINALLY REJECTED

You may have taken your patent application through numerous office actions, perhaps even filed a Continuation in Part for clarification, but the examiner still refuses to accept your application's subject matter as being patentable. You have received a "Final Office Action", which contains a final rejection by the examiner. Upon receipt of this final notice, you still have two more alternatives.

First, you can prepare an immediate response and try to restate your position and clarify (argue) the differences. You will usually do this if you feel the examiner's rejections are in error. Hopefully, you can provide additional facts to support your position. Promptly pursued, you can send this correspondence to the examiner and ask him/her to reconsider. You should have a response within 30 days.

Second, if you (and most likely your attorney) feel strongly that your material is patentable and the examiner's judgment in rejecting the subject matter is wrong, you can file an appeal with the Court of Appeals for the Federal Circuit. This is a special appeals court in Washington, D.C. that handles only patent-related matters. To appeal, you need a well-prepared legal argument to present your case. Your argument should include other related cases supporting it.

This appeal process can be costly, but it usually occurs after you have realized some success and profit from the manufacture and sale of your invention. Keep in mind that a patent granted after it has endured the appeal process in the U.S. court system will be more difficult to invalidate at a later date. If infringement occurs, the appeal process should help to strengthen your patent's integrity.

YOUR PATENT IS PROPERTY

When you receive your U.S. Patent, you will have accomplished something that few people in history have ever accomplished. Feel good about it and celebrate. Your patents are intellectual property and are personal assets, like a boat, a house or business. When someone infringes your patent, it feels the same as though someone stole your boat or robbed your house. For twenty years, this intellectual property is exclusively yours.

As with real estate, you can sell your patent or license it, which is comparable to leasing real estate. You can earn substantial income from the sale or license of a patent.

INVENTORSHIP, OWNERSHIP AND PATENT ASSIGNMENT

Only true inventors can be named patentees, but any individual, firm, corporation or partnership can own a patent. An inventor automatically owns his/her patent when granted, unless it is assigned to another entity.

For someone other than the original inventor to own a patent, the inventor's rights must be transferred via a patent assignment. It is just like signing over a pink slip to an automobile or boat. The assignment of a patent is also registered at the U.S. Patent Office, although this is not a legal requirement.

If you are an inventor and intend to assign your patent to an individual or a company, make sure you are getting a fair deal. Remember that patents are now worth 20-50 times more than just 15 years ago. Ask yourself if you are satisfied with the amount of

Zigzag Stitch

Was invented by Helen Augusta Blanchard of Portland, Maine. She earned at least 28 patents, many of which were for improvements to sewing machines, including the first zigzag stitch machine. She also patented related items such as hat-sewing machines and surgical needles.

Patents are similar to deeds in a way. If you have a patent and someone wants to buy it, but wants to pay on installments, never assign it until you have received the last payment. Just like a deed to a house, you would not assign it to a purchaser before it was paid in full.

...Bob DeMatteis

49 U.S. Patents

Beulah Louise Henry of Tennessee was dubbed "Lady Edison" in the 1930s. She earned 49 patents, but her inventions numbered around 110. Her patents include a vacuum ice cream freezer and an umbrella with different colred snap-on cloth covers.

Literally overnight she invented the first bobbinless sewing machine in 1940.

From Patent to Profit
Workshops

From Patent to Profit workshops are given in many parts of the U.S. in colleges and universities and in cooperation with many SBDCs.

If you have a chance to attend one, it can be a highly informative and valuable experience.

compensation you are receiving in exchange for giving up your title and rights to the asset.

When you work for a company and invent something related to your company's business, on company time and for its use, you cannot ask for compensation. Your continued employment is your compensation for the invention. After all, your inventive discovery probably occurred in the job environment and you would not have been able to make it otherwise.

If your invention was conceived before you joined the company and you are patenting it for the company's use, you can ask your employer for extra compensation. However, making this request after your employment begins may put a strain on your relationship and end the relationship.

Ending your relationship with your employer may not be bad news. If you provided the company with solid patents that were shaping its future and your efforts went unrecognized, don't worry. The competitors will find you and make you a better offer.

Federal laws state that if you are employed by a firm and receive a patent on an unrelated idea in another field, and development was not on company time, your employer cannot claim any rights.

HOW CAN YOU LEARN MORE ABOUT PATENTING?

There are not a lot of sources of information about patents. You will find it somewhat difficult to find for the following reasons:

1. **Classes and seminars on patenting are rare.** Other than a few short courses that focus on certain legal aspects of patenting, it is very difficult to find classes or seminars in which you can thoroughly learn about the patenting process.

The workshop series *From Patent to Profit* offered by IPT, Inventions, Patents and Trademarks Company, includes all the basic laws about patents and information regarding how to develop your patenting strategy. These seminars teach in reasonable detail all types of intellectual property, how to write a patent application and what to do when your patent is infringed.

More importantly, the *From Patent to Profit* workshops focus on patenting as it relates to invention development, manufacturing, marketing and licensing. This approach ensures that an inventor will file for claims on the invention's correct and very best attributes. They focus on how an inventor can make money from his/her inventions, not just get a patent.

You've seen it before and will continue to see it throughout this manual…it is unwise to write a patent or pay a lot to have a patent written, without a clear idea of the value, and merit and marketability of

100

your invention. Why would you want to spend thousands of dollars without knowing whether you can earn a single cent?

Learn all you can about patenting, inventing and marketing and make some sound decisions before you spend a lot of money.

2. **Patent attorneys can help.** There are many competent patent attorneys willing to provide information and guidance, but they generally charge $200-$300 per hour! A phone call to learn about some simple aspect of patenting can cost you $100. This is a high price to pay to learn the basics.

In addition, keep in mind that while patent attorneys can help you with patenting, they are generally not able to guide you creatively or offer manufacturing and sales expertise. Even if they could, they would not be cheap. Most patent attorneys don't even ask about whether you think you can market your invention and earn real income from it. Don't get lofty ideas that having a patent automatically means that you will make a lot of money. Remember, only about 5% of all granted patents ever earn an inventor any substantial income.

Patent attorneys are generally a pleasure to work with and usually bring you good news, but you should use them in a cost-effective manner. Many attorneys have the gift to gab...at your expense. Keep this in mind as you learn about patenting.

3. **You cannot always use another inventor to help.** There are successful inventors who could help, but there are many reasons why they cannot. First, you do not want a co-inventor on the patent. Besides, most successful inventors are busy with their own inventions. If they are good and have the time, they may charge as much as a patent attorney.

Finally, keep in mind that an inventor from a different field may not understand your sphere of knowledge. Can an inventor working on jet propulsion systems help someone invent a machine to mass manufacture bagels?

4. **Books and Handbooks.** There are some good specialized handbooks on patenting, but very few focus on patenting from the perspective of a first time inventor who employs an attorney to ensure having legal claims with broad coverage.

This manual is written for the layperson and provides a complete overview of the patenting and inventing process. *From Patent to Profit* is the only manual available that combines patenting and patent strategy with the invention development strategy and the all-important manufacturing, marketing and licensing processes. It is based on the experience of successful inventors. Use it as your guide and you can be successful as well.

Avoid Invention Assistance Company Attorneys

You have to remember that invention assistance companies only want your up-front money and rarely have your best long-term interests in mind. (Frankly if they did, they would immediately shut their doors in good faith)

Similarly, attorneys to these companies can only survive with this business and are not looking after your interests, but those of their true client--the invention assistance company!

Learning on the Internet

Some of the Internet News Groups in the Appendix can be helpful. Just be extremely careful to steer clear of any company offering assistance for pay. These are worthless invention assistance companies.

Only accept advice from experts who know. In this perspective, keep in mind that patent attorneys are not inventors nor are they marketing experts. And vice versa...inventors are not patent attorneys. Neither should be giving advice on the other's field of expertise!

I don't know of a single success story related to any submission company. In fact, in the past 2 years I have repeatedly challenged them on the Internet newsgroups to show us some real successes, and none has ever responded! In fact, about 5 years ago, I called one of the largest companies and interviewed with their West Coast rep. When I told her I made money from my inventions, she gasped and replied, "I have never met an inventor who actually earned any money from them."
...Bob DeMatteis

The FTC recently indicted 7 owners of dozens of invention development companies. While many of them may seem to be competing for your business, creating the image that this is a booming business, the truth of the matter is that they are frauds.

For more information about these indictments go to the FTC Web site at: www.ftc.gov

If you have any questions about a company you want to employ to help you out, go to the Inventor's Awareness Group Web site hosted at the From Patent to Profit Web site. There you will find all the key questions to ask. That address is: frompatenttoprofit.com/iag.html.

This publication is intended to teach you how to plan your strategy, protect your idea, write a patent application and get it filed in a timely manner. It also explains how to hire a patent attorney and defer major patenting costs while you are developing your invention into a new profit center.

5. **The Internet.** This is one of the best information sources on invention and patent-related matters in the world. Still new, it is rapidly becoming a most respectable place to seek valuable information on patenting and licensing. For an update on *From Patent to Profit*™ news and activities, visit our Internet site at **frompatenttoprofit.com**

ABOUT INVENTION ASSISTANCE COMPANIES

The fact is that invention assistance companies promise help to inventors, but provide little. Several invention assistance companies advertise on radio, television and in magazines promising to help inventors develop their ideas and/or find licensees. It is doubtful that any of these companies can provide you with help that has any real value. In fact, they may even do considerable harm.

Invention assistance companies want you to think they are well-connected with multi-million dollar corporations and that these corporations are ready--right now--to license your idea and pay you hundreds of thousands, even millions of dollars for it. Don't believe them. The best you will get for your money is a book containing "boiler plate" copy providing information you already knew or could readily find out. It will be a well-written dissertation using lots of positive phrases intended to make you feel good and to convince you that you are going to become a millionaire if you spend thousands of dollars with them. Your odds of winning the lottery are much better!

Read the company's advertising and see for yourself. Check their references and you will be shocked at the extremely low rate of success. The reality is you have to pilot your invention yourself. You can't rely upon someone else to bring success to you on a silver platter. Don't waste your time or money.

6

YOUR PATENTING STRATEGY

*There are many more ways to gain
patent protection than you may think!*

THE BIG PICTURE FIRST

The first prerequisite to your patent strategy is having an idea that could make money for you. It must be worth the investment. Part One, Chapter 2, contains the basic tools to help you evaluate your invention's money earning potential.

Being confident that your invention is worth pursuing, you should protect it by establishing the date of original conception, which is fortunately inexpensive and only takes a couple of hours at most. Then, you will follow through, reduce it to practice and subsequently file patent applications.

As you recall, the United States is a "first to invent" country, which means that only the first inventor will have a valid patent. Your first action to protect your first to invent status is to establish your date of original conception by writing an invention disclosure. But before you do so, you should know about the types of patent protection you can seek. Then write your disclosure to cover these various inventive

Remember to follow the Strategic Guide in the back and apply its tenets, so you do not spend a lot of money on patenting before you begin making it on sales.

By following the Strategic Guide tenets, you will also find that you will not make the serious error of filing prematurely before you know what the inventive attributes of the invention are.

aspects. This patent development strategy should dovetail with your invention development strategy. What you discover as you invent is what you will want to include in your patent applications.

SPECIFICALLY, WHAT PATENT PROTECTION CAN YOU GET?

Patents are usually thought of solely as products--something physical. But patents are commonly grouped into other categories that can have a greater sphere of influence in an industry. For instance, cost-cutting systems and processes of manufacturing can make an otherwise costly, hard-to-use product an extremely valuable one.

It would be wise to study and understand the following patenting approaches. The seven patent categories refer to utility patents. The names and definitions are well-known jargon among patent attorneys, agents, examiners and experienced inventors.

PRODUCT OR APPARATUS PATENTS

The Light Bulb

Thomas Edison's patent No. 223,898 on "An Electric Lamp for the Giving of Light by Incandescence" was granted on January 27, 1880.

...DewRay Calendar, January 1996

Product, apparatus or device patents refer to the actual product or group of products themselves. Examples are Edison's light bulb, a paper clip, the MacIntosh® mouse, a plastic sack with handles and The Pump® basketball shoes.

Product patents are usually fairly straightforward and easy to understand. They are probably the most common and the easiest to conceptualize. Since they are easy to envision, they are also usually the easiest for which to draft a patent application. Product patents are usually the easiest to determine if they are being infringed. But product patents may not necessarily give you the best, tightest patent coverage, as you will see.

PROCESS PATENTS

Pasteurization Was a Process Patent

U.S. Patent No. 135,245, patent by Louis Pasteur of Paris, France, in 1873, revealed the fundamentals of the food sterilization process now known as pasteurization. This patent related to beer making, not to dairy products!

...DewRay Calendar, January 1996

Process patents generally refer to processes of manufacturing. Examples are a process for extracting cotton seeds (Eli Whitney's cotton gin), cutting and cooking large quantities of tortillas, mixing large batches of ice cream (without a churn) or making large quantities of bagels. A process patent may also include the intangible process of reading DNA in genes.

Process patents are commonly used for patent protection and can be powerful assets. Can you imagine if all tortillas were handmade or ice cream was made in churns? Their retail prices would be much higher. Can you imagine the cost of a pair of jeans if cottonseeds were manually extracted? How about the tremendous benefits of reading DNA and how it is affecting medicine, law and justice?

Process patents frequently offer significant improvements to our quality of life. The timesaving afforded from high-speed manufacturing processes means we have more time to do other things. The reading of DNA for disease prevention holds the promise of eliminating many diseases and birth defects.

If an industry is to make a significant advancement in product improvement, it must also have a cost-effective means to do it. Hence, it is easy to see that a process patent at times may be more valuable than the (patented) product that is being produced!

SYSTEMS (OR METHOD) PATENT

This is a patent that defines the unique system, sometimes referred to as a method in which a product is used. While patents cannot be obtained on a commonly known product, a patent may be obtained when it is used in a certain novel, unique method.

A unique method of use will typically consist of a combination of components used together that result in a "system". One or all of these components may be prior art. For instance, systems patents have been granted on the methods in which a clerk uses a common, prior art, plastic grocery sack on a rack-style holder to facilitate loading of the sack. Patents have also been granted on the systems used to scan groceries in supermarkets, using prior art laser technology. These two examples have saved millions of hours of labor and lots of time waiting in checkout lines!

Systems patents usually make products "people friendly". Scientific discoveries like polyethylene plastic used in grocery sacks have started the supermarket checkout revolution, but it was the systems approach that made them people friendly. It was the electronic age that brought us into the era of the computer, but it was all the people friendly discoveries that made them sell so well. People friendly computer applications have made computers more popular than televisions.

Systems patents can also provide broader patent coverage. For instance, would it be better to have the first patent on the common style of plastic grocery sack with handles or on a system that uses them in an efficacious manner--dramatically increasing usage? Take the system. If plastic grocery sacks are hard to use, they will not be used. This was evident as the first patents on the plastic grocery sack were granted in the mid- to late-1960's. It wasn't until the late 1980's, when plastic grocery sack systems made them easy to use, that they began to replace paper sacks.

Systems patents represent a great opportunity for inventors and businesses. In many of your patenting activities, you may be thinking of a product patent, but may conclude that it is wiser to get a systems patent instead. Of course, you can file for both.

The Cyclotron System

Patent No. 1,948,384 was granted on February 20, 1934, to Ernest O. Lawrence of Berkeley, California, for the Cyclotron system, a method for the acceleration of ions.
    ...DewRay Calendar, February 1996

Famous inventor Jerome Lemelson's first patent was on a "flexible manufacturing system". He later developed hundreds of other systems related patents.
    Systems patents seem to be very common amongst prolific inventors.

We know prior art articles cannot be patented, but some systems patents use prior art articles. If a company supplies prior art articles that are used "in your system" without your authorization, they may be liable for "inducement of infringement".
    ...Bob DeMatteis

MACHINE PATENTS

The First Gas Motor Engine Patent

German inventor, Nicolaus Otto, was granted Patent No. 365,701 in 1887 for the first, four stroke, gasoline engine.

When several elements are put together and comprise a machine that does something useful, it is referred to as a "machine patent". Examples may be a machine to automatically make bagels with a round hole in the middle, a high-speed machine to cut out and bake tortillas or a machine to sort plastic waste.

Frequently, machine patents may have accompanying process patents. Many times, when new machine technology is being explored and developed, several other inventions and discoveries on the many individual aspects of the machine may also result in patents.

COMPOSITION OF MATTER (CHEMICAL COMPOSITIONS)

Bakelite Invented

The forerunner to modern plastics was patented on December 7, 1909, in U.S. Patent No. 942,699. It was granted to a scientist, L.H. Baekeland of Yonkers, New York.
...DewRay Calendar, January 1996

Chemical compositions are truly scientific by nature. Excellent examples of patents granted in this field are the various types of plastics. A newer area of patenting may include some of the genetic and biological engineering discoveries.

If you are developing patents in this field, you are probably a scientist working for Lawrence Livermore Labs or perhaps Stanford, Cal Berkeley or MIT.

SOFTWARE PATENTS

17,000 New Software Patents in 1998!

According to Greg Aharonian of PATNEWS, the USPTO will issue over 18,000 software patents in 1999...up from over 13,000 in 1997. A few years ago, some believed that the field of software patents was so heavily blanketed that few new discoveries could be made! Now, the PTO expects to grant 15,000 a year for the next several years!

This refers to the software as it is "written" and how the system works. For instance, the "one-touch" computer screen uses a unique software system. It is designed to be sensitive to the touch of the monitor and can guide even the most inexperienced computer user. Other software patents include the sophisticated random means of garbling Internet transmissions during credit card transactions to protect the buyer.

Some of the most famous software patents are those that originally differentiated Macintosh with its "window" and "mouse" applications. Today, this concept has become the standard means of operation for all computers. Another interesting computer patent is that of the "blinking cursor" developed by an independent inventor and licensed worldwide.

Software patents are more common today than ever before. When considering patenting in this field or making this part of your inventive matter, keep in mind that it is a rapidly changing field. Patents in this realm tend to become obsolete quickly, unless they are very broad and yet specific in scope like the "one-touch" screen patents.

IMPROVEMENT PATENTS

Most of the patent categories previously mentioned can also be considered "improvement patents".

Improvements to existing products or processes can be extremely valuable and change entire industries forever. These improvements frequently improve the lives of people. They can also improve safety and productivity on the job and comfort in the home.

There is an endless stream of improvement patents in our history-- power steering systems, pneumatic tires, improved tread designs, automatic opening systems for plastic grocery sacks, streamlined means of reading DNA, and on and on.

Improvement patents rely upon the existence of some other product or product attribute. If the other product or attribute was also patented prior to yours, there could be a danger of inducing infringement on this patent (referred to as the dominant patent).

Infringement depends upon a few factors. It will not infringe if the company you are licensing to use your new improvement patent is also licensed to use (or owns) the dominant patent. It will also not induce infringement if the dominant patent's term has expired or the maintenance fees are not current.

Improved Golf Tee

Patent No. 638,920 was granted in 1912 to African-American inventor George F. Grant of Boston, Massachusetts, for the tapered golf tee.
...DewRay Calendar, December, 1996

FILING FOR MULTIPLE INVENTIONS AND COVERAGES

You can save a lot of money by filing one utility patent application for more than one invention and more than one of your patenting objectives. The major consideration is to make sure that the subject matter is reasonably related. Don't try to combine a new fluorescent light bulb with an ice cream manufacturing process, unless the light bulb's function is specifically a part of the unique process.

When combining related attributes, you will pay a single application fee. After the examiner reviews your application, he/she will respond by sending you a rejection based upon your application containing "more than one invention" or "unrelated inventive material". The examiner will cite the different "inventive matter" and you can then select which one to prosecute first.

This action is referred to as a "divisional" patent application, in which the contents are "split-out" into two or more patent applications. When you file in this manner, the time required to review all the inventive aspects is lengthened.

I once filed a single patent application that contained five separate inventions. During prosecution, it was split out. Three of the patents were pursued and subsequently granted.
...Bob DeMatteis

MORE ABOUT DESIGN PATENTS

Design patents refer to ornamental design and not to functional design. For example, assume that you have a design patent on a plastic

Round Chessboard or Checkerboard

Design Patent No. D251826 was granted in 1977 to Norman Betros for a round game board used for playing Checkers or Chess.

This obscure, yet novel patent obviously did not take off in the marketplace. Upon looking at it, you would need to put your brain in a different perspective altogether.

While the patent covers the design of the round board, there is an underlying function that is inherent, which utilitarian function is not covered under the scope of the patent.

kitchen hook that is used for hanging pots and pans. If it has certain smooth, rounded lines, it can be easily designed around by eliminating the smooth, rounded lines. Unfortunately, design patents generally do not afford much patent protection, but there can be exceptions.

When a design patent also includes (but is not reliant upon) a certain functional structure, the patented article might have some excellent strength qualities. For instance, using the preceding hook example, what if the smooth, rounded lines were attractive arched supports underneath the hook element? The attractive arched supports also provide strong bracing that allows the hook to hold over 500 pounds! However, design patents do not protect function itself, only the ornamental design.

The clever use of design patents is also illustrated by Nike, the sports shoe company that has used design patents to its benefit over the years. Their purpose for using design patents is to keep others from cloning their attractive shoe designs. While not utilitarian, design patents certainly help preserve their original, proprietary look and have a positive effect on marketability.

Utility patent protection is generally considered the best overall patent protection, but there are times when a simple design patent may serve the purpose. Generally speaking, it is wise to strive for utility patent protection, if possible. It is wise to seek design patent protection only if the ornamental design itself will have some important, lasting proprietary effect on marketability that is not easy to design around.

MORE ABOUT PLANT PATENTS

Plant patents are granted to "botanical inventors" who create new plant variations asexually. Plant patents are commonly granted for award-winning roses such as "Queen Anne", "New Day" and "Pascali" roses. If you are creating patentable roses, you might consider working for Armstrong.

Although photographs are not normally supplied with patent applications, the applications for plant patents are an exception.

WHAT YOU DO NOT WANT TO PATENT

We want to make money from our patents, not just collect pieces of paper. In Chapter 2, we discussed evaluating your inventions and making money from them. In concert with the moneymaking theme, here is a list of items you do not want to patent:

Trade Secrets

Don't patent your trade secrets as long as they can be tightly held. Tightly held trade secrets can be more powerful than patents. As long as they are tightly held, they can be advantageously used for a much longer time than patents. After 17 or 20 years, patents expire and anyone can make the product. On the other hand, trade secrets can be held for years, even centuries.

Examples of valuable trade secrets are Coca-Cola's formula(s) and Lea and Perrin's Worcestershire Sauce. It has been reported that a few individuals hold Coca-Cola's secret formulas in confidence. Each individual holds the key to only a portion of the formula and process.

Trade secrets are also common in manufacturing processes. These trade secrets may be more difficult to guard, but they can easily make the difference between profit and loss.

A recent product, which has become a mainstay in almost every child's toy chest, is Play Dough®. Today, its formula and process of manufacture is a trade secret. An independent inventor originally created it.

How many magic tricks have been patented? Licensed? Or kept as a trade secret?

Fads

Pursuing patents on fads is a waste of time and money. By the time you receive your patent, the fad will be over. Save your money and look for something that is worthy of long-term patent protection.

Low Sales Volume

If your marketing report shows that your invention will not generate significant sales volume, it does not merit the costs of patenting. Even if you see factors that will improve the moneymaking ability of your invention, be careful not to invest a lot of time, money and effort in something that will provide marginal income.

A student who attended a From Patent to Profit seminar recently had a great Mexican salsa recipe. After learning about his options, he realized that his best protection was to keep it as a trade secret.

By using confidentiality agreements, he entered into serious licensing negotiations with a substantial Mexican fast food chain in California.

Inventions of Insufficient Improvement

This will result in low sales volume or patent coverage that is too narrow, allowing others to easily design around your invention. You should give careful consideration to the coverage you can attain before spending too much time and money. This can usually be determined through a patent search.

INVENTION DISCLOSURES

You are ready to protect your invention and your first to invent status. The best way to establish first to invent status is to start with a written disclosure. An invention disclosure typically consists of 1-3 written pages of text and 1-3 pages of drawings. It can be handwritten or typewritten. Disclosures are brief summaries and not nearly as long

As you will see in Part Three, Manufacturing and Marketing, there might be an exception to this rule.

An inventor may sell certain specialized inventions on the Internet that would not otherwise generate enough sales for an established company.

The key to doing this is to make certain that the profit margin is large enough to warrant establishing a home based business for the product. Generally this is about 5-6 times cost.

as patent applications. You don't need a functioning model at this time. All that is required is a reasonably good idea of how it will work.

You should write your disclosure as soon as possible after the date your discovery was made. Your invention disclosure is the best means of establishing the date of original conception. A preprinted invention disclosure form that you can copy is available in the *From Patent to Profit* Resource Guide.

Your disclosure should include the following:

1. **Title of invention.** Descriptive titles are best. For instance, "Sanitary Pot Scrubbing Device". Do not use a title that might be a trademark and is not descriptive. For instance, "Potzella" may be the trademark of your new scrubbing device, but it describes nothing at all.

2. **Background of the invention.** In a paragraph or two, discuss the products that are currently in use. For instance, in the genre of pot scrubbing, you may say that sponges, Brillo® soap pads and assorted scrub brushes are most commonly used.

3. **Brief description of the invention.** For clarity, describe it from two different perspectives. For instance, your pot scrubber may be described as a "nylon mesh pad shaped like a ball and easy to hold in your hand". It can be further described as "being made from a continuous length of nylon webbing about 10 inches wide and 30 feet long, folded back upon itself and when bunched together at the mid section, forms a ball."

4. **Sketches.** Sketches are almost always necessary. It does not matter how well you can draw, as long as the sketches can be understood. If you have any doubts, have someone assist you. This person can also be a witness who signs the invention disclosure to verify the date of original conception.

5. **Detailed description of the invention.** Explain in detail how it works. Include numbers and lead lines on the drawing and reference them as best you can. For instance, for the pot scrubber you could show a long length of plastic webbed material being bunched up. A second sketch could show how it is sewn in the middle and a third sketch could show the final ball shaped scrubber. You can make additional sketches to show some variations on the theme. For instance, perhaps it would be advantageous to have a "submarine shaped scrubber" instead.

6. **List the unique attributes.** List them in summary in one section or discuss them throughout the document as you describe the invention. If you write them into the body of the disclosure, use words

---

The Right Invention Disclosure

The invention disclosure in the From Patent to Profit Resource Guide *is the perfect tool to help you think about your invention in the right light. It also follows the same context and content you will eventually use in patent applications, both provisional and non-provisional.*
...Bob DeMatteis

Invention Disclosures Are Important First Steps

Many lawsuits have been settled in favor of inventors who have been able to prove their original date of conception along with their proof of reduction to practice.

The only other key element is to verify that you, the inventor, did not abandon the project.

Prepare a legal verifiable disclosure and keep it in a safe place.

such as "unique", "faster", "easier to use", "more efficient", "convenient", etc.

7. **Other possible uses and variations.** Try to list as many as you can imagine. You may find some alternative uses that may prove to have more potential than the original intended use. Also include alternate materials, ways of making it and ways of designing it.

8. **Name, address, date and signature.** Clearly print your name and address and those of all others, if applicable. Include your phone number and e-mail address if you have one, which may come in handy if it is used as your disclosure for a patent search. If all the inventors are not available to sign the disclosure, make reference to their participation in the disclosure and at least verify your signature. The others can confirm their inventorship later.

VALIDATING AN INVENTION DISCLOSURE DOCUMENT

There are several ways to validate the disclosure's date and content. Use one of the following methods. You need only one.

1. One of the best ways is for two reliable witnesses (not an interested party or a relative) to sign and date the disclosure. A reliable witness may be anyone, such as a college professor, a bank officer or community businessperson. It should not be someone who stands to gain from the invention, like your wife, brother-in-law or someone with whom you may go into business. This method of witnessing is usually the easiest way to verify the date of original conception.

It is wise to show the witnesses the description of the invention, so they understand it. Have them sign a confidentiality agreement before you disclose details. (See Chapter 10.) Have them initial or sign each page to verify that they read it and understood it.

2. Have the disclosure notarized. Notary laws are getting tougher every year. In the state of California for instance, laws for notaries are very strict and penalties against fraud severe. A notary's seal and signature on your document will probably cost $10 or more, but will certainly verify your disclosure date. This may be the quickest and easiest way of getting the date validated, if you prefer to use a disinterested third party as a witness.

The only problem associated with using a notary is that he/she may not understand your invention. It may be difficult to prove that the notarized disclosure was not altered. To avoid this problem, make a copy of the original disclosure and have the copy notarized. It would then be obvious if alterations were made. Keep the original as additional proof.

An Interesting Alternate Use

Play Dough was originally developed as a wallpaper cleaner. But when the wife of the inventor noticed their daughter playing with it--modeling it like clay, but without the mess--the light bulb went off.

The cleaning compound was made in colors to make it more attractive to children and marketed as safe, reusable alternative to clay.

The inventor became a multi-millionaire before he reached 27.

Model airplanes began as a means for airline manufacturers to sell their real airplanes.

Interesting Report

Greg Aharonian, PATNEWS, reports the following statistics:

Year	Software Patents	Total # Viruses
1998	17,500	15,500
1997	13,000	10,000
1996	9,000	8,000
1995	6,100	5,000
1994	4,500	4,000
1993	2,400	2,600
1992	1,600	1,000

Correlation? According to Greg, there might be. Viruses cause economic problems for everyone except their inventors. So, the question is...which came first, the software patent or the software virus?

Early in my invention career, I actually avoided a litigation incident with a company that was going to develop one of my inventions after I had disclosed it to them, but without compensation to me.

The central issue was, "whose idea was it really...mine or theirs?"

In order to prove that I was the original inventor, I produced a copy of a dated, sealed envelope along with 9 other supporting documents, including a log and bag samples, from my archives.

Upon receipt, they immediately entered into negotiations with me.

I am thankful that I maintained my log sufficiently well and kept all my samples and drawings.

...Bob DeMatteis

Using the U.S. Patent Office for filing disclosures is the preferred method of many inventors including George Margolin.

He says, "What's better than having it on record with the U.S. Patent Office? Even if they do throw it away after two years, you will still have a copy and a receipt from the PTO with the date it was originally received."

It's a good argument.

3. The least preferred method is to seal it tightly in an envelope, take it to the post office, request a U.S. Postal Service date-time stamp and mail it to yourself. ***Do not open*** the envelope when you receive it. Keep another copy of the disclosure that you can use for your on-going development activities. Keep the date-time stamped copy in case it is ever needed. **IMPORTANT:** Although this method has been defeated in court, there should be no problem if a subsequent, immediate and substantial paper trail follows. The combination of the two has withstood legal scrutiny.

4. Fax it to your patent attorney. The date on his fax receipt will be a valid date of disclosure. You should ask him/her to let you do this at no charge, until you take action on the invention. The attorney can establish a file for your disclosures. Your patent attorney should welcome this approach as an indication that you are going to use him/her to file and prosecute the regular application.

The U.S. Patent Office provides a service for registering a disclosure and charges a small fee (currently $10). The paper size of your disclosure must not exceed 8.5 inches x 13 inches and you must include a self-addressed stamped envelope. You have two years to act on your disclosure or it will be discarded. It is best ***not*** to file your disclosures with the U.S. Patent Office. Two years can be limiting. For about the same amount of money, you can have your invention notarized regardless of paper size.

There is no time limit on how long you can wait to file a patent application after you have written a disclosure. If you are busy finalizing the development of other inventions and patents and arranging their marketing, long delays can be justified--even several years! The only danger is that in the interim, someone else may begin the development and patenting of the same inventive material and challenge your first to invent position. See Interference on page 95.

The most important activity during this initial stage of disclosure is to maintain a log of the invention's development and all drawings, sketches and prototypes. A log will help substantiate your first to invent position. You can read more about logs and maintaining records in Chapter 2.

DISCLOSURES HELP YOU UNDERSTAND YOUR INVENTION BETTER

Writing a brief summary of your invention helps to establish the direction of your developmental process. Writing a disclosure may also help solve some of the basic problems associated with the invention. It can give you a clearer picture of your objective and the outcome you seek. As discussed, there are several ways to achieve patent protection without increasing costs. As you write your disclosure, consider as many of these ways as you can.

When you have some experience, you can consider using a more formal version of the disclosure, as a tool to attract partners for a project prior to the patent application stage. While best done with trusted relationships, when used in conjunction with a tightly written confidentiality agreement you will improve the preservation of secrecy. You can read about using confidentiality agreements in Chapter 10.

Part of the wisdom of filling out a disclosure, is that it is a similar format as an actual patent application.

By following this format, you can go back and use the disclosure as an aid to writing your patent application.

PATENT SEARCHES

After your disclosure is filed, you will most likely want to conduct a patent search. Nothing is more discouraging than filing a patent application only to find out later that there is already an existing patent or it will have narrow, ineffective coverage. A patent search can save you time, money and a lot of anguish.

A thorough search can help support the validity of your patent. If you are uncertain about the novelty of your invention, almost every patent expert, inventor and attorney recommends a thorough patent search before you spend too much time and money on development. The patent search can indicate if there is prior art that will affect your patentability and can help to determine if your invention may infringe on existing patents. It is wise to know early on, as this can be extremely embarrassing later. Can you imagine going into production or licensing a manufacturer, then after 1-2 years discovering that your products are infringing another patent? Not only is this illegal; it could destroy everything you have been working on.

A patent search will also determine if related art exists that may cause the patentability of your invention to be narrow in scope. In other words, you may be unable to get the broad coverage you want and may have to settle for something that can be designed around. If it is too easy to design around, it may not be worthwhile to patent. You can read more about narrow and broad patent claims and coverage in Chapter 7.

You can do manual and computer searches at one of the many patent depository libraries throughout the U.S. or at the U.S. Patent Office library in Arlington, Virginia. If your inventive technology is a type that could have been used overseas, the search should include patents from foreign countries. Remember that prior art anywhere in the world will void your ability to patent in the U.S.

Without question or exception, an experienced search professional can conduct the most effective patent search possible at the U.S. Patent Office in Arlington. The USPTO's library is known throughout the world as the largest single information source anywhere, period. This makes it one of the best sources for international searches. The USPTO

The United States patent Office is like a global information supermarket. It's virtually a technology shoppers' warehouse with an ever-expanding inventory of new technical information, and a well-versed staff constantly refreshed by new ideas.

...Donald Grant Kelly, Director, U.S. Patent Office

If you have made the unfortunate mistake of having a patent search done by one of the invention assistance companies, I suggest you spend a few hundred additional dollars and have it reviewed by a qualified patent searching expert or patent attorney to evaluate its content.

Unfortunately, many of the searches done by these companies, which I have seen, were inadequate. In fact, detrimental to the inventor's best interests, they even overlooked the utility patent potential of the invention!

...Bob DeMatteis

PATENT SEARCHING AT A PATENT AND TRADEMARK DEPOSITORY LIBRARY (PTDL)

There are currently over 80 large public, state and academic libraries designated as Patent and Trademark Depository Libraries (PTDLs) by the U.S. Patent and Trademark Office (USPTO). These libraries are located in all 50 states, the District of Columbia and Puerto Rico. You may request information on which library is the closest to you by calling the following USPTO toll-free line: 1-800-PTO-9199. A current list of PTDLs is also found in the weekly USPTO "Official Gazette" and on the USPTO's Web site at: **http://www.uspto.gov/**.

PTDLs are a key component of USPTO's information dissemination strategy and, as such, they receive a vast array of products and services on a depository basis from the USPTO. In exchange for receiving the information, the library must agree to provide public access to the materials and provide assistance in their use. Be mindful that providing assistance does not include conducting the patent search. PTDLs generally do not conduct subject matter patent searches, although fee-based service areas within a library may offer patent searching on commercial databases provided that search terms and search strategies are developed by the requestor.

In addition to providing free access to depository materials and assisting the public in their efficient use, standards for PTDLs also include acquiring a minimum 20-year backfile of patents from the year of PTDL designation, protecting the integrity of depository collections, and training PTDL librarians at annual seminars. These standards ensure that current and accurate information is being provided by the PTDLs to their users. Remember that the USPTO has no field or regional offices. The PTDLs are the only "field" presence for the USPTO.

When visiting a PTDL you will find information collections that are considered "core" collections and are standard to all PTDLs. A partial list follows:

1. Weekly issues of complete patent documents including utility, plant, design, and reissue patents, Statutory Invention Registrations, Reexaminations and other status changes impacting issued patents.
2. Official Gazette of the USPTO for both patents and trademarks.
3. Complete Cassis CD-ROM series of products.
4. Trilateral CD-ROM products such as Patent Abstracts of Japan.
5. Manual of Classification.
6. Index to the U.S. Patent Classification system.
7. Classification Definitions.
8. Classification Orders.
9. Manual of Patent Examining Procedure.
10. Current USPTO fee schedules.
11. All USPTO directories.
12. All USPTO general information brochures.
13. PCT Applicants Guide by the World Intellectual Property Office.
14. Plant Patent Directory by the American Association of Nurserymen.

Outside of this "core" list, collections can vary widely from one library to the next. Almost 40% of PTDLs have complete patent backfiles dating back to 1790 on microfilm. A similar percentage maintain a subscription to the USPTO's online Automated Patent System (APS), which offers full-text (no images) patent searching back to 1971. Some PTDLs maintain collections of foreign patent documents. Many acquire a number of related publications in the form of self-help books, court decisions, and business collections. The best way to learn more about these resources is to visit the library. It is advised that you call first to find out about library hours, directions and parking instructions. Some PTDLs offer appointments for first-time users of patent information.

Copies of patent documents at PTDLs are numerically arranged, so it is necessary to use a step-by-step process in identifying patent documents in a particular area of technology when conducting a subject matter search. The following outline lists the tools used in this process and was developed as a handout to accompany the videotape "conducting a Patent Search at a PTDL", available for viewing at PTDLs and available for sale. Information on purchasing this $20 videotape may be obtained from a PTDL, from the USPTO's Web site or by calling the toll-free number listed earlier and requesting a copy of the most recent "Products and Services Catalog" of USPTO's Information Dissemination Organizations.

THE USPTO's SEVEN STEP STRATEGY TO CONDUCTING A PATENT SEARCH

1. **Index to the U.S. Patent Classification** (paper or CD-ROM)
   Begin with this alphabetical subject index to the *Manual of Classification*. Look up common terms describing the invention and its function, effect, end-product, structure, and use. Note class and subclass numbers.

2. **Manual of Classification** (paper or CD-ROM)
   Locate class and subclass numbers in the Manual. Note where the terms fall within the U.S. Patent Classification System. Scan the entire class schedule, paying attention to the dot indent. Revise search strategy as needed.

3. **Classification Definitions** (microfiche or CD-ROM)
   Read the definitions to establish the scope of class(es) and subclass(es) relevant to the search. The definitions include important search notes and suggestions for further search.

4. **Patents BIB CD-ROM or APS (Automated Patent System) TEXT**
   Find out if you are on the right path: retrieve and browse through titles of patents issued in a given class and subclass. Or redirect the search: retrieve lists of patents containing applicable keywords; note their class and subclass numbers and go back to step 2.

5. **Subclass Listing** (CD-ROM or APS TEXT)
   Once relevant class(es)/subclass(es) are identified, obtain a list of all patent numbers granted for every class and subclass to be searched.

6. *Official Gazette* **– Patent Section** (paper or microform)
   Go to the *Gazette* and look up summaries and a representative drawing for all patents on the list(s) to eliminate patents unrelated to the invention.

7. **Complete Patent Document** (microfilm, paper, CD-ROM, or APS IMAGE)
   Search the complete text and drawing(s) of closely related patents to find out how different they are from the invention.

Conducting your own preliminary patent search at a PTDL before making decisions about whether to pursue your invention is almost always a valuable exercise. While the quality of your search depends entirely upon your ability to understand and utilize the process, and the time you are willing to devote to it, conducting a preliminary search at a PTDL will never fail to educate!

As a final note, the USPTO has designated three of the PTDLs as Partnership PTDLs. These PTDLs, located in Sunnyvale, Detroit and Houston, offer additional services on a fee basis. These include access to USPTO's full patent image AOS database (the same that is available in USPTO's onsite search facilities); video conference facilities used for interviews with patent examiners and for expert lectures; expedited foreign patent copy fulfillment; certified and uncertified USPTO document fulfillment, and; the local filing of USPTO Disclosure Documents. More information on the Partnerships may be obtained by directly contacting the PTDL or by looking at USPTO's Web site.

*This information is provided courtesy of the PTDL.

library includes patents from every country in the world. It also includes the largest collection of supplementary reference materials, including scientific documents and databases outside the realm of patents.

A smart search expert will use both computers and manual investigation. Since computer searches only contain patents going back to the early 1970's, some manual searching is inevitable. Invariably, modern inventions will have some relevant art from decades, or even a century ago! Don't be discouraged if you discover age-old prior art. Just use your creativity and patent the next generation.

A search expert should also consult with a patent examiner in the field to assure that discovery is being conducted in the right field(s). There are about 125,000 product classification groups to search. A search expert will know what fields to search (invariably more than one), and will usually know if your type of inventive matter might be found in foreign patents.

A professional search conducted at the USPTO library may cost a bit more, but it can save time, money and embarrassment. The total cost of a patent search on a relatively simple invention is usually $300 to $600. The range is usually affected by whether or not a legal opinion is given.

Before you have a search done, ask some questions. Does it include foreign patent discovery and a legal opinion on patentability or are you going to receive a lot of patent copies that you will have to sort through and make your own determination? How long will it take to complete? A search usually takes 3-5 weeks, but it can be expedited for an upcharge.

To initiate a search on your invention, you may submit a copy of your signed invention disclosure to the search expert. If the expert is not an attorney, ask him/her to sign a confidentiality agreement.

ABOUT DOING YOUR OWN PRELIMINARY PATENT SEARCH

All patent searches are preliminary by nature. That is, they are also subject to the search of the patent examiner who will review your application. However, if you want to do what I will call "your own very preliminary search", you can do this at a Patent and Trademark Depository Library (PTDL) or on the Internet. Some PTDL's have supplementary reference publications, although not as many as that of the USPTO.

Many of the libraries give lessons on how to do a patent search and have instructions you can follow. But be advised patent searching is not easy to do. This is not a simple, exact science. If you have any doubts you should hire an expert who knows what he/she is doing.

You can conduct a more limited search on the Internet. The USPTO and IBM have Web sites that allow users to conduct patent

---

A Patent Search Nightmare!

My invention career almost ended with my first invention. I spent two full days conducting my own search at a USPTDL and then spent thousands of dollars writing and filing an application.

Six months later, my licensee found a patent that my invention had been infringing. The patent was owned by the invention's largest competitor! Did I ever have egg on my face! Do you think I'll rely 100% on my own patent search again?

...Bob DeMatteis

Donald Kelly, Director at the U.S. Patent Office says, "Patent examiners are among the busiest people you're ever likely to meet because they're generally up to their shoulder blades in patents pending. But on the other hand, they readily interrupt their work to offer inventors assistance in outlining an appropriate field of search among the myriad of possibilities."

If you ever get the opportunity to search a patent at the U.S. Patent Library in Crystal City, consider asking a patent examiner where you might search for technology related to your invention.

...Bob DeMatteis

searches by using a Boolean or simple word search, or searching for inventors, fields, patent assignees, etc. The domain names on the Internet are http://uspto.com for the USPTO and http://patent.womplex.ibm.com for IBM.

When doing your own search, it is critical to not overlook similar, related words. For instance, the word "glue" could also be described as:

bonding means	binder
adhesive	stick
adherent	fastening material
tackifier	epoxy
paste	gum
sticking substance	mucilage
conjoining compound	means of adjoinment

How many more can you think of? Can you see that the process is tricky? Do you realize how it can be subject to error--especially for a first time inventor?

HOW TO READ A PATENT SEARCH

Arrange your schedule so that you can read the patent search without being interrupted. A letter from the search expert with an analysis of the related patents should accompany your search. Read it carefully since you are probably more experienced in the field of your invention than the searcher. In addition, you are the one who must make decisions about how to proceed.

In this sequence, read the pertinent patents.

1. Glance at the picture on the cover page, but don't rely upon it. Even when it may look similar, more often than not, it will be about different subject matter.

2. Read the abstract. If the invention appears to be related to your invention,

3. Look at the following patent drawings and skim the body of the patent, particularly the "Summary of the Invention", which should be on the first written page.

4. Go directly to the back and read the claims--very carefully. The claims are what dictate the patent's scope and legal clout. Claims are not usually easy to read. Dedicate some time to reading them and you will soon understand their meaning. As you read the claims, ask yourself if any of them "read on" your invention. In other words, is the

In counseling inventors over the years, they have frequently requested my evaluation of their invention/concept, which I sometimes have obliged.

Usually the first thing I will ask is if they have done a preliminary patent search at a U.S. Patent and Trademark Depository Library or at the IBM Web site. Of those who say "no", I have urged to at least do this preliminary patent search before they proceed and waste a lot of time on the project.

A surprise comes to at least 1/3 of those who do it. Of course, this surprise is that there is very similar or exactly the same art on their invention! Does this mean it is time to quit?

...Bob DeMatteis

inventive matter you want to pursue already claimed in one of the patents in the patent search?

5. If you think a patent's claim reads on your invention, go back to the body and read it more carefully. Re-read the claims to make absolutely certain--one more time--that it describes the same subject matter.

You will usually find that a patent or prior art does not exist on your invention, but almost invariably there are related patents. They may not be in the same field or for the same use, but they must be considered when evaluating the ability to obtain the patent coverage you seek.

Once you understand the search report, you will be in a much better position to plan your course of action.

WHAT IF THERE IS PRIOR ART OR YOUR INVENTION INFRINGES ANOTHER PATENT?

Just because a product or process exists and does a fair job doesn't mean that there aren't other ways that may do it far better or cheaper or safer or easier. Or, all the above.
...George Margolin

You have four major choices: (1) You can improve upon the existing patent. (2) You can design around it. (3) You can license it. (4) You can drop the project. Before you decide, take some time to analyze the conflicting patent(s).

1. How is it different from your invention?
2. What are its strengths?
3. What are its weaknesses?
4. What words and phrases are specifically included in the claims that have narrowed the scope of the patent?

Unbeknownst to prolific inventor, Jerome Lemelson, his first invention for a "universal robot", that could rivet, weld, measure, drill and pick up objects and reposition them was found to infringe a patent application filed just two weeks before his. Lemelson immediately set out to work on a second application of the robot, his "flexible manufacturing system" which became today's automated machine shop.

As you scrutinize the claims, you may find that certain operable words have specifically defined the scope of a patent. If so, these words can indicate how you may discover improvements or a means to design around it.

For example, let's say we have identified the operable words and phrases used in a claim for a plastic grocery sack style in the following four phrases:

1. Handle straps extending upwards from, and adjacent to, the bag mouth
2. Apertures intermediately located on strap handles
3. Upwardly extended, centrally located tab
4. Said tab defined by a severable line between it and the bag body

You now have four or more possible alternatives to design around this bag style. Hopefully, you can design around at least one attribute that will give you a competitive advantage. Four potential design-arounds are:

1.   Handle straps that do not extend upwards from the bag
2.   Apertures that are not located in the handle
3.   A tab that does not extend upwards (or perhaps two tabs laterally spaced)
4.   A tab that does not sever itself from the bag

When reading claims and attempting to design around other patents, remember that the Doctrine of Equivalence is highlighted and discussed in more detail in the next Section. If you decide to design around an existing patent, review Chapter 3 in Part One to better understand the merits of applying new inventive attributes.

After your analysis, you may no longer want to pursue the original invention or you may want to consider licensing the dominant patent from its owner. Before you pursue the licensing, it would be wise to contact the U.S. Patent Office and see if the dominant patent's maintenance fees are current. You can call the USPTO's maintenance fee department at 703-308-9752, 703-308-1156 or 703-308-5068.

DOCTRINE OF EQUIVALENCE … LITERAL VERSUS FIGURATIVE INTERPRETATION

The Doctrine of Equivalence that recently withstood a test by the U.S. Supreme Court in the Hilton-Davis case states that:

If the elements of a product do not literally infringe a patent's claims, but essentially serve the same function, then it infringes anyway.

Patents can be interpreted two ways: literally or figuratively. If you plan to design around an existing patent, you must thoroughly understand the scope of the infringed claims.

We now know that relying on the literal interpretation of claims can be dangerous and we must use a broader interpretation of their meanings. Nevertheless, some patent claims might be interpreted more literally than other claims. This is usually the case when claims have very specific attributes that had to be included for the examiner to award the patent.

In applying the Doctrine of Equivalence to the preceding potential design-around attributes, a question arises about serving the same function. You would be wise to get an attorney's opinion. Your

Lillian Moller Gilbreth (1878-1972), the mother of 12 children, had good reason to improve the efficiency and convenience of household items.

She patented many devices including an electric food mixer, the trash can with the step-on lid-opener and an ergonomically efficient kitchen that benefited homemakers and disabled persons.

Until the U.S. Supreme Court ruled upon it, the Hilton-Davis case caused many patent infringement court cases to be put on hold.

Afterward, prosecution as an infringement attorney became a lot easier.

objective is to create a new, improved functionality from your design-around. Hence, it should not infringe the prior art patent.

Here are a few examples of literal versus figurative interpretation:

Operable Word	Literal	Equivalent
hole	a round hole	any shape, slit or aperture in any configuration or size
strap handle	"loop handle"	any extended grip or rope-like piece
table leg	attached legs	any support means regardless of shape or attachment
gauge	dial with arms	any gauge, regardless of whether it is a dial, digital readout, idiot light, etc.

Other commonly used phrases that reflect equivalence are "under the scope of", or "in the spirit of", The most important point to remember is that you can use the Doctrine of Equivalence to your advantage. If your patent has well-written claims, you will be in a superior position to defend your interests.

USING A PATENT SEARCH TO YOUR ADVANTAGE

By reading the patents related to your invention, you can use the information to your advantage in the following ways:

1. **Prove that your invention is not obvious.** In other words, there is no prior art and you should be granted a patent with the broadest possible scope.

2. **Prove the novelty of your invention.** A search may reveal several patents that point to the inventive matter in your application as being inferior or not possible (based on the prior technology). If you now have a solution that shows that the new process or material is superior or viable, you will have solid claims.

3. **Discover other fields of uses for your invention.** Can it be used in other industries that you did not previously consider? You may want to try to broaden your patent coverage.

4. **Help guide the development of your invention.** You may learn what to do or not to do from reading related patents.

5. **More clearly define the novelty of your invention in the patent application.** The patent examiner will most likely not object to

Patent Searches as Part of a Proposal

When approaching possible manufacturing and marketing partners early on in the development process, a common mistake made by many first-time inventors is that they say, "I have a patent pending", which they don't. We know this is not a wise thing to say (in fact, it's fraud).

A simple alternative that carries as much--perhaps even more weight--is to say, "Our patent search has revealed that we should be able to get broad patent protection for the new innovation. My attorneys and I are incorporating this broad scope into the patent application".

It is honest and powerful. Remember, we are a first to invent country, not first to file.

prior art you cited in your application that you carefully designed around. In fact, the examiner's acceptance infers that he/she agrees that your inventive material is different. While this does not necessarily provide assurance you are not infringing the prior art patent, it does improve your argument.

6. **Understand the terminology in your field.** Read the several prior art patents and select one or two as models to write your patent application. This method will provide a good background about the proper terminology to use and saves time and money.

WHEN IS A SEARCH NOT NECESSARY?

You may not need to do a patent search if your invention is so unique that its novelty is apparent. Some examples of unique inventions are Eli Whitney's cotton gin, the first laser, the television picture tube and the transistor.

If you have been developing patents related to a certain invention or field for a few years, you may have accumulated a sufficient library of related patents and an understanding of the field. If you paid for a search, you would be paying for copies of documents you already have, in a field in which you are already the leading expert.

If you have not conducted a search recently or want to get some current knowledge about your competitors, it would be wise to conduct a search.

WHEN DO YOU START WRITING A PATENT APPLICATION?

After you have conducted a patent search and you are confident that you want to proceed with development, start thinking about writing your provisional application right away. It is best to begin writing during the initial stages of invention development. Don't expect to complete it in the first few days or even weeks. It may take months, depending upon which of the following two strategies you use. The reason you will want to dovetail these two processes is to ensure your ability to include the correct inventive material.

WHEN IS THE BEST TIME TO FILE A PROVISIONAL?

There is some disagreement about the best time to file a provisional patent application. Your timing depends upon how fast you can develop the invention, your manufacturing and marketing strategy and your financial capacity.

I would be very cautious of any attorney who says you don't need to do a patent search since when you submit your patent application, the patent examiner will do one anyway. Pursuing the strategy based upon this comment can cost you thousands of dollars and can waste months, even years of your time.

I begin the marketing and licensing of all my inventions before and during the patent pending stage. In this manner, I have a return on my investment before any major out-of-pocket patenting expenses. Aggressive licensees like it too. This way, they get to bet on the "come" instead of wondering "what if".
...Bob DeMatteis

At times, it may be wise to use a provisional patent application instead of a confidentiality agreement. Most giant corporations will not sign confidentiality agreements. With a provisional filed, you are in a patent pending status; hence, you have the ability to reveal your invention to corporations with less fear of theft.

The best news is that there's no end to inventors' imagination. For the first five years of the twenty-first century, U.S. independent inventors and small businesses will file nearly 70,000 patent applications. At our previous "turn of the century," America's independent inventors took this country for a real wild ride. We must not expect less during this one.
...Donald Grant Kelly, Director, U.S. Patent Office

A Totally Absurd Patent

A patent for a "brain buzzer" issued in 1998 to Thinky Corp. in Japan proves that not only Americans can think up totally absurd ideas. It is for anyone who falls asleep at inopportune moments. For instance, dozing off during class, while driving a car, or during a not-so-hot date. The "Brain Buzzer", which looks something like an electric tooth brush, keeps the Sandman at bay, yet will not disturb others. How does it work? Bite down on the vibrating wand and vibrations are transmitted to the brain, buzzing you awake.
...totallyabsurd.com

Some will say that, based upon the new provisional laws, patents should be filed immediately, regardless of content. When new inventive matters are discovered, new provisional applications can be filed. Some attorneys, and maybe a few inventors, believe that it is then merely an "administrative affair" to file the final, permanent, non-provisional applications and get the claims they want.

On page 100 we discussed interferences and indicated that being in the "senior" position might have a very slight advantage. That is the only reason to file provisional applications in a "shotgun" manner. If filing many provisionals is your strategy, you had better be prepared to spend a lot of money. The filing of provisional applications are only $75 for a small entity and $150 for a large entity, but who is going to write all these patents? Your legal costs could get very expensive.

Most experienced inventors (many attorneys concur), tend to wait until later in the invention development process to file. There are three good reasons for this approach. First, during development, an inventor better understands the inventive material and can include the most accurate, broadly written attributes of the invention itself. Second, by waiting until just before product launch, just before the invention is publicly disclosed, an inexpensive, provisional patent application gets you an entire year's protection before incurring the high cost of filing the permanent, non-provisional application. Third, filing one provisional application instead of several costs less and saves time.

WHEN TO FILE THE REGULAR PATENT APPLICATION

After you file your provisional, you have one year to file a regular, non-provisional application. Remember that the one-year rule also applies. You must file either a provisional application or the permanent application before the end of one year. As previously discussed, filing the provisional application just before the end of one year, can give you an extra year to run up sales before incurring the more expensive costs of filing the permanent application.

At times, you may want to file your regular application long before the provisional patent application expires. For instance, your potential licensee may have some doubt as to the patentability of your invention.

Another consideration is infringement. To enforce your rights, you must have a patent granted and issued. If you were infringed, it would be wise to proceed immediately to get your patent issued, so you can protect your rights and stop the infringer.

STRATEGY, WORLDWIDE PATENT RIGHTS AND PCT'S

Whatever your strategy, if you want to preserve your worldwide patent rights, file your provisional or regular, non-provisional application before your invention is publicly disclosed. Once you have done this, you have one year to file for patents in countries that are part of the Berne convention or take the more popular approach and file a PCT. To preserve the foreign filing rights, the PCT must be filed no later than one year after the filing of either a provisional or regular, non-provisional patent application..

PCT refers to the "Patent Cooperation Treaty" that allows you to designate foreign countries (that are a part of the pact) in which you may want to file for patents. Most countries are part of the PCT. By filing a PCT, you can get time extensions of up to 36 months to file your foreign patent applications. In patenting overseas, PCT's are commonly used to extend dates and preserve cash.

As for the few countries that do not recognize PCT's or patents at all--don't let them stop you. These countries will not be able to export to countries that do honor the PCT anyway. More and more third-world countries honor the patent systems of the developed countries of the world as a step to improve their international relations.

CONSIDERATION FOR INTERNATIONAL FILING OF PATENTS

Less than 10% of all patents filed in the U.S. are filed internationally. Most foreign filings are by large corporations on inventions that have worldwide appeal. The most important factor regarding your decision to file overseas is finances. The costs can be staggering! Overseas filings require translations, foreign attorneys' fees and filing fees. The cost can be $100,000 or more.

One way to save a substantial amount of money is to file for a "European Patent", which allows you to file in nineteen countries simultaneously. There is no extra cost for translations or filings. A European Patent can cost as much as $30,000. However, this is inexpensive compared to individually filing for patents in each European country.

The cost to seek out and license a foreign entity can also be costly. Who will travel there and search out licensees? Who will work with and train the licensee about how to make the invention? Who will locate or train the sales-marketing team? Who will monitor the accounting? Who will follow up and make sure that there is no patent infringement by others?

The best way for an independent inventor or small company to license patents overseas is to find an experienced overseas sales-marketing company that is confident it can sell your inventions. Let them license the patent(s) and pay all the costs of patenting, etc. They will have a better understanding of the patent system in their country and can save you time and money. In exchange for their dedicated efforts, take a small royalty and/or money up front and let them handle

The advantage of PCT prosecution is that you can delay the expensive process of national phase prosecution (country by country) for up to 36 months. After that time period, you may have a better idea of which foreign countries you wish to file.

Prosecution in foreign countries is very expensive and may provide only limited patent protection, and thus I do not recommend it for inventors or start-up companies unless special circumstances warrant such expense.
...Robert Platt Bell, Esq.

An interesting fact about PCTs, pointed out by Greg Aharonian, PATNEWS, is that they are published after 18 months. Thus, PCT applications are a good way to get an advanced look at pending applications here in the U.S., which otherwise remain secret.

We find that the markets for America's genius long ago outgrew her national borders. Inventors struggle along with corporation to compete in a world where the potential buyers of new products and processes live in nations around the world.
...Donald Grant Kelly, Director, U.S. Patent Office

the invention. With a vested interest, they will have the incentive to make things happen.

Remember that the U.S. is the world's biggest marketplace. Every company wants to sell its goods here. If you are successful in launching your invention here, you should have more than enough income as a result. Consider whatever you earn from foreign licensing as "gravy".

WHO SHOULD WRITE THE PATENT APPLICATION?

There are three choices: you, someone associated with you or a patent attorney. Most experienced inventors agree that it is best for the inventor to write the majority of the patent application. In the case of a provisional application, an experienced inventor can write the entire document. It is best to begin the writing process during development and complete it later when the inventive matter is best understood.

There are significant benefits to writing your own patent application. Four important benefits are:

- You can learn a lot about patents and patenting.
- By writing it during development, you will learn more about your invention and potential design-arounds.
- During the writing process, you will make new discoveries.
- Writing your own application will save you thousands of dollars.

Most patent attorneys agree with this patent-writing approach. It really enhances an inventor's ability to include the best, most inventive material relevant to the invention's success and to the patent's coverage and integrity.

If you feel uncomfortable about writing an application, at least consider writing a thorough draft using the standard writing format covered in the next chapter or have someone you trust help you. If writing is just not possible, you have three other choices:

1. Make a videotape of the invention and narrate it. An associate or attorney can draft the application from the video.

2. Describe the invention in audiocassettes. An associate or your attorney can use them to draft the application.

3. Schedule a physical interview with an associate or attorney and he/she can either record your meeting or take notes.

Once a patent application, provisional or regular, is written, it must be edited and scrutinized for errors. Prior to filing the regular, non-provisional application, experienced inventors agree that it is wise to have an attorney or patent agent write the final draft. It is particularly

*Most good patent attorneys will tell you that inventors seldom know what the **INVENTION** is. They may know what they meant to accomplish--what problem it was meant to solve--but the **INVENTION** itself usually remains a mystery to them. A good patent application provides the framework on which to hang together those aspects of what the invention does and how to show its novelty and usefulness. The application illustrates the **inventive leap** that goes beyond what persons skilled in the same art had done and had been able to do before the creation of the newest invention.*

...George Margolin

important to have an attorney write the claims on the regular, non-provisional patent application.

The claims are the most important part of the patent application. They must be legally written and must properly and adequately reflect the inventive matter you want protected. It is best to have an expert write them. Most patent attorneys concur; this is where they earn their money…by writing bulletproof claims and getting you the broadest coverage possible.

After your attorney has written the final draft, you must proofread it *very, very carefully.* A simple overlooked detail may change an entire meaning that could affect the integrity of the patent. A misplaced period or improper punctuation could change an entire chemical formula or give a sentence an entirely different meaning. It could invalidate the patent. Two examples of entirely different meanings are:

> *The formula uses a half-processed protein.*
> *The formula uses a half processed protein.*

> *Do not touch the part or roll in the solution.*
> *Do not touch the part, or roll in the solution.*

If you are going to file the patent application yourself and rely upon your own ability to write the claims, you are taking a big risk. If this is your choice, you should first read *Patent It Yourself* by David Pressman, Nolo Press, Berkeley, California. In my opinion, at least you will have a chance to succeed in your effort.

If you have properly developed your invention according to the guidelines in this manual, you should have a cash flow before any major costs of patenting are incurred. When it is time to write the regular, non-provisional application with the legal claims that will give you twenty years of protection, it should be affordable.

IS IT BEST TO USE A PATENT ATTORNEY TO FILE OR IS IT BEST TO FILE "PRO PER"?

Experienced inventors invariably use patent attorneys to file for them. After they file, they will prosecute your application. Another reason to hire an attorney to prosecute your patent application is that when infringement occurs, you will have an attorney on your team who knows your patent intimately. During the writing and filing process, your attorney will become an expert on your patent's subject matter and its field. If you have to hire another legal firm to defend you, their review and evaluation of your position could be costly. The patent attorney who knows your patent is best able to protect you when infringement occurs.

Use an Expert Patent Attorney to Help Protect Your Next 20 Years!

Although my attorneys always tell me that I write great patent applications, I can't imagine filing them myself. I will continue to rely on my legal experts to proofread my final drafts, write the claims, and file and prosecute the applications. I believe that relying on anyone else when it comes to my patent's integrity is a mistake. I might be an expert inventor, but I am not a patent attorney or an expert in patent claim writing.
…Bob DeMatteis

125

There is no doubt that many inventors can, and do, successfully draft and file their own patent applications. But, given the importance and relative complexity of the application and prosecution process, the PTO strongly advises prospective applications to engage the services of a registered patent attorney or agent.
...Donald Grant Kelly, Director, U.S. Patent Office

Filing Patent Applications - An Alternative Strategy

Here's an alternative strategy to consider. I recommend NOT giving an attorney the power of attorney to file for you. Instead, you, the inventor, insist on filing the patent application yourself.

Even though you would be wise to have your attorney or patent agent write the claims, this approach may help secure the desired coverage as laws say the patent examiner must then help out.

More important is that all office actions and notices are sent directly to you and not the attorney. There will be no margin of error or excuses with missed deadlines or miscommunication if a practitioner or the inventor passes away. Instead of bankers managing the estate, and the patent application, your appointee can.

If your attorney or agent is not enthused about this approach, find one that is.
...George Morgan, Registered Patent Agent, Inventor of Disc Brakes

By filing by yourself, "pro per", you take the risk of not knowing how to best respond to the PTO's actions. Some recommend filing "pro per" because the law states that the Patent Office examiner must help you write at least one claim. While this may sound appealing, it is foolish to rely on a patent examiner for your future security. Examiners are usually very bright, but they don't have any vested interest in you, your invention's success or your patent's coverage, scope and protection. Why would you want to trust anyone except an expert who cares about the future integrity and security of your invention and your livelihood? Do it right and hire a competent patent attorney.

WHEN AND HOW TO HIRE AN ATTORNEY WITHOUT SPENDING MONEY

When most neophyte inventors have an idea they want to pursue, the first thing they do is consult with a patent attorney. After the patent attorney advises him/her that the first step is to file for patent protection, the inventor budgets the amount. Frequently, a novice inventor will spend a few thousand dollars before he/she knows if the development and marketing of the idea will be feasible. This is not a wise invention development approach, unless you have a lot of money to waste.

While there is little disagreement about the merits of patent protection, there are other steps that should be taken first. More specifically, start the development of your invention. Too often, hastily filed patents result in inadequate or wrong coverage. As you now know, inventions must be developed sufficiently to have patents that cover the broadest and very best inventive subject matter.

Hiring an attorney will not cost you a cent if you do it right. Just follow this simple procedure:

1.   When hiring a patent attorney, never pay for the first visit. *You* are interviewing him/her, not the other way around. When you call for the initial appointment, say, "I am interviewing patent attorneys." Also confirm during this phone conversation that you do not expect to be billed for the interview. It is best to confirm in advance, before the attorney's daily log reaches the bookkeeper, who may automatically bill you.

Most attorneys will agree not to charge for the first visit. There are more patent attorneys than there is business to go around and many are looking for new clients.

2.   Tell the attorney that you have a limited budget. Even if you are wealthy, don't represent that you have an endless stream of cash.

3. If the attorney you select is not familiar with your field, tell him/her you do not expect to pay him/her for the time it takes to learn about your field. He/she will agree if he/she wants your business.

4. Ask the attorney if you are going to be charged for all phone calls, including quick answers to your simple questions. You do not want to see 5-minute phone calls turn into expensive monthly bills.

During the interview, ask for cost estimates to file and prosecute a patent application. They should include:

1. The cost to write the final application draft (provisional or otherwise). Tell him how much of the original draft you will provide or that you will provide a copy of your provisional application, if you are writing it yourself.
2. The cost to prepare drawings to the PTO's standard.
3. The filing costs.
4. Prosecution cost estimate.
5. Patent issuing costs.
6. A total estimate of how much he/she thinks it will cost to get a patent filed, prosecuted and granted.

If he/she wants a retainer, ask him/her to start without one, since it will be awhile before any costs are incurred. Let him/her know that you are not sure how long it will take you to finish writing the application, complete prototyping, developing, etc. This could take months. Besides, if you have good credit, a retainer is just not necessary. Assume that your patenting costs will be 25% higher than quoted.

The interview is a good time to state your marketing and licensing intentions. If there are areas in which you have questions, ask for his advice (at no charge). It is easy to get a few pointers, if the attorney really wants your business.

In your search for a patent attorney, find one who understands your needs and with whom you can communicate. Beware of any attorney who tells you that the first thing you must do is protect yourself with a patent--especially if it is the more costly, regular patent application. If you have taken the precautions described in this manual, you will have more than adequate protection. Encouraging an inventor to pursue a costly regular patent application without knowing the invention's commercial value borders on unethical.

After you have chosen an attorney, send a letter confirming your intention to hire him/her and saying that you look forward to working with the attorney and his/her staff. He/she will respond with a letter confirming fees and terms, etc.

Be careful about calling your attorney with a lot of questions. Instead, find the answers in this manual, other books or on the Internet.

In my From Patent to Profit seminars and workshops, some participants will invariably listen with a curious grin on their face. They are thinking something like, "How did this guy ever figure out how to con patent attorneys like this?"

Thus, I invariably explain to the group, that I did not invent any of these "tricks"...that they were all volunteered to me by patent attorneys themselves.

Following the Strategic Guide, you will normally want to hire an attorney fairly early on, so that you have one there for counsel as it may be required. But keep in mind that they will not be spending much time on your project (nor will you be incurring any major bills) until sometime later.

Usually they will not be needed for patent matters until they either review your final provisional patent application before filing or begin reviewing and writing the claims for your final application.

From this perspective of the Strategic Guide, you will not be spending much money until much later on.

When you do call with questions, keep them concise. Otherwise, each answer can cost you $100 or more! If you become friendly with your attorney, see if you can meet over lunch from time to time. You can have a lot of expensive questions answered for a $50 lunch tab.

ABOUT PATENT INFRINGEMENT PROTECTION

Another important consideration when selecting an attorney is his/her position on patent infringement protection. If you are a small company without a lot of cash or if you are expecting an infringement problem with a large firm, the best time to ask about infringement protection is up front.

Ask the attorney if he/she will work on a contingency basis in the event of patent infringement. Many will, providing the scope of your coverage and the patent's integrity are sound. Remember that 80% of all court cases are ruled in favor of the inventor. Having this commitment is better than an insurance policy. It is one you can tout later if you think there may be an impending threat of infringement.

Assume that infringement costs can run up to $250,000 and into the millions and determine your contingency split at the outset. Your attorney will probably want something like this:

- 30% if settled out of court
- 35% if court documents need to be filed
- 40% if it goes to court

Three other points to keep in mind are:

- In most infringement cases, you have to pay the actual costs for filing court documents. These costs are deducted from the settlement before the contingency split is made. These expenses may be high, but only if the case goes to court. Remember that at least 95% are settled before going that far.
- If you have plenty of cash or are a medium- to large-sized company, you will probably not want a contingency arrangement with legal counsel.
- If you are a small company and have a contingency arrangement with strong defense counsel from an attorney who is successful in your field, you are in a sound position to develop your invention, mass produce it and get it sold…without the fear of infringement.

HAVING A PATENT ATTORNEY WORK FOR FREE

Some attorneys may work for free or for a "piece of the action", but this is rare. They will at least want you to cover the basic costs, such as

I am finding it is becoming more and more common that patent attorneys filing clients' patents would also defend them on a contingency basis in the event of infringement.

Of course the two key factors that warrant doing so are predicated upon receiving broad enough patent protection (or maybe you have multiple infringement of more than one patent) and having an infringement that has enough profit in order to justify the investment.

In my From Patent to Profit seminars and workshops, I am frequently asked about finding an attorney to "work for free". As you will find later on, the biggest deal-killer in license negotiations is to use an attorney.

Why would you want a deal-killer on your team controlling the very aspect that is ultimately going to make your project a success?

filing fees and copying and fax charges. The attorneys I have met who would consider these types of arrangements are generally not of high quality. You can find equity partners elsewhere, who will not be as controlling. Besides, it could cost you a small fortune just to have another attorney review your partnership draft.

WHO CONTACTS THE PATENT OFFICE TO FOLLOW UP ON THE APPLICATION?

If you have hired an attorney, only he/she will be able to follow up. The Patent Office wants to communicate with one person. This individual is usually you, if you filed pro per or your patent attorney, if he/she filed on your behalf. At filing, you will give your patent attorney "power of attorney" to file and prosecute your application.

Your attorney can send letters and faxes referencing your patent's serial number to request an update. He/she can also talk to the examiner by phone. For a charge, the patent office now offers an interview directly with the examiner via the Internet.

PROSECUTING THE APPLICATION

After about one year, you will receive your first office action. If your application is rejected, don't panic. Most patent applications are rejected on this first office action. Even high-quality patents are rarely accepted with the very first office action. Patent examiners usually ask for qualification of the inventive aspects. When you fight for them, you are improving the quality and integrity of your patent and its claims.

When the first response is returned, do the following:

1. Carefully read your attorney's response to the patent office action. Your attorney may inform you that some or all of the claims are acceptable with only minor changes. If so, ask yourself, "With these changes, am I going to get the overall coverage I want?"

For instance, your patent may refer to inventive matter related to making ice cream, but the examiner could cite similar art related to freezing of bacteria for medical purposes. In this case, it would be fairly easy to get clarification on your claims by adding words relevant to making ice cream for human consumption.

2. If the reason for rejection is not clear, you should carefully read the examiner's rejections and the accompanying patent references cited.

3. Jot down the reasons you believe the references cited do not apply to your invention. Be thorough and look at the rejection from many angles. For instance, is the examiner citing art that is much more

Internet Patent News Service

The Internet Patent News service is a mostly daily news service dealing with information about the patenting world. Topics include announcement from various Patent Offices around the world, stories about who is suing who, interesting new patents and styles of patent drafting, statistics on issued patents (with a focus on software patents), reviews of patent books and computer programs, and biting commentary if I happen to be in a lousy mood that morning.

Additionally, contributions are solicited from anyone with some patent issue they have an opinion on, as well as explanations from patent lawyers about some of the issues raised in the news items.

If you are interested in signing up for this free service, look up PATNEWS in the Appendix under Trade Magazines.

costly to produce? Is it impractical to use the teachings of the prior art on your invention? Does the prior art not apply because you know from considerable experience that it is not relevant to your invention's function?

4. Discuss the examiner's rejection(s) with your patent attorney. He/she should be very experienced in this area and able to help tremendously. Patent Office rejections and objections will not intimidate your attorney. He/she can tell you precisely what the examiner is rejecting.

5. Discuss the response strategy with your attorney. With your input on cost effectiveness, application and functional differences, a savvy patent attorney will know how to overcome the objections. Be ready to supply additional facts. To substantiate your point, you may have to prepare an affidavit on the state-of-the-art in the industry.

Most patent applications are rejected because the examiner cites prior art from one or more sources that he/she believes make your invention obvious. Another common basis for rejection is that your invention was "anticipated" by what is contained in a previous patent.

In both cases, you are in a better position to prove that the examiner's prior art references or anticipations are incorrect. You will frequently find that the references are irrelevant. They often pertain to archaic prior art and processes that could never be applied to your invention and its new technology.

Other common reasons for rejections and objections by patent examiners are:

1. **Application contains more than one invention.** As we discussed on page 107, your strategy may include filing a single application for more than one "inventive matter" or more than one invention. In this case, you will have to split out the application into two or more divisional applications. One invention is prosecuted immediately; the other(s) are prosecuted in the order you select after initial prosecution has been completed. Base your choice on your anticipated return on investment. Sometimes you want to prosecute weaker patents later, based upon their value as defensive patents.

You will probably never use defensive patents, but you don't want others to use them either. It is like having the two best patents in the field of your invention--developing the sales on the best one and blocking the sales of the next best one. Defensive patents can be an effective part of your long-term patent strategy.

2. **Drawings that are incorrectly drawn or have misapplied numeric references.** This is easy to overcome.

Mary S. of St. Louis, Missouri (1851-1880) was a genius inventor who was poverty stricken. Lacking finances and confidence, she sold the rights to her inventions (most of them mechanical) to various male agents for as little as $5 each.

These agents received 53 patents and a great deal of wealth! Mary S. died penniless at age 30. While the battle against sexism was not yet won, one principle is clearly declared. That is...women inventors were a force to be reckoned with in modern America.

Lemelson-MIT Invention Dimension

3. **Unclear references to the invention in the body of the text.** This is easy to overcome.

4. **Claims that do not adequately describe the invention.** This too is usually easy to overcome.

A SECOND REJECTION

After a second rejection, repeat the previous process and discuss strategy with your attorney more thoroughly. Reportedly, in 97% of the cases, the second action is the final action, regardless of whether the patent is granted. Experience indicates that although the second action may not result in the granting of a patent, it is not a dead end.

Try a telephone conversation between the examiner and your attorney. Request the examiner's advice about how to overcome the wording. If you have licensed the invention, use that fact as evidence to substantiate the merit of the patent and its claims.

If necessary, you can take your invention directly to the Patent Office to show the examiner how great and unique it is. Willingness to do this is an indication of your strength and determination. As discussed on page 121, you can also arrange an interview via the Internet with the examiner, although it may not have the same impact as a face-to-face meeting.

Frequently, a second rejection is due to the change of wording in the claims and subject matter in the response to the first office action. The examiner will cite that the changes bring up "new subject matter", which requires the filing of a Continuation In Part (CIP). This allows you to literally re-write the patent application so that it conforms to the new subject matter.

CIP in Layperson Terms

A continuation-in-part application (CIP) is the label given to a specification of a second application that has a different specification from the first application, but is related in some way. Most frequently, the CIP has some extra material added to the earlier specification. In other instances, the CIP may be completely rewritten but directed to the same general subject matter as the earlier specification. In yet other instances, the CIP may be a subset of the earlier specification.
...Greg Aharonian, PATNEWS

DURING PROSECUTION YOUR ATTORNEY EARNS HIS MONEY

Only your patent attorney should respond to the examiner's rejections. It must be done in a certain protocol. We inventors are emotionally bound to our creations. We might say to the examiner, "You're crazy and don't have a !B#F!ST*LK clue about what you're talking about." That outburst would most likely result in a second rejection of the application.

On the other hand, your patent attorney will respond tactfully, to negotiate the best possible outcome. He/she knows how to compose a respectful response, following the courtesies that must be extended to the patent examiners.

PATENT STRATEGY, LICENSING AND VENTURE CAPITAL

Ann Moore (b. 1940), worked for the Peace Corps in Togo, Africa in the early 1960's. She realized that native women carried their babies in slings, which provided a great deal of comfort and security, while keeping the parent's hands free.

After returning to the U.S. Moore and her mother, Lucy Aukerman, designed and patented the "Snugli" (1969), a rugged, adjustable, pouch-like infant carrier. In house production eventually led to a buy-out from a national corporation.

There are other issues to consider as you develop your patent strategy. For instance, if you plan to license your invention afterward, pay special attention to the details surrounding your patent's development and scope. A patent that is easy to design around will be difficult to license.

You will want to fight for all your claims and get the broadest possible coverage. A patent application that has been well fought for is usually more difficult to contest. Fight for your rights and patent claims until the bitter end. See Chapter 5, pages 98 and 99 for more discussion of this subject.

Solid patent positions can also improve your ability to secure venture capital, fund a company and secure expansion financing. If you intend to use your patents as part of the assets of your business, be sure to fight for every last claim that will give you protection.

THE MOST IMPORTANT STRATEGY – KEEP INVENTING

Famous inventor Yujiro Yamamoto reports that his first breakthrough idea was patent number 4 or 5, which became the telephone answering machine we all know so well today.

An inventor's first patent is rarely a breakthrough, moneymaking opportunity. The smartest thing an inventor can do is to continue to improve upon his/her invention and secure more patents. It is usually later that a breakthrough opportunity will arise.

There are three key benefits to this approach. First, in the event of infringement, you will be in a superior position to defend against infringement of your invention. It will be more difficult and costly for an infringer to try to invalidate two or more of your patents.

Second, with new improvements, you can extend the life of your licenses. If your licenses are based on the "expiration of the last of the patents", you may add years to the term.

The third benefit to continuing the invention process is that you get better at it. You could find new opportunities with related product groups. You may even be asked to invent something for a company or help design around and improve upon an existing product. The more you invent, the more opportunities you will find.

7

WRITING PATENT APPLICATIONS

*You will learn a lot about patents and your
invention while writing your application.*

UTILITY PATENT WRITING STRATEGY

There are two basic types of utility patent applications that can be filed at the U.S. Patent Office: the provisional patent application and the regular patent application. To review, the provisional patent application is a greatly simplified version of the regular application, is not reviewed by the PTO and is kept for a period of one year. The regular patent application must be filed to maintain the priority date established by the provisional.

As we discussed on page 122, you will probably file a provisional patent application, followed by a regular patent application within a year. Even if you skip the provisional and file only the regular application, there are several reasons for you to write as much of the application as possible. These reasons include improving the integrity of your patent, discovering potential design-arounds, making new discoveries and saving money. Your patent writing will dovetail with your invention development and enhance your ability to include material that is most inventive and relevant to the invention's success and the patent's scope.

Generally speaking, you will write the provisional application first and write the regular patent application within a year. The regular patent application will reference the provisional application. Although the laws regarding provisional applications are new, it would be wise to have your regular patent application "read on" your provisional application as much as possible. In other words, if they both have the same specifications and drawings, the preservation of the priority date should remain intact.

In contrast, if a subsequently filed regular patent application does not read well on the original provisional application's specifications, some of the content could be vulnerable to losing the priority date. If the material in the regular application is considered new and does not reference the prior provisional application, or is newly added material, the new material will not have the original priority date.

Another question regarding provisionals is how well written should a provisional patent application be? The answer is as good as possible. Nevertheless, you could argue that a poorly written provisional is better than none at all.

The decision about whether to write and file the provisional yourself is yours. Before deciding, consider that the better the document is written and the better the subsequent regular patent application reads on the original provisional, the better your chances of getting a patent. If you are unsure about your patent writing ability, write as much of the provisional application as you can and have your attorney edit, re-write and file the final provisional draft.

The same is true for filing the regular application, but here your attorney is far more important. Most everyone in the patent business agrees that a highly qualified attorney should at least edit and write your final draft and the claims.

MODELING AFTER ANOTHER PATENT

Before writing your patent application, you will probably conduct a patent search. As you review patents from your patent search, select one or two as models for your patent application. Copy their style and language. However, keep the content accurate and use the format that is required by the U.S. Patent Office.

DRAFTING YOUR APPLICATION ON A COMPUTER SAVES TIME AND MONEY

You will probably edit your patent draft continually. Don't be surprised if you print five or ten drafts before you have the one you

Plagiarizing Patents

All government publications are considered "in the public domain" and do not fall under copyright law.

When you do your patent search and you find one or two that are related to your invention, go ahead and plagiarize their content. It is entirely legal and is done all the time.

In fact, there is no reason to "re-invent the wheel" in this regard. It will save you a huge amount of valuable time and improve the content of your patent application.

want! Drafting your provisional or regular patent application on a computer word processor saves hours.

Another advantage to using a computer is that you can send the final draft to your attorney on a diskette. This can save days or even weeks in preparing and filing an application. All your attorney has to do is put your diskette in his computer, make the necessary corrections and return it to you for proofreading.

WRITING AND FILING A PROVISIONAL PATENT APPLICATION

A properly written provisional patent application filed at the U.S. Patent Office should include the following components:

1. Written specifications adequately describing the invention and the preferred embodiments. They are defined in U.S.C. 112, first paragraph. Use the following format, but write sections 1-7 only. The abstract, Oath of Inventorship and the most difficult part of a patent application, claim writing, are not included.

2. Drawings per section 1.81 and 1.83. Use the drawing format as defined in Section 7.

3. A provisional patent application cover sheet (one is included in the Resource Guide).

4. A declaration claiming small entity status, if applicable (one is included in the Resource Guide).

5. A check for $75 if you are a small entity or a check for $150 if you are a large entity.

One great advantage to writing and filing provisional patent applications is that during development, if you make new discoveries you can write and file another provisional patent application.

When doing so, you can usually start out with the computer draft of a previous application and change it accordingly.

This newly drafted patent application can then be either incorporated into the final, permanent application or can be filed as a separate application later.

Discuss this strategy with your patent counsel.

PATENT WRITING SIMPLIFIED

Writing patent applications (provisional or non-provisional) is somewhat like writing high school or college term papers, although more technical. Here are some guidelines:

1. Draft the written portion according to the standard manuscript format. For instance, it should be double-spaced (1.5 spaces is OK), with 1 inch margins on all sides.

2. Number the lines for easy reference.

3. The drawings should follow a basic drafting format. They should meet the Patent Office's standards for number and letter references. If the drawings don't satisfy PTO standards, the application will not necessarily be rejected. However, your drawings should be clear enough to make the inventive matter perfectly clear.

Since it is important for your regular, non-provisional patent application to read on your provisional application, use the same format in both, with as much of the same wording as possible. The following example is easy to understand; you can use many of the same words in your application. The text box comments will help to explain the writing process.

THE STANDARD FORMAT FOR WRITING A REGULAR PATENT APPLICATION

There are several variations of the standard format, but the one that follows represents the easiest way for an inventor to write a regular patent application. Since a patent attorney or patent agent will edit the final draft, he/she may choose to alter the format. If so, it will still follow the basic theme that follows.

Your regular patent application should begin with a descriptive title, not a trademark or nickname. These six topics plus the drawings, claims and abstract, should be included in the following order:

Remember that it is important for you, the inventor, to write the original patent application draft. Most experienced inventors agree that the patent-writing experience is invaluable. While writing, you will make new discoveries, find potential design-arounds and develop alternative means of making or using your invention. You should cover these alternatives in one patent application with the broadest language possible.

Section subtitles:
1. Field of the Invention
2. Background of the Invention
3. Description of Prior Art
4. Summary of the Invention
5. Brief Description of the Drawings
6. Detailed Description of the Drawings
7. Drawings
8. Claims
9. The Abstract

As you write each section, you will learn more about your invention. When you are finished, you should have an excellent understanding of how and why it works.

Patent applications that do not meet the Patent Office's rules and laws or are incomplete will be cited with a notice of objection. The notice will include a brief summary of the objections.

STORYTELLING

One of the easiest ways to write a patent application is by telling a story. The story will automatically cover the categories in the standard format in the proper sequence. Your story will begin with the field of your invention, and in a time line sequence, cover the past, the present and future. In other words, what was used (past), what is currently used (present) and what you have discovered (future).

These nine sequential short stories correspond to the nine standard format section subtitles:

1. **Field of the Invention:** Tell about the field related to your invention.

2. **Background of the Invention:** Tell about the problems with past and current art and why it would be beneficial to fix these problems.

3. **Description of Prior Art:** Describe the past and current state of the art. In other words, provide a brief history lesson about prior art and how it contributes to the problems you cited in the Background of the Invention.

4. **Summary of the Invention:** Tell about your invention and how it solves the problems associated with prior art.

5. **Brief Description of the Drawings:** Describe the invention in "big picture" terms.

6. **Detailed Description of the Drawings:** Describe in detail exactly how the invention works. This is equivalent to the written specifications in your provisional application.

7. **Drawings:** Draw pictures that illustrate the invention's specifications, as detailed in items 5 and 6 above.

8. **Claims:** Describe what you claim are your discoveries, inventions and improvements.

9. **The Abstract:** In one paragraph, summarize the invention.

If you want your attorney to write the entire patent application, he/she will ask you to tell the "story" about how it came about. Why not write it yourself?

Remember that according to the Strategic Guide, you should be developing your invention in concert with input from your manufacturing and marketing partners.

This strategy will make sure that you are developing the very best attributes, and of course, including these superior attributes in the patent application.

It is interesting to note that when incorporating the input of these two most-important experts, it dovetails perfectly with the "story-telling" sequence of writing a patent application.

For your protection, the claims must be written correctly and legally. This is how a patent attorney will earn his fee--by protecting you and your future with solid, defendable claims. Good patent attorneys and agents will provide that.

WRITING A REGULAR PATENT APPLICATION

You will most likely start writing your patent application while you are testing and qualifying your inventive discoveries. Well into the testing process, you will decide that you have accumulated enough information to begin writing the application. When you do, it is best to have quiet time alone, so you can think, analyze and draw as you write.

The following patent application was written on a computer using the "story telling" method. It is an actual patent filed by the author. You can use this example as a model for writing your patent application. To get started, remove the key words, such as "plastic sacks", and insert those words that apply to your inventive material, such as "kitchen cleaning devices".

The following model is written much like you might actually write it yourself. It is at 1.5 spaces per line, justified left, Times New Roman typeface with a font size of 12. Underline each heading with an extra space between paragraphs. This writing format will be easy for your attorney to convert to numbered lines as he/she edits and writes the final draft.

Comments are printed in Italics in the column text boxes to help guide you. Suggested copy you might use is in bold, standard typeface.

Improved Plastic Grocery Sack Bagging System

Field of the Invention

This invention relates to plastic sacks commonly used in supermarket, drug and discount stores in food and related trades, to carry merchandise from the store to home. More specifically, this invention relates to a plastic sack style and system that can be used to substantially improve load capacity and loading efficiency.

Background of the Invention

Plastic sacks have become the most popular style of bag to carry merchandise and their related loading systems are preferred in high volume outlets in North America and in much of Europe, Australia and Asia. In these high volume outlets, the systems incorporate a rack style holder which supports the thin gauged bags while a user loads the bags and removes the filled bags from the holder.

Being able to fill up plastic sacks by utilizing as much of the entire capacity as possible is important in high volume outlets. If the capacity is not properly utilized, i.e. under utilized, more bags will be used,

---

Field of the Invention

The story begins. Start by telling the field of your invention, such as pneumatic tires, tortilla manufacturing processes or kitchen cleaning devices. Begin your patent application like the model, such as:

This invention relates to kitchen cleaning devices commonly used in households and commercial applications.

Continue with greater specificity, such as:

More specifically, it relates to a cleaning device that substantially improves the ability to remove baked-on cooking residue and other hard-to-remove substances.

These two sentences should get you started in the right direction.

Background of the Invention

In this section, add a sentence or two about why your invention would be desirable. Note that in this section, the invention's "usefulness" is being clearly stated.

The end of this section should lead you into the next.

thereby increasing both bag and labor costs. A system that utilizes as much of the available capacity in a plastic sack as possible can represent an important cost-cutting measure.

Description of Prior Art

The most popular systems in use in the world today in high volume outlets is described in U.S. Re. Pat. 33,264. Plastic sacks of this variety have a centrally located detachable tab that extends upwardly, and holes intermediately located in each handle. These bags are generally in unitary packs of 50 or 100 bags. The unitary pack is mounted onto a rack style holder by threading the two sets of handle holes onto two rod supports and placing the centrally located upwardly extending detachable, apertured tab, onto a centrally located projecting element.

The projecting element holds the bag pack in place while the forward-most bag is being utilized. To prepare for utilization, the user separates the front wall of the forward-most bag and pulls it forward, while the bag is being supported by the rod supports which have been inserted through the handle holes, and the rear bag wall is being retained at the centrally located tab mounted onto the projecting element. The user then loads the bag in this supported position. As disclosed in U.S. Patent No. 4,529,090 tearing at the bag body upon separation of the bag walls from the tab can be avoided by utilizing detachable joinder sections located adjacent the bag mouth.

A problem associated with this prior art system is that when bags are mounted on the rack style holder, they hang down to an undesirable extent. This is confirmed by the fact that the upwardly extending tab which is hooked on the projecting element forces the bag mouth to be below the top of the rack style holder. It is further compounded by the fact that the plastic sack handles are generally 6" long and upon mounting the intermediate handle holes onto the holder's rod supports, the bag and the bag mouth are caused to hang down even to a greater extent.

Description of Prior Art

Tell the history of how it was done in the past and about the problems associated with the prior art.

For instance, begin by describing relevant prior art:
Wire mesh prior art cleaning devices tend to scratch metal pan surfaces...

Elaborate with some details about how the prior art is being used. If there is more than one piece of related prior art methodology, write about them.

Continue to tell about problems associated with prior art inventions.

You are later going to be describing how your invention overcomes these prior art-related problems.

It is not necessary to make the prior art section of the application too long. Examiners and attorneys do not seem to care much for it. If in doubt, it is better to list too much prior art. Why? One reason is that the attorney writing your final draft will probably know best what to edit.

More importantly, you do not want the examiner citing some prior art as a possible reason for rejection, when you could have cited it as a reason for approval!

Further, in order to open up the bag mouth to a sufficient width so a user can commence loading the bag, the rod supports must be spread outwards, beyond the normal distance spanning the handle holes. Thus, the handle holes mounted on the rod supports cause the handles to be stretched outwards about 11-12", with the handles pointing away from the center, whereas the handle holes on a bag in a lay-flat position are usually spaced about 7-7 1/2" apart and 3" above the bag mouth.

The result, upon opening the forward-most bag, is a bag and bag mouth hanging down below the rod supports, well below the top of the rack style holder and, with a relatively narrow, oblong shaped, open-mouth configuration. Such a hanging bag actually resists squaring itself out due to being forced to take on this unnatural, oblong configuration. This narrow oblong configuration generally causes the user to under utilize the actual capacity of the plastic sack.

As illustrated in the PRIOR ART Figure 1A of the drawings, the upwardly extending tab T determines where the central region of the bag mouth M will be situated on the rack style holder in its lowered position. The bag mouth's lowered position is further determined by intermediate handle holes H mounted onto rod supports S. Such mounting causes the bag to hang downward below the rod supports S on the rack style holder. The result is the oblong configuration C of bag mouth M.

Summary of the Invention

The plastic sack and rack mounting system of the present invention increases the ability of the user to access the sack's entire capacity. When the plastic sack of the present invention is placed on a rack style holder and opened up, it utilizes more of the bag system's cube for loading than is possible with prior art systems.

This is accomplished by using a unique design which lifts the sack high onto its rack holder and allows the bag mouth to open more widely. In fact, the bag mouth actually opens up to a configuration which provides more area than the original bag dimensions would

Conclude the section with a description of a prior art drawing. You will include this drawing with those you do of the present invention--but only if a prior art drawing is necessary. If you are discussing something obvious like a paper clip, this would most likely be unnecessary.

Summary of the Invention

Tell about what you have discovered and why it is so wonderful. Do so in two or three sentences, such as:

The present invention overcomes the problems associated with prior art by...
Due to the unique nature of the content of the...

Note that while summarizing your invention, you are describing your product's "uniqueness".
As you write this section, continue telling the story, but elaborate on the specifics regarding why the unique design accomplishes what you say it does.
Your paragraphs may be long and wordy, but this is OK for the sake of accuracy.
This is an important section of the patent. Use real numbers and specifications to illustrate your point if possible.

indicate to be possible. For instance, a plastic grocery sack which typically measures 12" across by 7" wide has an open mouth area of 84" square (12" times 7"); whereas this same sized bag in the form of the present invention can take on a squared out configuration of 9.5" across by 9.5" wide (9.5" times 9.5") or an open mouth area of 90.25" square.

Instead of an upwardly extending detachable tab, one style of the bag pack of the present invention is retained on the rack style holder by mounting a transverse slit on a centrally located detachable portion of the bag body wall, said slit being located below the portions of the body wall immediately adjacent the centrally located detachable portion, the upper edge of which detachable portion, together with the upper edges of adjacent body wall portion define the bag mouth. A retaining means, such as an upwardly extending element is passed through said slit when the bag is mounted on the rack style holder. When the detachable portion is disposed onto the central retaining means of the rack holder, the central part of the bag body is actually lifted up and the bag mouth is disposed at approximately the top of the rack holder instead of hanging down below it as in prior art systems. The outer regions of the bag body and mouth are also lifted up high onto the rack style holder by providing two laterally spaced apertures in the sides of the bag and passing the rod supports through such apertures. These two spaced apertures in the body are normal to the plane of the centrally located detachable portion and may be disposed near the outside edges of the plastic sack. They may be cut through the side gussets as well. When the apertures are placed onto the rod supports of the rack holder and the centrally located detachable portion is secured on the central retaining means, the result is a plastic sack which sits high up on the holder, and, when opened by the user, squares itself out naturally along the rod supports.

The lifting up of the bag walls and the squaring out effect increase the area of the open bag mouth substantially, and can result in the ability to load up to 20 to 30% more merchandise. When the sack is fully loaded, it is then a simple operation to locate and grasp the

> *Try closing the <u>Summary of the Invention</u> with a clinching paragraph, on a topic that you will clearly illustrate in the next two sections. For instance, reinforce your claims by describing the specifications and tests you conducted. You can explain how you did them and with whom. For example:*
>
> **Tests conducted show that the present invention virtually eliminates scratching of the metallic surfaces and yet lasts 50% longer than prior art...**

Brief Description of the Drawings

List your drawings and describe them in simple but broad terms using one-sentence paragraphs.

This section is usually the shortest. It simply references the drawings included in the application. All you need to consider is putting them in their proper sequence. Usually they begin with a drawing of the invention and then each subsequent drawing expands upon how it works.

Detailed Description of the Drawings

In this section, you will describe the details of how the invention works.

Without question, this is the most difficult section for most of us. If you find that it is a breeze, you are meticulous and probably an experienced inventor! There are four great difficulties with this section:

1. Explain in greater detail, but not too much. You need not get into the physics of why something happens, only explain what does happen. For instance, you may point out how two plastic pieces are bonded together by heat sealing, but you need not explain why or how the heat sealing action works.

2. Write in a logical sequence to carefully explain exactly what is happening. In other words, explain from beginning to end how your invention works. Your drawings will correspond to the written storytelling sequence.

Cont. on next page

handles which lay atop the rod supports, and remove the loaded sack from the rack holder. Thus, the plastic sack of the present invention lends itself to being loaded more fully and more easily, and is simple to use.

Brief Description of the Drawings

Fig. 1A is front perspective view of a prior art rack and such combination.

Fig. 1 a plan view of one type of bag of the present invention showing its centrally located detachable portion and rod receiving orifices.

Fig. 2 is a front perspective view of the bag of Fig. 1 mounted onto a rack holder.

Fig. 3 is an enlarged plan view of the centrally located detachable portion of the present invention.

Fig. 4 is a plan view of the preferred version of the present invention with its centrally located detachable portion and apertures in the bag's body.

Fig. 5 is a front perspective view of the bag of Fig. 4 mounted on a rack holder.

Fig. 6 is a front perspective view of the bag and rack holder in Fig. 5 with the forward-most bag opened and ready for loading.

Fig. 7 illustrates a further embodiment of the invention.

Detailed Description of the Drawings

Referring to Fig. 1, plastic bag 1 has a bottom 2, two handles 3 and 3', a bag mouth 4, a body 8, and side gusset panels 15. Centrally located below bag mouth 4 extends substantially horizontal from the base of handle 3 to the base of handle 3'. Centrally located below bag mouth 4 in body 8 is detachable portion 5, which has a slit 7 within its perimeter, said slit 7 also thereby being located below bag mouth 4. This perimeter is defined by perforation line 9 in the bag body 8 and a center portion of bag mouth 4. Handles 3 and 3' have handle holes 6 and 6' intermediately spaced along the handle's length.

As illustrated in Fig. 2, rack holder 10 has two rod supports 11 and 11', a central retaining element 12 and a base 13. Rod supports 11 and 11' are connected along the back side of rack holder 10 by brace 14, which generally, together with said rod supports represents the top of rack holder 10. Bag 1 is mounted onto rack holder 10 by passing handle holes 6 and 6' onto rod supports 11 and 11' respectively. When the detachable portion 5 is secured on retaining element 12 by slipping slit 7 over the retaining element 12, it lifts the entire bag body 8 up high onto rack holder 10. Bag mouth 4 is now proximate to the top of brace 14. The elevation of bag 1 on the rack holder 10 may be seen to have improved the potential loading capacity of said bag 1 over what is possible with the prior art system described above.

In Fig. 3 the detachable portion 5 is shown adjacent to bag mouth 4 with a centrally located traverse slit 7. Perforation line 9 is defined by scalloped cuts 21, 22, 23, 24, 25 and 26, with tit connections 28, 29, 30, 31, 32 and 33 located in between the scalloped cuts of said perforation line. The tit connections 27, 28, 29, 30, 31, 32 and 33 point inward towards the center of the detachable portion 5 and away from bag body 8. Upon separation of the detachable portion 5 from the bag body 8, the inwardly pointed tit connections will tear inwards towards the detachable portion 5 thus significantly reducing the possibility of tearing downwards into bag body 8. The use of detachable portion 5 with its perforation line 9 which only tears inward hence preserving the integrity of the bag body is of significant importance. By contrast, the use of tabs such as those of the 4,529,090 variety are impractical for lifting the bag body upwards, and; the use of traditional style straight-line perforations will leave the bag body vulnerable to tearing.

In Fig. 4 plastic bag 31 has a bottom 32, two handles 33 and 33', a bag mouth 34, a body 38, and side gusset panels 41 and 41'. Bag mouth 34 extends substantially horizontally from the base 33a of handle 33 to the base 33a' of the handle 33'. Centrally located in the bag mouth 34 is detachable portion 35, which has a slit 37 within its perimeter, which perimeter is defined by perforation line 39 below and bag mouth 34 above. All of the foregoing is much the same as the bag

---

Detailed Description of the Drawings (cont.)

3. Perfectly match your reference numbers (and letters) with the drawings.

4. Proofread the section many times to confirm its accuracy.

It may take several hours to complete this section and you may redo the drawings several times. However, one thing is for certain. Writing this section is one of the best ways to learn about your invention in depth. *It is usually during this process that you find flaws, problems and alternative methods or design-arounds.* If you discover alternative design-arounds, try to include them in the scope of your application.

Before you begin writing this section on __Detailed Description of the Drawings__, have plenty of drawing paper handy. In the previous section, you listed the drawings that you want. Now, you will draw the sketches while you are writing this section. Instead of making new ones, you may want to trace some of your previous sketches. While writing and drawing in this section, you can decide whether to add or subtract drawings to clarify the invention's functions.

You will also notice that run-on sentences are common. That is to be expected, since legal writing often employs long, rambling sentences for clarity. (This is ironic, because such writing frequently creates just the opposite effect!)

A rule in writing patent applications says to keep each related thought together in one continuous sentence.

After this section and the drawings are completed, you are in the home stretch. There is not much more to do. Regardless of how you may struggle with this section, do not worry.

The worst case is that your attorney will take a little extra time to re-write and finish the application for you.

The important issues are what you learned during this detailed writing experience and the possible design-arounds.

style in Figs. 1, 2 and 3. However, body apertures 36 and 36' are spaced laterally from detachable portion 35 and below handles 33 and 33' respectively. Body apertures 36 and 36' are cut through both front bag wall 56 and rear wall 55 (Fig. 6) of bag body 38 and through gusset panels 41 and 41' respectively. Body apertures 36 and 36' may be in a variety of round, oval or straight line configurations but are generally preferred to be about 1/4" wide by about 1 1/4" long. It is also preferred to have them located about 3/4" inside of the outer edges 40 and 40' of bag body 38, which coincides with being about 3/4" inside the gusset panels 41 and 41' as well.

In Fig. 5, bag 31 of Fig. 4 is mounted onto rack holder 50 (which holder is of the same style as that illustrated in Fig. 2) by passing body apertures 36 and 36' onto rod supports 51 and 51' respectively and by slipping slit 37 over retaining element 52 to secure detachable portion 35 to rack holder 50. Visually, it can be seen that bag 31 mounted onto rack holder 50, lifts the entire bag body 38 high on said holder 50, even higher than the bag of Figs. 1 and 2. It can be appreciated that the bag handles 33, 33' will lie neatly behind the rack holder 50 instead of protruding out sideways.

In sequence from Fig. 5, as illustrated in Fig. 6, bag 31 is opened and ready for loading with rear bag mouth location 55 seen as being clearly proximate to and slightly above brace 54 and rod supports 51 and 51'. In this open end position, front bag wall 56 has been separated from the detachable portion 35, and extended fully forward, thereby causing gusset panels 41 and 41', defined by dotted lines, to also expand fully forward and leave handles 33 and 33', laying atop rod supports 51 and 51' respectively. It will be appreciated that in this open position, with front bag wall 56 extended fully forward, the bag mouth opening 61 is considerably enlarged and squared out over what is achievable in the prior art system. Through the enlarged bag mouth opening 61 the user has easy access to load merchandise into the available cube capacity within bag 31. Upon completion of the loading process, the user may easily locate the two handles 33 and 33' laying atop rod supports 51 and 51' respectively, and pull the bag 31 forward to separate at rear bag wall 55 from its detachable portion 35 along its perforation line 39.

The same result may be attained with the modified embodiment of the invention illustrated in Fig. 7. In this embodiment, the upper edge 34a of the bag mouth 34' and the upper edge 35a of the centrally detachable portion 35' do not lie in a substantially horizontal line, as in the embodiments of Figs. 1 and 4-6, but are slightly arched from the intersection 36a of said edges 34a and the bag handles 33", 33'". The slit 37 then may be slightly above the lowermost section 37a' of said upper edges 34a, but will be below the sections 34b, 34b' of the edges 34a which abut the centrally detachable portions 35a. This slightly arched configuration of the upper edges 34a of the bag body 38' with the centrally detachable portion 35a and disposition of the slit 37a will not produce any different result from that attainable by the other embodiments of the invention.

DRAWINGS–ARTISTIC OR NOT

Compile your sketches while writing the two previous sections, Brief Description of Drawings and Detailed Description of Drawings. If you are artistic or have drafting experience, doing your own drawings will be fairly easy. If not, do your best and then turn your drawings over to someone who can improve them.

When you submit the accompanying drawings to the PTO, you have two choices. They can be sketches that are not professionally prepared but that clearly and accurately depict the invention and the inventive matter. The PTO will invariably object and cite your drawings as "not being up to standard". You will have to have a professional perfect them. The cost to have an attorney's artist prepare the drawings is about $300-$400 for a simple invention. You can save money by hiring a recent graduate or an engineering student at a local university.

Your second choice is to have a professional or student perfect your sketches and then file the application. If there is some rush to get the patent filed, you may want to save time and not have them perfected until the patent is through being prosecuted. This is common practice.

Organizing Your Drawings

Since the section on drawings and the corresponding written portion is such a fine way to learn about your invention, try to do as

If You Are Writing a Provisional Application

Celebrate! You can stop writing when you finish this section and its related drawings. Now, you have only the cover letter and the other related documents to prepare. See the checklist on page 93.

Inventor's Journal

The newly released Inventor's-Journal® from IPT is perfect for first time inventors and unskilled artists.

It has a special 1/4-inch grid pattern with 1/32-inch marks that allows you to easily construct your perspective patent drawings.

The grid is designed so that when you copy your drawings on a dark setting the words "Do Not Reproduce" print through. Or, you can copy it on a light setting and no grid lines will appear at all. It's perfect for patent application drawings!

See the Appendix for more information.

Tracing Drawings

Since granted patents are published by the U.S. Patent Office, there is no copyright protection. Therefore, you can copy or trace over existing artwork to help expedite your efforts. If you are referencing "prior art" in your application, simply trace over the art from the referenced patent and include it in your application.

many sketches as you can. You can sometimes model your sketches after existing patents--perhaps even trace and re-sketch them.

As you compile your sketches, incorporate the following:

1. Arrange the drawings in a natural progression. Use the "story-telling" sequence.

2. The first drawing should illustrate the invention with a simple plan view or perspective view.

3. The subsequent drawings should show how it works (what is happening) in a natural progression. You may include some detailed sketches showing key attributes and embodiments.

4. Last, show variations on the theme. These drawings may include some design-arounds that may be less desirable but will help to broaden and clarify the broader scope of your inventive matter.

5. One of the drawings should illustrate the "preferred embodiments". You are legally obligated to reveal the preferred version of your invention in the patent application.

Using Numbers in Your Drawings

Except for prior art illustrations, drawings should be referenced using a numerical format. By adopting the following format, you will make it easier for your patent attorney's artist to do the final drawings.

1. On the first drawing, Fig. 1, begin the number sequence with either 1 or 10. Use only even numbers with your first sketches. Since it is easy to forget some description of an attribute, this will allow you to add it later by using the odd numbers you omitted.

2. For subsequent drawings, Figs. 2, 3 and so on, begin at the next multiple of 10...for instance, 20, 30, etc. leaving numerical gaps of all the odd numbers. As an example, if the last number you used in a drawing was 24, begin the next drawing at 30.

3. If you later draw a variation of an earlier drawing, use the same number reference for consistency.

4. When your invention has a right and a left side, use the same number for components on each side. On one side add an apostrophe (') after the number (referred to as a "prime"). For instance, the number on a left side component is 36, the number for the same component on the right side would be 36'.

5. You can also attach letters to the numbers when referring to similar drawings. This can be done when referencing variations on a theme. For instance, in Fig. 4 certain attributes are illustrated as 38, 41 and 41' and the same, very similar attributes in Fig. 7 are illustrated as 38a, 41a and 41a'.

Using Letters in Your Drawings

Letters are commonly used in two ways. One is to designate attributes used on prior art drawings. For instance, in the prior art example, Fig. 1A "M" refers to mouth, "T" refers to tab and "S" refers to support.

Letters can also be used to illustrate forces throughout the sketches. They are helpful as a means to repeat an action. For instance:

1. "A" for "air flow"
2. "V" for "vacuum"
3. "F" for "force"

When using letters in your drawings, refer to them in writing as "force F" or "air flow A".

Syntax

Generally speaking, you should use standard engineering and drafting terms in your drawings.

Here are some of the common syntax and symbols:

1. A line with an arrow references the entire unit
2. A lead line without an arrow references an individual element
3. A lead line may be broken out into several smaller lines to show the same or consistent elements
4. Obvious symbols for things like electrical components, building materials and hydraulics

Be as thorough as you can. Even patent attorneys and professional artists make errors in drawings from time to time. That may not be so bad. If the only thing the patent examiner objects to is that your drawings are not in compliance with the accepted norms, that is good news. Some think that it is good to let them find such errors so there is something in the application to reject.

I have seen many first-time inventors waste weeks, even months trying to learn all the minute details about how to write a patent application and prepare legal drawings. The result is almost always the same. They get frustrated and end up with an application that has an inadequate scope or, as we know, was filed too soon to cover the inventive matter, which was subsequently discovered during product development.

The only resolution is for them to find an attorney to make the proper corrections.

If you are an inventor, who desires to make money on his/her invention, why even waste the time doing this in the first place?

It is just as easy to model your patent application after another, follow the story-telling sequence, and have your attorney edit and file it in a timely manner. This strategic method is faster, more accurate and more cost effective than trying to patent the invention yourself.

Drawings

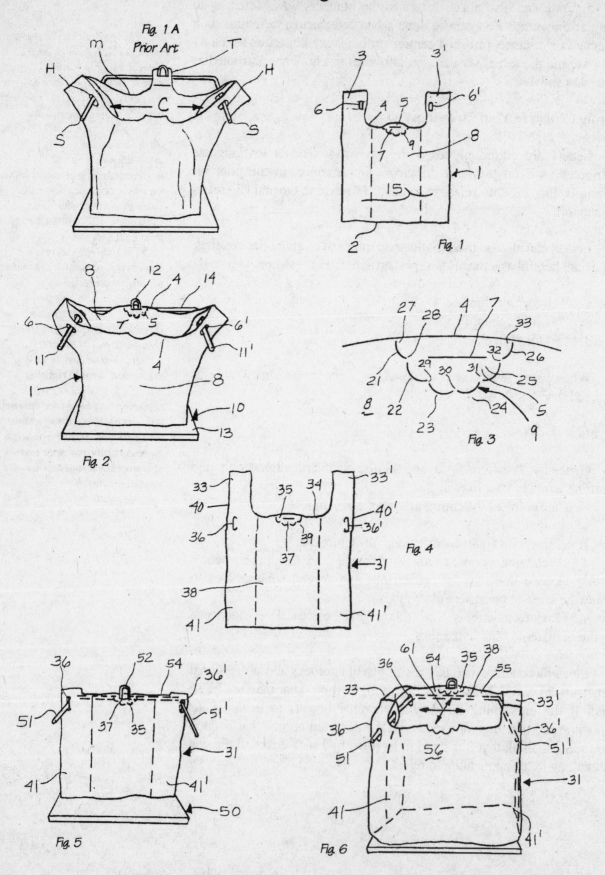

WRITING CLAIMS

This is at the heart of the patent protection you are seeking and the one area in which you would be wise to employ an experienced patent attorney. Let him/her write the final claims as accurately and as broadly as possible using correct legal language. However, before your attorney writes the claims, list them in simple English. Think carefully about the coverage that you need to be properly protected. You should know that some negotiation usually takes place with the patent office examiner. This is where your patent attorney can help a lot. He/she will probably have a claim-writing strategy in mind to maximize your protection. For instance, your attorney may consider extremely broad claims that "blanket the world" and then settle on a single "continent" during negotiation with the examiner.

Think ahead. Generally speaking, you should draft your claims as broadly as possible, but they should also be specific enough to be enforceable. To ensure maximum protection for your patent's claims, you will want to know these four key elements to claim structure:

Broad Claims

In summary, broad claims:

1. Give more coverage with a broader scope.

2. Are best, especially for totally new concepts. Velcro®, ZipLoc® bags and Kleenex® tissue are examples.

3. Must be carefully described, to avoid design-arounds. For instance, words such as "means of adjoinment" or "bonding means" should be used in place of "glue" or "paste".

4. Are vulnerable to subsequent improvements. Will the improvements be more important than the initial broad claims? For instance, the original ZipLoc® bags were a bit difficult to use, until they were made with the double and triple rails (a subsequent improvement patent over the original). They were also costly to make, until the manufacturer discovered how to extrude the rail profile right into the film, eliminating the entire step of bonding the two elements together. This too was a subsequent improvement patent.

5. Are generally more powerful than narrow ones. They are frequently called "dominant patents" when subsequent patents improve upon them.

*Drafting excellent claims is an art and takes experience. Learning the various ways to write and list claims is not easy. Having the claims you want--and **need**--will make or break your patent. Writing solid claims is how a patent attorney earns his/her fee.*

Claim Writing

Every experienced inventor I know uses the same method for claim writing. In simple English, he/she lists the claims as precisely as possible, to maximize the coverage. Then have your patent attorney write bulletproof claims in the application.

Narrow Claims

In summary, narrow claims:

1. Provide less overall coverage, since they tend to relate to more specific inventive details of existing products.
2. Are commonly seen as improvements to existing patents and product groups.
3. Are usually more vulnerable to design-arounds.
4. Can have a lot of power due to their specificity; hence they can be very valuable.

A simple example of the power of broad and narrow claims is:

- Patent 1, the first, dominant patent claims "a vehicle with 1 or more wheels".
- Patent 2, a more recent improvement patent claims "a vehicle with 4 wheels which is steerable". (It has a steering system.)

The broad coverage of Patent 1 covers all vehicles, including unicycles, regardless of whether they can be steered. In contrast, the narrower coverage of Patent 2 covers only those vehicles with four wheels and steering systems. You could argue that Patent 2 is more powerful than Patent 1 because without the ability to steer, Patent 1 is almost worthless. Consider that very few vehicles would be in use today if they could not be steered!

Independent Claims

Claims that "stand alone" are called "independent claims". This means that they contain the broadest possible inventive matter. In simple English, there are typically 1-4 independent claims in a patent when it is granted. Here are three examples of independent claims that might be found in three different patents:

- Claim 1.   A vehicle with 4 wheels.
- Claim 10.   A plastic bag with a reclosable bag mouth.
- Claim 20.   A non-tacky adhesive tape.

These independent claims have broad coverage, but are vulnerable to specific improvements. The improvements may be included in the same patent application as dependent claims.

Filing Pro Per Means Having a Patent with a Narrow Scope

Since the scope of a patent depends upon the breadth of its claims, this is an area in which inventors filing pro per (by themselves, without the assistance of a registered patent attorney or agent) invariably fail. They settle for claims that are simply too narrow to give them any real protection.

This is most unfortunate since at this late strategic point in the inventing/patenting phase, it could mean a complete waste of time and effort.

Think about it. Do you want to spend 18 months to two years trying to sell a product that ultimately has very narrow patent protection? That will be easy for much larger competitors to design around? Of course not.

Remember to follow the course in the Strategic Guide in the back of the book, and you won't have to.

By the time you are to this point, you should already have your marketing and manufacturing experts hired and sales generated.

Do you?

Dependent Claims

Dependent claims reference independent claims in the patent application. For instance, corresponding with the previous claims 1, 10 and 20:

- Claim 2. The vehicle in claim 1 whereas any two or more wheels are steerable.
- Claim 11. The plastic bag in claim 10 whereas said reclosable mouth means is a plastic profile zipper.
- Claim 21. The adhesive tape in claim 20 whereas the contact surface of said tape is a layer of ultra low-density polyethylene with a melt index less than 2, which layer will heat bond to other surfaces when exposed to temperatures in excess of 160 degrees.

Generally speaking, the best rule is to try to include the broadest possible coverage (independent claims) and include as many improvements as you can imagine (independent claims). Using the preceding vehicle example, you can see how the following series of claims empowers the patent and the products that can be made from it.

- Claim 1. A vehicle with one or more wheels.
- Claim 2. The vehicle of claim 1 whereas any two or more wheels are steerable.
- Claim 3. The vehicle of claim 1 whereas said wheels are made of rubber.
- Claim 4. The vehicle of claim 1 whereas any pair of wheels are at ends of an axle.
- Claim 5. The vehicle of claim 1 whereas said vehicle is made of metal.

The ability to write good claims comes with experience. What is more important is to have good patent counsel to write solid claims. You will be relying on these claims to protect your interests over the next 20 years. If there is one thing your patent attorney must do extremely well, it is to **make sure that you are protected with convincing claims.**

Written in simple English, the claims for the plastic bag example are:

What is claimed is:

1. A plastic sack with a detachable portion centrally located in the body of the bag, at the bag mouth.

2. The claim in 1 which includes a slit in the detachable portion.

Claim Writing

Based upon the review and the office action of the patent examiner, you may have an opportunity to actually expand upon the patent claim coverage. But don't assume this is automatic.

Once approved, you may be in a position to file a CIP (Continuation in Part) to apply the inventive matter to other related material.

Your patent attorney or agent will know exactly how to do this and how much broader it may expand the scope.

If you have been following the Strategic Guide model, and have sales and profits generated, to proceed with a C.I.P. will be an easy decision to make.

<u>Claims</u>

The simple English in the example uses broad language that attorney Bill Pavitt converted into legal claims. Some of the claims may appear duplicitous, but the key is to give your attorney all possibilities and combinations you can imagine.

In this particular patent application, the examiner accepted the legal claims written by Bill Pavitt. The patent issues on September 2, 1997--as U.S. Patent No. 5,662,225.

A Final Review

When you read the claims your attorney wrote in legal form, study them well to make sure you are covered. This is your last chance to add drawings and descriptions to improve upon the scope of the invention. Even if it takes another week to rewrite and include, do it now!

3. A plastic sack with two holes laterally spaced in its body and proximate to the bag mouth.

4. The claim in Fig. 3 with handles extending above the two laterally spaced holes.

5. A rack-style holder and bag whereas the bag body is supported by support rods, and retained by a detachable portion.

6. The claim in Fig. 5, with handles located at the outer corners.

Sometimes a patent attorney will include more claims than you may expect. This might be because you have overlooked some facets of the invention or perhaps the reasoning is what we spoke about earlier. That is, your patent attorney's strategy may be to "blanket the world" and "settle for a continent" in an attempt to give you the coverage you want in the first place.

A Patent Office examiner's job is to thoroughly peruse, analyze and evaluate your patent application and claims. If every claim were accepted, there would be no need to examine applications. It is the examiner's job to weed out claims that are obvious, anticipated or are simply prior art. Conversely, it is your patent attorney's job to prosecute and negotiate on your behalf to get the broadest possible coverage.

In this light, the strategy of some patent attorneys is to begin with incredibly broad claims knowing that the patent examiner will be rejecting them anyway. Then, he/she will negotiate with the examiner to get the real claims you wanted in the first place.

Regardless of the approach you and your patent counsel use, once the claims are written, you must review them and give the attorney your opinion and approval. It is your obligation to ensure that they accurately reflect your invention. Compare your simple English claims with the legal ones written by your attorney. Make sure you have not overlooked anything.

ABSTRACT

The abstract is the first page in your patent, once it is granted. It is a one-paragraph summary of your patent application. You will have a better idea of what to include in your abstract after the entire application has been written. So wait and write it last.

An abstract has little to do with the power or scope of a patent. It simply offers the reader a snapshot of the inventive matter in the patent. The abstract sometimes does not accurately disclose the true content of a patent. This is particularly true if one patent has been split-out into two or more applications. In such a case, you may find that one abstract covers both patents, although one may refer to a product or system and the other to a process of making the product.

The abstract for the previous draft is as follows:

Abstract

A bagging system comprised of a rack with support rods and a central retaining means and a bag pack which is mounted on the rack. The bag pack is of a T-shirt bag style with orifices laterally spaced in the outer edges of the bag body plus a centrally located detachable portion in the bag body. The orifices are mounted onto the bag rack support rods and the detachable portion is secured onto the retaining means. The result is a bag which is raised up and may be opened more widely for filling articles.

OATH OF INVENTORSHIP - POWER OF ATTORNEY

Once your regular patent application is written, it will be accompanied by an additional document, your Oath of Inventorship. In simple language, the Oath of Inventorship states that:

- I reside at the address listed on this document.
- I believe I am the original, first and sole inventor of ____(application title)_____.
- I acknowledge my duty to provide information material to this application.
- I claim foreign filing protection (if applicable).
- I hereby grant power of attorney to ____(your attorney's name)____.
- I hereby certify that all the above is true.

The power of attorney gives your patent attorney the right to file the application on your behalf and to subsequently prosecute it. Once the application is filed, the Patent Office will want to communicate only with the one person who is designated in the power of attorney.

SMALL ENTITY DECLARATION

If you are a small entity, file a "Declaration Claiming Small Entity Status", which allows you to file an application at one-half the cost of a large entity. Remember that a small entity is an independent inventor, a non-profit organization or a small business with 500 employees or less

Change of Entity Status

A common question: What happens if you have filed your patent application as a small entity and after the patent is pending or has been granted, you license it to a large entity?

The answer is: Once your entity status changes then all subsequent payments will then be as a large entity.

...Bill Pavitt, Esq.

(including all affiliates). Be careful, though. The law states that if you license a producer with more than 500 employees, your status will change to a large entity. If in doubt, consult with your attorney to determine your entity status.

8

PROTECTING YOUR RIGHTS

It is another problem-solving adventure...
at times disheartening, at times exciting!

KNOCK-OFFS, PATENT INFRINGEMENT, AND
THE CHESS GAME BEGINS

After all your efforts to induce a successful birth and pilot your product towards maturity and success, there may be others who will attempt to discredit you and your invention by making derogatory comments. Others may try to copy you via infringement of your patent. While copying your inventive art is a compliment of sorts, it can be a costly problem as well. Don't let these people or issues bother you. Just stay cool.

First, if you planned your invention and patent development well, built the right team and did all your marketing research, you know that your patent (and the resultant products) is a wonderful piece of intellectual property that promises growing value. Once your product is on the market, you may be perceived as a threat to those who currently own the market.

It can be painful to see another company blatantly copy your inventive ideas. Infringement on (theft of) your intellectual property feels the same as having your car stolen or your house robbed. Expect infringement to happen, but keep in mind that you are well positioned to combat it. Exactly what do you do?

HANDLING NEGATIVE COMMENTS

This is such a common occurrence that we must cover it in this book. Keep in mind that people who try to destroy you and your patent are usually misinformed. They may attempt to intimidate you into thinking that you do not have a valid patent. Others are jealous of creativity and want to discredit the original creations of others. Finally, some are motivated by greed and want to profit from your genius without compensating you. Most of these people are unaware of the numerous court decisions in the last 10-15 years that have been in favor of patent holders.

For some serious and yet light-hearted entertainment, here are some of the common comments you might hear and what they really mean:

"I've seen that before."

1. They do not mean that they have seen *exactly* your product before, but perhaps a similar one. For instance, regarding your revolutionary high-speed tortilla machine, they may mean that they have seen a tortilla machine before or;

2. They have seen a similar process before, but it was 5 years ago and not with tortillas, but in a tile manufacturing plant. Keep in mind that most laypeople do not understand what makes one product patentable over another.

3. If they truly claim to have seen what you created, get the details. If *exactly* what you have declared in your patent has been done before, your patent (or one or more of the claims) may be invalid. Ask where you can find one. Then you can determine if it is a similar product (97% chance), recent infringement (2.97% chance) or previously unknown prior art product (.03% chance).

"You can't patent that...it's too simple."

"You can't patent a hole in a plastic bag." Oh yes you can! Frequently, people look only at the simplicity of a hole in a bag and not at the outcome it produces. If the hole does something unique, we know it can be patented.

Pessimist's Point of View:
"Investing assets/money in a patent is only investing in a future lawsuit to protect/enforce the patent."

Optimist's Point of View:
"Investing assets/money in a patent grants one a solidly defined and protected piece of Intellectual Property that one can sell/assign or lease/license to a much larger entity to obtain a steady flow of vested income from rents/royalties from an entity that can afford to defend/litigate against infringers, if any"...(larger corporations have litigation war chests and insurance to cover such contingencies).
...Doug English, Patent Attorney

For instance, the holes placed in the right location in the plastic bag in the example in Chapter 7 produced a bag design that has been proven to allow users to load 20%-30% more merchandise. Furthermore, the holes in the plastic bag are of a special configuration that does not propagate tears in the thin plastic film.

Negative comments about simple patents are really compliments! Why? Because you received a patent on something so simple, yet so unobvious, and it does something so wonderful. In contrast, the positive person says the opposite: "Wow, it's so simple, why didn't they do it like this in the first place?"

"Your patent isn't valid."

This is another negative comment from someone trying to either put you down or intimidate you. The person is probably a little dense and also unaware of patent law. Even if the individual who makes this statement knows something about patents, do not be concerned. They must prove that the patent is invalid, and that will cost a lot of money. Your patent application has already been scrutinized by experts and was granted.

"Well, until you get a patent we'll go ahead and make the product."

This comment is usually made by a company larger than yours is. They may be trying to bully themselves into position. But once your patent is granted, and you give them notice, they can be liable for willful infringement. Willful infringement can be subject to treble damages. You can be in for a huge windfall!

"You just copied someone."

Anyone who says this does not have a clue. If they are trying to insult you, consider laughing, because the insult applies to their intelligence.

POSITIONING YOUR RESPONSES

Regardless of the negative comments you hear, having a patent (or patent pending) puts you in the stronger position. The burden of proof to invalidate your patent is on the infringer. In addition, it is extremely costly to pursue such a case and the chances of winning are in your favor. Remember that over 95% of all patent infringement matters are settled before going to court. Of the patent infringement suits taken to court, 80% are decided in favor of the patentee.

"Your Patent Isn't Valid"

This is one of my personal favorites. I have heard this comment time and again, but no speaker has ever challenged the validity of my patents in court. This comment is mostly an intimidation tactic.
...Bob DeMatteis

YOUR PATENT INFRINGEMENT STRATEGY

When your patent is infringed, it does not mean you have to give up or abandon your rights. Regardless of the size of the infringing company, you can prevail if your patent has legitimate claims.

Keep in mind that patent infringement does not have to be a bad experience. It frequently has a very positive outcome. In a few cases, it can even become a gold mine.

When infringement occurs, several issues will determine your best strategy. They are:

1. **Your invention development strategy.** Are you planning on developing, manufacturing and marketing the invention yourself or will you be licensing it?

2. **The size of the infringing company and how many are infringing.** You will probably have an entirely different strategy if there are several small infringing companies as opposed to a few larger ones. Remember infringement includes those manufacturing, using and selling products under the scope of your patent.

The inventor of the sewing machine was not Singer but Elias Howe. Howe had difficulty marketing his invention, but Singer--a brilliant marketer--went ahead and infringed Howe's patent and created an empire.

Howe sued Singer and was granted a royalty of $25 per sewing machine!

After all was said, Howe didn't do too badly for not having a means of selling his invention.

3. **Your patent's integrity and the nature of the infringement.** Is your patent solid with excellent claims that are being infringed? Is the infringement literal or would it fall under the Doctrine of Equivalence? If it is literal infringement, it's a lot tougher for an infringer to challenge.

4. **How much money is involved?** Is the infringement of minor or major consequences? Does it represent annual sales of $20,000 or $20 million?

5. **The financial condition of the infringers.** Are the infringing companies able to defend themselves?

6. **Your financial condition.** Are you able to afford a patent infringement suit? If you cannot afford to hire an attorney, get one to represent you on a contingency basis. Providing that the scope and integrity of your patent are adequate, finding a contingency attorney should not be difficult.

WHEN INFRINGEMENT OCCURS

Since the statute of limitations allows you 6 years to take action, you have plenty of time to respond. Don't panic. You may want to take several years to respond. Here is what you do:

1. **Find out everything you can about the infringing product.** Get a sample of it, look it over carefully and determine if it is indeed an

infringement. You cannot press a claim for a product that does not infringe. This could result in a huge damage claim against you.

2.   **Send a sample of the infringing product to your attorney.** He/she can confirm your suspicions.

3.   **Find out everything you can about the infringing parties.** Since this includes all those manufacturing, using and selling products under the scope of your patents, make a list of all manufacturers, distributors, sales companies, individuals and end users. What are their intentions? Do all of these entities know they are infringing your patent? Are any of them purposely infringing?

Is an infringer the leader in the industry in which your product represents a serious threat to their sales? Are they an aggressive company trying to cash in on your success in a big way? Are they a small company trying to cash in on your success in a small way?

Get all the inside information you can. Perhaps they are responding to their customers' requests for your products without regard to your patent(s). Take good notes on what you hear from others in the field. Try to get the infringer's financial report to determine their current economic strength.

4.   **How big is the infringement problem?** After investigating the infringing companies, find out the magnitude of the infringement. How many units have been sold? What is the sell price?

5.   **How will they respond to your actions?** Try to learn if the infringing companies really need your invention or if they would switch if forced to do so. Will they try to protect their market share at all costs? Will they want to continue making, selling or using the product in the future?

DECIDING ON A PLAN OF ATTACK

Once you have accumulated all available facts, you will be able to determine the nature and timing of your action. In a strategy session with your legal counsel, you can make some sound decisions. Here are some general points to consider:

1.   Use a strategy that meshes with your invention development strategy. For instance, if you are granting non-exclusive licenses, your tack will be a lot different than if you are going into business with partners.

Patent Infringement Counsel

One reason I prefer using a highly qualified patent attorney to file and prosecute my patent applications is because if infringement occurs, this same attorney will be familiar with my patent, its claims and its potential weaknesses, if any. An experienced patent attorney can help you plan your strategy and turn an infringement issue into a happy ending.
...Bob DeMatteis

Ironically, patent infringement is usually good news...not bad.
Why? Well sooner or later, the infringer is going to have to address the issue. In today's business climate, we know that patent infringement is a serious issue and record judgments have been granted in favor of the patent holder.
Your job--from the onset--is to make certain your patent's coverage--its scope--is going to be interpreted as broadly as possible. Don't allow for any margin of error.
...Bob DeMatteis

Willful Infringement

Remember that if you can prove willful infringement, the damages will be substantial. Provable, malicious infringement has recently resulted in several gargantuan monetary rewards in favor of patent holders. If you can locate an attorney who is willing to take your case on a contingency basis, you may be in for some real windfall profits!

Any evidence that supports willful infringement can result in treble damages.

A good way to inform a producer it is infringing is by sending a letter referencing your patent, and offer it for license.

A Creative Strategy to Stop Infringement

In one particular case in which I was counsel for a patent holder, we sued a small company that was infringing my client's patent.

In order to protect itself, the small company hired a very large well-known law firm to defend it.

Not long afterward, the small company's cost to defend itself rose to over $1 million. Unable to pay, it was forced out of business.

So, instead of stopping the infringement, the defendant forced itself right out of business altogether.

...Doug English

2. Take a position that will improve your and your development team's position and may even improve the credibility of the patent. Weigh the short-term financial gains against your long-term objectives.

3. If you wish to grant non-exclusive licenses and there are several infringers who you are certain want to continue to make, use or sell products under the scope of your patents, you may want to start by "picking a fight" with one or two of the weaker ones who cannot afford litigation costs. You can license them and set a precedent. If they are small enough companies, they are unlikely to want to spend their limited resources challenging your patent's validity. This will provide some income and set a precedent for other infringers to follow later.

4. You may be able to discuss the patent infringement issue with the head of the infringing company. If so, can you turn it into an opportunity? Just because someone is infringing your patents does not mean he/she is your enemy. You may be able to amicably discuss the problem and conclude your visit with the intent to enter into a long-term, mutually advantageous license agreement.

5. If you have to take on a "giant" corporation with significant financial resources and your resources are limited in comparison, take them on last. If not, you will need an absolute knowledge of infringement and should have your counsel working for you on a contingency basis. You can also look for angles that may be easier. For instance, perhaps the user is not as large as the manufacturer and you could start your infringement claim there.

6. If you take on the giant last, after defending your position with several smaller companies, and perhaps licensing them, you will be better able to beat the giant corporation if the case goes to court.

7. If you have greater financial resources than the infringers, take on the largest, most visual infringer(s) first. When your victory over the strongest infringer is made public, you will be in a powerful position to quickly stop the smaller ones and get them to enter into license agreements as well.

WHAT IF YOU ARE IN AN EXPANDING, START-UP INDUSTRY?

It is interesting that infringers can actually help you "run-up" sales at no cost to you. If you are trying to overtake an old-fashioned industry with your modern, patented products, it is a lot easier to do so with more than one company selling the change. Infringers can help you do this. Delaying infringement issues for a few years may be a tactic you will want to consider.

BE NICE OR FIGHT?

There are four general approaches to addressing infringement issues with infringers. In order of "niceness", they are:

1. **Nice:** You send them a letter offering a license and letting them know that they are infringing.

2. **Not as nice:** Your attorney can send a letter offering a license and letting them know that they are infringing.

3. **Willing to fight:** You can file a complaint in court that will ask for substantial money, based upon what you have learned.

4. **Let's fight:** You can have your attorney file a cease and desist order.

THE ROLE OF YOUR ATTORNEY

However you approach a patent infringement issue, consult with your attorney and coordinate your activities through him/her. Unless you have significant financial resources, begin by evaluating your position and strategy before incurring legal bills. Ultimately, you will determine how to proceed to reach the most advantageous outcome. Get all the information you can about the extent of the infringement and who the infringers are before you meet with your legal counsel.

WHAT TO DO IF SOMEONE SAYS YOUR PATENT INFRINGES THEIRS

While not very common, it does happen. Your patent may have "slipped through the cracks" and there may be an unknown "dominant patent" which it infringes. If someone sends you notice or points out a patent that yours may be infringing, here is what to do:

1. Don't panic. Get a copy of the patent to learn the date it was filed and the date it was granted. Does the filing date pre-date your patent? If not, theirs may be infringing yours. If your filing date precedes theirs, you are probably in a good position.

2. Read the abstract, skim the summary and read the claims. Does the patent *really* talk about the same subject matter or does it reflect similar technology being used in a different field? If their claims refer to a water-cooled apparatus and yours is air cooled, there probably is no patent infringement.

Being a Litigant in a Lawsuit

If one should be in the unfortunate situation of being a litigant in a lawsuit, try to picture a cow with the plaintiff pulling the cow's horns and defendant pulling the cow's tail, the judge standing aside watching with humor, and plaintiff's and defendant's counsel gleefully smiling whilst they take turns milking the cow. This will remind one that despite one's differences, it is in plaintiff's and defendant's best interest, though not their counsel's, to quickly negotiate an agreement they can live with, albeit not with glee.
...Doug English, Patent Attorney

3. If you still believe that there may be a conflict, read the claims again--slowly and carefully--with your product nearby. As you read the claims, follow the language and decide if _every_ point in any single claim covers your product. Remember the Doctrine of Equivalence.

4. Send a copy of the patent with a written explanation to your patent attorney for his/her review. You need not request a written, legal opinion at this time. Just ask your attorney if he/she thinks there is a serious problem.

WHAT IF YOUR PATENT INFRINGES ANOTHER?

If your patent appears to infringe the other patent and your attorney agrees, you have several choices. First, if it is an older patent, call the USPTO and verify that the maintenance fees are current (some phone numbers to call are 703-308-9752, 703-308-1156 and 703-308-5068). If not, the patent is no longer valid. Confirm this with your attorney.

Next, you can order the entire file (called the file wrapper) from the U.S. Patent Office. This will help clarify the scope of the claims and determine if there is some vulnerability to the patent and its claims.

If you still infringe, decide if you can make a modification that avoids the other patent. Reread the infringing claims and try to extract the important "operable" words that must be included in the infringed product...that possibly do not need to be included in the way you make your product. (Review the details about how to do this on pages 118 and 119.)

You can also consider licensing the other patent. Is it of mutual benefit to cross-license one another?

If you conclude that you are infringing another patent, but the owner of the patent has not sent you notice, get the answers to these questions:

- Who owns the patent?
- Where do they live?
- Are the maintenance fees up to date?
- Do you think they know that you are infringing? If so, why have they not taken action?
- Are they interested in pursuing the patent and its protection?

Most patent owners, whether they are large corporations or independent inventors, are not interested in legal battles. If their patent is not something they are actively pursuing and you want to actively pursue it, you can probably reach an amicable settlement. A license from them will only strengthen the value of your patent position.

Abandoned Patents

You can ask the Patent Office Maintenance Fee Department to fax you a status report on the payment of maintenance fees on a particular patent. Just to make sure--and to have it for your records.

This could be helpful to put your manufacturing and marketing partners at ease.

The fax number at the Maintenance Department to request copies is 703-308-5077.

When Infringement and Legal Action is Eminent

Try to avoid this at all costs. You don't need to go spending your good time and money on fighting others in court.

Ask yourself what would be a Win/Win situation? How can we both benefit from this unfortunate situation?

Do all you can to spirit the other entity into wanting a mutually beneficial solution.

After all, as you already know, two heads are exponentially better than one.

It is also possible that a larger corporation that owns many other patents may own the infringed patent. They may have little interest in pursuing it because they subsequently developed other technology they consider a much larger market. They may think that the sales and profits are too small for them to develop. Hence, the large corporation may license the patent to you. They may even intend to abandon the patent (by not paying the maintenance fees) in light of their focus on high-volume projects.

PROBLEMS BECOME OPPORTUNITIES

In your invention development process, you overcame problems and turned them into opportunities. With patent infringement issues, you must show the same patience, creativity and savvy.

As an inventor, you have an obligation to yourself and your development partners to continue to improve and take your inventions to the next level. As long as you continue to develop the next generation of products from your initial concept, you will propel your efforts past other competitive (or problematic) patents.

In your patenting efforts, remember that:

The greatest rejection in patenting is to never have been infringed. You will best learn the wisdom of securing patents by experiencing the tribulations of infringement.

Once you have attained your first inventing-patenting success, continue to improve the product and invent into the future. As you improve your product, you will also improve your position. You will get better and better and become the premier, innovative expert in your field. The more you do so, the less likely it is that there will ever be infringement issues.

If after all your hard earned effort, you find that it is just not worth the effort to overcome the infringement of another patent, this should still be good news. What would be worse than continuing the pursuit of a project that will evolve into a serious problem?

Instead, cut your losses and spend your time on developing another product.

PART THREE
MANUFACTURING & MARKETING

9

INVENTION MARKETING BASICS

*Marketing new ideas and inventions requires
lots of effort and takes a special kind of team.*

THE RIGHT INVENTION MARKETING PHILOSOPHY

Marketing new inventions requires a philosophy much different than marketing existing products or new ones that are spin-offs of the same old line. Marketing new ideas and concepts requires having excellent contacts and a strong team effort. There are so many details to consider at this point that your team's effort will be crucial to your success. You will always pilot the effort, but as you will see, the team will eventually take over most of the responsibilities, expand itself and really make things happen!

Before the first test marketing and subsequent product launch, your invention must be packaged and priced, with the appropriate brochures and specification sheets ready to go. Depending on the marketing strategy you choose, much of this work will be done by your licensees, with your guidance. These basic marketing tools will reflect the positioning of your new invention. Your product's positioning will create a new market and lots of excitement. You will want to carefully incorporate several possible marketing advantages to launch your new

Nothing is more exciting than working with your marketing and manufacturing experts when launching a new innovation.

As your marketing expert tells you about the millions in sales that can be generated, the manufacturer is gearing up for mass-production. All the while, you are waiting in the wings, watching the excitement build!

167

invention. In other words, you will want to give your customers as many good reasons to buy it as possible.

Your marketing philosophy will dovetail with your Customer Driven Innovation philosophy. Perfectly, in fact. All the attributes you have created in your CDI invention, including your mindset, will now be reflected in how you take your new invention to market. It is best that the members of your marketing and support team share your CDI philosophy.

CDI, MARKET CREATION AND ESTABLISHING YOUR NICHE

Creating new markets through innovative products goes hand-in-hand with inventing and Customer Driven Innovation. Through CDI, you can create niches that make it difficult for competitors, large or small, to adapt. In his book, *Thriving on Chaos*, Tom Peters writes about "niche or be niched". This trend in the 90's and into the 21st century carries a clear-cut message for survival. New ideas that give producers the ability to capture new niche markets are the winning ideas that will shape tomorrow's business climate.

Think about it. Commodity product lines are usually dominated by generic giants. If you can secure a small niche (just 1%) in a billion-dollar market, it is not a threat to the dominant competitors. If the niche is based on added value to the customer, it will be much easier for the smaller producer to protect it. Focus on your niche, turn your inventions into the most wonderful products you can imagine and then let sales rise via "customer pull-through".

By using a CDI approach and tailoring inventions to value-added, high-performance, niche markets, you should be successful for years to come. You may even see your niche grow into a major market share!

THE CDI PHILOSOPHY IS TAILORED
TO SMALLER, FLEXIBLE ENTITIES

Unlike many larger corporations, inventors and smaller entities are not bogged down with bureaucracy, large decision-making committees and detached R&D departments. Small entities are inherently more flexible and naturally more entrepreneurial. They can invariably beat the large, inflexible ones to market with new innovations. Small entities can make decisions, gear up, adapt and follow through much faster than their large, generic competitors. While large firms typically take three years and more to release new products, small ones can do it in a fraction of the time and at a fraction of the cost.

The large, independent and detached R&D departments of corporate giants can be easily out-maneuvered by small innovative entities with their hands-on R&D operations. Besides, the focus of

All New Products Start as Niches

Remember that every new invention, regardless of its nature, begins as a niche product. Small cars in America, lasers, even TV's, computers and cellular telephones are examples. The continual improvements of these inventions catapulted them into becoming generic products.

The key is to focus on the niche and let it grow through customer pull-through.

America Does It Best

Our country is flooded with success stories of start-up entrepreneurs--Eli Whitney, Levi, Edison, Singer, Ford, Hoover, Jobs, Wozniak--because it is in our nature.

The team of Benjamin Franklin, Monroe, Madison and Washington, et al, set the theme over 200 years ago by literally inventing a new country, America.

Franklin was a supreme inventor (bifocals, electricity and much more), Madison and Monroe were administrators, and Washington (who established the U.S. Patent Office in 1793) was the field marshal who pointed the way.

large corporate R&D departments is frequently *not* on customer-driven innovations, but on scientific and engineering improvements. These improvements are frequently directed toward production processes and cost-cutting designs and not CDI.

In addition, large R&D departments frequently have a propensity to over-engineer new products, sometimes to the product's ultimate death. It is easy for them to take years to release new products and exceed their budget.

Another factor that contributes to the ability of small entities to out-innovate large ones is that many large firms hire uncreative people to maintain existing business, not creative people to create new business. Couple this defensive posture with the bureaucracy and inflexibility of larger corporations and it is understandable that it is almost impossible for them to innovate and launch anything new.

Small, flexible, entrepreneurial entities are also better equipped to sell new, innovative products into new markets, instead of trying to nibble on existing market share. Unlike their larger competitors, the focus of small entity sales forces is on selling value-added innovations that benefit customers. These smaller (sometimes considered "guerilla warfare" type of sales units) can adopt the CDI philosophy, almost always out-maneuver the giants and seize new opportunities.

One thing is for certain: independent inventors and small companies cannot create new markets if their innovations are merely simple modifications of existing generic products. In the last several years in the United States, we have seen a continual onslaught of cheap, generic products. These products come from domestic giants, as well as producers from all over the world. Generic producers are literally in a dogfight, struggling to maintain the remnants of dwindling market share. Any business that does not differentiate its product line today and prepare for tomorrow, will be left out.

Every inventor must learn to create new products that are truly Customer Driven Innovations. They must learn to create innovations that the large, generic entities cannot easily duplicate. To do this, inventors need a narrow and flexible marketing focus on innovative products that *customers want to buy*. To be successful in the world of invention and innovation today, CDI must be your key inventive focus.

CHOOSING THE RIGHT SIZED MARKETING AND MANUFACTURING PARTNERS

Ted Levitt's product concept flower revealed in Chapter 3 shows the product focus potential of both generic and innovative firms. To expand on this concept, the long-term strategy of traditional U.S. manufacturing companies focusing on generic products tends to look like the flower in Fig. 9-1. In contrast, the long-term activities of smaller inventive, innovative companies tend to look like the flower in

A Smart Mega-Giant Corporation That Knows!

Worthington Industries of Columbus, Ohio has about 6000 employees, yet no more than 100 at any single location. Mr. John McDonnel, Chairman of the Board of Worthington says, "Get more than 100 employees under the same roof and the quality and service go to hell."

As a result of being structured like a small, fast and flexible company, Worthington Industries has become well known for its quality, service and innovative ability to solve its customers' problems.

Fig. 9-2--focusing on the augmented and potential product. This is where your focus should be.

Figure 9-1   **Figure 9-2**

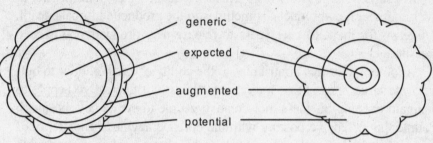

generic
expected
augmented
potential

Working with Mega-giant Corporations

When approaching mega-giant or giant corporations as potential marketers, you will find that they will be more amenable to talking to you after your patent(s) have been granted.

But if you have a patent pending, you can use an approach that Yujiro Yamamoto has used to a great deal of success. That is, to enter into a short-term (6 months to a year) contractual agreement with them to mutually develop the technology.

During the duration of the project, confidential information is then exchanged on an item by item, need-to-know basis. In other words, the two parties will exchange just enough confidential information in order to complete the project.

Upon completion of the project, the royalty stream would begin...and most likely at a reduced rate. But this is usually a good outcome since their volume is so great.

...Bob DeMatteis

Keep in mind that it is very difficult for large, cumbersome, established firms to change their production philosophy. It usually takes years and sometimes never happens! From the examples in Fig. 9-1 and Fig. 9-2, it is easy to see that there are excellent opportunities for inventors and their associated small, flexible marketing entities to cash in through innovation. For start-up businesses, this example helps to focus in exactly the right direction. When interviewing potential manufacturing and marketing companies, focus your efforts on those with the right philosophy, just like yours.

Table 9-1 illustrates the size of companies, based on annual sales volume. Following is a summary of the manufacturing and marketing position and philosophy in each category.

Mega-giants. The mega-giants tend to be the generic producers in any given field in industry. They dominate the industry, have in-house R&D departments and a defensive posture towards their existing products. They are rarely, if ever, interested in licensing outside innovations and inventions. If nothing else, it would be embarrassing to admit that an outsider did a better job at creating future innovations than their own, billion dollar in-house R&D team. You would be wise not to waste your time pursuing these companies as manufacturing or marketing partners.

Giant Corporations. Like the mega-giants, giant corporations tend to be generically based producers. They too have in-house R&D departments and all the same innovation- and invention-related ills as their big brothers. Don't waste too much time with them. The chances that they will license your ideas are not very good.

Large Corporations. These companies represent excellent licensing potential. Most large corporations are not the dominant leaders in their fields, but are niche players, focusing on value-added benefits. They generally do not have in-house R&D departments (the exceptions might be those that are drug- or computer-related) and are more willing to listen to outside inventors and innovators. They are also more accessible at the top level, which is where you want to strike a deal. This sized entity usually has well-established contacts and plenty of cash to invest into new product developments. You want to pursue them.

Medium-sized Corporations. Just like large corporations, they are excellent licensing potentials. They are also niche players in the market and usually eager to look for ways they can capture more sales via new, innovative products. Rarely do they have R&D departments and thus, they make excellent targets for inventors and innovators. Medium-sized companies frequently are younger, more aggressive companies that like to make things happen. The top management level is usually quite accessible and will listen to you. Likewise, they should have adequate cash to invest in your new projects.

Table 9-1

Company Size	Annual Sales
Mega-giant Corporations	$5 billion +
Giant Corporations	$250 million – $5 billion
* Large Corporations	$50 – $250 million
* Medium-sized Corporations	$10 – $50 million
* Small Corporations	$3 – $10 million
"Mom and Pops"	Under $3 million

Small Corporations. These too can be fine licensing candidates. Many are newer companies with fresh ideas and are eager to carve out their niche. Your ideas and inventions may be perfect for their growth plans. They do not have R&D departments and it will not be difficult to talk to the top people. The only problem you may find is that they may not have the necessary finances to effectively launch a new idea. But they usually make up for it with the willingness to try hard!

"Mom and Pops". Under most circumstances, you can eliminate them as potential candidates. They are usually too busy trying to survive or to grow. They may also find it difficult to fund a new invention with their limited working capital. If your invention is simple and small, you can consider them, but then you must also ask yourself if the sales of your invention are too small to consider pursuing.

Mega-Giant Corporations as Manufacturers

While they may not be your number one choice, they can be excellent suppliers for certain high volume products.

Due to their large size and their "generic manufacturing" mentality (not fast and flexible), it will require more of your and your marketing experts' time to help get them ready for market.

But generally speaking, once they are in place they can be formidable!

Project Manager

When discussing start-up with your manufacturer, make sure that a "dedicated Project Manager" is appointed to lead the manufacturing effort. This could be a plant manager (a small company), an engineer (a large corporation), or a product manager (a giant corporation). If this individual's first responsibility is your project, that is even better yet.

MAKE YOUR MANUFACTURING AND MARKETING PHILOSOPHY "SMALL"

Smaller entities can quickly maneuver and bring about the birth of new innovations. How large can these entities be? Like Worthington Industries, no facility (or entity) should exceed 100 employees. This includes all work shifts, which invariably must work together toward a common goal. If your manufacturing and marketing interviewees have more than 100 employees, you should be cautious. Small entities should reflect the following attributes:

- A flat organizational chart
- Common CDI goals and missions
- Open and swift communication among *all* employees
- Hands-on R&D, management and supervision

Common goals in your marketing and manufacturing philosophy should reflect your CDI mission and the assurance that your customers are satisfied with your superior products and services.

FAST, FLEXIBLE NICHE COMPANIES

Smaller companies must be fast and flexible too. Fig. 9-4 is a chart identifying various marketing philosophies. Make a list of the dominant and less-than-dominant suppliers and evaluate them based on their positions. The companies in the niche marketing category are the best potential partners. Any company that rates higher than 5 should understand the importance of CDI and will be more receptive to hearing about and discussing your inventions.

Your challenge is to seek out and create niches you can protect.

Figure 9-4 Niche Marketing Philosophy

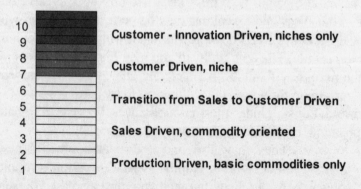

Inventors Are Underdogs

If you find that you prefer to cheer on the underdog in sports activities, you have the true spirit of an inventor/innovator.

Starting out as a niche is like being the underdog in the marketplace.

But don't worry, just like in sports, there are many excellent examples of being the underdog and winning the "whole enchilada" in the marketplace.

A Small, Fast and Flexible History Lesson

There are many examples in history of being small, fast and flexible in history and being successful.

Centuries ago, David slayed Goliath...just to prove it was possible.

In the 17th century, the small, fast ships in the English Navy outmaneuvered the much larger Spanish Naval ships and thus dominated the seas.

Today, smaller, faster sports teams frequently win over the much larger ones...whether it is football, basketball, baseball or hockey...even boxing! Remember..."the bigger they are, the harder they fall".

The niches that are the most profitable, the easiest to protect and that have long-term security, are those created by unique and highly specialized *Customer Driven Innovations.*

With the commodity giants committed to large runs, look for the niches you can secure through smaller marketing companies and smaller, flexible manufacturing processes. It may take some time to find the right marketing and manufacturing partners, but be patient. Having the right partners is so very important--especially if the future of your invention depends on it!

Small manufacturing entities can also quickly run down the learning curve of efficiency. In fact, it is not uncommon for niche manufacturers to have lower scrap rates and faster changeover times than their large competitors. This is exactly the type of match you want.

YOUR MARKETING EXPERT BECOMES YOUR R&D LIAISON

The sales-marketing expert, one of the leaders of your team, can use his/her sales force to gather valuable R&D information to improve existing products and develop new ones. The focus of a smart sales company is on information gathering and innovation liaison and ultimately becomes counseling or advising, as new ideas and technologies unfold.

In the early stages of new CDI developments, sales associates should work closely with the customer. This hands-on activity serves as a valuable training vehicle. With industrial and commercial applications, their initial activities may include gathering information from the customer's operations, manufacturing, and even accounting departments. With retail-oriented products, this will mean close contacts with the managers and supervisors who sell your products and the end users themselves. The objective is to identify problematic areas, which we know are really CDI opportunities! The more sales gets involved with the customer, the more you will all learn and be able to assist with new CDI developments in the field.

Your sales team can arrange key meetings between customer personnel. They can also arrange the initial testing of new innovations and monitor the results in industrial and commercial applications. After its first success, the team will be in a position to use this process, and much of what they learned, with other customers. After a while, your sales force will become the premier experts in the field. They will be called on to counsel customers, new and old, on all important future product developments.

As a marketing expert, I like to look at any product from the viewpoint of how to maximize its sales.

It is easy for me to tell you that you have a great idea and that it is better than what is out there. But there must be some significant sales advantage that the others don't have that will make it sell like crazy.

Instead of marketing a product that can represent a niche of 1%-2% of an existing market, I like to figure out how to position a product so that it can become 10%-20% of the market, or more.

Better yet, I like to see how the product can be adapted and modified in order to create its own niche and can seize 100% of it.

...Joe "Truckload" Bowers

Timely Feedback

If you truly want to develop a new product that will be a big success and make a lot of money, listen to your marketing experts.

Even if the problems they state seem insurmountable ...overcome them and you will be all alone in the sales leadership position.

Remember that if anything is too easy to do...it most likely will have already been done. Only those things that are unique and seem almost impossible to achieve make huge impacts in the marketplace and our lives.

...Joe Justin, Pinnacle Group

IDENTIFY YOUR TARGET MARKETS...
WHICH ONE ARE YOU GOING TO CAPTURE FIRST?

In concert with your sales experts, you will want to narrowly define your initial target market. While you may look for opportunities in the various related fields of your invention, you should identify one for your first product launch. It is very important that you have clear-cut specifications for each target audience that may be within the scope of your invention. Your invention's specifications--size, shape, etc.--must be broad enough so that the product can be produced cost effectively, but specific enough so that it is not generic. Your sales experts can help. Don't let your manufacturing processes dictate mediocrity, when creativity and uniqueness are so important.

CATEGORIZING YOUR SPECIFIC NICHE

You know that your new invention occupies a small niche that your marketing team will try to capture. You know the niche, you have described it, now you must clearly categorize it. Successful marketing campaigns focus on a category and then describe it. If you cannot describe your niche's category in a few words, the customer is not likely to remember it.

Customers remember categories quite easily. They will identify with your product and feel good about buying it. For instance, here are some marketing categories that also correspond with the company's innovation and product-related categories:

- High-quality suit: Hart, Shafner and Marks
- Affordable T-shirt: Fruit of the Loom
- The safe automobile: Volvo
- The low-priced automobile: Hyundai
- The thick pasta sauce: Prego
- The al dente pasta: Barilla
- The only auto alarm police use: Lo-jack
- The "un-cola": Seven-Up
- The baking soda toothpaste: Arm and Hammer
- The whitening toothpaste: Rembrandt
- The tastiest avocado: Haas
- The crunchiest corn chip: Dorito

No matter what your category, you have to clearly define your niche and then market accordingly. Focus your advertising efforts on identifying your category and clarifying why customers want to buy from your category.

The first target market I look for is the one that has the most unique sales position. It is the one that can be captured with the least amount of resistance from the existing suppliers and can be held onto afterward. This is usually accomplished with some sort of technological advantage that the existing suppliers just don't have.

The advantage can be in the form of manufacturing processes that are different from the existing competitors' processes, or it could be a certain marketing advantage, such as having a better, lower cost distribution means.

I always look for those unique sales angles.

...Joe Justin, Pinnacle Group

Before WWII only 25% of homes had refrigerators. After WWII it soared to 95%! With market saturation in the early 1950's, the refrigerator manufacturers looked for other markets and began developing air conditioners for automobiles. This new product expanded into window box air conditioners for homes and businesses, and then the central air conditioners we know today.

HOW TO DETERMINE A WHOLESALE AND RETAIL PRICE

Determine wholesale and retail prices early on. The best way to determine what the market will bear is to discuss it with your sales and marketing expert. Then make sure your manufacturing partner can do what is necessary to get it made at the right cost.

Most new inventions should be priced close to a competitive product or substitute. You can't assume that a new product will be so great that consumers will spend double the price just to enjoy its benefits. Sometimes this is true, but not usually.

The worst way to determine price is to calculate how much it costs to manufacture and then mark it up accordingly. It is usually best to do it backwards, and then figure out how to get it made with all the right attributes at the right price. Remember, most competitive suppliers in an industry are priced about the same. It does you no good to simply make something and offer it for sale at just any price. If it is too costly to make, you may have no sales at all.

Also remember that if you license one company to manufacture and another company to market, you must include your royalties and the sales commissions as part of the cost. Specific strategies regarding this philosophy are covered in detail in Chapters 11-14.

Industrial/Commercial Price Scenarios

After you have discussed pricing with your sales/marketing expert, you can use the chart in Figure 9-5 as a guide to determining what the cost should be. Keep in mind that these cost analyses are general and do not apply to all industries. Also, some products within an industry tend to have larger discount structures than others. Your sales expert can quickly tell you the current discount structures.

Independent inventors and entrepreneurs literally invented the world in which we live. In every major city, marquees dot the skyline with the names of those who, themselves, once were mere up-starts: Edison; Bell; Ford...the list is endless.
...Donald Grant Kelly, Director, U.S. Patent Office

KISS
(Keep it Simple, Stupid)

Keep your pricing scenarios and structures simple. Let your manufacturers pay all the associated costs, since they must do the billing of the finished product. They are used to doing it.
Just let them know what to include in the cost and they can quickly figure it out for you.
If you are a novice at business, don't get into an administrative nightmare and try to buy, sell, warehouse, pay commissions and ship.

Figure 9-5 Industrial / Commercial Cost Model

Sell price (to end user customer):	$10.00
Distributor cost (25% volume discount):	7.50
Less terms (2% 10 days)	- .15
Less freight (5% is a median cost)	- .38
Less royalties (3%)	- .23
Less commission (5%)	- .38
Net sales price:	$ 6.36
Manufacturer's cost (10% profit):	$ 5.73

As illustrated in Fig. 9-5, most industries use "discount schedules" as opposed to "mark-ups". Talk in terms of discounts, since this is what distributors and dealers will most likely want to know.

In the industrial/commercial model, the manufacturer is billing the distributor direct and the manufacturer's actual cost ($5.73) is not really of interest to you. All you know is that the sell price to the distributor must include all royalty, commission and related costs.

Make sure that the price a distributor quotes to you and your marketing experts includes the terms used in the industry, plus payment of freight, royalties and commissions. Based on the preceding model, the price a manufacturer should quote to you is $7.50, the price the distributor is going to pay. When talking with end users who may be purchasing from the distributor, be careful to quote the end user price of $10, not the distributor cost.

Another common industrial/commercial scenario is for large end user customers to purchase direct from the manufacturer. In this event, have a sliding scale based on volume. The greater the volume, the larger the discount. Using the model in Fig. 9-5, it is safe to say that the sell price to the end user would be about $10 in small quantities (there'll be extra freight and handling in small shipments), and about $7.50 in large quantities. There might even be 3-4 price breaks as well.

Royalties and commissions are usually paid on the sell price from the manufacturer, whether it is to the distributor or end user. It is very difficult to try to collect royalties in any other way. How would it be done? Would you invoice every end user separately? Would the distributor collect them and then pay you? Keep it simple and collect a fair royalty from the manufacturer's sell price. At that point, it is an easy transaction based solely on large volume sales.

Retail Pricing Scenario

This differs from industrial and commercial applications, since it will usually have a larger mark-up to cover the higher costs of getting a product to market and to the retail end user. In the scenario in Fig. 9-6, we begin with a retail price that has a psychological effect. While $10 may be appropriate in an industrial application, the psychology of $9.95 works better in retail.

In this retail scenario, the ratio of the retail sell price to the actual cost is about 3 to 1. Notice that the manufacturer's sell price to the distributor is about 55% off the retail list price. This is a fairly standard margin in most industries. The dealer price is commonly referred to as the wholesale price.

If a large discount store like Target or Walmart is purchasing in volume, they will want to eliminate the distributor and buy directly from the manufacturer. These large retailers usually have internal distribution systems. When they purchase in volume, they also tend to discount the retail price. It is easy to see that a large retailer can buy in

In sharp contrast to retail and infomercial pricing scenarios, most high-volume, commercial and industrial pricing is priced at about double that of the cost of raw materials.

For instance, a case of 1000 plastic grocery sacks uses about $4.40 in plastic resin, $.30 in ink, $.30 in shipping cartons and materials, or a total of about $5.00. This same case of plastic bags sells for about $10.00 in truckload quantities.

The best products for short form infomercials are unique, easy to use, make the user feel good about her or himself, have an element of magic and retail for $29.95 or under.

...Joan Lefkowitz, Accessory Brainstorms, NYC

Infomercial Profit Margins

Most direct response infomercial companies need to take a five to ten times markup on the cost of a product because of the high cost of purchasing TV airtime. You need to evaluate this if you plan to sell your product to or even if you want one of these companies to do the manufacturing of your product. Will the market bear the retail prices?

...Joan Lefkowitz, Accessory Brainstorms, NYC

Figure 9-6 Retail Cost Model

Retail sell price:	$9.95
Dealer cost (40% discount):	5.98
Less distributor discount (25%)	- 1.50
Distributor cost:	$4.49
Less terms (2% 10 days, net 30)	- .09
Less freight (5% is a median cost)	- .22
Less royalties (3%)	- .13
Less commission (5%)	- .22
Net sales price:	$3.81
Manufacturer's cost (10% profit):	$3.43

volume, discount retail prices by 10%-20% and still have a reasonable profit margin. For instance, by purchasing a product at a cost of $4.49 and selling it at a 20% discount ($7.96), the profit margin is 43.5%.

In each industrial/commercial model, the actual manufacturer's cost will be somewhat lower than is shown here. These costs include a 10% profit for the producer, which is reasonable. However, these costs might also have to include amortization of their start-up expenses and the cost of the debt service required to launch the new product. These costs could be another 10%-15%. In other words, the net cost of the retail item in Fig. 9-6 could be as low as $2.91.

Heavy Advertising Required?

When pricing for retail applications, a simple rule of thumb that can be applied is that the retail price is about 3-4 times that of the net cost. The higher priced the item, the lower the ratio.

But with products that are heavily advertised most producers look for higher percentages...as much as a 6 to 1 or 8 to 1 ratio.

Don't think that with these large profit margin they are making all the money and you are not. The fact is the advertisers must get paid and TV, radio and other mass marketing media advertising is not cheap!

ESTABLISH A TRADEMARK

Trademarks can become more valuable than patents! Some excellent examples are KLEENEX™, ZipLoc™ and Styrofoam™. When your invention becomes a success and even more so after years of improvements, it will be well known by its trademark. Try to develop a trademark early and make it part of your marketing plan.

Trademarks are generally easy to establish. Read more about the simple process in Chapter 6. Simply put, here is what to do to get your trademark established:

Whenever you use your trademark, include a "TM" superscript at the end of the word(s). Remember, trademarks are like copyrights; the minute you start using this unique mark, you own it. Putting a "TM" at the end is a means of publicly noting that it is your "mark".

Once in use, you will eventually want to further protect your marks. For $245, you can file your mark with the USPTO or an attorney can do it for about $500. Registered trademark documents are relatively easy to complete. You can get more information from a free booklet entitled BASIC FACTS ABOUT REGISTERING A TRADEMARK.

When Are Trademarks More Valuable than Patents?

After several years, the value of a patent declines and the value of a trademark increases. If you can create a trademark and make it part of your license agreement, your license may endure even after the expiration of the last of the patents. You can use the patents as a means to establish the trademark.

It is available from the U.S. Patent Office. This PTO booklet includes all the necessary documents you need to register a trademark.

HOW TO DEVELOP A CATCHY TRADEMARK

Inventors are usually not short on ideas for trademarks. You can develop your own, but it may take some time and experience to learn what it takes to create a good one. Here are a few suggestions:

1. Use the project's nickname--the same code word that has been identifying the project all along. For instance, "FLAGGER^{TM}" for a new marking system, "STICK-EMS^{TM}" for a new label maker or "BIGMOUTH^{TM}" for a new bag with a large opening.

2. Listen carefully for words people use to refer to your invention and see if you can use some combination or offshoot of them. Can they be joined together in a catchy way? Common words themselves cannot be trademarked, but a unique spelling or combination can be. For example, BOXXERS^{TM}, DIZPENSERS^{TM} or SOFT-EEE^{TM}.

3. If you use common words together without contest for a period of five years, you can have them trademarked. For instance, "DUAL-TAB^{TM}", defining a bag with two tabs or "BIG-RED^{TM}" for a type of fire truck.

4. Borrow ideas from other trademarks, but make sure that you change them sufficiently so they do not appear to be similar or conflicting. They must not cause confusion.

5. Brainstorm with other creative people involved in your project.

6. Ask your children. They can surprise you with some great, creative ideas.

7. Hire an advertising agency.

PACKAGING YOUR INVENTION

In industrial and commercial applications, packaging your invention is relatively easy. Flashy, eye-catching packaging is usually unnecessary. The primary consideration with industrial and commercial packaging is to ensure that the product arrives without damage and can be easily handled once it arrives. Your manufacturing and marketing experts can help. If you are going to be involved in the packaging of the new industrial/commercial product, here are a few considerations:

1. Most cases or master cartons should not weigh over 50 lbs.--a maximum of 30 pounds is best. If your product is relatively small in size, use a case count that will make the cartons convenient to handle.

I have found that trademarks are usually developed sometime well after the product development begins. It is usually some word or combination that those working on the project adopt.

Don't be too concerned if you don't find a name you like right away. It may take a year or more to discover this magic mark.

...Bob DeMatteis

For consumer products, professionally designed packaging and sales materials are a savvy investment. It denotes a seriously commercial entity.

...Joan Lefkowitz, Accessory Brainstorms, NYC

2. Bulk packaging is only for OEM (original equipment manufacturing) or strictly industrial applications. It is not popular or desired in most commercial or retail applications.

3. Don't scrimp on carton strength to save a few pennies. Carton crushing is always a potential problem and can result in returns.

4. Palletizing of the product should weigh no more than about 1200 pounds. If the volume is relatively large, establish a pallet count and stack (referred to as "tie and high") with cartons that fill out the pallet as much as possible and have level layers. Stacking of pallets is common. Corner braces can also be used to help protect the underneath product when another pallet is stacked on top.

5. Use good pallet quality. The image of used pallets reflects poorly on any product.

Packaging in retail applications is much different. Give extra consideration to the type of package, whether it is a bag or a box. The graphics are also critical.

A well-designed product should ship compactly and occupy as little shelf space as possible.
...Paul Berman, T2 Design

Packaging in Plastic Bags

- Bags (which may hang on a pegboard hanger) are used for inexpensive, lightweight items. They can convey a better image if they are printed with great graphics. They can convey an even better image if the graphics are printed on a chipboard insert.

- Most plastic bags are made from low-density polyethylene plastic. The bags you use should be from "high clarity" film. Cellophane or polypropylene can convey a better image, but cost more. Be careful with cellophane, as it tears easily.

- There are two types of headers to attach to the tops of bags for hanging on the pegs. One is made from chipboard; the other is a plastic reinforced header. Chipboard is much classier and easier to assemble, even in small quantities. Plastic-reinforced header bags cost less, but the quantity must be larger. Since they are not as stiff as the chipboard headers, they tend to droop at the sides and over time can look used and worn on a pegboard display. Chipboard headers are superior in almost all aspects of plastic bag packaging.

Product and packaging color is an important factor in marketability. Study the intended demographics for your product before determining color selection and combination.
...Joan Lefkowitz, Accessory Brainstorms, NYC

Blister Packaging

A highly popular alternative to using a box is blister packaging. There are thousands of companies throughout the U.S. that do this type of packaging. You can easily locate them in the yellow pages.

Many of these companies will be able to help you make inexpensive, prototype packaging if you have the artwork already completed.

Packaging in Boxes

Boxes usually convey a better image than plastic bags. The cost is usually much greater as well. A product packaged in a $.03 plastic bag might cost $.15 in a box. But the reality is that U.S. consumers like to purchase their retail products in boxes. An example is retail trash bags, which are sold throughout most of the world in bags, but sold in the U.S. in boxes.

There are many varieties of boxes used in retail packaging. A smart packaging expert can help you determine what the costs will be. This is one person who can help your team effort tremendously and can steer you and your marketing and manufacturing experts in the right direction.

A smart packaging expert can help you position your product to capture the intended target market…maybe even more than you expected! Keep in mind that it can take up to several months to get the packaging designed and in place. Prepare for these delays. Here are some basic considerations when using boxes for packaging:

- Most high quality printed boxes you see in supermarkets and retail stores are made of inexpensive chipboard. Lower-quality boxes are usually gray on the inside, since this is the color of the recycled material used in construction. High-quality chipboard usually has an inside white liner or is 100% bleached board. There are various thicknesses available…the thicker the board, the higher the quality.

- Chipboard boxes are attractively printed and then treated with a special coating on the outside. Usually referred to as UV (ultraviolet), this coating is very shiny and usually the best choice for a high quality image. Varnish is also used as the outer layer, but is not as glossy.

- Cardboard can also be used for heavier items, but cannot be attractively printed. White cartons cost more than standard brown (referred to as Kraft). However, a separate sheet can be printed and then glued (or laminated) to a carton's sides. The flashy, narrow gauge (referred to as "E-flute") cardboard cartons that are attractively printed on an outer laminated sheet can be very costly, but they convey the best overall quality.

- There is growing use of plastic boxes in retail applications. They are usually made from a stiff, high-clarity polypropylene material or styrene plastic. The cost of this packaging is still much greater than paperboard boxes. Printing is usually done on a printed insert placed inside the container.

INFOMERCIALS

Increasingly, more and more products are being sold on television using infomercials. It is becoming a huge marketplace! Infomercials range anywhere from money generating schemes, to "oldies but goodies" song collections to new, slick fishing lures.

According to my infomercial experts, you are going to need a real slick gimmicky product that has some very attractive profit margins. Ken Robbins, Product Development Consultant with BKV in Atlanta, Georgia scouts out new products for several companies including Dirt Devil. According to Ken, billions of dollars worth of products are sold annually through direct response TV, a.k.a. infomercials. Here are the

Hiring a pubic relations firm or establishing an in-house heavy public relations effort in your company can make a significant difference in the recognition of your product in the marketplace.

Good "Press" is often a determining factor in a buyer purchasing your product or passing it up for something they deem more "important".

Joan Lefkowitz, Accessory Brainstorms, NYC

Home Shopping Network and Other TV Marketing Shows

Generally speaking, these shows can generate a lot of sales. But the problem for the first-time inventor is that the amount of inventory that is required to be on one of these shows is huge. As much as $250,000 or more is usually required to be maintained in their warehouse long before (up to two months) the show will air. They want to guarantee sales to their callers.

For inventors /innovators, the best way to begin is to have your manufacturing and marketing experts develop your innovation for other markets first, whether that be for retail outlets or infomercials. Then, after you have a track record and can finance a large inventory, let your marketing experts get it launched on the HSN-type companies.

Also keep in mind that 90% of the HSN sales are products geared for women.

requirements that Ken says every TV marketer looks for, in order of importance:

1. The product is a new-to-the world consumer product.
2. It is highly demonstrable or has raving testimonials.
3. The product appeals to the profit motive, vanity motive or ease of burden.
4. The product is patented or copyrighted.
5. The product is available nowhere else.
6. It is priced between $20 and $300.
7. It does not require professional installation.

If you believe you have a new innovation that meets these criteria, check out the companies in the Appendix of this book, or search out others either in the yellow pages of major metropolitan areas or on the Internet.

10

YOUR MARKETING AND MANUFACTURING STRATEGY

Choosing the right partners may be
the most important decision you make!

The challenge of getting a
product from idea to market can
be daunting. It's a process fraught
with difficult decisions demanding
reliable information and advice at
every stop.
...Donald Grant Kelly,
U.S. Patent Office Director

You may have the finest, most unique, creative invention in the world, but it will be a total failure without the right manufacturing and marketing strategy. This strategy involves selecting a team that includes a manufacturing expert, a marketing expert, a legal expert and others who may play minor roles. These team members are your associates--your partners--and are crucial to your success. They will make or break your new invention!

WHY SEPARATE YOUR MANUFACTURING AND MARKETING STRATEGIES?

The simple reality is that most manufacturers are not good at marketing. If they had their way, producers would only manufacture large quantities of their own generic products. And most marketing experts are not manufacturers either. The sooner you separate these two entities in your invention-related activities, the sooner you will be successful. You cannot invest all your time with manufacturing experts speculating about whether your invention will sell. In addition, you cannot invest all your time with marketing people who know little about cost-effective manufacturing.

These two experts must work closely with you to determine what will be the invention's best, most cost-effective attributes and how it will be sold. While finding a manufacturer to make a product is easy, finding the right one is not so easy.

But where most first time inventors fail miserably in their invention-related activities is marketing. It is frequently neglected until after a lot of money has been spent and prototypes have been made. When the prototypes receive a poor response in sales presentations, the inventor wonders why. Marketing is the most important aspect of inventing and, as illustrated in the *Strategic Guide,* should be one of the first steps to take, not one of the last.

FIVE STRATEGIC APPROACHES TO MAKING MONEY FROM YOUR INVENTION

Before selecting your team members, formulate a reasonably clear idea of the best way to take your new invention to market. Keep in mind it is wise to stay flexible and open minded, as interesting offers may come your way.

Generally speaking, there are five basic approaches to consider. They are:

1. **Your company manufactures, your company sells.** With this approach, you build an internal team of close associates to oversee the manufacturing and marketing of the new products. This approach requires the largest cash outlay, to create a start-up project (or perhaps an entirely new company). But it does give you the best control over the ultimate outcome.

2. **Your company manufactures, you hire outside sales/ marketing experts.** By hiring outside sales/marketing experts, you can save expensive start-up marketing costs and a lot of time. You can either hire them on a commission-only basis or pay a salary. You will maintain excellent control over product quality, but lose some control over sales and the direct relationship with the customer.

Charles Darrow, an unemployed heating contractor invented the board game, Monopoly in 1933. The many toy companies he contacted repeatedly rejected him.

They said the game was too complicated to learn, took too long to complete and "who ever heard of a board game that kept going round and round. There is supposed to be a beginning and an end."

He struck out on his own and began marketing the game. Two years later, Parker Brothers saw the light, bought out his rights, and today, it is the most popular board game in the world.

Stay Flexible

While marketing one of my first inventions, I came across an opportunity to join forces with one of my competitors. They wanted my creative mind...and they had money. We worked together and embarked on an exciting future, running sales up to $10 million a year in just a couple of years.

In your invention activities, keep an open mind and always look for options and possibilities. You never know what offers you may receive!

...Bob DeMatteis

Question: What do Mr. Potato Head® Viewmaster®, Frisbee®, Lionel Trains®, Operation®, Colorforms® and Play Dough® have in common?

Answer: They were all created by independent inventors that either licensed their creations or established some form of strategic business partnership.

Alternative Home-Based Business Approach

If you are an outgoing inventor with an invention that would not be too difficult to get manufactured at a suitable profit margin, and that is targeted toward a service oriented market, you can consider the teaching circuit.

Give seminars in the extended education departments of colleges and universities and teach others about the service you provide. Of course, one of the by-products from the service is your innovation, which is sold at the workshop for profit.

You will be amazed at how word of mouth travels and sales blossom!

...June Davidson, American

Other Choices

There are a few other choices to consider regarding your approach, but they are not ones you would normally pursue.

As we discussed in Chapter 1, you can develop your invention, patent it and then sell it. However, your time will not be well spent, since there are so few buyers who will have the same vision as you do.

Another approach is to just wait and see if anyone starts to infringe your patent and then try to license them.

3. **Your company sells, you sub-contract the manufacturing.** If you are strong in marketing and weak when it comes to manufacturing, this is your best approach. You will be in the enviable position of bringing in orders and commitments at an early stage. By bringing in orders and commitments, it should not be difficult to have your selected sub-contractor make prototypes, which will save you time and money. This approach keeps you in close contact with the all-important customer, but you lose some control over product quality.

With this approach, you can also consider supplying your invention in bulk to various full-line product suppliers (or perhaps one or two exclusive suppliers) that would include it in their product lines. This approach is simple and easy and requires no license agreement, just their obvious commitment to purchase the goods from you.

4. **You license a manufacturer(s) and it markets.** This is the best way to alleviate all or most of your start-up costs. Depending on the nature of your invention, you may want one or a few exclusive licensee(s) or several non-exclusive licensees. With this approach, your job becomes one of coordinating support behind the scenes with the producer-marketer. Unfortunately, this scenario is not as easy to find as you might expect.

5. **You license a marketing organization and authorize a manufacturer to supply it.** This approach will also alleviate the majority of your start-up costs. By licensing a committed sales expert in the field of your invention, it is frequently much easier to find and authorize (or you can grant a limited "manufacturing only" license) a manufacturer to support it.

The most important underlying consideration in your approach to licensing and marketing is that of personal finances.

IT'S A TEAM EFFORT

First, you physically cannot do everything yourself. Even if you could, it is doubtful that you would be skilled in every facet of bringing a new invention to market. You may be a clever inventor, but are you an expert in manufacturing, marketing and patent law as well? Even if you are, do you really want to work 25 hours a day? Of course, this is impossible, but it would probably take 25 hours a day to manage the production, sales and marketing, and legal aspects of your new invention--*in addition* to your full time job of overseeing the product's development! Sooner or later, in the course of developing your invention, you will want to involve other team members, so that you can really make things happen.

Another reason you will want partners is that they can help enormously in defraying costs. If you did it all yourself, the start-up costs for a new product innovation would probably be at least $100,000. Think about the money you would spend buying manufacturing equipment, renting a facility, hiring people, flying around the country to make sales presentations and meeting with suppliers.

With some savvy you can defray all, or almost all, of these start-up costs by building the right marketing and manufacturing team. Frankly, there is no reason to spend much (if any) of your money to get your concept to market. Good ideas that are attractive to others will generate plenty of interest from innovative marketing and manufacturing entities. You just want to find the right match for you.

The reason they will be interested is simple: your team members will have a lot to gain by assisting you. The right team members will have the means at their fingertips to help propel your project forward, which would otherwise be very costly to you. This includes making prototypes and lining up sales. Finding partners does not have to be painful; everyone wants to get in on ground floor opportunities. You just have to find the right partners.

You may already have an idea of some partners you want on your team or your future team members may be people you have never met. But one thing is for certain, the team members you select must be experts in the field of your invention and they must have the right attributes to get the job done. You will be establishing long-term relationships with these individuals and you will be relying on them for your future. With you as the team captain and parent of the invention, these experts will help you induce the birth of a "baby".

WHO WILL BE ON THE TEAM?

First, think of the team you are developing as a new franchise football team, without as many limitations and restrictions. You are the team captain and you want to develop the finest team players you can. You do not want "has beens", rookies or team hoppers.

You want an all-star offense (innovators are inherently offensive) consisting mostly of seasoned professionals. Your sales team should consist of running backs and wide receivers who will score points (get orders). You want the Joe Montanas, the Emmitt Smiths and the Jerry Rices on your team. The offensive line (manufacturing) will support the backs and wide receivers by manufacturing top-quality products. You want 2000 pounds of human muscle. The front office (your legal team) will make sure that the contracts you negotiate with these top-rate players are based on winning performances.

To assemble a winning team, in either sports or business, look for quality "players" who fit the style of "game" you play, have proven performance records and exhibit the enthusiasm and spirit to make things happen.

SBA BBS on Angel Investors

Most inventors at some point need money to take their ideas into the marketplace. This can be through the license or an invention or some form of start-up business relationship.

Venture capital is one source, but increasingly, start-up inventors and partnerships are too small for VCs to pay much attention (since VCs like to invest a larger amount of money).

Angel investing has recently become a popular funding mechanism. The U.S. Small Business Administration Office of Advocacy is sponsoring the ACE-Net, the Angel Capital Electronic Network, offering a chance for entrepreneurs to raise sums ranging from $250,000 to $3,000,000. Check it out--your tax dollars at work.

The SBA Web site is: http://www.sba.gov/advo.
...Greg Aharonian, PATNEWS

Invention Assistance: Companies Are Never Your Team Members

They might say they are...but it's really a one-sided relationship in their favor. Why? They get all their money up front and chances are, you get nothing in return. Not a company to manufacture your invention or one to market it...nothing. It is a WIN/LOSE situation.

What kind of a team relationship is that, if you are supplying the invention and the money?

In sharp contrast--your team members--manufacturing and marketing experts--will be spending their money to develop your ideas and inventions...not the other way around! This is the WIN/WIN situation you want!

Lemelson and Team Building

This famous inventor knew the value of teamwork. His foundation sponsors the NCIIA in dozens of colleges and universities in the U.S. with grants helping college students develop their inventions into licensable and marketable innovations.

The establishment of "E-Teams" ("E" stands for excellence and entrepreneurship) is the primary mechanism in this effort.

Lemelson's inspiration for the E-Team model was the collaborative interdisciplinary development teams used during WWII to rapidly develop innovative technical solutions to urgent wartime needs.

E-Teams were pioneered at Hampshire College in Massachusetts. They consisted of students formed into groups to develop solutions to real world problems with commercial application.

Since Lemelson knew the importance of commerce, E-Teams invariably become linked to the business community through relationships with non-academic mentors and advisors, thus fostering connections between the institution's most entrepreneurial graduates and local business and technical communities.

It's no wonder Lemelson was as successful as he was!

Now back to inventing...with you as the team captain, the three key team players should be:

1.   **A legal firm.** It will file and prosecute your patent applications. It will put its stamp of approval on your licensing activities. It will also protect you in the event of infringement.

2.   **Manufacturing entity.** If this is not your company, it will be an existing sub-contractor or manufacturer. What might take a new start-up firm months, even years to complete, the right existing manufacturer can do in a fraction of the time. With very little added expense, a small, flexible manufacturing facility can create your prototypes and first working models quickly.

3.   **Marketing and sales.** This team member is either the sales and marketing associates with your company, one or more independent sales agencies or the sales force associated with a manufacturing firm (which you may ultimately license). They are not so-called marketing companies that will create an image for you or invention submission companies that will help you find manufacturers and sales agents, nor are they distributors.

You will devote most of your time and attention to your manufacturing and marketing partners. The three of you will work together to get the new invention launched, manufactured and sold!

WHEN DO YOU START BUILDING THE TEAM?

By now, you understand the importance of involving your sales and manufacturing partners as soon as possible. Once you feel confident that your idea is a good one, dedicate your time to locating your three chief partners. The sooner you do this, the sooner your invention will be born and the sooner it will have all the right features and benefits for the all-important end user. Take a look at the *Strategic Guide* at the end of the book to better understand your timing.

Early on, manufacturing partners can avoid potential manufacturing problems. Sales and marketing experts can provide valuable input about what customers want. With the right manufacturing and marketing team in place, you will have a much greater chance of quickly and successfully launching your new innovation.

Most inventors look for manufacturing partners before looking for marketing partners. However, it would be wiser to look for your marketing partner first, particularly if you are able to make prototypes without a manufacturer, so that you can begin "pre-selling" activities first. The value of doing this is covered in detail in Chapter 2.

THE ROLE OF YOUR ATTORNEY

Regardless of your strategic approach to getting your invention sold and producing income, it is best not to make commitments to your manufacturing and marketing team members until your legal counsel is in place. The attorney who will help you in licensing activities will probably also be your patent attorney. Besides, you will want to interview your manufacturing and marketing team members with the power of "already having personal legal counsel". Sometime later, you will want your attorney to give his/her blessings to your license agreement negotiations.

You would be wise to learn all you can about licensing and patenting before engaging legal services. At $200-$300 per hour, attorneys are expensive teachers. Even after all your learning, it will still be up to you to make the decisions that are best for you. Legal counsel for an inexperienced licensor can run into the tens of thousands of dollars! And unfortunately, most of the questions have nothing to do with the law, but have everything to do with your manufacturing and marketing development and strategy. The best strategy is to learn all you can beforehand.

Your patent attorney should have a real interest in you, your invention, your patent(s) and your licensing activities. He/she should communicate well, in a style you understand.

POSITIONING YOUR INVENTION AND YOUR DESIRES

Before you start looking for partners, it would be wise to think about your approach to manufacturing and marketing. Think about how you will position and present yourself and your invention. You should be positive and display enough knowledge to properly convey your desires. It is important to remember that you will be dealing with sharks and barracudas, which may want to try to steal your good ideas. Keep your initial conversations sufficiently masked to avoid trouble.

Follow these five guidelines to be in a position of strength:

1. **Establish yourself in a position of strength**. Do this with straightforward talk highlighting some of the strong points about you, your experience and your invention. If you do not have a lot of experience in inventing or new product launches, focus more on the features and benefits of your invention and perhaps some of the test results. In a few sentences, describe a few accomplishments in your field of work, in product design, sales or whatever is relevant. If you have patents and licensees, say so. If you have assisted other people or companies in the success of their patented ideas or new product launches, talk about these as well. If you have a long history of successes, focus on the most recent ones.

Team Building = $$$

Many inventors look for outside investors and sources to finance the development of their inventions. This may include borrowing from relatives, bankers (2nd Trust Deeds), stock purchases, venture capitalists and so on.

In contrast to this, I have never asked anyone for money to develop my inventions. Instead, I have built team/partner relationships in which the other team members have funded the manufacturing and/or marketing effort.

From the financial perspective of needing money to develop an idea…it makes that much more sense to start building your team as soon as possible.

But best of all, in building a team effort, everyone is happy. You are usually trading their monetary investment for a favored position in the license to manufacture and market the new product--and you are not sacrificing ownership of the patent and its rights. In other words, you retain 100% ownership of the patent rights.

…Bob DeMatteis

Don't Say You Have a Patent Pending if You Don't!

This only shows your inexperience and reflects a lack of sincerity and integrity. If you say you have a patent pending and you really don't, what are you going to say when it is time to file? That you have been lying? You might destroy your credibility. Besides, it is a fraud, which is punishable by fine.

Ant Farm® Story

Milton Levine created the Ant Farm in the 1950's. It was all made possible with the development of modern plastics.

He originally sold it for under $3 in newspapers. It has changed very little over the past 40 years--only in price.

Of over 9000 species of ants, only one is suitable for the Ant Farm concept--a vegetarian ant.

The ant farm teaches teamwork, organization, perseverance and innovation...all of which are desirable traits for inventing!

2. **Use key power words**. The right words and phrases will elevate you and your invention to a position of strength. Some examples of power words (underlined and in boldface) and how to use them when discussing your invention are provided below.

"I recently invented and tested a new plastic bag that increases loading capacity by 20%-30%." Continue with words such as "In my **patent application,** I revealed two systems that accomplish this."

- "I am presently working on the **patent application with my patent attorneys. We expect to have it filed** in the next two weeks."

- "We have **filed disclosures for patents** covering at least four unique, state-of-the-art improvements. I am interested in discussing the manufacture of them with you."

- "**My attorneys and I have been discussing the various forms of patent coverage**. One in particular reflects the embodiments we would use in the invention I am proposing to you."

- "I am discussing **patent strategy with my attorney.** We believe it is best to…"

- "The **patent search and legal opinion reveal** that we will be able to secure key patent protection with our new invention."

- "My **attorney** would never allow me to discuss the details of my invention without a signed Confidentiality Agreement."

The use of these words lets potential licensees know you are serious and your idea-invention is well developed.

3. **Be on the offense**. You have the carrot and you can dangle it. Ask the manufacturers and sales agents what they can do for you; don't allow them to control the conversation by asking you for information. They are the ones who need to make a solid commitment in your favor. When dangling a carrot, don't be misleading either. You don't want to build up false hopes or make them angry.

4. **Remember that you want to be on the same side of the fence.** Simply put, you do not want to create animosities with anyone. Interview your new partners with the intention of building a totally mutual relationship. If there is a problem with the relationship later on, you will want to be able to openly discuss it. Successful team

relationships must be built on trust and understanding. You are seeking long-term relationships.

5. **Keep the customer in focus.** When selecting manufacturers and sales agencies, keep your customer in mind. You know the CDI attributes your customers want--make sure your producer can deliver and your sales team can sell. Frame your interview questions around the needs of your anticipated customers, so they will be happy with your choice of manufacturers and sales agencies. Remember, it will ultimately be your customers who "pull through" the sales and keep them going.

IF YOU HAVE FILED FOR PATENTS OR ALREADY HAVE ONE

If so, use language that reflects it. This gives you more power than just having a disclosure written and perhaps a patent search conducted. Your patent pending status tells others that you are seriously moving ahead. Refer to your product as having a "**patent pending**" or "**patents pending**" if there is more than one.

If you already have a patent, say so. If they want a copy, give them one. Most people will only want to see the first page with the abstract and your name on it. If you are sending out letters of inquiry, send a copy of the patent abstract along with it.

IN GENERAL, MASKED TERMS, TALK ABOUT YOUR INVENTION AND ITS SALES POTENTIAL

When you begin your search, talk about how you realized there was a problem with existing products or that no products were available to solve a particular problem. Tell them you discovered a unique solution and why you believe your invention is a good opportunity. You can say all this without having a signed confidentiality agreement in place.

Tell them about the size of the market it could impact, but don't be over-zealous. Use comments such as, "It is useful in a $150 million market and can save money over existing paper and plastic products. I think we could capture a niche as great as 2%-5% in a few years. I believe with a more aggressive sales campaign and a sufficient monetary investment, it could be even greater."

Don't talk about it being a "must have" invention. These are few and far between. The last two "must have" inventions were probably the wheel and the discovery of fire. To say that you are going to revolutionize the industry and take over all $150 million in sales in three years shows inexperience and a lack of understanding. It's not

Talking Confidentially About Your Creation

Many inventors believe that there is "nothing" like their invention in which it can be compared to. That it is not possible to talk about it in masked terms without revealing the exact subject matter. But this is rarely the case.

For instance, if you just discovered the automobile, would you not talk about it in terms of being a superior transportation means that does not require the use of horses or oxen?

If you just discovered the television set, would you not talk about it being somewhat like a radio, but not only can you hear voices, you can see the people like in a picture show.

If you just discovered the photograph, would you not call it a way to quickly make a lot of copies of a picture with the people and scenery perfectly duplicated?

Use your creativity and you can find a way to describe your inventions in "masked terms".

Make a Video of Your Innovation

If you have a production model or a working prototype of your invention, try making a demo video. This shows a prospective licensee that the idea performs as expected and details how the product is made. Remember these essentials to making a great demonstration video:

Script the Video:
1. *Make a list of what the product does.*
2. *Make a list of the important parts of the product.*
3. *Make a list of the benefits of using the product.*

While Shooting:
1. *Your home video camera will work fine.*
2. *Do not make a video longer than 10 minutes (5 minutes is even better)*
3. *Keep the camera steady.*
4. *Show how the product is made.*
5. *Show the product in action.*
6. *Explain if there are any other uses for the product.*
7. *Tell what stage the product is in, e.g., "the widget is patent pending and presently we have two prototypes of the product."*
8. *Tell if you have any manufacturing estimates: "I have priced this widget with a local manufacturer and it would cost me $33.00 each to make."*

After Shooting:
1. *Copy your original tape to another VHS copy.*
2. *Send the copy to potential suitor companies with a brief description letter.*

...Ken Robbins, Product Development Agent, Dirt Devil

going to happen. Established businesses are not going to roll over and let you put them out of business.

It would be equally incorrect to exaggerate the size of the market. If you do not have exact figures, do some research and find out. Pie-in-the-sky estimates will cost you more time and money than they will cost your potential partners.

Here are a few ways you can learn the size of your market:

- Ask your marketing expert
- Visit the research section at the local library or ask the librarian
- Get sales figures from a single company, find out what percent of the market they represent, and then calculate the total market
- Ask a manufacturer
- If it is a retail item, ask a store manager or a district manager
- Do an Internet search

TALK ABOUT CUSTOMER BENEFITS AND TEST RESULTS

In Chapters 3 and 4, you learned about Customer Driven Innovation--CDI benefits--and how they apply to making outstanding inventions. Now you can use some of this language in your conversations and letters. It is easy to do, without revealing confidential design attributes. The use of facts conveys serious intent and a professional, knowledgeable attitude. Here is a list of possible phrases you can use in your activities:

- It is environmentally sound; it reduces waste, since it is made of recycled material
- It saves time, space and money
- It is safe to use and does not produce toxic emissions
- More convenient than ever…it only takes 2 minutes to assemble, instead of 15!
- More comfortable than the most expensive one on the market
- Dramatically improves accuracy
- It's the most entertaining machine on the market
- It's easy to learn
- Appeals to the senses
- Improves looks
- Improves productivity
- A three-step system
- People friendly

If you have tested some prototypes (no matter how crude), you can talk about the test results, without revealing specifics. When you refer to testing, say that it was done "*in the lab*" regardless of whether the lab is your garage or in an actual testing situation. For instance:

- Tests show the 33% recycled content did not negatively affect performance
- There is a 20%-30% savings due to a larger capacity. (This speaks for itself. You do not need to say how you tested it right now.)
- Tests show it takes an average of 2.17 minutes to assemble!
- Every test subject agreed it was far more comfortable than all the others they have used
- Accuracy of the cuts was improved by 7.23%
- All the testers laughed out loud
- Tests revealed that instructions were not necessary
- Every test subject felt it improved his/her looks
- Productivity went up by 31%
- Test observations showed that people could figure out how it worked without any additional help

INVENTION SUMMARIES

An invention summary will help position your invention by listing all the right attributes. It may illustrate the preliminary market analyses you may have done. It will not reveal any pertinent details, but will reflect the CDI benefits listed in the preceding section. Your invention summary should be concise and reflect a highly professional approach. Don't use out-dated clip art, cartoons or "hip jargon". This is considered unprofessional.

You can send an invention summary to those you have interviewed on the phone and with letters of inquiry you mail to prospective candidates. It can serve as a personal guide to help you say the right things as you talk to potential candidates by phone. An example of an invention summary is in Fig. 10-1.

FINDING AND INTERVIEWING
YOUR MANUFACTURING AND MARKETING CANDIDATES

Your invention disclosure establishing the date of original conception is written, you have hired an attorney and you are now eager to locate some manufacturing and marketing partners. First, make a list of all the potential candidates you would like to interview. Then,

---

How Necessary Is Testing?

I hate to say it...but I find a lot of inventors have not sufficiently tested their prototypes in order to answer some basic marketing questions. For instance:

- *What did the testers (not family members!) think?*
- *Did they know how to use it?*
- *Did it work as anticipated?*

How can an inventor expect a potential licensee to invest hundreds of thousands of dollars on a product that has not had minimal testing?

Invention Summaries

It is best to prepare concise summaries with "bulleted benefits". Don't use gimmicky or old-fashioned pictures or cartoons. Serious business people will view them as being unprofessional.

If you have a patent or patent pending, consider having the summary color copied with a photo image of the invention.

YCN Your Company Name *Company address, city, phone and fax numbers, Web site*

Product Summary
High Productivity Bagging System

Background of the Invention

According to industry standards reported by the California Supermarket Association, present day, plastic bagging systems used in supermarkets average 2.9 items per plastic sack when loaded. The low item count (paper averages 7-8 items) is due to the standard sack being lightweight and undersized with an associated system that actually promotes inefficient use.

Some companies have introduced larger plastic sacks of the same system with twice the capacity, at twice the price and average about twice the item count, hence no real savings. This tells us that the system plays a major role in contributing to inefficient bag loading.

Summary of the Present Invention

The present invention uses a system that enables baggers to access more available sack capacity. When a bag is opened on the system of the present invention, the entire rack dimensions become "loading capacity". The opened bag mouth presents a substantially larger opening for loading groceries.

Test results in 6 separate studies over 3-6 months have proven the actual savings to be from 22%-44% off the bottom line! The reason is due to the new sack and system, allowing the user to naturally increase item count...even double it...without doubling bag costs.

Benefits of the Invention

There are many benefits for supermarkets. Here is just a partial list:

- Lower overall bag costs
- Lower labor costs
- Improved productivity
- Convenient, easy to use
- No training required
- New, attractive racks improve front-end appearance
- Bags are super strong

Patent Status

Current status is patent pending in the U.S. and Canada. U.S. patents will issue around September 1997. The trademark, BIGMOUTH™, is also established in the U.S.

The Opportunity

Licenses have already been granted in the U.S. A strategic licensee in Canada is being sought to enter into a favorable, preferably exclusive or dedicated agreement. A highly beneficial, long-term license agreement can be struck with the right licensee.

Figure 10-1

begin interviewing these potential associates (usually on the phone) without disclosing any confidential information. (Confidentiality agreements will not be needed until later.) If your first discussions with a candidate go well, follow up with a second conference, either by phone or in person.

It usually does not matter whether you first interview sales and marketing experts or potential manufacturers. You may start with existing contacts or seek out total strangers. What is important is to begin the process by locating as many viable entities as possible and gathering as much information as you can. You want to find the "right fit" for your invention, your team and you.

When speaking with manufacturers, you will evaluate their ability to manufacture **and** market your invention. This may require you to talk to two people in an organization. As you know, many times you will find that companies are only manufacturing oriented and not sales oriented. When you talk with manufacturers, they will be able to recommend marketing experts. When you are interviewing sales experts, ask them if they know manufacturers. Networking will help you quickly locate several potential manufacturing and sales partners.

In Chapters 11 and 12, you will learn where to find marketing and manufacturing team members and how to evaluate them.

Internet Opportunities for Home Based Inventors

If your invention has a very small target market, and can be made with an attractive profit margin, then you may want to consider starting a home based business and put it on the Internet.

You can go into business with an attractive Web site for just a few thousand dollars. Many servers will even provide credit card access as well.

On the Internet, you have an opportunity to reach the smallest of markets everywhere in the world. Best of all, you will be selling to them at a full retail price.

Don't be surprised if your business develops into a full-time operation in just a year or two. It is ideal for creative ventures.

The Internet--*The Inventor's Power Tool!*℠

Successful inventing in today's competitive business environment requires inventors to use every available tool to get ahead. Investors who learn how to use the Internet effectively dramatically increase the chance of success and profits.

With just a few hours per week at the home computer, inventors can save hundreds, or even thousands of dollars, avoid scam invention companies, and gain access to more up-to-date research materials than a University library--all on the Internet!

Here are just a few of the resources inventors can access Online:

* Inventor Organizations
* Marketing Your Invention
* Free Patent Searching
* Government Grants & Venture Funding
* Companies
* Looking for Inventions

* Market Research Resources
* Industry Associations
* Discussion Groups
* E-Zines
* Inventor Newsgroups
* And much, much more!

One of the most comprehensive Internet Web sites for inventors seeking information is the Inventor's Resource at http://www.gibbsgroup.com, updated regularly. Get Online now, and supercharge your invention efforts!

* * * * * * * * * * *

Andy Gibbs' Inventor's Resource Web site has earned more than 2 dozen prestigious awards, 18 of them in the first 3 months of 1998. His Web site is the perfect companion to From Patent to Profit. As a successful inventor, entrepreneur, past VP of Business Development for a Fortune 50 Div., he knows how to use the proper business tools for the job.

Personal Preferences - Phone vs. Letters

While many inventors may prefer to send out letters of inquiry, others will prefer to call on the phone or meet in person. Generally speaking, calling on the phone is more personal and more effective as well. In this age of swift communications, telephone is the preferred method. Let's not forget, we are building relationships and there is no better way to do this than by hearing a real voice.

If you feel comfortable calling the executives of potential licensees on the phone, you should do it. You can even leave voice mail messages, which usually get a return call. Even if you have a tough time connecting with the president, at least you will be remembered if you follow up with a letter and invention summary afterward.

When starting out to call prospects on the phone, try practicing on some local companies first. When you've got the spiel down, then start calling the more serious candidates.

Make Your Own Letterhead

Send letters that are on your own letterhead. It is easy to make your own using a computer. You can quickly model your letterhead after any style you like.

One additional suggestion: You can use your own name and add "Company" to it without creating any problems with mail delivery, business licenses, etc. For instance, if your name is Ralph Smith, call your company the Ralph Smith Company and add your home address.

SEARCHING BY PHONE

Telephone interviewing-networking-prospecting is the most effective means of quickly locating potential team members. It is fast, inexpensive and easy. Focus on locating your marketing expert first.

When you are doing telephone interviews, ask for the President of the company, regardless of the company's size. He/she is the one who must ultimately sign your license agreement. Besides, you will most likely be dealing with small, medium and large companies in which the President is going to be accessible.

If you cannot speak to the President, try to talk to the Vice President of Marketing or the National Sales Manager. Never present your new ideas and inventions to the head of R&D or New Products departments without first going through the President or marketing head. The head of R&D is not paid to evaluate the ideas of outsiders. Besides, R&D people rarely decide what products are going to be manufactured and sold. Don't waste your time by talking to these individuals.

If it is a company's policy to run all new ideas through R&D before being reviewed by sales, this is probably not a company for you. This is a production-driven company with a NIH (not invented here) attitude. Move on to other possibilities.

Once you find an interested candidate on the phone, follow-up the conversation by faxing or mailing your invention summary.

USING LETTERS OF INQUIRY

While it is best to establish initial contacts by phone, the task can be accomplished with a mail inquiry instead. Letters of inquiry should be concise and professional. Make sure to include an invention summary with your letter.

Address a letter of inquiry to the President of the company. This will give you a perfect reason to follow up by phone afterward. When you call, ask for the President by name. If asked, tell the person who answers who you are and that you want to make sure he received your letter. If you still can't get through, leave a voice mail message. Your pleasant persistence in trying to get through is a trait that many company heads appreciate. In fact, this same persistence will also indicate to them that you are committed to the success of your idea.

Fig. 10-2 is an example of a letter of inquiry that is targeted for a domestic marketing company. Fig. 10-3 is an example of a letter of inquiry that is targeted for a domestic manufacturer. Fig. 10-4 is an example of a letter that is intended to locate importers. Either the indented or block style format illustrated is acceptable. Make sure your letters are typed using a similar professional format with clean, crisp typewritten copy. Do not hand write letters or summaries.

YCN Your Company Name *Company address, city, phone and fax numbers, Web site*

April 24, 1998

Mr. President (preferably the person's name)
Domestic Company
123 Wonderful Street
New York, FL 45678

Subject: Seeking a Marketing Company

Dear Mr. President:

I am seeking a strong, national marketing company for my new novelty product. Yours has been identified as a possibility, since your sales are in a related field.

The novelty product will be made from a metal stamping process and will include a small plastic injection molded part. I am presently exploring both domestic and foreign production. Once you have seen this new product, you very possibly may have a preferred source of your own.

This new novelty item is really quite unique and a lot of fun to use. The initial responses in some key test groups reveal that it is not only very handy but an amusing conversation piece as well! A brief summary of the product is enclosed.

I am interested in revealing this new product to you for your evaluation and possible licensing. Since I am in the process of securing patent protection, I have been advised that I must interview marketing companies on a confidential basis. If you are interested in seeing this novelty product--and discussing the licensing opportunity --please feel free to call me anytime.

I look forward to hearing from you soon.

Sincerely,

Your Name

Figure 10-2

YCN Your Company Name *Company address, city, phone and fax numbers, Web site*

April 24, 1997

Mr. President (preferably the person's name)
Domestic Company
123 Wonderful Street
New York, FL 45678

Subject: Seeking a Dedicated Manufacturer

Dear Mr. President,

I am interested in locating a dedicated manufacturing entity that can consistently produce high-quality metal stampings (coupled with a plastic injection molded part) for my new novelty product. Your company has been identified as a possible supplier, since your products are in a related field. I am seeking marketing experts for the invention as well. Once you have seen this new innovation, you possibly may know some.

This item is really quite unique and a lot of fun to use. The initial responses in test groups reveal that it is a desirable item and an amusing conversation piece. For your convenience, I have enclosed a brief product summary.

I am interested in showing the prototype of this new product to you for your evaluation and possible manufacturing and licensing. Since I am in the process of securing patent protection, I have been advised that I must interview manufacturers on a confidential basis. If you are interested in seeing the product and plans, I have enclosed two pre-signed Confidentiality Agreements, which you can countersign, keep one for yourself, and mail or fax the other back to me. Since premature public disclosure or offering of the invention could be damaging, it is important that these matters remain confidential during the initial development.

When your signed agreement is received, I will forward to you a detailed summary, along with some manufacturing specifications. We can then talk on the phone about the details and discuss your level of interest.

I look forward to hearing from you soon.

Sincerely,

Your Name

Figure 10-3

YCN Your Company Name *Company address, city, phone and fax numbers, Web site*

April 24, 1997

Chinese Culture Center (or any other country)
832 Stockton St.
San Francisco, CA

Subject: Locating a Manufacturer in China

Dear Consulate:

We are seeking a manufacturer for a new novelty product. It will be made from a metal stamping process and will include a small plastic injection molded part as well. Some of the less than ten components will be stock items that can be easily out-sourced. I am fairly certain that this novelty product can be made cost effectively in your country.

It would be much appreciated if you could have one of your Trade Consulate employees advise me of the means to locate manufacturers in China. I would also much appreciate knowing if you have any references for import agents here in the U.S., preferably from Northern or Southern California, who are active in importing small novelty items such as mine. Do you know of any?

Since I am in the process of securing patent protection, working with an import agent here in the U.S. would greatly help expedite matters due to the confidentiality of the new product. Since premature public disclosure or offering of the invention could be damaging to me, it is important that these matters are kept confidential during the development.

I would like to thank you in advance for your assistance in this matter. I look forward to hearing from you soon.

Sincerely,

Your name

Figure 10-4

NEXT: INTERVIEWS WITH CONFIDENTIALITY AGREEMENTS

Sending Confidentiality Agreements to Candidates

When writing to potential manufacturers of your new invention, it can be acceptable to send a confidentiality agreement with the initial inquiry. This is acceptable as many manufacturing experts work confidentially with clients and sign these agreements all the time.

When sending agreements to marketing experts, it is best to talk to them first on the phone and then follow the guidelines on page 202.

Confidentiality Agreements and letters of rejection are an excellent part of your paper trail...keep them in your files!

Many companies do not want to deal with inventors because they believe them to be too difficult to work with. The typical inventor is expected to buck corporate policy, be difficult and unsophisticated. It's OK to be that way if you are financing your own production. If you want to play in the leagues of a Fortune 500 manufacturer, clean up your act. Your first step should be to take "inventor" off your business card and put "Product Developer" or "Product Designer" in its place. Big companies hate dealing with inventors, but they love dealing with product developers.

...Ken Robbins, Dirt Devil

After phone interviews, you will want to meet some of your potential team members/licensees. You will want to explain the opportunity in greater detail and gather more information about these candidates. During these more serious discussions, you will have to disclose confidential details of your invention. Before you do, have a confidentiality agreement (sometimes referred to as a non-disclosure agreement) signed by the heads of the companies you are considering.

You will also want to use confidentiality agreements with any other entity that will occupy a supporting role to your efforts, regardless of whether you are already doing business with them. This could pertain to sub-contractors, parts suppliers or engineers. You never know when you may stop doing business with them or they may be sold.

There are three types of confidentiality agreements. The most common is a "broad-based" non-disclosure agreement that can be used with just about anyone. The second type is a "Plant Visitor Disclosure" for those visiting your (or a licensee's facility). The third is an employee agreement that is usually part of a company's "Employee Patent Program".

Confidentiality agreements protect you and also show your professionalism. For a few hundred dollars, you can ask your attorney to pull one out of his/her computer and tailor it to your needs or you can use or adapt the following agreement. Regardless of which agreement you use, *you* send it when it is required. If you have your attorney send it every time it is needed, it could get costly.

BROAD-BASED CONFIDENTIALITY AGREEMENTS

While not 100% foolproof, a broad-based confidentiality agreement can play an important part in your invention-related activities and reinforce your reduction to practice scheme. It is certainly a lot better to have those you talk to and work with sign one than to use none at all.

In summary, a confidentiality agreement is between two parties, the DISCLOSOR (you) and the DISCLOSEE (the second party). It is a broad, far-reaching agreement signed by both parties, stating that "you" (the DISCLOSOR) will disclose certain confidential information to "him/her" (the DISCLOSEE), which "you" request is kept confidential.

The Confidentiality Agreement in Fig.10-5 is a well-written, broad and universal document that covers most circumstances related to the protection of an inventor's proprietary information. The key points it covers are:

Figure 10-5 Sample Confidentiality Agreement

CONFIDENTIAL INFORMATION AND NON-DISCLOSURE AGREEMENT

This is an agreement between _____, having a place of business at _____ (hereinafter "DISCLOSOR") and _____ having its principal place of business at _____ (hereinafter "DISCLOSEE".)

DISCLOSOR has developed certain proprietary patents, applications, processes, trade secrets, information and intellectual property, which proprietary property relates to _____ _____(hereinafter "INVENTIONS".) Considerable damage could accrue to DISCLOSOR from the premature public disclosure of the existence of the proprietary information and complete loss of commercial advantage could result from disclosure of the information itself.

DISCLOSOR wishes to disclose to DISCLOSEE certain of its confidential material for the sole purpose of permitting DISCLOSEE to determine the suitability or feasibility of performing certain tasks for DISCLOSOR, to bid on performing such tasks, and/or to perform such tasks related to DISCLOSOR's proprietary property as may be further agreed on between the parties hereto.

DISCLOSOR wishes to maintain the confidentiality of the material disclosed to DISCLOSEE and to preserve to himself the commercial benefits from utilization of such material except as may hereafter be specifically agreed in writing between the parties.

DISCLOSEE desires to evaluate the feasibility of performing certain tasks and procedures concerning DISCLOSOR's proprietary property, to bid on performing such tasks, and/or to perform such tasks as may be agreed on between the parties hereto.

THEREFORE the parties agree as follows:

"Confidential material" includes DISCLOSOR's trade secrets, pending or abandoned patent applications, invention disclosures, blue prints, documents, engineering specifications, models, customers, suppliers, distributors, licensees, marketing studies, profits, costs, pricing, tooling, process descriptions, manufacturing processes, and all other material, whether written or oral, tangible or intangible, which DISCLOSOR holds confidential and has not been publicly disclosed by DISCLOSOR or a third party, that are directly related to INVENTIONS.

Unless DISCLOSEE specifically identifies with written consent of DISCLOSOR that certain material is not encompassed by this agreement, all material disclosed by DISCLOSOR to DISCLOSEE relating to INVENTIONS will be presumed to be confidential and will be so regarded by DISCLOSEE unless such materials are publicly available.

DISCLOSEE agrees:
(1) That it will maintain the confidentiality of DISCLOSOR's confidential material and of existence of same;
(2) That it will direct its employees to maintain such confidentialities and will limit access to confidential information to the minimum number of employees necessary to complete DISCLOSEE's tasks, all of which employees shall be identified in writing to DISCLOSOR on his request;
(3) That it will not disclose to any third party, including subcontractors of DISCLOSEE, without written authorization from DISCLOSOR, any of DISCLOSOR's confidential material;
(4) That it will use DISCLOSOR's confidential material solely to perform or determine the feasibility of performing certain tasks to be explicitly specified by DISCLOSOR;

Sample Confidentiality Agreement (continued)

(5) That it will not use for its own benefit or the benefit of any third party any of DISCLOSOR's confidential material;

(6) That it will not contract or negotiate with customers of DISCLOSOR for DISCLOSEE to provide to such customers products manufactured by, or caused to be manufactured by, DISCLOSEE which incorporate or utilize any confidential material of DISCLOSOR; and

(7) That, except as may be further directed or requested by DISCLOSOR, it will not sell, other than to DISCLOSOR, any products manufactured from tooling or molds provided by DISCLOSOR, or developed in accordance with or in response to DISCLOSOR's confidential material.

(8) That on the termination of the relationship between the parties, which may be accomplished via 15-day written notice by either party with or without cause, at the stage of negotiation, DISCLOSEE shall return any and all documents of any nature, originals and copies, to DISCLOSOR. Furthermore, any information, technical or engineering procedure devised for concept which is developed at any stage during these negotiations or other contractual relationship between the parties shall be the sole property and for the sole benefit of DISCLOSOR (except as may be specifically agreed to in writing hereafter) and shall not be used for any other purpose by the DISCLOSEE, its agents, or representatives.

DISCLOSOR and DISCLOSEE further agree:

(1) That should this agreement be breached, money damages would be inadequate compensation, and therefore any court of competent jurisdiction may also enjoin the breaching party from disclosing or utilizing confidential material encompassed by this agreement;

(2) The prevailing party shall be entitled to reasonable attorney fees, in addition to any other amounts awarded as damages;

(3) The laws of the State of California shall govern this agreement and it shall be deemed executed in Chino Hills, California; and,

(4) All amendments or exceptions to this agreement must be in writing.

Both undersigned parties hereby represent that they have authority as agents or representatives of the respective parties to bind the parties to this agreement.

Executed by the parties this _____ day of _____, 199____.

_____
DISCLOSOR

_____
DISCLOSEE (COMPANY NAME)

_____
NAME AND TITLE

1. DISCLOSEE promises to keep information confidential.

2. DISCLOSEE will not disclose to others in DISCLOSEE's company, any information they do not need to know.

3. Great harm may come to DISCLOSEE if information is "leaked" and that DISCLOSOR can and will hold DISCLOSEE liable.

4. DISCLOSOR requests that DISCLOSEE have a confidentiality program or an "Employee Patent Program" to protect DISCLOSOR's proprietary information and property.

5. Any innovations or improvements to DISCLOSOR's invention that are developed with the DISCLOSEE's assistance will become the sole property of the DISCLOSOR.

6. DISCLOSEE will not compete against DISCLOSOR.

7. DISCLOSEE will not try to design around DISCLOSOR.

The only problem with this agreement is that the DISCLOSEE may sometimes want his/her attorney to read it first. The attorney will invariably want to change some wording. If this happens, read the changes carefully. The changes are usually innocuous. For instance, they may want to insert language to indicate that the agreement does not pertain to information the DISCLOSEE already knows or that is "publicly known". This statement is obvious, because the agreement only refers to new, confidential information. Generally, this agreement will be signed, unaltered, 80%-90% of the time if you are sending it to small-, medium- or large-sized corporations.

BASIC RULES OF USING CONFIDENTIALITY AGREEMENTS

There are a few words of caution about using Confidentiality Agreements. Keep them in mind:

1. Always give a copy of the signed agreement to the DISCLOSEE. It will not be in force otherwise.

2. Do not disclose any technical details that will jeopardize your inventive matter until it is signed with a signed copy in your possession.

3. If you don't understand any changes that are made, you may want to talk to your attorney. Most of the changes will be simple and won't require your attorney's involvement, but be careful.

4. If there are state laws governing these agreements, make sure they are a part of the agreement.

5. Make sure your agreements are clean and neatly drafted.

6. The city and state in which it is executed should be yours. If there is ever a challenge to the document, it must then be addressed in your area, instead of in the DISCLOSEE's, which might be 3000 miles away.

Using Confidentiality Agreements with Manufacturing and Marketing Candidates

Most giant corporations will not sign the confidentiality agreements of others. Being afraid of being sued, they will want you to sign theirs instead. If you elect to do this, talk to your attorney first.

Invariably their agreement protects them a lot more than you...if at all. Be careful, some confidentiality agreements have clauses that say something like, "if any of the subject matter discussed was or is now being worked on by them, all proprietary rights will be theirs."

The problem with this clause is the burden of proof needs to be clarified. You don't want to give them the opportunity to say "we already knew about it" and that's the end of subject. You must have some means of verifying their claim so you will not be pitted against their multi-million dollar law firm.

Simpler Versions

You can use simpler versions of a confidentiality agreement in your efforts. Just remember that they may contain less protection and may put the burden of proof on you. However, if you are dealing with larger mega-giant corporations, this is better than nothing at all...and a lot better than signing theirs!

At the very least, having them sign a one-sentence statement saying, "I promise to keep your invention secret" has some power.

...Bob DeMatteis

ASKING OTHERS TO SIGN YOUR CONFIDENTIALITY AGREEMENTS

Having Friends Sign Agreements

*If you want someone to sign a confidentiality agreement who considers himself/herself a good friend and thinks it is not necessary—but **you** want him/her to sign because you don't trust the person—tell him/her that it is "something **your attorney** requires with everyone… **including your mother**"! Then laugh. This helps lighten up the situation.*

Having Trouble Getting Signatures?

The most common reasons I find that companies won't sign confidentiality agreements are:

1. *They are mega-giants that are really not interested.*
2. *It was a blind mailing…you did not talk to them on the phone to "warm them up".*
3. *They are too paranoid that they will "miss out on the opportunity if they sign it" (truth is, they will miss out if they **don't** sign it!).*
4. *They think you are just a "flaky inventor". Don't worry--change your approach and call yourself a "product developer".*

If you are still having problems getting a candidate to sign the long version of the confidentiality agreement, try using a shorter version, like the one in the From Patent to Profit Resource Guide.

Follow these simple guidelines and you will find that those you talk to will usually sign your confidentiality agreements with no modifications at all.

1. Before you send a confidentiality agreement to someone, you should have already had conversations that indicate their interest. Make sure these conversations are friendly. Talk in terms of team efforts and partnerships, not as adversaries.

2. If you are interviewing marketing and manufacturing candidates, you will have revealed much about the benefits to your invention without revealing any specifics. Soon, you will want to meet with them or send them more information. Before you meet with them, tell them that you will need to fax a standard confidentiality agreement.

3. Whether you will be meeting in a couple of days or a couple of weeks, neatly fill out a form and fax it as soon as possible. It becomes less intimidating over time.

4. Sometime before the meeting, call the person to confirm the meeting and that he/she received the agreement. If there is some resistance, you will hear it now. You may have to re-confirm that it is just the standard agreement. You may have to tell him/her that your legal counsel will not allow you to divulge any information until it is signed. If necessary, tell the other party that signing confidentiality agreements is something that your attorney requires from everyone… not just him/her.

5. Just before the meeting, call again to confirm the meeting. If you have not received a signed copy via fax, let the other party know. If his/her attorney made any changes, he/she must fax the agreement to you right away, so you can review it. When you receive the faxed copy with the changes, you may have to consult with your attorney.

6. Be prepared to cancel the meeting if there are major changes. You will only look inexperienced and vulnerable if you don't cancel (or postpone) it.

7. Remember that using confidentiality agreements is something your legal counsel will advise you to do and is important to the future of your project. Don't sacrifice or jeopardize your proprietary position by acting irresponsibly.

TAILORING A (BROAD-BASED) CONFIDENTIALITY AGREEMENT TO YOUR NEEDS

The confidentiality agreement in Fig. 10-5 is easy to modify to fit your specific needs. The obvious changes you may want to make are:

1. Instead of "DISCLOSOR", use your or your company's name...this provides a professional touch.

2. Instead of "DISCLOSEE", insert the actual name of the DISCLOSEE.

3. In the second paragraph, insert the field in which the "proprietary property" relates. For instance, "thermoplastic bags and related bagging systems" or "tortilla manufacturing and related machinery used for cutting and cooking".

4. In paragraph 4, in the section where DISCLOSEE and DISCLOSOR further agree, print the name of your state. If the DISCLOSEE is out of state, do not let the state be changed to his/her location. Any disputes over the agreement would then need to be settled in the DISCLOSEE's state.

If you have any questions as to this document's credibility or acceptability in your trade, you should consult your legal counsel.

VISITOR'S NON-DISCLOSURE

This form of confidentiality agreement is similar to the broad-based non-disclosure, but is limited to the activities viewed inside a plant. It is signed before a visitor visits your facility where he/she will see confidential material owned by you or your company. This confidential material may include your inventions, prototypes or manufacturing processes. This agreement requires a visitor to not discuss confidential matters with anyone. It is slightly narrower in interpretation, as it refers to the visit and not to current or future discussions. Use it with those who are not a threat to your invention--incidental visitors who service equipment or are involved in other non-invention-related matters. If a person is an integral part of your development team, he/she should sign the broad-based non-disclosure instead.

When you visit a prospective licensee, you may be required to sign a confidentiality agreement. If so, make sure that it does not conflict with your agreement.

Confidentiality Agreements have been an important part of business for many years. If you use one in your efforts, which almost all inventors do use from time to time, make sure it is one that is tailored for new product development.

When revealing your new product to others, don't use a general form such as a plant visitor agreement or a "universal confidentiality agreement". This can be confusing if ever challenged in court.

EMPLOYEE PATENT PROGRAM (AND AGREEMENT)

This agreement instructs employees not to discuss plant activities with others outside of the plant. It also advises employees that if they make a discovery (or invention) related to the business matters of the company, it will be the property of the company. Further, it says that employees will cooperate in filing and assigning to the company, any and all documents, if patent applications are filed and pursued.

Also referred to as a Trade Secret Program, this program is usually revealed in a two-step process.

- First, an announcement by the President of the company discusses the importance of the new trade secret program.
- Second, the employee is asked to sign a non-disclosure agreement, which includes an agreement to assign to the company all relevant inventions and patents in which he may participate or develop.

Inexperienced employees can inadvertently "leak information" when they socialize with others from competing plants. The Trade Secret Program explains the sensitivity of confidential matters within the plant. Without it, employees have no way of knowing what is confidential.

This agreement is what you will use in your company, if you start one, and what you will ask your licensees to use in their plants.

INVENTION (OR PRODUCT) PROSPECTUS

With a confidentiality agreement in place, you can elect to send a prospectus based on your market studies, lab tests and even your intuition. More and more, prospectuses are becoming an important part of a successful invention/product development strategy. A prospectus is not a business plan; it is an analysis of current market conditions, products available and the opportunity your invention presents. An invention prospectus should contain the following:

SECTION I: PRODUCT OPPORTUNITY SUMMARY

The first section is a more in-depth description than the invention summary you previously sent. It will include:

1. **Field of the Product.** One paragraph describing the field of the invention/product.
2. **Background of the Product.** Summary of the state-of-the-art in the industry.
3. **Description of the Present State of the Art.** Tell about the current products available and their shortcomings.
4. **Product Summary.** How your new product overcomes the shortcomings of the other products.
5. **Test Results.** Provide a factual analysis.

An Invention Prospectus Is Important

This is becoming an increasingly important part of the invention-licensing process. A well-written prospectus is the inventor's version of a business plan.

I don't think there is any doubt about it. Give a prospective licensee a prospectus and you are greatly increasing your ability to be successful.

...Stephen Gnass

PRODUCT OPPORTUNITY SUMMARY

Section I of your prospectus is the invention summary, which is similar to the one-page summary you may have included with the letter of inquiry, but with a bit more detail. Below the title, insert language that specifically requests that confidentiality be maintained.

If you have a patent application written or filed, you can use some of the application language in your summary.

6. Patent Status. Offer an accurate report with honest expectations.

7. About the Product Developer. Include a brief biographical statement about yourself.

SECTION II: INDUSTRY ANALYSIS

1. Introduction.

2. Current Position of Existing Producers. Their attitudes toward the marketplace.

3. The Best Approach to Sales and Protection of Your Niche. How do you plan to capture your niche?

4. A Breakthrough Opportunity. Do not falsely claim that it is.

5. The Licensing Opportunity. In general terms.

6. Barriers to Entry. What resistance will there be? If you don't know, you have not done enough research.

7. Long-term Opportunity.

SECTION III: TARGET MARKET

1. Introduction.

2. Market Description. Clearly identified, narrow targets.

3. Market Size and Trends. It has to be relevant to some market. Is it entertaining? A learning aid?

4. Additional Considerations.

5. Market Readiness. How is the timing?

6. Marketing Plan Assistance. How are you going to assist in their efforts?

7. Sales Projections. Establish realistic targets.

SECTION IV: START-UP COSTS

Present a reasonable cost analysis. If you don't know what it may be, employ the producer's assistance to find out.

A MODEL PROSPECTUS

The following is an invention/product prospectus you can use as a model. It is based on the same plastic grocery sack that was used as an example in Chapter 7 on how to write a patent application. You can write your prospectus with more or less detail, but be concise and try to capture the reader's interest.

As you read this prospectus, note how the categories match previous parts of your invention activities, such as your initial invention disclosure, and can even read right on your patent application. Thinking in this story telling vein will allow you to move swiftly through all your inventing-, patenting-, marketing- and licensing-related activities.

Invention Vs. Product

In the model prospectus, note how almost all the words regarding an "invention" read "product" instead.

To Attract a Manufacturer… It Works!

As an expert marketer, we launched a new product recently and needed to attract at least one mega-giant or giant corporation as a manufacturer to supply our customers in a $300 million dollar market.

We needed to send them a detailed proposal, but sending them a copy of our business plan would have been inappropriate. Sending them our business plan would mean sending them confidential information about our sales and marketing plan that we did not want them to know.

What we did instead was to model our proposal after the invention/product prospectus in the book. It was easy, fast and very effective.

We titled it, "Manufacturing Prospectus", eliminated some of the information regarding the industry analysis and our specific target markets and that was about all.

The result was astounding. The prospectus landed us three serious candidates vying for position. One of which became the suitor.

…Joe Justin, Pinnacle

The text boxes contain hints about how to write this important document.

SECTION I: PRODUCT OPPORTUNITY SUMMARY
(The following confidential information is not to be copied without prior written permission by the Bob DeMatteis Company.)

Field of the Product

This one-paragraph summary is similar to what you wrote (or will write) in your patent application. The more you can focus on these descriptions, the better your patent-related writing will be.

Field of the Product

This product relates to plastic sacks commonly used in supermarket, drug and discount stores in food and related trades, to carry merchandise from the store to home. More specifically, this product relates to a plastic sack style and system that can be used to substantially improve load capacity and loading efficiency. This new innovation is called the Bigmouth™ sack and system.

Background of the Product

Plastic sacks have become the most popular style of bag to carry merchandise and their related loading systems are preferred in high-volume outlets in North America and much of Europe, Australia and Asia. In these high-volume outlets, the systems incorporate a rack style holder, which supports the thin-gauged bags while a user loads the bags and removes the filled bags from the holder.

Background of the Invention

This too reflects what is written in your patent application.

Being able to fill plastic sacks by utilizing as much of the entire capacity as possible is important in high-volume outlets. If the capacity is not properly utilized, i.e. under utilized, more bags will be used, thereby increasing both bag and labor costs. A system that utilizes as much of the available capacity in a plastic sack as possible can represent an important cost-cutting measure.

Description of the Present State of the Art

The most popular system in use in the world's high-volume outlets is described in U.S. Re. Pat. 33,264. Plastic sacks of this variety have a centrally located detachable tab that extends upwardly, and holes intermediately located in each handle. These bags are generally in unitary packs of 50 or 100 bags, which are mounted onto a rack-style holder by threading the two sets of handle holes onto two rod supports and placing the centrally located upwardly extending detachable, apertured tab, onto a centrally located retaining means.

Description of the Present State-of-the-Art

If you are using language from your patent application, you may want to rewrite some of it, so it reads easier and is not "patent-like" legalese. A lot depends on the nature of your invention and those you are addressing. If it is technically oriented, be more technical and to the point. This example is more technical than most.

The retaining means holds the bag pack in place while the forward-most bag is being utilized. To prepare for utilization, the user separates the front wall of the forward-most bag and pulls it forward, while the bag is being supported by the rod supports and the rear bag wall is being retained at the centrally located tab mounted onto the projecting element of the rack. The user then loads the bag in this supported position.

A problem associated with this prior art system is that when bags are mounted on the rack-style holder, they hang down to an undesirable extent. This is confirmed by the fact that the upwardly extending tab which is hooked on the projecting element forces the bag mouth to be below the top of the rack style holder. It is further compounded by the fact that the plastic sack handles are generally 6" long and on mounting the intermediate handle holes onto the holder's rod supports, the bag and the bag mouth are caused to hang down to an even greater extent.

Further compounding the problem is that in order to open up the bag mouth to a sufficient width so a user can load the bag, the rod supports must be spread outward, beyond the normal distance spanning the handle holes. Thus, the handle holes mounted on the rod supports cause the handles to be stretched outward about 11-12", with the handle ends pointing outward as well.

The result, on opening a forward-most bag, is a bag and bag mouth hanging down below the rod supports, well below the top of the rack holder and with a relatively narrow, oblong-shaped, open-mouth configuration. The hanging bag actually resists squaring itself out due to being forced to take on this unnatural, oblong configuration. This narrow oblong configuration generally causes the user to under-utilize the actual capacity of the plastic sack.

As illustrated in the PRIOR ART Figure 1 of the drawings, the upwardly extending tab T determines where the central region of the bag mouth M will be situated on the rack style holder in its lowered position. The bag mouth's lowered position is further determined by intermediate handle holes H mounted onto rod supports S. Such mounting causes the bag to hang downward below the rod supports S on the rack-style holder. The result is the oblong configuration C of bag mouth M.

The PRIOR ART Figure 1A shows that the support members of the rack have a back support B, rack retainer R, in which the bag pack is retained, side rod supports S and S' on which handle apertures H and H' are threaded. The handles typically lay on the outside of the rod supports as illustrated, which pushes the sack's body down and inward. The confined bag mouth is illustrated by the arrows, which touch the outer extremities of the opened bag mouth.

This confining effect is typically due to three factors. One, when the bag is opened, the bag mouth opening is restricted by the short span between the stretched apart handle holes, typically only 4"-6", illustrated as X. The second factor is that with the short span X, it causes the bag's rear wall W to also pull forward and away from the bag pack P, further confining the bag mouth opening. The third factor is that the rod supports S and S' are typically about 7"-8" long, which is less than the required dimension to allow a bag to fully expand its potential bag mouth opening.

Product Summary

The plastic sack and rack mounting system of the present product innovation increase the ability of the user to access the sack's entire capacity. When the plastic sack of the present product innovation is placed on a rack-style holder and opened up, it utilizes more of the bag system's cube for loading than is possible with prior art systems.

This is accomplished by using a unique design that lifts the sack high onto its rack holder and allows the bag mouth to be opened more widely. In fact, the bag mouth actually opens up to a configuration that

What Liberty Can You Take?

Keep in mind that if your invention has an emotional flare, it is perfectly acceptable to convey some pizzazz to reflect the emotion it elicits. However, be careful with the use of "cutesy" words and gimmicky artwork. Keep your content professional.
...Bob DeMatteis

Product Summary

These paragraphs should reflect in substantial detail how your invention actually works. They should also reflect what you wrote in your patent application.

This section will probably include drawings that you reference as you describe the invention and compare it to prior art. You can use some of the same drawings you used in your patent application, which will help validate the authenticity of your claims.

At times, you may include an actual prototype. If a prototype is not available, that may be one reason you are pursuing your invention with this company. You can ask in your prospectus for assistance in prototyping.

Most prospectuses will not be as detailed as this model, for which a patent was granted in September, 1997. The material in this prospectus was used in actual license solicitations months prior to the granting of the patent, with positive results.

provides more area than the original bag dimensions would indicate to be possible. For instance, a plastic grocery sack which typically measures 12" across by 7" wide has an open mouth area of 84" square (12" times 7"); whereas this same sized bag in the form of the present product innovation can take on a squared out configuration of 9.5" across by 9.5" wide (9.5" times 9.5") or an open mouth area of 90.25" square.

Instead of an upwardly extending detachable tab, one style of the bag pack of the present product innovation is retained on the rack-style holder by mounting a transverse slit on a centrally located detachable portion of the bag body which is located below the bag mouth. The detachable portion is then retained on the central retaining means of the rack holder. The result is a bag that is actually lifted up with the bag mouth disposed at approximately the top of the rack holder instead of hanging down below it as in prior art systems.

The outer regions of the bag body and mouth are also lifted up high onto the rack-style holder by providing two laterally spaced apertures in the sides of the bag and passing the rod supports through the apertures. These two spaced apertures in the body are normal to the plane of the centrally located detachable portion and may be disposed near the outside edges of the plastic sack. When the apertures are placed onto the rod supports of the rack holder and the centrally located detachable portion is secured on the central retaining means, the result is a plastic sack which sits high up on the rack holder. When opened by the user, it squares itself out naturally along the rod supports.

The lifting up of the bag walls and the squaring out effect increase the area of the open bag mouth substantially and can result in the ability to load up to 20% to 30% more merchandise. When the sack is fully loaded, it is then a simple operation to locate and grasp the handles, which lay atop the rod supports, and remove the loaded sack from the rack holder. Thus, the plastic sack of the present product innovation lends itself to being loaded more fully and more easily, and is simple to use.

As illustrated in the drawing of the present product innovation of Figure 2, plastic bag 31 has a bottom 32, two handles 33 and 33', a bag mouth 34, a body 38, and side gusset panels 41 and 41'. Bag mouth 34 extends substantially horizontally from the base 33a of handle 33 to the base 33a' of the handle 33'. Centrally located in the bag mouth 34 is detachable portion 35, which has a slit 37 within its perimeter, which perimeter is defined by perforation line 39 below and bag mouth 34 above. Body apertures 36 and 36' are spaced laterally from detachable portion 35 and below handles 33 and 33' respectively. Body apertures 36 and 36' are cut through both front bag wall 56 and rear wall 55 (Fig. 6) of bag body 38 and through gusset panels 41 and 41' respectively.

The present product innovation, as illustrated in Fig. 3, shows bag 31 is opened and ready for loading with rear bag mouth location 55 seen as being clearly proximate to and slightly above brace 54 and rod supports 51 and 51'. In this open end position, front bag wall 56 has been separated from the detachable portion 35, and extended fully forward, thereby causing gusset panels 41 and 41', defined by dotted lines, to also expand fully forward and leave handles 33 and 33', laying atop rod supports 51 and 51' respectively. It will be appreciated that in this open position, with front bag wall 56 extended fully forward, the bag mouth opening 61 is considerably enlarged and squared out over what is achievable in the prior art system. Through the enlarged bag mouth opening 61, the user has easy access to load merchandise into the available cube capacity within bag 31.

Actual Test Results of the Bigmouth™ Sack

In summary, sales of the Bigmouth™ sack over the past year have resulted in substantial savings to end user customers. The actual, bottom line savings reported by customers is 22%-44%.

What is perhaps most interesting is that this saving is based on the Bigmouth™ sack being sold at a price substantially higher than current, light-gauged, $1/6^{th}$ or $1/7^{th}$ barrel bags. The saving, of course, has been due to the end user using far fewer bags. Furthermore, testing has also produced the same results with larger bags. For instance, with the current onslaught of jumbo grocery sacks which cost 40%-50% more than the Bigmouth™ sack, the saving has still been evident. The facts show that checkers and packers load about the same amount of merchandise in both the Bigmouth™ sacks and the jumbo sacks!

Patent Status

The new innovation, the Bigmouth™ sack, has two U.S. and Canadian Patents pending. The two U.S. Patents have been approved. One patent will issue on September 2, 1997 as U.S. Patent No. 5,662,225. The other should follow shortly afterward.

The scope of the patents based on the inventive matter revealed in this prospectus is quite broad. It covers at least the location of detachable portions below the bag mouth, the location of apertures in the bag body and the use of these two embodiments in a system.

Furthermore, the patents do not infringe or cause the infringement of any existing patents, including all those of Mobil Chemical and Sonoco Products Company.

The patent attorney who has prosecuted the patent applications is Bill Pavitt, Esq., in Los Angeles, California. Bill is very experienced in the field of plastics packaging and in particular, plastic grocery sacks.

About the Product Developer

Bob DeMatteis is an experienced product developer in the field of plastics packaging. He has 14 U.S. Patents and several others pending. Sales of his patented products today are in excess of $25 million annually and are sold to Sears, Kroger, Wal-Mart and other major and minor retailers. Time and again, his patents have withstood the threat of infringement. He has developed, patented and licensed niche products used throughout the U.S. and Canada in three primary areas of plastics packaging: merchandise bags, T-shirt grocery sacks and bags on rolls.

Actual Test Results

Hard facts can be most helpful in your ability to get interest from potential licensees. Financial decisions are usually based on verifiable facts. If you do not have any test results, you will want to pursue the testing with your potential partners.

It would be smart to include in your prospectus that you would like to work with them to establish actual test results. This can be an important part of your Marketing Plan, which is presented later in the prospectus.

Patent Status

Summarize your patent status. Do not falsely claim that there is a patent pending. (Refer to the previous sections on how to position your invention.)

If you can give an honest analysis of the patent protection you expect to achieve, you would be wise to do so.

About the Product Developer

Include a brief summary highlighting your experience. Include information that is relevant to your inventing and new product launching activities. Do not say, "I have always wanted to be an inventor and hope to find someone to license my ideas." You want to be perceived as a specialist in your particular niche.

SECTION II: INDUSTRY ANALYSIS

Introduction

The new innovation is positioned to take advantage of the current attitudes of many major manufacturers in the plastics packaging arena. In the past 5-6 years, these producers have incorrectly responded to soaring front-end costs their customers have experienced. Kowtowing to their demands to lower front-end costs, major manufacturers have lowered the cost per unit (cost per case of 1000 bags, for instance) by lowering quality by literally reducing the size and gauge of the standard grocery sack. In confirmation of this point, a plastic grocery sack has shrunk in size by over 20% and in gauge by more than 50% in just the past 10 years. During the last few years, this ludicrous trend has increased and pushed bag sizes and gauges to the threshold of being practically non-functional.

It has become apparent that most major manufacturers are intent on playing a shell game of sorts, trying to mass manufacture the existing "generic product" only, instead of tackling the real problem. This problem as perceived by the end users is soaring front-end bag costs. The solution as perceived by most of the customer's buyers and the manufacturers is to lower the price per case of bags, in order to reduce the soaring costs.

The real problem is not soaring bag costs. In fact, that is only a symptom of the real problem. The real problem (at its root) is four-fold. First, it lies in the simple fact that the smaller the bag's size, the less they will contain. Second, the thinner they are made, the less confidence a user in loading them full, hence under-filling them. Third, and perhaps the most important issue, is that the current generic system advocates improper bagging techniques...the result of which is a poorly under-packed bag. The fourth reason is that retail store operations cannot continue to train employees--full-time, part-time or seasonal--in proper bagging techniques.

We all know very well how under-packed our grocery sacks are when we come home from a shopping trip. Two to three items per bag is an average count. No wonder bag costs are soaring when the item count should be at least 2-3 times that amount! And no wonder that what was once estimated to be a 25 billion bag marketplace ballooned way up to over 60-70 billion bags in just a few years!

High Volume T-shirt Bag Producer's Make-up

Most every producer targets high-volume, major chain markets. Why? When products are being sold based on "cost per case" only, long runs are the only possible means of making a profit. For this reason, virtually every manufacturer focuses on long-run, generic-based business.

One other characteristic of these high-volume producers is that they tend to sell their generic products to either distributors (not the real customer) or to buyers. Then tend to skip over (even avoid) the operations people and are rarely concerned with what is actually happening with their products. True to form, these generic producers

---

SECTION II: INDUSTRY ANALYSIS

This title should be the heading at the top of a page. The purpose of this section is to provide an in-depth analysis of the industry in which your invention relates.

Don't summarize the current suppliers and try to anticipate their competitive responses. If you don't have accurate information about the industry leaders, you will be vulnerable to other opinions.

The Generic Leader's Make-up

This is a must. Since the industry leaders are most likely not your potential licensees, provide an accurate analysis of them and their probable responses to your invention.

MANUFACTURING AND MARKETING

are all chasing the same generic market, trying to squeeze out a little more market share than the next company.

The Best Approach to Sales and Protection of the Bigmouth™ Sack Niche

Based on the current results in the United States, it is believed there will not be serious challenges by the major producers in the near future based on several factors.

- First, they sell to the wrong parties--typically distributors and buyers. It is difficult to change bad habits in mid-stream.
- Second, by not immediately targeting long-run business, they do not make the large generic runs their equipment (and mentality) is set up to do.
- Third, the Bigmouth™ sack is impossible to make on a lot of the existing bag-making equipment without major modifications. Only about 20% of existing bag machines can make the product.
- Fourth, with patents that will issue shortly, eventual patent infringement will become an issue in an industry that has experienced several damaging infringement claims.
- Fifth, our legal counsel has already defeated the largest producer in an unrelated patent issue and has successfully stopped infringement against several other major retailers and manufacturers.
- Sixth, this same counsel, on behalf of Bob DeMatteis, has also successfully defended his patents with at least four victories in the past few years.

A Breakthrough Opportunity

The Bigmouth™ sack is a proven, successful sack and system with resounding success in actual tests that consistently reported savings from 22%-44%. It overcomes the real problems associated with front-end systems. Sales of the Bigmouth™ sack and system can also be made with the confidence of knowing that the existing major producers will most likely not jump in and henceforth pursue making the same problem-solving products. This would be especially true in light of the solid patent protection with a broad enough scope to keep out clones and copycats. Furthermore, patent infringement protection will be supported by expert patent counsel, Bill Pavitt, Esq.

The Licensing Opportunity

Bob DeMatteis Company is interested in licensing one or two U.S. or Canadian producers with strong marketing skills for the exclusive manufacturing and sales rights in Canada. The license will be for production of either low-density films, high-density films, or both. An exclusive license to a marketing company will also be considered. Dedicated producers will subsequently be appointed to supply the marketing entity.

This license agreement can be structured in several ways, but generally speaking, it will be structured to have favorable, declining

---

The Best Niche

Remember all new inventions and products start out as niches. In this section, you want to narrowly define the niche that you are suggesting your team can capture.

Of course, this may change once your team is in place and is fine tuning your marketing plan.

A Breakthrough Opportunity

Keep breakthrough opportunities confined to your niche, not to the entire market.

Use simple, straightforward language that substantiates the potential. If your invention is not considered a real breakthrough, don't call it one.

The Licensing Opportunity

*Describe the basis of the licensing arrangement you are pursuing. Be somewhat specific, but leave the details open for discussion. This is **not** the place to say, "I want a 10% royalty and an up-front deposit of $500,000."*

royalties based on sales volume and certain guarantees on performance to maintain the exclusive rights. The license will include the use of the established trademark, Bigmouth™, and the term of the license can be for up to 20 years.

Other favorable terms and conditions may be available to the right licensee under certain circumstances. For instance, the Bigmouth™ Sack can represent a very favorable means for a customer to justify the higher costs of low-density bags.

In no condition whatsoever is this Prospectus an offering of license in any form to any one person or entity. Any license offer will expressly be made in subsequent written form.

Barriers to Entry

There are four barriers to entry for a Canadian licensee. They are:

- **The right equipment.** Does your company currently possess the right bag-making equipment to make the Bigmouth™ sack or will modifications be required? How costly will that be? The turnkey bag machines are Amplas, some Limos and some Elbas. Others can be adapted easily and some perhaps not so easily.
- **The right sales approach.** Does your sales team or your existing manufacturer's representatives call on the operations people at the end user? This is where you will find tremendous success, not through buyers or distributors. If not, are you committed to re-training your sales team or hiring new sales people?
- **Training aids.** It would be wise to create new brochures, training posters, etc. to help train the end users. Fortunately, once the initial start-up (a few days) has passed, the learning curve is very fast. It is natural to load the bags full, which means that excessive training of new employees or part-time and seasonal employees is not necessary.
- **New racks.** The Bigmouth™ system requires new racks. While this can initially be considered a negative because of the start-up expense, most consider it a positive. The reason is three-fold. First, the cost of the new racks has been amortized and completely paid for by the first two months' sales of Bigmouth™ Sacks. Second, the other, generic bags don't work as well on the new rack, helping to maintain your sales advantage in the event that you will be sharing the business. Third, you are doing your customer a great favor by providing the new systems.

A supplier of racks has been appointed and can handle an assortment of custom rack requirements.

Barriers to Entry

Make a list of the requirements needed to get your project launched.

You are the team captain. If you don't know what these barriers are, you will have to find out. They can include equipment, the right marketing approach and much more.

The list you make here may overlap into your marketing plan, where you will develop new training aids, brochures, etc. Other barriers may include the need to license other technology, secure an adequate supply of raw material and at times to develop a means of distribution, albeit that is not usually difficult if your product is in demand.

Long-term Opportunity

A licensee of the Bigmouth™ Sack that can successfully take the product to market will have other proprietary, patented innovations offered to them as well. Other innovations, whose patents are owned by the Bob DeMatteis Company, may include Dual-Tab® bags, some roll bag systems and trash liners.

SECTION II: TARGET MARKET

Market Description

The target market for Bigmouth™ sacks includes retailers and supermarkets that focus on productivity in their operations. Some of these may be larger chain operations, but experience tells us that it is usually the medium-sized chains that have a better understanding of productivity. Productivity-oriented companies tend to base their bag costs on actual bottom line savings, not on a per case cost. Per case, the Bigmouth™ Sack costs more than traditional 1/6th and 1/7th Barrel bags, but in any given time period, the actual expenditures on plastics sacks will be less.

Perhaps the biggest side benefit to any customer using the Bigmouth™ system is that they will also improve their productivity, due to using fewer sacks, less handling, etc.

Market Size and Trends

While the target market is a potentially nondescript market to identify--in other words, you could say that every retailer wants to improve productivity--the focus would be on only the most progressive, the top 20%, of those retailers. You could also say that the focus would be on retailers that recognize a need to improve their front-end performance, hence lower bag costs.

From this viewpoint, capturing about 20% of the target market short-term (3 years), is about 2% of the overall market and should be realistic. The entire Canadian grocery sack market is estimated at about 5 billion sacks annually. At an average price of $15 per case, this amounts to $75 million annually. Therefore, 20% of the total market would be about $15 million annually and 20% of this target would be about $3 million.

Capturing 20% of Canada's target market in three years might look like this:

Supermarket	$2.2 million
Drug	.3 million
Hardware	.2 million
Others	.3 million
Total	$3.0 million

Long-term Opportunity

If there is a long-term opportunity with your invention, summarize it here. But do not rely on this as an incentive to license your invention. Position yourself with the attitude that "if they can do a good job with this opportunity, it will be the basis to open a long-term opportunity".

TARGET MARKET

This section is a reiteration of the niche you plan to capture but goes into more detail.

Market Description

Start with a brief description of the target market, the niche, you plan to capture.

Market Size and Trends

Be accurate in identifying your market and its size. Notice that in the model, the target market is not based on geography or type of store, but on only those retailers that are conscientious and have productivity-focused businesses.

Get the facts, so you can present reasonable numbers. Over-zealous projections will affect your credibility.

Other Considerations about the Target Market

Here you can add some comments about why your target may even be larger than anticipated. Illustrate that you are not relying on it as part of your industry analysis.

Market Readiness

Comment about why you think the timing is good.

Marketing Plan Assistance

How can you help them in their endeavor? Be specific.

Sales Projections

Based on your analysis of the target market and its potential, you can now list the sales projections. They should be based on monthly sales over at least a 2-3 year period. Base the projections on the available supply of raw materials and a company's financial and physical ability to gear up and respond.

START-UP COSTS

This final section should be a simple summary of the costs required to launch the project. Remember that most companies will expect to invest money in new projects, so do not be afraid to ask for it here.
In particular, add a fair deposit for the license agreement. This deposit will be credited against future royalties.

Other Considerations about the Target Market

It is possible that the right marketing effort can bring to the forefront a "fast food" opportunity with the new Bigmouth™ Sack. The ease of loading the Bigmouth™ Sack means that sales could quickly take an additional giant step forward. The fast food industry is one of the last using papers bags. One of the new Bigmouth™ products (called the LittleBigmouth™) may be able to make a substantial dent in this traditional paper-bag volume.

It is also possible that market conditions will cause the identification of the root problems associated with the high cost of using the current, generic front-end systems. A few years back, Joseph Lerch, Esq., a patent attorney with Darby and Darby, wrote his legal opinion on the Bigmouth™ patent disclosure and said, "Well, it is obvious that everyone will be going to this new product...that it will be the preferred system...if it does what it appears it will do." All reports this past year have confirmed that it is doing exactly as anticipated.

Market Readiness

Soaring plastic resin costs have caused bag prices to rise. This has only compounded the problem of high bag costs. A large number of retailers will listen to those who offer solutions that can be verified.

Marketing Plan Assistance

Bob DeMatteis Company can assist in the training of your sales team and the preparation of a marketing plan that will fit your needs. This assistance would be coordinated through the direction of a national sales coordinator. It may include the hiring of reps and the preparation of trade show sales aids and related brochures, posters and videos.

Sales Projections

The following sales and financial projections are predicated on an adequate sales thrust in 1998 that allows for time to travel, hire and train sales representatives and buy rack supplies and inventory. The cost analysis is based on current price levels in U.S. dollars, and is subject to change, although profit percentages or margins should not be significantly affected.

SECTION II: START-UP COSTS

The following start-up costs are based on one-time expenses that will impact the first two months of operation. The following cash flow summaries reflect these one-time costs:

1. Hiring an artist to create brochures and promotional materials: Cost projected at $2000, payable over the first two months. On-going costs are reflected in the promotional account.
2. Initial printing of the promotional materials and assembly into catalogs: Cost projected at $2000, payable over the first two months. On-going costs are reflected in promotional account.

3. Initial rack inventory: Cost is $3000, payable in the first two months of operation. On-going costs are reflected in the hardware account.
4. Miscellaneous start-up expenses, including travel and training, are projected at $5000.
5. Licensing deposit against royalties: Cost is estimated at $20,000.

Start-up costs for the first three months would be:

ITEM		MONTH 1	MONTH 2
1.	Hire an artist	$ 1,000	$ 1,000
2.	Initial printing of promotional materials	$ 1,000	$ 1,000
3.	Initial rack inventory	$ 1,500	$ 1,500
4.	Misc. start-up and travel exp.	$ 2,500	$ 2,500
5.	License deposit	$10,000	$10,000
	Total expenses	$16,000	$16,000
	Grand total		$32,000

FORMALIZING YOUR PROSPECTUS

Once completed, your prospectus should be neatly packaged in a folder or bound in an inexpensive comb-style binding. Use attractive, friendly colors, such as blues and greens, for more technically oriented prospectuses. Colors such as chartreuse, lavender and pink should be used only in situations that call for some unusual flare, such as products appealing to women and cosmetics. Remember that your audience consists of conservative executives, production managers and sales professionals.

Send a brief cover letter with each prospectus. You may use language such as, "I have enjoyed talking to you these past few days," and "I look forward to discussing your interest on the project in the enclosed prospectus."

Deliver the prospectus via the mail or an overnight delivery service. Do not fax it. Remember that if your prospectus contains confidential information, send it only if you have a confidentiality agreement signed by the other party.

Sales Projections

May or may not be included. After all, sales projections would have to be those of your marketing expert, since that will be its commitment.

If you include some sales projections, make sure it is only in a narrowly defined niche that you feel comfortable can be captured.

Your entire Prospectus (that took you hours or days to prepare) can be tossed in the trash in one second if your projections are not believable. The reader would think, "With these laughable sales figures, I imagine the rest of the information in this prospectus is also fabricated."

11

YOUR MANUFACTURING EXPERT

*Look for one that truly understands the quality
and service you need. Make sure they have the
track record you expect. Don't settle for a promise.*

*Holding a patent on a new
product and bringing that new
product to market are two
different things. Some patents
describe well intentioned but
unrealistic technology that would
be difficult or impractical to
produce.*

*...Donald Grant Kelly,
U.S. Patent Office Director*

If you are not going to produce the invention yourself, you must locate manufacturers with the ability to get the job done and done **right**! It takes a lot of manufacturing savvy to induce the birth of a new invention. A manufacturer with savvy can make things happen a lot faster than if you go into the manufacturing business.

The right manufacturing partner can quickly make prototypes and gear up for production. As discussed in Chapter 2, the right manufacturer can save you a lot in start-up costs and prototyping. Even if you plan to license several producers non-exclusively, select a favorite producer that can work with you early on. You can grant them a "jump on the market" with a short-term exclusive in exchange for their prototyping assistance and working models for tests and trials.

If you plan to manufacture and sub-contract some or all of the components, your sub-contractors can also help in the same manner. The key is to find manufacturing partners with motivated, smart people who can solve start-up problems and then propel production ahead.

YOUR MANUFACTURING OBJECTIVE

Your primary marketing goal is to locate a willing manufacturing company with all the right attributes that can mass-produce your invention. It is most important that you find a producer able to make your invention the way you want it made--not the other way around. You simply cannot allow a manufacturer to dictate how your invention will be made.

The manufacturer can provide input, but if you modify your invention to make it more and more generic, you will destroy its uniqueness. This could be a disaster. Keep in mind that you are "customer driven" and your invention is a Customer-Driven Innovation. You will significantly decrease your potential for success by being "production driven". To have a successful invention means applying CDI and not kowtowing to the mediocrity of manufacturers who prefer generic production processes.

Separate a company's ability to manufacture from its ability to market. Remember that companies with a manufacturing focus are usually not very good at sales. When evaluating manufacturing abilities, use manufacturing-related questions. As you read this chapter, make a list of the crucial needs and attributes of your invention.

When searching for manufacturers, do not limit your search to the United States. Look everywhere in the world. Be patient, keep networking and searching and you will find the right fit.

HOW MANY MANUFACTURERS WILL YOU NEED?

The answer to this question will be determined by your marketing and licensing approach. The four possible approaches are:

1. Exclusive marketing and licensing of the entire scope of the patent(s) to a single entity. One company will take it and run!
2. Exclusive licensing of the scope of the patent(s) in various unrelated and non-competitive fields. One single company will take it and run within a given field.
3. The non-exclusive licensing of the invention in one or more fields. You will license more than one entity, regardless of the field.
4. An exclusive license in one field and non-exclusive licenses in one or more other fields, such that the non-exclusive licenses specifically exclude the scope of the exclusive license.

As you analyze your approach, here are some factors to consider:

A Big Expense for You Is a Small Expense for Them

What could cost you a small fortune for R&D and prototyping, the right manufacturer can do at a fraction of the cost and in a fraction of the time. If you are not a manufacturer, you need a close association with one that is flexible, future thinking and highly competent.

Simplicity Vs. Sacrifice

Although keeping the design of your product simple is almost always a good idea, don't unnecessarily sacrifice product functionality for simplicity. If you manufacture your product in Asia, the lower labor costs will allow the use of a lot more parts without significant impact on the cost of the product.

The cost of an injection-molded product produced in Asia is mostly a function of the amount of plastic used, and the shipping volume.

...Paul Berman, T2 Designs

When seeking out manufacturers, you might want to keep in mind "minority based enterprises" (MBE). Since the purchasing power of minorities is expected to pass that of majorities by the year 2000, there are many incentives for customers to buy from minority owned enterprises. There are usually cost advantages as well. In other words, you may be able to get a slightly higher price.

...Mike Griffin, Pinnacle Group

Non-exclusive Licensing Relationships

With non-exclusive licensing relationships throughout an industry or field, licensees can do as they please and use your invention as they please. You will have a relatively hands-off relationship with them. They may provide less incentive for a producer to push your invention. Your position would be to license anyone and everyone and hope they use the invention wisely. A good example of non-exclusive licensing is the "flip-top" can invention that allows the flip-top to remain attached to the can. It replaced all the throwaway flip-tops because of its positive environmental impact.

You will read more about the relative values of non-exclusive or exclusive licenses in Chapters 13 and 14.

Exclusive Licensing Relationships

Exclusive licenses provide the licensee with an incentive to make things happen because the licensee has some proprietary patent protection. In return, these licenses usually include a guarantee of sales volume and minimum royalties. It is common to have different exclusive licensees in different fields. When granting exclusive licenses, do not waste your time on a candidate that will not put up front money or give a long-term guarantee on sales and income.

Exclusive licenses may not be advisable for a commodity-type product. For instance, it destroyed Sony's Beta Max, and contributed to the downfall of Apple Computer. But if you are carving out a specific commodity niche that you want to protect, it is usually best to have a dedicated, exclusive relationship.

HOW DO YOU FIND MANUFACTURING PARTNERS?

There are many good avenues to search. As you search, keep an open mind and look for every potential manufacturing candidate in the entire world. Do not limit yourself to your metropolitan area or just the U.S., Canada and Mexico.

Consider:
1. **Companies you already know.** If you work in the field of your invention, you may already know some qualified candidates.

2. **Personal recommendations.** Network with friends and business associates.

3. **Trade shows.** Go to trade shows as a visitor, not as an exhibitor. You can effectively network with experts in your industry in a short period of time. Most decision makers attend shows to visit with

---

Exclusives Can Kill a Product!

Just remember that companies like Apple Computer, who were the leaders early on, did not license their technology, which eventually caused them to lose tremendous market share.

This blunder opened up the market for all the IBM clones and their competitive software.

Today we are all quite familiar with the software company that took advantage of this opportunity...Microsoft!

Slinky Toy Inventor, Helen Malsed, Dies

One of America's most prolific woman inventors, Helen Malsed, died recently at the age of 88.

In 1958 she earned $5000 for inventing large, irregular-shaped interlocking beads sold as "jewelry" for children. Unlike the tiny plastic pieces of similar toys, her beads were made too big to fit into a toddler's mouth.

Her biggest success came from inventing Slinky Toys for which she reportedly earned over $60,000 annually from royalties on her licensed patents. Years after the Slinky was invented in 1944 by Richard James (who formed James Industries to market the product), Mrs. Malsed approached the company, suggesting a line of Slinky Toys with wheels. They liked it and licensed her patents.

...Greg Aharonian, PATNEWS

customers and to see what competitors are doing. You will also be able to meet privately with those to whom you sent an invention summary or with those who have signed confidentiality agreements.

4. **The Thomas Register.** Many companies, small and large, have an entire set of these valuable resource books. They list millions of U.S. companies in virtually every imaginable field. You can also find the Thomas Register on the Internet (see appendix in the back of the book) at most major libraries. The Register includes the company's size, phone numbers, names of contact people, etc.

5. **Ask potential customers.** If your invention is a retail product, talk with a potential retailer and ask for recommendations of manufacturers. If it is an industrial or commercial product, talk with the operations department or the decision makers of these potential customers. When you are talking to them, you can use the approach and the wording that was discussed in the last chapter. With their interest piqued, you will also be establishing a valuable customer base, which will improve your ability to reach an agreement with a potential producer.

6. **Yellow Pages.** If you are in a metropolitan area, you may be able to contact several companies. For instance, if your invention is a plastic injection molded product, locating several injection molding companies will be easy.

7. **Local shopping center.** You can identify several candidates by walking through stores that carry the type of product you are developing. Look in related, overlapping categories as well. For instance, if you have a bath brush product, visit stores that sell both kitchen and household brushes as well.

8. **Recommendations from your sales experts.** If you are working with sales experts, they can be a valuable resource. Frequently, they will already have established relationships with qualified manufacturers.

9. **Importers.** Telephone directories and International Trade Centers can provide many leads. The problem with the listings in telephone directories is that they do not usually define the importer's category. However, you may be able to get the category by contacting the Trade Center in a metropolitan area or networking using directories. It takes more time, but it works.

Purchasing a tradeshow booth and exhibiting your new product could easily cost $10,000 or more. In fact, it is not uncommon to spend $25,000 and up on booths at prominent trade shows.

And all you would do is anger the visitors anyway. Why? Attendees at trade shows like to BUY, not just visit. If you don't have inventory ready to ship…your product will get a big black eye.

Instead, do a deal with a manufacturer and/or marketing company and let them handle those details.

The Best Place to Begin

The best place to begin your pursuit of manufacturing and marketing experts/partners is at a tradeshow in the field of your invention. There you will be able to see what is currently on the market and can meet with many potential candidates. It is a sure bet a tradeshow will jumpstart your networking activities.

Instead of filing for costly patents from the outset of your activities, tradeshows are a much better investment. Follow the Strategic Guide and you'll protect yourself anyway.
…Bob DeMatteis

The Emerging Internet

My favorite source of finding manufacturers on the Internet is "Big Book". Look them up at www.bigbook.com.
…Bob DeMatteis

SBDC - It All Starts with a Dream...Your Dream

And now you are looking to make money from that dream. You may have never thought about yourself like this...but if you are an inventor, you are a businessperson by default. You might have invented the world's best widget, but you will have many business-related decisions to make: How can you protect your invention? Should you manufacture it yourself? How do you market your invention? Who is your target market?...and so on. SBDCs can help you with these questions and a lot more.

"We're the government, and we're here to help." I bet you've heard that before. Well this time, it's true! There are over 1000 offices nationwide offering existing and prospective small business owners free, confidential consulting, educational seminars and workshops, databases, and more. Whether you're new to business or looking to expand, chances are, we can help. Here's an A-Z list of our specialties:

Advertising
Business Feasibility and Planning
Cash Flow Management
Dealing with Customers
Export / Import Assistance
Financial Management
Growing Your Business
Home Based Business
Internet Access / Training
January Tax Preparations
Keeping Books & Records
Legal Structure of Business
Marketing Plans
New Technology
Office Automation
Procurement Assistance
Qualifying for a Loan
Retail Marketing
Strategic Planning
Trademarks and Patents
Understanding Entrepreneurship
--Cont. on next page

10. **Trade Development Councils.** Virtually every embassy has a list of manufacturers in its country that are interested in exporting to the U.S. The lists can be faxed to you in a matter of hours.

11. **The Internet.** Search the many search engines and you will find an unlimited string of potential candidates. There is really no end to the possibilities. If you are not on the Internet then you must get on it soon. In just a few years this will very clearly be your best ally for finding and evaluating manufacturing candidates! A few of the better search engines to use for business related matters are Alta Vista, Hotbot and Lycos.

12. **The Government.** Yes! The U.S. and many state governments have a myriad of agencies available to help you find the kinds of manufacturers you seek. Your best start is with the SBDC (Small Business Development Center), a division of the SBA (Small Business Administration). Look in the local phone book or go to their Internet Web site at: http://www.asbdc-us.org. Through the SBDC you will also be able to connect with state agencies that assist in manufacturing. For instance in California, there is MAP (Manufacturing Assistance Program) and CMTC (California Manufacturing Technology Center). Let an expert with the SBDC match you up with the right group.

13. **Manufacturers that cannot make your product.** During the initial interview/networking process, you may have some friendly conversations with producers that cannot make your new invention, but may know a company that can. **Every time you talk to a manufacturer that says it can't make your new invention, ask, *"Do you know a company that can?"***

You can also search creatively to locate potential licensees. For instance:

- Companies in related fields that may be interested in expanding "sideways"
- Companies with cash interested in diversifying
- Start-up companies with a management team that has several successes, cash and desire for new opportunities
- Aggressive sales organizations with significant past success that may have the cash and be interested in opening a small production facility

As you network, don't be surprised if you get a call from one of your prior contacts who has changed jobs and is now with a company looking for new products like yours to market! It happens. That's why it is important to tell the experts in your field about your invention.

EVALUATING A MANUFACTURER

It is best to base your decision on the entire company's ability to produce, not on the executive with whom you are dealing. While you may like a particular individual, he/she must have the right team. Remember to maintain a CDI approach during interviews and discussions. Your CDI focus will help you make all the right decisions.

To find the best possible manufacturing expert for your team, evaluate the candidates based on these primary considerations:

1. **Quality First**. The quality of your invention will make or break its success. A manufacturer absolutely must be qualified to give you and more importantly, *the customers*, the quality they expect. A manufacturer's track record must prove it can do exactly that. After reviewing its capabilities and evaluating its production ability, you can continue your evaluation.

If a manufacturer cannot deliver the expected quality now, it could take years to do so. It is extremely difficult to convert a so-so quality company into one that makes excellent quality. Chevrolet is not going to compete with Mercedes in the near future, nor is Timex going to compete with Rolex. If a potential candidate cannot give you the quality you need, do not waste your time. Keep searching.

If a manufacturer can produce the required quality, you must also qualify if they can do it consistently. A modern Quality Management system and philosophy will most likely give you that result. If a manufacturer is just beginning a Q.M. system due to quality problems in the past, be cautious. It could take 2-3 years before the system is securely in place and the quality of its output is consistent.

2. **Price.** A producer must be able to manufacture your new product at competitive prices. You can get a good idea if it can by comparing the prices of some of its other products. If a producer talks about how it only sells products with large profit margins, beware. On the other hand, if it is the low-cost producer in the industry, ask why. Is it because it has generally mediocre quality and a generic approach to manufacturing?

You want to locate companies that are not low-cost generic producers, but those that focus on cost-effective, quality manufacturing. Competitive companies within an industry usually have similar pricing. You need to know that your manufacturer is "lean and mean" and not loaded with excessive profit demands.

3. **Service.** Are they known for excellent customer service? Do they return phone calls promptly? Do they have an 800 phone number? Are they polite and courteous? Do they do what they say they will do? Are their deliveries on time? A retailer or industrial/commercial

SBDC, cont.

Venture Capital Access
Women Business Owners
X-Pert Training
Your Family Business Succession
Zeroing in on Success

Are there specialized centers?
Yes! We have centers specializing in high technology, manufacturing, export/import and, most importantly, intellectual property. For instance in Northern California, the Redwood Empire SBDC operates the Sawyer Center, which provides information and assistance on the inventive process. It helps businesses and individuals develop ideas into marketable products by offering assistance with patent searches, copyrights, and trademarks. They're on the Internet at http://www.santarosa.edu/sbdc.

A typical success story:
John Kaptinski, recalls "I had a design for a hat box. It seemed like a simple item, but I thought it was a good idea and wanted to protect it." The resources at the Center enabled him to do a preliminary key word search through an on-line CD-ROM network from the U.S. Patent Office in over 100,000 categories. After reviewing the results with the Center's consultant, John applied for a utility patent on his hatbox, the Kap-Pak. This custom hatbox and travel case design protects military caps, keeping them inspection-ready, even under adverse conditions.

The National Association of Small Business Development Centers can put you in touch with SBDCs in all 50 states and the Trust Territories. For additional information, call 703-271-8700 or visit: http://www.asbdc-us.org.
...Bonnie Cornwall, Director and Brian Veazey, Asst. SBDC

The consumer product death knell elicits in the user, "I overpaid for this".
    ...Joan Lefkowitz, Accessory Brainstorms, NYC

Want to Make Excellent Decisions...All the Time?

If you keep in mind one concept--"make all your decisions based upon what is best for my customer"--you will only make wise decisions.
    ...Bob DeMatteis

SBIR Grant $$$ Available

The Small Business Innovation Research Program was created by the federal government and has granted more than $600 million in the past 15 years. In 1999, it has $75 million budgeted for grants.

In summary, they grant money for energy and high tech related projects. There is stiff competition for this money, but if this fits your invention/innovation, it may be worth pursuing.

For information, visit http://sbir.er.doe.gov/sbir/ or call them at: 301- 903-1414.

customer must feel good about purchasing a new product, especially if it is from an untried supplier. Do not settle for anything less than dazzling customer service from your manufacturer!

4. **Capacity.** If a producer does not have the capacity to take on additional output, you are probably wasting your time. If it cannot give customers the quantity they require with a timely delivery, consistent orders will not follow. If the potential manufacturer says it can expand quickly in another location, get all the specifics. At the very least, make sure your manufacturing expert has sufficient capacity to handle the start-up production requirements.

5. **Finances.** What is the present financial condition of the manufacturer? This is particularly important if a producer must expand to accommodate your requirements. If necessary, request a P&L statement or an annual report. If they are reluctant, explain that "it is something your accountant requires." They'll do it. Another strategy is to ask others in the industry about the company's financial reputation and history. Believe it or not, some companies file for bankruptcy protection every 10 years or so.

6. **Reputation.** Thoroughly research the producer's reputation for customer service, quality and reliability. A reliable manufacturer must have a good reputation or else it could make your new customers angry and kill your invention. Find out if the company goes through frequent management changes. If so, you could be in for a roller coaster ride. A new president may not see the potential of your product in the same light as did the old president.

What is its reputation regarding patents and licenses? Is it a licensee for other products? Have they ever knowingly infringed on a patent? When talking to them about patents, listen carefully. Ask around to learn what their attitude has been toward other intellectual property. If they have infringed on others, they will probably look for a way to get at you.

7. **Trust and Philosophy.** Can you trust its owners and management? During the interview, look the executives straight in the eye. If they cannot look back at you, you will have a tough time ahead.

A company's business philosophy must be similar to yours. Are they people with whom you would do business? Remember that they will be your partners for a long, long time. The last thing you want is a company that is late with royalty payments and then pesters you to death with excuses for their inability to perform.

8. **Innovative or generic.** Is this company innovative or is it just another old-fashioned, generic producer? Most innovative companies

can quickly gear up and make new products. They are good problem solvers and tend to be more responsive to your needs. If a producer has a generic attitude, it would be difficult to suddenly change it. Evaluate other products the company has produced, see the production hands-on and feel confident they are capable of providing you and your potential customers with high-quality CDI products.

9. **Other Considerations.** Is the producer's niche compatible with your product's niche? How willing is it to assist with prototyping and manufacturing the first test products? Find out what other prototyping and new product development the company has done. Do they show eagerness to take on your project?

10. **Commitment.** Above all, is the manufacturer willing to make a *total, absolute commitment* to your cause? The only way anything will happen in a timely manner is with their total commitment to you. You must ask for this and they must give you the right, aggressive response. Your success depends on it!

Ideally, you want manufacturing partners that correctly answer all these questions. Sometimes, however, we do not have this luxury; it is not a perfect world. If a candidate does not fulfill most of the preceding attributes, keep looking. Remember: if a manufacturer does not meet your standards, but wants your new invention badly enough, it will come to you willing to change. Make sure that they prove it to you first.

Whether you are seeking a manufacturer or a marketer for your product, learn to take "no" for an answer.

Your best bet is probably to move on to another company if you have submitted your product to no avail. Companies have many considerations beyond a product just "being right for them". They may love your product, but only have money to allocate to prior commitments. The product may be in a category the company is moving out of. Your invention may skewer the need for a product on which they already have placed their corporate bet. The truth is that you are not entitled to know all the whys--just the end result. "We saw it. Thanks, but no thanks." Now pick up the phone to their competitors and get busy with them!

...Ken Robbins, Product Development Agent, Dirt Devil

12

YOUR MARKETING EXPERT

*Nothing happens until your product
gets sold. Get the right sales expert
on your team from the outset.*

**"What Is the One Thing an
Inventor Should Do First?"**

*Early in my seminar career,
a participant asked me this
question. The answer is to get a
marketing expert on your team at
the earliest possible moment. The
expert will allow you to develop
you invention with all the right
attributes for the customer.*

*I now realize that my first
thought has been permanently
embedded ever since.*

...Bob DeMatteis

This is the most important requirement for a successful invention
and is usually the last aspect most first time inventors consider. It is
usually not until long after they have spent a lot of time and money on
patenting and prototyping that they even think about marketing and
sales. While technically different, sales and marketing are interrelated,
because a successful marketing approach results in sales.

Your sales-marketing expert may be a single individual or an entire
marketing company. It may be a manufacturer's rep organization or the
sales department of a manufacturer. In each case, a key contact will
focus on your new invention. For best results, the expert should be on
your team from the beginning of development.

224

YOUR SALES-MARKETING OBJECTIVES

The single smartest thing an inventor can do is to get a marketing expert on the team as soon as possible. This expert will be invaluable in the following ways:

- **Qualifying the inventive attributes.** The right marketing expert in a given industry can quickly tell you if the inventive attributes you have discovered and are developing are salable. They can also give you feedback about how they could be improved. One thing is for certain--you do not want to waste a lot of time and money on developing inventions with attributes that do not have solid marketability. Keep creating and inventing instead!

- **Help determine the target market.** Being perfectly positioned with sales contacts, your sales expert will also be perfectly positioned to help determine the target market for your new invention. They can advise you about which target markets to avoid due to competitive responses.

- **Determine the quality required.** A marketing expert can help determine the exact quality a new invention should have and perhaps even know a producer to make it.

- **Determine price.** Your objective is to use the correct target price and thereby maximize sales. Your sales expert can help determine the target price.

- **Help in the initial evaluation of the invention.** Having the marketing expert on your team early on can help you get your invention's potential evaluated by an end user.

- **Help locate a manufacturer.** Your marketing expert is likely to have several good contacts.

- **Set up test marketing.** They can arrange for and coordinate the testing of your new invention.

With the right marketing expert on your team, and if you are able to make and test your own prototypes, your expert can line up some sales. This can be done regardless of whether you have a particular manufacturer in mind. With orders, you will have a lot less trouble finding manufacturers. By beginning your sales activities before you have a producer, you will be developing orders and generating potential cash flow before incurring any manufacturing costs. With guaranteed orders, a manufacturer has a lot more incentive to manufacture your new products quickly. In addition, you significantly improve your negotiating position with them.

Your sales and marketing experts are not distributors, but they will arrange distribution for you. They are not graphics artists, but they can work with graphic artists to help prepare the right sales aids and

An Inventor's Best Friend-- Your Marketing Expert

Inventors tend to get attached to their creations and lose their objectivity. They tend to use tunnel vision and see their creation's use or sales only in a certain perspective.

By listening carefully to a smart marketing expert, an inventor can learn all he/she needs to know in order to change, modify or improve the invention to become a high-volume winner.

If the marketing experts you talk to just can't buy into your invention...you might want to put it on the backburner and start developing something else.

The Best Business Plan of All!

*An inventor can plan, consult and learn all there is to know about manufacturing, marketing and going into business. But the quickest route to success is to **find a sales-marketing expert who looks at your invention and says, "I can sell that!"***

To me, that is the best business plan of all. The only remaining questions are who'll make the new product and how much can be sold?

...Bob DeMatteis

Unable to See the Light

In the late '70's and early '80's, GM did not see the direction in which the auto industry was headed. Resisting the transition to smaller, higher-quality cars, Chevrolet lost its sales leadership. To illustrate how backward their vision was, in early 1997, Chevrolet finally announced that it would no longer make large cars!

The willingness of a company to develop and market a new product depends, in part, on how secure its patent protection is. Does the patent provide broad coverage of the technology or is it possible to circumvent the patent with a minor design modification?
...Donald Grant Kelly, U.S. Patent Office Director

A good infomercial product should be easy to understand, have a high perceived value, and cater to a gigantic demographic.
...Joan Lefkowitz, Accessory Brainstorms, NYC

Your Best Team Players

Your marketing expert is usually the easiest team player with whom to work. He/she wants to do exactly what you need--get your invention sold and producing income! You will find that having a trusted marketing expert on your team will be a wonderful asset to your invention's development and lead to its ultimate success.

promotional brochures. They are experienced professionals who will get the right appointments with the right accounts and save you a huge amount of time and money!

CAN THEY REALLY SELL YOUR PRODUCT?

It is important to find the right team players to develop the sales and ultimately the distribution of new inventions. Many good ideas and inventions have gone astray because of the lack of a committed or properly trained sales team. Great new inventions and products go nowhere if sales teams do not want to sell them or lack the knowledge to sell them.

There are two classic examples in history of a lack of commitment from sales teams that created opportunities for more innovative companies. First, the American auto industry figured they could make more money selling large cars than smaller, higher-quality cars. It took years for the U.S. auto industry to only partially recover. Second, in the '70's and '80's, the IBM sales team directed IBM's future away from PC's because they did not offer the large commissions available from the sale of super computers. In both examples, these industrial leaders should have had the guts to "attack themselves" to retain their leadership position.

You want sales experts who are not afraid to attack themselves, not complacent with the past or committed to selling only existing products. You want those that have the ability to introduce and sell Customer-Driven Innovations. After all, by the year 2010, all products sold in the U.S. will be CDI products in one form or another.

Regardless of whether your sales team is the sales organization (or extension thereof) of the manufacturer you license, your own hired team (employees or manufacturers' reps) or a dynamic sales agency, it must have the right ingredients for the success of your invention.

TWO TYPES OF SALESPEOPLE

Generally speaking, there are two types of salespeople. The first wants to take orders, maintain the status quo and look for additional market share. The second type wants to sell new products, create new markets and be entrepreneurial partners. This is the kind of sales expert you want on your team. They are "market creators", can sell into the future and are not content with just taking orders. They sell by value-added instead of lower prices. They are not afraid to "attack themselves" and can spot future trends long before others.

Beware of sales organizations that call themselves "market creators" when they are really looking for added market share. These firms cannot follow through on selling your value-added niche products and will invariably fold to price pressures. Their justification for failed sales is almost always "the price is too high".

These are "false innovators" that simply do not have the patience to persevere and are not persuasive enough to convince the customer to try your new (value-added) products and to experience the benefits for themselves. For instance, a "bottom line savings" is far more important than a per unit price. But it takes savvy and knowledge to present this argument effectively.

Market creation sales take considerably longer at the beginning. But they result in loyal customers and sales that are easier to maintain over the long term. Companies that are good at market creation sales know this and when they speak this language, you will know that you have a good potential partner.

ONE OF THE BEST KEPT SALES SECRETS ON THE PLANET

Many independent manufacturers' representatives are interested in working with inventors and many have the attributes that inventors need. Why? Well, first, they work for themselves and are naturally entrepreneurial. Second, many understand what it takes to get a new product to market. They usually represent many lines of products, some of which are smaller companies. Unlike large, established companies with in-house, defense minded sales teams, manufacturers' reps tend to understand the strategies and tactics required to launch new products. They also know how to protect these smaller niches once established.

Most experienced reps have been hired by major companies to build up sales and were subsequently fired once the job was complete. It is not uncommon for a national company to hire these sales experts to get immediate market penetration and then fire them when new management takes over (a cost reduction move). If they can work with an inventor and help them get their new products launched, they can establish a relationship with long-term security.

The best news of all is that manufacturers' reps work on commission. You do not have to pay them a salary when they are hired; you arrange for the manufacturer to pay them a commission instead. A standard industry commission is 5%, sometimes higher with specialty items and sometimes lower with high-volume commodity sales.

You will discover in Part Three how you can license an exceptional manufacturers' representative organization. Not all of them may be interested, but when you find one that is, it can be very rewarding for you and for them. Just keep in mind that when you find an aggressive, successful manufacturers' rep organization, they will be your best friends!

This Guy Can *SELL!*

Early this century, Murray Spangler worked in a department store selling carpets, but developed an allergy to carpet dust. Since cleaning carpets was done by hanging them over a line and then whacking them with a dust paddle, Spangler's problem worsened to a degree that he might have had to quit if he couldn't find a solution.

Thus, he invented the vacuum cleaner.

He had a difficult time trying to sell them due to the high cost. But when his cousin, Hoover, saw the vacuum work, he immediately saw the light and said, "I can sell that!"

To overcome the high price objection, he cut out the middlemen and sold them direct to the users in a door to door (home to home) sales campaign.

The rest is history.

Don't Confuse Distributors with Sales Experts

Distributors are not specialists in any given field. Salespeople for distributors generally sell thousands of products and are excellent order takers. They "resell" small amounts of many products to many retailers or users.

In contrast, the sales expert you want on your team will handle a small number of specialized products and sell large amounts to a smaller number of distributors or large end users.

LOCATING THE RIGHT SALES AND MARKETING EXPERT FOR YOUR INVENTION

Inventors often ask me where to find other product scouts. The title "product scout" doesn't exist in corporate flow charts. It exists as the VP of Marketing, VP of Engineering or VP of Product Development or even sometimes as the CEO. The unequivocal best place to find these people is AT THE TRADE SHOW INDUSTRY. The head of product development for a company with sales over $100 million probably will not take your phone call but he will spend five minutes with you, face to face, on the floor of the Housewares show in Chicago for example. At a trade show you can walk the floor and see all the competitors, pick up business cards of potential licensees and even make an appointment to speak later. Companies attend shows to sell their wares and are always in pleasant, "let's do business" moods. Don't try to accomplish too much. The purpose should be to find the right contact that you can call or meet later.

....Ken Robbins, Product Development Agent, Dirt Devil

Inventors must avoid the marketing scams--those late-night television ads that ask: "Do you have an idea?" They're a national disgrace. Some $200 million will be spent by independent inventors on these bogus marketing scams this year--and they get nothing in return.

...Donald Grant Kelly, U.S. Patent Office Director

There are several excellent ways to locate sales agencies. The best ones are:

1. **Personal recommendations.** Talk to friends, acquaintances and business associates about your new invention. Ask them if they know any smart marketing people in its field.

2. **Recommendations from the manufacturers you interview**. You will interview those in charge of sales separately from the production people with a given manufacturer. If their sales approach is not right for your product, ask them for the names of sales reps and marketing companies in the industry.

3. **Trade shows.** Go to a trade show as a visitor, not an exhibitor. Many sales-marketing-oriented companies will have booths at the show. Some of them may be manufacturers' representatives and not be producers of the products they sell. You will also find that a large number of independent manufacturers' representatives attend these shows and work in the booths of major manufacturers they represent. Seek them out!

4. **Trade journals.** You can place an inexpensive classified advertisement seeking sales help in the back of most journals. To find out about trade journals in your industry, ask a store manager for retail products or a plant manager for wholesale products for an old issue. Get one or two of the most popular publications and then call the 800 number and ask for a complimentary copy.

5. **Ask a future customer.** If you have a certain customer in mind that might do well with your new product, contact the person in charge of marketing or merchandising, if retail, or the head of operations, if wholesale. Ask them about the manufacturers' representatives who call on them. If you cannot get these names on a local level, try calling the district office and ask a district manager.

6. **Ask distributors**. While you will not normally focus your efforts on seeking distributors, you can still ask some who their favorite manufacturers' representatives are.

7. **Yellow pages**. This is the least likely place to look, even though many manufacturers' reps are listed. The problem is that it does not list their field of expertise.

8. **Internet.** More and more companies are on the Internet, looking for business. This is becoming more popular for sales-related organizations as well. Master the Internet in your field and you are securing your ability to finding strong marketing experts. The Appendix contains a list of some Internet sites you may want to consider.

9. **The Appendix.** In the Appendix, there is a list of companies that have marketing ability in certain specific areas. If your invention falls in one of the categories listed, inquire with the appropriate companies and find out for yourself.

10. **The Invention Convention®.** This dedicated trade show for inventors is another resource for inventors to seek out licensees and network. If it is in your budget, it may be worth the investment.

11. **Small Business Development Centers (SBDC).** This valuable government agency is a friend to innovators and start-up companies. Make sure to talk to your local SBDC consultant (remember it is free) and see if he/she might be able to help.

THE ATTRIBUTES OF A WINNING SALES ORGANIZATION

For a sales partner to have the ability to market and sell your products, the person or company must have all the right ingredients. There are ten factors for you to evaluate:

1. **Quality.** Is this salesperson or company currently selling the type of quality product you have invented? If not, they may not be capable of selling value-added products. Used car salespeople don't usually jump into the new car market selling Mercedes or BMWs with much success.

2. **Sales philosophy.** Does it have a defensive sales strategy, trying to hold onto existing business and market share? (Bad news.) Is it hungry, offensive and aggressively looking for new markets to create? (Good news.) Do its leaders talk about the new markets they have created? (Good news.) Do they only talk about "picking up additional market share?" (Bad news.) When referring to your invention, do they say, "I can sell that?" (Good news.) Are they more interested in hearing what you can do for them? (Bad news.) Do they show the positive attitude, eagerness and enthusiasm needed to launch a new product? (Good news.)

3. **Niche marketers**. Is this potential partner a small company, cutting out niches and holding onto them as it goes? Is its niche your

The Hook

Hal Meyer has a company called The Hook Appropriate Technology in Connecticut. He is experienced in invention marketing and works with inventors on a performance basis. If you have at least a patent pending (Hal likes products that are in the well-developed stage) and would like to explore some possibilities with Hal, look on the Internet at www.thehooktek.com.

There is additional information in the Appendix.

A recent From Patent to Profit Workshop participant told about how he placed a press release in a trade journal describing his innovation. His phone was ringing off the hook the day it hit the press!

Internet Web Site Promotion

If you have a patent pending or issued, you might consider building a Web site promoting your new innovation/product.

Instead of just "offering it for license", try posting thorough specifications, features and benefits, photos showing how it works, plus an anticipated sell price. Make sure that interested parties can send you inquiries regarding availability, comments and questions. This feedback can be valuable.

Based upon the number of customer inquiries you get, you will find it a lot easier to sell your manufacturing and marketing partners on taking on the project. A marketing expert checking out the state of the industry on the Internet may also discover your Web site.

niche as well? A "yes" answer to these two questions is a big plus. If the interviewee is a big company that is losing market share and it thinks your new opportunity may just be the ticket to get some back, turn around and run. Invariably, its bad habits will return, price will become the sole issue, and it will not be able to sell your new invention any longer.

4. **Track record.** What are some *recent* past successes? Salespeople and companies with stories about pioneering products 10, 15 and 20 years ago will never make it today. Anyone could do it back then. The fact that they have not had any recent pioneering successes illustrates their satisfaction with the status quo. If the candidate has some recent successes, the chances are that it will be successful again...with your innovation.

5. **Innovative.** Is the sales candidate innovative in its marketing efforts or is that left to others? You want partners who have the ability to help direct these very important issues. New inventions invariably require innovative approaches to problem solving. Your sales expert is your first and most important liaison with the customers and end users. They will be called on to help solve problems as they arise.

6. **Ability to Promote.** Is the candidate willing and able to promote? Does it have positions at trade shows? Positions at retail establishments? Can it help make sales and training videos? Develop sales brochures? While not all sales organizations have the ability to do this kind of work, many do. If they can't, you will have to do it yourself, do it with the manufacturer or arrange to have it done elsewhere.

7. **Time and Manpower.** Does the sales organization or person have the time and the people power to promote your product right now? If not, forget it.

8. **Well connected.** Is the potential candidate well connected with your potential customers' top-level management? Decisions to change are made at the top, not in a buyer's office. Buyers only follow instructions from their superiors. Are the sales associates well connected at the end-user level as well? In industrial and commercial applications, the best way to do this is directly through your sales expert. Is your sales expert team willing to make the arrangements to work with the end user, so you can get the valuable feedback you will need?

9. **Finances.** Is the organization or the expert financially sound? Does it have the resources to do what it says it can do? Remember that

Here is a proven way to use Press Releases to relevant trade publications and news media to get in front of people in the right industry when trying to license your ideas. First, you call the publication and ask for a media kit. This will include a free copy, profiles of readership, statistics on distribution and the name of the editorial contact. This editorial person is your target. Next, learn how to write a one-page, proper press release from any of the many books on the subject at the library. This is your ammunition. Finally, you send out a press release for each and every event during development, for example: 1. Ohio inventor solves an age-old problem of cats shredding couches. 2. Couch protector receives Notice of Allowance. 3. Couch Guard under consideration by several major manufacturers. 4. Couch Guard exhibited at Furniture market in NC. Every step becomes a media story by which an inventor (Product Developer) can receive free press.
...Ken Robbins, Product Development Agent, Dirt Devil

If your expert candidate is driving a BMW, Mercedes or the like, chances are he/she is financially sound. If the expert is driving a 1983 Toyota pick-up, you may want to find out why.

innovative efforts require time and money in the early stages. Later, your sales experts will have the luxury of having protection because of the proprietary nature of your product.

10. **Total, absolute commitment.** Will your sales-marketing expert make a total, absolute commitment to do a bang-up job with your product and do it now? Just as with manufacturing, you need a totally committed response to do all it takes to make things happen.

This is a tall order for sales teams, but they really must have these attributes. If they are short one or two, will they still do OK? Probably just that--OK. But it is best to cover their deficiencies ahead of time and see if there is something you can do to fill in the gaps. Find out if they will consider changing their sales approach to accommodate your new innovation's needs. If they can, and they will make the total commitment to the change, you probably have a winner.

CONFIRMATION OF APPOINTMENT OF A SALES EXPERT

When you are comfortable with your selection of a sales expert--an organization or an individual--confirm their appointment in writing. If you are hiring a manufacturers' representative to do sales, but not billing, he/she will need a letter from the manufacturer you license. This letter will confirm that the manufacturer will pay the sales commissions as it bills the paying customer. In certain cases, the sales organization itself may be doing the billing and will enter into a buy-sell arrangement with the manufacturer.

Your sales expert and manufacturing expert must feel comfortable with each other. Once the team relationship is established, your sales expert will be working more closely with the manufacturer as the project develops. Then, once orders start flowing, your contact with sales and manufacturing will slowly diminish as the contact between the two picks up substantially.

Your written confirmation of a sales expert should be in one of two ways. You can send a letter of intent, which is predicated on the confirmation of having a commission agreement with a manufacturer or an outright letter of confirmation. Either one should be a simple 1-2 page letter stating both parties' understandings. Use layman's terms and avoid legalese. In any confirmation, there should be an "out clause" which enables any party to quit the agreement. Usually this "out clause" requires a 90-180 day notice. In the event of non-performance, you will want it.

You will find that some manufacturers' representatives work on a "handshake" agreement, while most will want a written contract. A contract may be a standard form (which they may have) or a simple one-page written agreement. Hopefully it is not something generated by an attorney.

If a company says it does not accept outside invention ideas but you really feel they could make a hit of it, try this back door approach: Look up the company's other patents on the Internet. Each patent will show the law firm that handled the patent filing. Contact this firm and ask questions like, "With whom could you put me in contact regarding product development?" or "I have a novel improvement to patent number ... which you filed. Whom should I contact to discuss licensing it?" You are very likely to end up with a private phone extension inside the company to a sympathetic ear that will listen. At the very least you will be able to say, "____ at your law firm suggested I call you to discuss this."

Ken Robbins, Product Development Agent, Dirt Devil

Top producing, innovative sales organizations can also be licensed. They are tailor-made for exclusive agreements in their respective territories with sales performance clauses. You will read more about this in Part Four, Licensing.

Almost always you will find your sales expert and your team players the easiest of all to work with. They like to do what you need the most... sell your inventions!

13

INDUCING A BIRTH

This can be the most difficult process of all. Just keep focused on the means and you will have the end results you want.

INTRODUCING A NEW PRODUCT

"Inducing a birth" more accurately reflects what you are doing in the invention process than any other description. You want your invention to be healthy, just as you would want your newborn to be healthy. And just as you nurture your children and help them grow into well-adjusted adults, you will want to "nurture" your invention so it becomes a well-received, mature product. A child without proper parenting will not survive well in the world; a new invention (or product) also cannot survive without proper guidance.

There is one tremendous difference between raising a child and raising an invention and that difference is of great benefit to you as the inventor. When children mature into adults, they normally continue to cost you money. But a well thought out invention whose birth has been properly induced will earn you money!

232

Therefore, your mission as the "parent" of your invention is to induce a healthy birth, control its developmental environment and give it guidance and direction to become a gainful, useful, successful product. Do this and you will be rewarded with wealth and long-term security.

You should always remember that as the pilot of your invention, it is your primary responsibility to oversee its development, guidance and direction. You must never stop guiding its development until it truly is able to continue on its own. Even then you should continue to improve it.

In the process of inducing a birth, you must depend on many other people and companies to help get the job done. If you develop key team players, stay aware of developments and continually monitor and direct your invention's progress, it will become successful. In fact, it will happen almost by magic.

INDUCING A BIRTH AND SUSTAINING IT IS A FIVE-PHASE PROCESS

There are five overlapping phases to inducing the birth of a new product. Trying to jump ahead too fast will spell disaster. The five phases are:

1. **Build prototypes.** As discussed in detail in Chapter 2, you develop simple prototypes that evolve into working models and then into production models. In certain respects, your first sales may be considered prototypes as well.

2. **Test prototypes.** This begins with small "controlled" tests in-house in preparation for full-scale tests and customer trials.

3. **Controlled hands-on, user trials.** These are conducted with unbiased end users. Start small and then expand sufficiently to prove and repeat results. Make sure to do initial customer trials that allow hands-on participation.

4. **Expansion of sales.** Gradually expand sales within a customer's operations or within a region, then ultimately nationwide and perhaps internationally.

5. **Continuous improvement.** Continuous improvement of every aspect of the product, including quality, service and price will ensure that the induced birth will continue to grow on its own.

My Favorite Invention

My favorite invention was born 5 years ago. She is innovative, has lots of character, and so many worthy features and benefits that they cannot be listed here. She always brings me joy and makes me smile. Even when times are tough or difficult. She is my daughter, Lindsey.

At the end of the day--no matter how tough a day it was for me--I can always look forward to her greeting me with a smile...or a laugh.

If there is anytime that her smile is appreciated above all, it is during the invention/birth process. So many trials and tribulations to overcome.

The moral to this story...keep your family close at heart. When going through the machinations of inventing, they can be a welcome diversion.

...Bob DeMatteis

STEPS 1 AND 2: BUILDING PROTOTYPES AND TESTING

You will probably build more than one prototype. They usually begin as crude models and develop through various phases to the invention's ultimate form. It is common to make several prototypes before developing functional, working models.

The first prototypes are usually nothing more than a way to get an idea of the size, shape and basic design features. Testing is limited. Then, little by little, you fine-tune your prototypes into models that can be thoroughly tested. The first aspects that are tested may include strength, endurance and functionality. The final prototypes are usually those that have sustained extended tests in your lab prior to release into the marketplace. The later testing is usually targeted toward getting out some of the final "bugs" and being user friendly.

In your invention-related activities, define "testing" as those tests you conduct **before** you allow end users to try the invention on their own. After you have completed a series of obvious tests, you will want to set up hands-on tests using "guinea pigs" you can observe. This testing will probably begin in the lab or at a plant and then continue at a user's site, if necessary.

The importance of thorough testing cannot be stressed enough. If you think testing is unnecessary, you are overlooking something. You may be taking too much for granted. If you do not test your invention, sure death follows. You are far wiser to over-test your new invention and be totally determined to find and resolve every last problem.

The best approach to test observations and problem solving is to be super-observational. Watch your guinea pigs carefully and ask the appropriate questions. Consult your manufacturing and marketing experts on how to solve certain problems. Keep your end users' needs in focus, make the necessary changes and then...test it again and fix it again, over and over, until it is *right!*

Never introduce marginal-quality products into the marketplace. It will only result in a negative experience being associated with your invention, regardless of whether the problems are subsequently resolved. Remember that first impressions are hard to change.

The testing and fixing process can be lengthy, so be patient. The process of monitoring tests of your new invention usually results in uncovering unforeseen problems and unforeseen opportunities! Rarely do all problems surface during the very first test. Invariably, you will make several changes and modifications to the product and to the manufacturing process. Sometimes, the process may end in abandonment of the project. But most of the time, you will find success if you are determined to see it through. Just remember to:

Test it again and again.
Fix it again and again.

Doing Your Own Research

*Start-up inventors can and should do their own research on product needs, on the state of the technology, capital availability, manufacturing options, and self-promotion. Homework, bookwork, network, legwork-- hard work, but it's **their** work. On the other hand, when it comes to complex legal work, including drafting patent claims or threatening legal action for infringement, or crafting substantive contracts, they'd best call in the "suits".*
...Donald Grant Kelly, U.S. Patent Office Director

Measure twice, cut once!
...George Margolin, "words to invent by..."

STEP 3: HANDS-ON TRIALS

Sooner or later, you will have the test results you want and will be ready to do some customer trials. Use the word "trials" when talking to new end users, not "tests". Most people don't want to be guinea pigs with new products. At this phase, you can accurately say that the testing is done and now is the time for customer trials.

When you are confident that a good product will be produced, start your sales slowly and methodically. Begin with a small trial first. This could be a single customer or a single plant, machine or application. Initially, you should observe. Customers will invariably use products differently than you and your guinea pigs used them in a lab. Because there are so many unknown contributing factors to consider, it is best to start out cautiously.

If something needs fixing during these customer trials, fix it quickly. Communicate directly to the plant and to those who will make the necessary changes. The chances are that anything that needs fixing now is not of great consequence. Fix it anyway. Do your best to resolve any potential customer complaints before they arise. If you do, your customers will be impressed.

During customer trials, be friendly and enthusiastic. Do not hype the new product, but be encouraging to the users. The positive attitude you convey gets them involved and makes them part of the success equation. They will be eager to help solve problems and give you honest feedback.

If your customer is industrial or commercial and has a training department, get them involved as well. You can "train the trainer", so they can take over afterwards.

Last, customer trials are a great opportunity to have your sales experts observe the results. You can be sure that the experience will whet their appetites! By involving your sales experts in these start-up customer trials, you are training them to take over and "train the trainer" in the future.

STRIVING TO "MAKE IT RIGHT"

Just like good genetic engineering can determine a baby's future, you too want your new invention to be well engineered. In fact, your first objective is to consistently make it right. But just exactly how do you do this? Frankly, there are two approaches. Make it right from the beginning before your major market release or stumble around trying to make it right later.

Your primary manufacturer must be totally *committed* to solving all the start-up problems while continuously striving to make the perfect product. You had this commitment from them before you started and now they are living it.

Using Seminars for Tests and Trials

Seminars can be an effective way for you or your marketing expert to introduce a new innovation. You can establish a home based business or your marketing expert can use this approach in industry.

Seminars are a super way of introducing timesaving, productivity enhancing, self-teaching innovations.

Not only do you sell them at the seminar, but if you establish them at colleges and universities, you will be getting paid for the seminars as well.

The feedback you will get from your seminar participants will be incredibly valuable, virtually ensuring you of an ultimate success!

...June Davidson, President, American Seminar Leaders Asso.

First impressions are lasting impressions...

As you work together as a team, you must always remember that you are the key interpreter of quality. Everyone will look to you to determine if the quality is acceptable. The quality you want is the quality you believe the customers expect. Do not confuse expected quality with your personal opinion or the opinions of plant employees or salespeople.

How do you know when the quality is right? There are many signs you can read from your customers' responses to determine if your product's quality is acceptable. Here is a partial list of the signals you should look for during tests and trials:

1. It works the way it is supposed to.
2. People smile when they use it.
3. People know how to use it.
4. Your intuition tells you it is right.
5. It raises a positive emotion with the users, the marketers and those who are associated with it. Remember the importance of elicited emotions in new inventions!
6. They ask where they can buy more.

Before you can release your product to the mass market, you must be comfortable that it is made correctly and is ready for a major marketing push.

HOW DO YOU KNOW WHEN IT IS NOT RIGHT? ("RED FLAGS")

More important than knowing when your new invention is made right is knowing when it is not made right. If you spot problems and difficulties, your new invention is not ready to release to the mass market. Be sensitive to "red flags" that tell you something is wrong with the invention. Remember how "red flags" were defined in Chapter 3? These warning signs are more important than ever.

Don't downplay and avoid agonizing little problems. Overcome them and they will become a gift in disguise. Here are some things to look for:

1. It does not do *everything* it is supposed to do or does not do it quite right.
2. It does not look quite right.
3. It is too difficult to make. It requires too much labor, generates too much scrap or the technology is just not there yet. Do not confuse difficulty to make with the "learning curve" associated with manufacturing new products.
4. It raises a negative emotion with users of the product.
5. It is hard to use, or difficult to figure out how to use.

Work Your Plan…and Keep Focused

Once you have a concept and market defined, target your market by effectively making a plan, then work your plan…and stay with it 'til Hell freezes over. Or…at least until you make more money than you know what to do with, then call me!

…Doug English, Patent Attorney

Red Flags = Opportunity

If you have an established relationship with your marketing expert, you know that he/she can point out many red flags long before you will ever discover them on your own.

Never overlook these wonderful "blessings in disguise". Because when you solve them, opportunity abounds!

6. It is not a real great improvement. "I like it, but I don't know if I would switch."

7. There are no re-orders after the first trial.

These kinds of problems must be resolved or understood before you can move forward. Sometimes, just knowing what the problem is, and knowing that it can be resolved, is good enough. Your innovative team will want to resolve problems, prove it can be done, and will be driven to make things happen.

Another excellent way to find out about the receptivity of your new product is to conduct a blind survey, one in which those surveyed are anonymous. Keep the survey short--just 2 or 3 pages--and allow plenty of space for comments.

Surveys Made Easy

When we need a survey done, we contact Florida St. University and ask the appropriate faculty member if we might employ some students to do a customer survey.

Then we use the results to assist and improve our sales effort.

The best news is that the surveys are extremely accurate and cost effective.

...Joe Justin, Pinnacle Group

A $12-Million Red Flag

Chicago, January 17, 1991. On a cold winter day in early 1991, I traveled to the Chicago area to oversee a test my associates and I were conducting at Sears. The test was for a new bagging system we were developing and the stakes were high--$12-million in business. During the past week, and on the flight to Chicago, I had a nagging feeling, a "red flag" emerging over the performance of the new system. I was not sure what it was all about but I did not feel good about it.

When I landed in Chicago, it was snowing hard. I knew I had just enough time to rent a car, drive to the Sears test store, see how things were going and race to the hotel before I got snowed in. In the test store, I carefully viewed the clerks using the new bagging system, and tactfully asked them questions regarding its performance and what they did and did not like.

During the store visit, the red flag continued to nag me. While the clerks liked the new system over the other two systems we were competing against, to me it was just not right. Finally, I had to leave the test store and get to the nearby hotel before it was too late.

At the hotel, the snow pelted the window and built up to form a solid white block of ice. I was feeling depressed because the new bagging system was just not quite right and we really wanted this contract. After I walked around the hotel for awhile and then returned to my room, suddenly a light went off.

The red flag was a warning that the system was not natural. It would require some training to use effectively. Then the video tape in my brain began and I visualized what would be more natural. I visualized a system that dispensed "backwards" in a simple one-step fashion.

We made the changes and after two months of testing against two other competitors, which were larger, more generic-oriented firms, the survey revealed that we were the choice of the employees and management. We got the contract from Sears we wanted. We then filed for three patents to protect our interests... Bob DeMatteis

---

WATCH CAREFULLY FOR "RED FLAGS" UNRELATED TO THE INVENTION

You have been very sensitive to red flags during the development process pertaining to your invention's performance. These red flags have helped you develop a fine new product. Now, during the start-up process, you will need to be in tune to warning signs that are not necessarily relevant to your invention. They too can kill a product's successful introduction. Examples of unrelated red flags may be:

1. The overall quality is just not good enough.
2. Wrong color. What if most end users prefer a different color?
3. Wrong size. The end users may want it to be bigger or smaller.
4. The product is not strong enough.
5. It requires too much maintenance.
6. It works well, but assembly is aggravating.
7. Where's the sizzle, the pizzazz?
8. An environmental concern (justified or not) is not being met.
9. The manufacturer's leadtime is too long.
10. The customer service (sales or manufacturing) is poor.

If your invention was in my field of influence--plastics packaging--I imagine that I could resolve all these potential Red Flag problems in a matter of days...which might otherwise take you months or years.

...Joe Truckload Bowers, Marketing Expert

Try to be super-sensitive to the various comments you hear. As some may say, "try to be the bug on the wall" and listen to all the unsolicited comments.

STEP 4: EXPAND SALES

After you are comfortable with the initial end-user trials, expand them. Expand to several users, or if your invention is commercial or industrial, expand to an entire business. Next, expand with other new customers to make sure your initial trials are duplicated. During this expansion phase continue to be super-observational and super-sensitive to red flags.

Expansion of sales is usually slow and methodical...slower than what we want. Sales must be coordinated with production and production needs time to gear up. Only after sufficient production is available can sales be expanded into larger regions, nationally or internationally. If demand is overly great, it will only help keep prices and profits up.

During this phase, your sales organization may be ready to "blow the top off of sales" but they may need to be restrained until your manufacturer can gear up for added supply. In your piloting position behind the scenes, keep the pressure on the manufacturer to meet production deadlines while you gracefully keep your sales team informed and focused.

Ramp-Up

One qualifying factor I insist upon when designating a manufacturer for a new innovation/product, is its ability to supply large quantities quickly. Why?

What happens with a successful product launch with large users, is that after they test it and they like it--they want instant supply nationwide!

It's called "ramp up". The producer has to be able to provide a reasonable timetable to ramp up supply nationwide. If they can't, then the test will die.

You should consider this well in advance. If the manufacturer of your new innovation is a small entity and you expect me to sell it to a potentially huge user, how is this small producer going to supply them?

My reputation is on the line. I will never knowingly commit to selling a new innovation to a huge end user without extensively qualifying the manufacturing ability of the producer to ramp up once we have been successful.

...Joe Truckload Bowers, Marketing Expert

STEP 5: CONTINUOUS IMPROVEMENT

Just like with Quality Management (QM) processes, continuous improvement is your theme to guarantee continued success. Properly approached, "continuous improvement" can literally mean "product security". You will always have product security and will stay ahead of the competition with a continuous improvement strategy. Why?

1. Having the end-user in mind and improving your products accordingly will keep the users buying them. Remember the words, "new and improved".

2. You will probably make new discoveries for which you can file for (additional?) patents...hence, improve your proprietary position. A new improvement patent can mean another 20 years of protection!

3. If for some reason, you do not get your first patent, you will still be light years ahead of the others, and may have some important improvement patents to later protect your position.

4. New improvements can also mean breakthroughs in production processes, which means lower costs and putting competition at a further disadvantage.

During the process of taking your product to market and expanding the market, you should always be observing the product's performance and acceptance. You should always look for red flags and convert them to your advantage. Now that you have only good product going to market, you can improve and continually maintain your market edge through the same innovative, inventive process that got you there in the first place. That is, your CDI focus and being super sensitive to customers' and end-users' true needs.

When you have some improvements you want to try, start over with the same testing process. Basically speaking, you will:

1. Test it.
2. Then improve it.
3. Then test it and improve it...again and again.

Remember the "continuous improvement cycle" from Chapter 4? Here it is again as Figure 13-1 (see page 240), but as it pertains to the process of inducing the birth of a new product.

Each improvement that is made prolongs the life of an invention and usually improves sales. Improvements enhance the ability of your invention to become the preferred product, regardless of other competitive products being introduced into the market. Your invention will also become more cost effective to produce, since your manufacturing organization is now further down the learning curve.

Staying Close to the Customer

If there is any time that it is most important to "stay close to the customer", this is it...during the inducement of the birth of a new innovation.

During this run-up period, the environment is fertile for important improvements that can have a positive effect on your future business.

It is a perfect time to get the last bugs out and to really position the new innovation--and your business relationships--for years to come.

...Joe Justin, Pinnacle Group

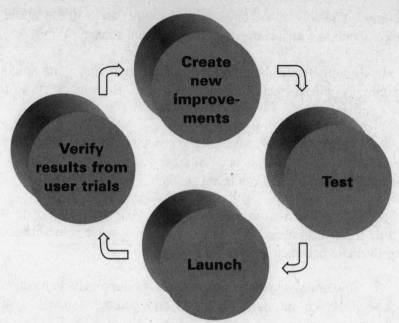

Figure 13-1 Continuous Improvement

KEEP THE SALES FORCE "SELLING INTO THE FUTURE"

Smart strategists know that when you "sell into the future," orders will continue.

Your challenge is now crystal clear. It is to continually improve your inventions and develop new creations so your sales team can continue to introduce new improvements and "future models". With your sales team as a liaison, with customers and end users, you can expand a product's sales and influence in many different ways. Here are a few possibilities:

1. Offer more sizes...small, medium and large, not just one.
2. Introduce new colors or designs.
3. Provide better graphics.
4. Install a just-in-time delivery system.
5. Provide local warehousing for immediate delivery.
6. Issue coupons for volume.
7. Create computer-generated presentations using programs such as Power-Point.
8. Develop national co-op advertising campaigns.
9. Sponsor corporate golf tournaments.
10. Give local or regional seminars.

Strategic Selling

Good marketing experts will naturally want to do this. They will want to expand the product line--and sales--every way they can.

At this time in your strategic development, you have already been thinking in terms of product improvements. Keep your marketing experts abreast of these improvements and let them determine which ones to incorporate and how they should be launched.

After all, expert marketers love to expand sales and capture new markets...this is what they do best!

A BIRTH IS INDUCED, AND STRONG GROWTH IS PREDICTED

When you see success with your invention, adequate production in a timely manner frequently becomes your most difficult problem. If there is not adequate production, here are a few alternatives to consider:

1. License new producers. Your first (or present) licensee is probably going to be protective of its business. Perhaps it can suggest a supplemental licensee that is not a threat. Maybe it can be in another region where the present licensee cannot ship cost effectively. Keep your present licensee abreast of your discussions with others.

2. Can you "sublicense" a manufacturer until the present producer can increase its capacity?

3. Can you hold off on expansion until the present producer can purchase more equipment? This is not always a good choice. When something's hot, it's hot!

If you're concerned about your manufacturer's ability to supply your customers--you should be!

We always like to have back-up manufacturers/suppliers in the event a customer is going to require a fast ramp-up.

If a fast ramp-up is a possibility with your new invention, make sure you have alternative suppliers ready to go.

...Joe Justin, Pinnacle Group

THE USE OF IMPORTERS TO SUPPLEMENT SUPPLY

With many products available from all over the world, you may want to consider importing to supplement supply and increase profits. If you can source acceptable import quality, it can be an excellent means of supply during expansion. It can also be a perfect way to fulfill seasonal requirements, while domestic production maintains a steady flow of supply.

Imports can also be an excellent way to supply some of the more difficult to make components or variations of your invention. For instance, the quality of smaller items is usually much better when made overseas. Domestic producers generally do not make small production items very well.

When importing to augment expansion supply, it is best done in concert with domestic licensees so they may benefit as well. An importer may serve well as a supplier to your domestic manufacturer during this time period.

Regardless of how product is imported, you will want to interview importers to qualify their ability to perform. This may include a visit overseas, which would be a most enjoyable opportunity.

Setting up the import of a product is a time consuming process. If you are not careful, one little error can be disastrous. You must make sure that materials are of the same or better quality. It may be necessary to install a quality assurance program for the manufacturer to test the various aspects of your product.

When you take time to celebrate, try to include your marketing experts. Why?

Easy...they are usually very, very good at it!

...Joe Justin, Pinnacle Group

MANUFACTURING AND MARKETING

TAKE TIME TO CELEBRATE

Hard charging innovator-inventors need time for leisure and relaxation. After all, inducing a birth is a lot of work! Take time to enjoy yourself in the process, whenever you can. Inducing the birth of new inventions will take you to many new places and you will meet many new people. Enjoy them and enjoy the scenery. Besides, during rest and relaxation many new, exciting ideas and discoveries are made!

PART FOUR
LICENSING

14

ALL ABOUT LICENSING

*Licensing is the best way to mass produce and
market your ideas without spending a lot of money.*

Licensing appeals to many inventors because it solves many of the problems associated with making money from inventions. Licensing can be a welcome alternative to spending hundreds of thousands of dollars and thousands of hours gearing up to go into business. Licensing an invention can be relatively easy, once an inventor has built his/her team of experts. This is particularly true if the manufacturing and marketing experts are two different companies. With a marketing expert wanting the exclusive sales rights and with a willing manufacturer eager to produce, licensing your proprietary rights is a relatively straightforward matter.

Inventors considering the licensing of their inventions should learn all they can before entering into an agreement. If this is your choice, take the time to learn the many nuances of licensing.

If you think that licensing is not the best way to earn money from an invention, think again. Prolific inventor Jerome Lemelson licensed his patents (over 500!).

He was the founder of the Lemelson Foundation, Lemelson National Program in Invention, Innovation and Creativity and the National Collegiate Inventors and Innovators Alliance.

WHAT IS A LICENSE?

A license is nothing more than an agreement, a contract. Just as a patent conveys rights to an inventor, so does a license agreement convey rights to a licensee. Simply stated, a licensor (you, the grantor of the rights) gives a licensee (the receiver of the rights) the right to manufacture, and/or sell, and/or use your invention. Either party may be an individual, company, corporation or other legal entity.

A license is literally a written authorization for a licensee to make, use or sell products under the scope of your inventions or trademarks. It also sets up the terms and conditions with which the licensee must abide to keep the license in force.

The key terms and conditions of a license typically include:

1. Payment of royalties
2. Maintaining manufacturing and sales records
3. Marking of patent number(s) on products
4. Maintaining insurance
5. Provisions in the event of the company's sale
6. Provisions in the event of bankruptcy
7. A time frame

It can also include:

1. Acceptable quality standards
2. Minimum sales volumes
3. Minimum royalties
4. A right to subcontract
5. The use of a certain trademark

In a license agreement, you should carefully position the provisions that apply to your needs. They must be carefully written to avoid ambiguity, so they are clearly understood by both parties.

WHAT RIGHTS DO LICENSES GRANT?

Licenses usually grant proprietary property rights to the licensee. This is usually some form of intellectual property and can be the rights you have based on the granting of a patent, trademark or copyright. It can also be proprietary property based on trade secrets, customer lists and of course, patents that are granted or pending.

It is not necessary to have a patent granted to execute a license agreement. In fact, it is usually wise to license your invention during the patent pending phase and not wait until after it is granted.

Technology Transfer

Greg Aharonian of PATNEWS points out a great resource worth knowing about, AUTM--Association of University Technology Managers.

Its members are representatives of universities, nonprofit research institutions, government, and industry who work in the field of licensing, new business development, patent law, and R&D functions.

AUTM is a valuable resource that sponsors conferences and educational courses, reviews publications and keeps abreast of patent legislation.

Their principal role is to:

- *Educate members about technology transfer*
- *Assist technology transfer professionals and nonprofit research institutions in managing the licensing of technology and encourage the commercialization of their intellectual property*
- *Make recommendations to enhance effective transfer of inventiveness and literary creativity to the public*
- *Network with other professional societies in the area of technology transfer*

For membership information visit their Web site: autm.rice.edu/autm/index.html or call them at 203-845-9015.

WHY ARE LICENSES NEEDED?

Frankly, licenses are not always needed, as may be the case between good friends or family members. In other situations, licenses are multi-page documents negotiated by attorneys. This might be the case with the sharing of major technology, such as reactor processing technology to make plastic resins or the "cold draft" process from Sapporo, which Miller's uses to make Miller's Genuine Draft.

Licenses do not have to be long, legal documents. Instead, they can be simple 2-3 page documents. What is most important is that they clearly cover the subject matter, to avoid misunderstandings between you and your licensee.

Most misunderstandings involve the reporting of royalties. In addition, if a company changes management or is sold, you want to make sure that the payments and product qualities continue. The best way to do this is with a straightforward license agreement.

If you want to get down to economic basics, licenses are assets for both licensors and licensees.

So, why wouldn't someone want to have a license instead of a simple manufacturing or marketing agreement?

...Joe Justin, Pinnacle Group

FOUR TYPES OF LICENSES AND TWO APPROACHES TO LICENSING

Choose the type of license that directly reflects your manufacturing and marketing strategy. The decision of whether to grant them exclusively or non-exclusively is your second consideration. Generally speaking, there are four types of licenses:

1. **Licenses to manufacture, sell and use.** This is the most common type, and is used with a manufacturing entity, regardless of whether it will use its own sales organization to sell your invention. With this arrangement, the licensed entity usually pays you royalties based upon the number of licensed products it sells.

2. **A sales-only license.** This is used when licensing to a sales organization. In concert with this license, you must also issue "manufacturing only" licenses (or a simple manufacturing authorization) to those appointed producers to make product for your sales organization. Either the sales company or the manufacturer can be designated to pay the royalties in this type of licensing arrangement.

3. **A manufacturing-only license.** This is usually a simple authorization to manufacture for a designated "sales-only" licensee or for your own sales organization. It can also be a sublicense to augment the production of another licensed manufacturer. Technically speaking, a manufacturing-only license allows the manufacturer to also sell the product, but the sales are restricted to those generated by the authorized sales licensee.

4. **A license to use.** This is common in computer software sales. When you purchase software, you enter into a license agreement upon installation of the software into your computer. This license agreement

There is another type of license that should be considered as well. That is, a "sub-license".

In some of our new product development activities we have licensed other patents and technology in order to develop these products in our industry. In doing so, we like to reserve the right to sub-license the technology to certain other companies so they may pursue the technology in other, non-competing arenas.

Of course, when we do this, the patent holder shares in the royalty stream from the sub-licenses. This is usually a good deal for the inventor/product developer since he/she does not have to spend any time pursuing the sub-licensees or get involved in the negotiations. Instead, it is just a pure income stream.

...Joe Justin, Pinnacle Group

http://web.mit.edu/invent/

This is one of the best Web sites on the Internet for invention related information, awards, links and on and on.

Once again a Lemelson sponsored entity hosts this informative site along with MIT, Massachusetts Institute of Technology.

One of the most prolific non-exclusive licensing arrangements came from the invention of the flip-top aluminum can that stays attached to the top.

If you recall, on prior art flip top cans, the flip top became detached upon opening and was usually discarded.

Environmentalists roared when problems arose. This included litter in our national parks, animals eating the small aluminum rings, or the rings getting caught in the beaks of birds.

The improved flip top ring was developed by an Ohio inventor, and was licensed to anyone and everyone for a very low, very modest royalty.

The result was instant success. With royalties so low, it was not worth it for any single producer to buck the system and to try to design around the new flip-top system. Yet, the cumulative royalty stream from all the soft drink and beer manufacturers was enormous!

states that the software is for your use only and not to be copied for the use of others.

A license may combine two approaches, such as a license to manufacture and use, but this is uncommon.

EXCLUSIVE LICENSES

Exclusive licenses are probably the most common licenses granted. They are generally for niche markets (we know that most new products begin as niches). An exclusive license granted to an entity protects the entity's interests and investment. If you are granting an exclusive license, it must also have built-in protection for you, since you will be relying solely upon a single licensee for your income.

As briefly discussed in Chapter 11, exclusive licenses can also be granted within the scope of a certain industry, field or region. For instance, you may have patents that cover products that apply to non-competing industries, such as a food product sold to hospitals, fast food chains and supermarkets. These three unrelated fields would most likely have three different marketing approaches.

In addition to the standard licensing clauses, exclusive licenses should include:

1. Guaranteed sales
2. Guaranteed royalties
3. Immediate recourse if sales and royalties are not met

Most new invention efforts are realized through the use of exclusive licenses. The fact that they are exclusive means that there is a dedicated team effort, which is at the heart of bringing about the success of a new invention.

NON-EXCLUSIVE LICENSES

If you are licensing several users, you will use a non-exclusive license. Non-exclusive licenses are typically used for commodity-type products, such as an aluminum can's flip top. Take care to license non-exclusive licensees at an "arms-length". Manufacturers tend to be very possessive of their sales and customer base and would frown upon your showing favoritism to a particular licensee. Non-exclusive licenses will usually contain:

1. No sales minimums
2. No guaranteed royalties, just a set rate
3. Recourse in the event of non-payment, infringement, etc.

15

YOUR LICENSING STRATEGY

*A mirror image of your manufacturing
and marketing strategy.*

Once you have a clear picture of your manufacturing and marketing strategies, and how you will take your invention to market, your license agreements will reflect it. It will be carefully tailored to protect both your sales and marketing partners and your interests. Your license agreement will dovetail perfectly with your manufacturing and marketing strategy.

THE RIGHT LICENSING APPROACH FOR YOU

If your invention is commodity oriented, you may want several licensees. If it is a specialty niche product, perhaps only one or two licensees are best. You may even have a potential licensee in mind. A well-thought out plan will save time, money and hard feelings later.

If your product has potential in more than one field, you may want non-exclusive licenses in one or more fields or exclusive licenses. Using the previous food example, consideration for the three licenses in the three fields can vary. For instance, you may want to grant an

Licensing Launches Disney

In 1928 Disney created Mickey Mouse. A woman approached Disney and asked if he would license the rights to her to make Mickey Mouse stuffed dolls. Disney agreed, and in fact, liked her work so much that he offered more characters for her to make.

The licensing income from Mickey Mouse, and eventually other characters and other products, launched the Disney Kingdom we know of today.

Even now, Disney's fortune is based in large part on royalties from licensing. The Disney royalties are typically between 5% to 7.5%.

249

Realistic Expectations

You and your licensee should determine performance requirements based on conservative, realistic expectations. Hopefully, this will dovetail with your earnings expectations. Unrealistic expectations may result in failure for you and your licensee.

Hopefully, your marketing study will be accurate enough to give you both a good idea of earnings potential.

Three Keys to Negotiating

According to Master Negotiator, Herb Cohen, here are the three key elements to getting what you want:

*1.   **Power.** If you have an invincible patent position and a ready market for your new idea/invention, then the power to make a deal is on your side. So, know your patent position up front!*

*2.   **Information.** The person with the most information will have the best tactical advantage. So, know the industry well and know who is doing what.*

*3.   **Time.** The person who is in a hurry to make a deal, will usually make a bad deal. So, take your time!*

exclusive in hospital food to a sole manufacturer (and sales organization), but a non-exclusive in the other fields. But if you do, make sure there is an exclusion for sales to hospitals in the other non-exclusive licenses you strike.

When licensing your inventions, here are some general strategic guidelines to follow:

Exclusive Licenses

1.   If you are carving out a specific commodity niche that you want to protect, it is probably advisable to have a dedicated, exclusive relationship. For instance, the producer markets new drugs exclusively.

2.   Exclusive licenses may not be advisable for a commodity-type product. It destroyed Beta Max, for instance.

3.   You may want to start with a limited exclusive license, giving a dedicated producer a jump on the marketplace, and then open it up to others. This is the case with the licensing of Direct TV rights. It started with RCA and later went to Sony and then others.

4   If a license is exclusive to give the licensee a jump on the market, how long does it last? Granting an exclusive for 1-3 years may be wise, if the company gives you an up-front guarantee on sales and/or income.

5.   Exclusive licenses must be predicated on performance and guaranteed earnings year after year. Make sure that your guarantees and your earnings begin early on.

6.   Do not waste your time on a potential candidate who wants an exclusive license, but will not put up any front money or give a long-term guarantee.

Non-exclusive Licenses

1.   If your invention is a commodity-type product, it may be best to grant a simple, non-exclusive license.

2.   There may be less incentive for a company to support your invention if "anyone can make the product".

3.   If you have a major breakthrough that is of great benefit to mankind, you may want to consider only non-exclusive licenses.

If you are not sure of your marketing and manufacturing approach, you will not be sure of your licensing approach either. If this applies to you, learn as you go and be cautious.

YOUR LICENSING FOCUS

Licenses are the granting of your rights to others. Early on, you learned about your primary objectives, two of which are to earn money and gain security. Licenses are the means to both. But inventors commonly look at licenses first as a means of achieving security and secondly as a way to earn money.

Most inventors seek to license manufacturers, and when they do, few orders follow. Why? This illustrates the wrong perspective toward licensing. Remember that manufacturers are notoriously poor at sales. They make products based upon what customers tell them they want; they don't usually create and promote new products well. Don't waste your time looking for or negotiating with potential licensees based on their manufacturing ability.

The principal focus of your licensing activities should be to establish a mutually beneficial relationship between you (the owner of intellectual property) and the licensee, the *seller* of the product under the scope of your intellectual property. In this way, both of you will be beneficiaries. Why is the focus on sales? You know quite well that you will not be happy until your invention is sold and begins producing income. That is your chief objective. The proper incentive for a license to produce income is based on sales, not manufacturing. Focus on sales incentives with your sales experts and there will be mutuality in your goals and desires.

THE SEVEN POINT CHECKLIST TO AN EXCLUSIVE LICENSE

The following seven points are based on the qualities you have pursued in selecting potential manufacturing and marketing partners, as explained in Chapters 11 and 12. Consistent with basing your licensing focus on the ability to market, not manufacture, the following is a checklist to use as a quick review when granting an exclusive license. The dedicated marketing expert who is going to be a licensee should have the following attributes:

1. **Size.** Is its current sales and marketing network big enough to handle your needs? If not, does it have the ability to expand?
2. **Cutting edge capabilities.** Is its marketing approach really dedicated to innovation? Does it have the graphics and marketing abilities your new product needs to succeed?
3. **Financial clout.** Does it have the financial ability to spend the necessary amount to be successful?
4. **History and reputation.** Does the company have similar relationships with other companies? Is it now selling or has it ever sold a product that has infringed a patent or been known to have infringed one? Does it have the ethical reputation you will need to introduce and drive your product?
5. **Testing and trials.** With the added responsibility, is this candidate prepared to handle hands-on product tests and trials? With a dedicated, exclusive relationship, it is more important than ever that the

Who Receives the Highest Royalties?

For name endorsement, Michael Jordon is known to receive the highest royalties. What are they?

Reportedly, they are about 17.5% with substantial up front money as well.

Authors also tend to get higher royalties than inventors. ...varying between 10% to 20%. But much of this depends upon who the author is, the volume the finished works will sell and how much work the publisher has to do to get the manuscript ready for print.

Do you suppose you could get the same royalties that Michael Jordan or Stephen King receive?

Wait for the Perfect Deal?

Don't wait for the "perfect deal" to come along. If it is perfect, be suspect. When a reasonable opportunity with fair-minded people comes along, nail it!

...Joan Lefkowitz, Accessory Brainstorms, NYC

candidate spearhead the effort to arrange customer trials and help monitor results.

6. **Trust.** The trust issue is crucial. You are trusting this entity with an important part of your financial future.

7. **Leadership.** Does the candidate have leadership with vision and determination to succeed, or does it just want to get in on the action and corner your invention to see if it sells?

Exclusive licensing relationships can make or break your new invention. If the organization had the ability to make things happen in the past, it will probably be able to make things happen with your invention. Make sure that your exclusive arrangements have performance requirements and a means of getting out in the event of non-performance.

WHEN IS THE BEST TIME TO LICENSE YOUR INVENTION?

The best time to start your licensing activities is as soon as possible. There is no need to wait for patents to issue. A patent is not required to license an invention. It is usually best to begin your licensing activities during the patent pending phase. If you do it while working under confidentiality agreements with your marketing experts and then introduce your new invention in a timely manner, you will maximize the profit potential.

As an inventor, you don't want to spend a lot of money pursuing patents on something that doesn't sell. A smart marketing expert doesn't want to wait. "Time is money" for both of you.

If a company wants to wait to license your technology, it will probably miss out on the opportunity. Smart marketing experts can see the opportunity at hand. They are willing to "bet on the outcome" instead of waiting to see what happens. Wise marketers and innovators know that you can't bet on the horse after it races.

WHO NEGOTIATES A LICENSE AGREEMENT?

Negotiating license agreements through attorneys can be extremely costly. It can also result in "building a fence" between the parties. The best licensing agreements are those in which all parties trust one another and work together toward a common goal. A trust relationship should not require the involvement of an attorney.

The best approach to licensing by a first time inventor is for the parties to discuss the agreement and come to an understanding of what they want and need. Work toward building a stronger relationship as you discuss licensing objectives. Remember that your licensees will be your partners for years to come. Your goal is to have mutually attainable goals.

Prepare Ahead

Before you take your seat at the negotiating table, make a detailed list of what is most important to you, what is least important to you and how flexible you are willing to be on each item. For instance, you might be willing to take a slightly lower royalty if they will guarantee to get the product to market a year ahead of schedule. Work out the math on the possible scenarios beforehand so you can make informed decisions during the meeting. If you're guessing under pressure in the meeting, you may make a careless error that costs you dearly in the long run.
...Robin Renee

How About "No Negotiating"

*Try telling this to your potential licensee...that you prefer **not** to negotiate a license.*
Instead, let the licensee know that you would rather just sit down with him/her and talk about the possibilities.
From this type of approach, you will not only be building a team, but you may end up with an agreement that not only gives you royalties, but gives you stock ownership in the company in exchange for an exclusive.
This is not an uncommon occurrence.

Your partnership approach to finalizing a license agreement with a potential licensee should allow the two of you to consummate the majority of the license. If you imagine that you are sitting side by side at a table, not across from one another, the two of you will work out the details of the partnership. Once it is drafted, the two parties can hire an attorney to "tie up any loose ends" before signing.

HOW TO INTRODUCE A LICENSE TO A POTENTIAL CANDIDATE

At the initial stages of licensing your invention, you probably discussed the possibilities with a candidate. Now you want to formalize the relationship. Here is a five-step approach you can use to do this in an amiable way:

1. Once the two of you have determined that you would like to enter into a license agreement, tell the other party that you will send him/her a draft of a license so that each of you can "fill in the blanks". This approach is better than sending the other party a license draft that contains a list of your demands. When you send a license draft, tell the recipient that it is a standard license agreement that can be modified to meet your mutual needs.

2. Send him/her a copy of your license agreement, not theirs. Leave blanks in several key places. The two most obvious are the royalty percentage and minimum royalty payments (or sales guarantees). You can also leave blanks for the term of the license, the field of the sales of the invention, and the licensee's name, address, etc.

3. Once the potential candidate receives the document, you each can "fill in the blanks" over the phone. Better yet, meet in person, talk it over and complete the agreement. Take your time. Don't pressure anyone. You want a carefully thought out mutual agreement.

4. Prepare another draft based upon your discussions and fax it to the other party for review. In this draft, you will have replaced the blanks with accurate information. Allow enough time for the other party to review it. You may have to repeat this step a few times to get the draft you want.

Last, the two of you can send the draft to your attorneys for a final review. It is wise to have established an understanding with your new partner that your mutual objective is to have a friendly agreement and that you are using your attorneys to make sure that you have the proper legal content.

When drafting a contract, in addition to concepts of Offer, Acceptance and Legal Consideration, always try to maintain an awareness for some degree of common sense. Any contract can be breached by either or both parties, even if said contract is legally enforceable, and will be breached by the party who is not getting something of value out of the contractual relationship.

In other words, always shoot for a Win/Win relationship...a situation for which a legal contract would not be necessary because it is in the best interests of both parties to keep the working relationship.

...Doug English, Patent Attorney

The License Format

Make sure the license format that you use is one agreed upon by both parties. I once spent six months negotiating a contract with the president of the company. When he handed it over to his attorneys, they tossed it out stating, "We only work with contracts that follow our standard format." Not only did we have to adapt to their contract format, but more importantly, we had to begin the negotiation process from scratch.

...Robin Renee

LICENSING INCENTIVES

In your licensing activities, think in terms of providing incentives for sales volume that will result in more, faster and easier sales and higher income for you. Here are some incentives you should consider:

1. **Royalties.** A new product with added benefits to end-users can usually bring a higher price. But this does not mean a dramatically higher price. The concept at work is "price elasticity", and means that some product lines, such as plastic trash bags, sugar and salt, will not sell if they are priced much higher than a competitive brand. In retail stores, this usually equates to a 2% premium. The more price competitive a product is, the higher the sales. Don't make the mistake of asking for high royalties and then wondering why no sales are generated.

2. **Sliding Scales.** Royalty rates frequently decline as sales volumes increase. This is an incentive for a producer to promote and sell a lot of product. A typical sliding scale may be:

Less than $2,000,000 in sales	3%
$2,000,000-$5,000,000	2%
Over $5,000,000	1.5%

3. **Exclusives.** Even in a commodity market in which you may ultimately license many entities, it might be wise to grant at least a temporary exclusive to a key company. In exchange for the exclusive, the company will invest capital to make sure the product launch succeeds. Being first to market is just as important as having proprietary product protection. And frankly, what should you care if your licensee has an exclusive for twenty years or more? If it is based on guaranteed sales and royalty income to you, you should be satisfied.

4. **Participation in licensing others.** You can include a clause in a license agreement that allows the licensee to sublicense others in the future. It can be structured so that both parties can share the income from the sub-licensing. This can be an attractive award if your licensee does a good job of taking the product to market. It allows the entire market to convert to your new technology if it so desires.

5. **Participation in patent infringement rewards.** If a licensee has an exclusive license and your patents are infringed, it may be in a position to defend the patents and sue the infringer for the loss of sales and income. In such a lawsuit, your licensee has much more to gain than you do, because lost royalties amount to a fraction of lost sales. If

Typical Royalties

If there is one royalty rate that is considered "standard", it has to be 3%. This conclusion is based on many discussions over the years with attorneys and inventors.

Generally speaking, if sales of your invention are relatively low, a higher royalty is best. If you are selling a high-volume commodity, a lower royalty is best, so others do not try to design around you.

Don't Get Greedy!

When considering royalties, keep in mind that most companies earn about 10% profit after all costs are paid. By requesting a 10% royalty, you are asking to make as much as they make. Can you justify this amount? Did you put in as much time and effort and financial risk as they have? Most likely you have not.

*Licensees are the ones that must spend their money--earned from the sales of **other** products-- in order to launch your new invention.*

Don't get greedy! Very few high-volume products have large profit margins. An overly aggressive royalty will kill a new idea fast. Besides, a small percentage of a multi-million dollar market is a lot better than 10% of nothing.

...Bob DeMatteis

you have this clause in your agreement, ask for a percentage of any reward the licensee receives. A reasonable request is 15%-25%.

6. Grant the right of first refusal on new developments. You can also give a licensee the right of first refusal on any improvements to the licensed invention. If you invent any new improvements to the invention, the licensee has the first right to license it or not license it.

7. Termination of the license agreement if a patent does not issue. Some licensees may be leery of entering into an agreement because if your patent does not issue, they would be vulnerable to others who later enter the market. If this is the case, you can offer to terminate the license in a pre-determined time period, such as 5 years.

8. Creating trade dress protection. If your product has the potential for trade dress protection, declare it immediately and make it part of your license agreement. By doing so, you help to establish your trade dress potential. While trade dress cannot convey functional attributes, there are some questionable areas as to what constitutes the functions associated with trade dress.

For instance, the shape of a bottle has trade dress rights, but bottles are functional. It can be argued that although any sort of container, regardless of shape, has a function, some shapes function better than others. If a particular shape allows the user to hold it more easily, does that mean it cannot establish trade dress? Whatever the case, you are better off establishing your trade dress ownership now rather than fighting over what might be later.

Licensing trade dress is in the best interests of you and your licensee. Long-term, both stand to benefit. With trade dress protection being a relatively newer concept, more and more "functional" shapes and attributes may be considered as part of trade dress.

TAILORING A STANDARD LICENSE TO YOUR NEEDS

With your sales and manufacturing objectives determined, you can tailor a standard license to your needs. You may want to consult an attorney to help with your license draft, but remember that it should be based on your needs and relevant to your industry. Your attorney may be unfamiliar with these issues.

The best approach is to start with a generic license, modify it according to your needs, make sure you add some incentives and then have your attorney help with the final draft. You would be wise to learn all you can before you employ your attorney in licensing matters. A good patent attorney does not want to spend hours teaching you about licensing. He/she will prefer you know what you want from the outset so an agreement can be tailored to your needs. As you will see, while

---

An Example of Suing for Lost Royalties vs. Lost Sales

Let's assume that your licensee is exclusively licensed and is being infringed upon by another company. The other company, which has been notified of patent infringement, has sales of $10 million a year.

If for a period of three years, no action was taken, the potential loss is $30 million. (The statute of limitations on patent infringement is 6 years.) This means a lawsuit can be filed for $90 million since willful infringement can gain treble damages!

Compare this to the amount of royalties you could sue for. At a 3% rate, you could only sue for $900,000 x 3 or a total of $2.7 million.

If your licensee is suing for $90 million and you share in 20% of the award, you stand to gain $18 million. Your licensee is also footing the bill.

Which would you prefer?
...Bob DeMatteis

Your Entity Status

If you or your company enjoy small entity status, remember that if the company that licenses your technology is a large entity (500 employees or more) you automatically become a large entity and your fees double. Bring this up in the negotiation and ask that they assume the payments, as they will be gaining the lion's share of the revenues when your product goes on sale.
...Robin Renee

most elements of a license agreement are very simple, some are not so easily understood.

The following license will serve as an excellent start for most new, simple inventions. It is a license to manufacture, sell and use. As you read it, analyze your needs based on the margin comments. This license is not considered short or long. Its best attributes are that it is easy to understand and contains a minimum of "legalese". Since most licenses are similar, you can save thousands of dollars by adapting this model to your needs.

STANDARD LICENSE AGREEMENT - SAMPLE

THIS AGREEMENT made and entered into in duplicate originals as of this _____ day of _____, 19___, by and between _____ (hereinafter referred to as Licensee) having its principal place of business at _____ _____; and _____ (hereinafter referred to as Licensor), having its principal office and place of business at _____.

WITNESSETH THAT

Licensor is the owner of certain technology and know-how pertaining to _____; and

Licensor wishes to grant and Licensee desires to secure an exclusive license under the Licensed Patent Rights.

In consideration of the premises and of the mutual covenants set forth herein, it is agreed by and between the parties as follows:

1.   For purposes of the present Agreement, the following terms shall have the meanings indicated:

A.   "Licensed Patent Rights" shall mean _____. Licensor defines its intellectual property rights (Rights) as those falling under the above referenced patent application and also includes the trademark, _____ _____™ and any trade dress that results from the manufacture and marketing of the Invention.

B.   "Licensed Products" shall mean any goods, materials and products covered by or coming within the scope of the

A license starts with basic information: names, addresses, date, etc. This information can be neatly printed or typed.

If you modify the document using a computer, you can replace the word "Licensor" with an actual name. For instance, Atlas Inc. (hereinafter referred to as "Atlas"). The designation "Atlas" will then replace "Licensee" throughout the document.

In this paragraph, insert the field of the invention in the blank. For instance, "plastic bags" or "ice cream manufacturing".

In Paragraph 1A, insert your patent application number, attorney docket number or invention's title here. If you have a patent issued, change it to read, "...including U.S. Patent No. _____". Also add any trademarks or trade dress you may be licensing.

Paragraphs 1A through 1D state the definitions of the terms used in the license agreement.

Licensed Patent Rights.

        C.   "Sale" shall include sale, gift, delivery, lease or consignment, as the case may be, whether for domestic use or export, and goods subject to royalty shall be considered "sold" when shipped, delivered, invoiced or paid for, whichever shall occur first.

        D.   "Sales Price" shall mean the price invoiced in the regular course of business in a genuine arm's length transaction and shall include a corresponding lease, rental or consigned price.

        2A.   Licensor hereby grants to Licensee on the terms and conditions set forth in this Agreement a personal, indivisible, non-transferable, exclusive license under the Licensed Patent Rights to make, use and sell Licensed Products, with no right to grant sublicenses.

        B.   The exclusive license shall be for all sales made by Licensee in the field of, and specifically restricted to,

_____.

        C.   This license shall be effective as of _____, 19___, and shall continue for the duration of this Agreement.

        D.   Nothing contained in this Agreement shall be construed as conferring, by implication, estoppel, or otherwise, any license or other right under any patent or patent right except the license expressly granted herein.

        3A.   Licensee shall pay royalties to Licensor on all Licensed Products sold by Licensee. The rate of royalty shall be three percent (3%) of the total Sales Price of Licensed Products sold by Licensee, less all returns and credits.

        B.   Within ten (10) days following each month's end, during the term of this Agreement, Licensee shall submit to Licensor a report certifying (i) the total number of goods subject to royalty sold during the previous month, (ii) the Sales Price or Prices of such products, (iii) the aggregate dollar volume of Sales for such period and (iv) the payment to be made thereon under Paragraph 3A hereof. The first such report shall include the period from the effective date of this Agreement until _____. Each such report shall

---

Paragraphs 1C and 1D discuss sales and sales price, which refers to "gross wholesale" sales price.

Paragraph 2A grants the Licensee an exclusive license to use, manufacture and sell. If it is to be non-exclusive or restricted, change it. To keep control of the patent rights, you don't want the licensee to strike sublicenses on its own. If they need extra production, you qualify the other producer and you strike a "manufacturing only" license with them.

2B If the license is restricted to sales in a given field, such as food supplies to hospitals, insert the field in Paragraph 2B.

2C is the effective date of the agreement. It is usually the same as the date on page one, but it can be otherwise.

2D says you are only conveying license for the patent or patent application listed. It says that you are not granting any other rights, such as trade secrets or trademarks you may own.

3A states that royalties are paid on sales, less returns and credits. Freight may also be deducted, but sales commissions usually are not.

Monthly and quarterly accountings are most common. While quarterly accountings may be easier for an accountant, monthly is better for your cash flow. This also gives an early warning sign if one of your licensees is having problems.

be accompanied by payment of the royalties due for a given period.

> C.   A similar statement shall be made within 10 days after termination of this license or of this Agreement for any reason, covering the period from the end of the last month reported until such date of termination.

> D.   In order for Licensee to maintain the exclusivity of the license, it must maintain minimum sales and royalties, which are calculated on a quarterly basis. If for any reason Licensee does not meet the minimum quarterly sales volume, it has the right to maintain the exclusive license by payment of the corresponding minimum royalty. Minimum sales are:

	1st Quarter	2nd Quarter	3rd Quarter	4th Quarter
Year 1:				
Year 2:				
Year 3:				
Year 4:				
Year 5:				

> E.   A deposit against future royalties of _____ is hereby acknowledged, attached to, and credited against future royalty payments.

> F.   In the event the Licensed Patents Rights are ever deemed invalid in a court in the United States of America, then this license is null and void and Licensee is under no further obligation to continue with the terms and conditions of the license, unless, however; Licensor elects to contest the judgement of invalidity in a court of appeals, in which case the terms and conditions of the license will remain intact until Licensor has exhausted its last possible avenue of appeal.

> 4.   Licensee shall keep complete and accurate records of its manufacture and sale of goods subject to royalty sufficient to verify the accuracy of the reports and payments required to be made by it. Such records and other operations of Licensee shall be available

A final accounting is also required at the end of the term.

If you are going to use a sliding scale for the royalty rate, insert it in or after paragraph 3A.

Paragraph 3D provides for a simple means for the Licensee to maintain the exclusive license. If this is a non-exclusive license, this paragraph will probably be deleted.
This paragraph is essential for exclusive licenses.

Paragraph 3E is for a deposit, which is to be credited against future royalties. The deposit check should accompany the signed license. It is best to receive the signed license and check within 3-5 days.

Paragraph 3F states that if the patent becomes invalid at some future date, the Licensee's obligation to pay you ceases.

Paragraph 4 allows you or your accountant to review the record keeping of the Licensee to ensure it is accurate. If you think you are dealing with dishonest parties, you may want to add a clause stating that: 1) Any shortage of royalties due to inadequate record keeping shall be payable at twice the regular royalty rate and 2) the entire cost of the Licensor's audit shall be paid by the Licensee.

during ordinary business hours for examination by an authorized employee or representative of Licensor for the purpose of verifying Licensee's compliance with all conditions and obligations of this Agreement.

5. During the term of the license granted by the present Agreement, Licensee agrees to have marked permanently and legibly all Licensed Products manufactured and sold by it, with the number of the Licensed Patent, and in compliance with 35 U.S.C. #287, and in a form subject to the prior approval of Licensor. In such notices, licensee shall not use the name of Licensor in any literature, advertising or other sales promotion.

The marking of patent numbers is a legal requirement. It actually protects both parties' interests. Without proper patent number markings on products, an infringer might claim, "I didn't know I was infringing."

6A. Unless sooner terminated in accordance with the terms hereof, this Agreement shall remain in full force and effect until the expiration of the last of the Licensed Patents.

6A The time period for the license can be whatever the parties agree upon. Remember that long-term licenses mean long-term relationships. With shorter terms, such as 3 years or 5 years, you will renegotiate frequently.

B. Should Licensee (i) fail or refuse to make any payment required under Paragraph 3 of this Agreement or be in breach or default of any other provision of this Agreement, or (ii) initiate any proceeding for dissolution or winding up its business, or (iii) apply for relief under any law relating to bankruptcy or insolvency, or (iv) become the subject of any proceeding relating to bankruptcy or insolvency, then Licensor, in addition to all other remedies available to it, shall have the right by written notice to Licensee to terminate forthwith this Agreement or any licenses granted hereby, as Licensor may elect.

Paragraph 6B allows the license to be negated in the event the Licensee stops paying you, goes bankrupt or shuts down.

C. Upon termination of this Agreement for any reason, all rights and licenses granted hereunder to Licensee to sell and market Licensed Products shall terminate.

Along with paragraph 6B above, the Licensee must stop producing licensed products. While the legality of provisions 6B and 6C can be argued, include them anyway. Let them prove otherwise, instead of being locked into court proceedings without royalty payments. If bankruptcy occurs, you want to consult legal counsel.

D. Any termination of this Agreement shall not relieve Licensee from its obligation to make a final statement and report, or from its liability for the sales on goods subject to royalty, made or sold prior to the date of such termination, and shall not prejudice any remedy, cause of action or claim of Licensor accrued or to accrue or which Licensor may have on account of any failure, refusal, breach or default by Licensee.

Relevant to paragraphs 6B and 6C, even though a Licensee is no longer producing your products, it still must file a final report and pay you. Also, you are ensured that you have recourse in the event it stops payment.

Paragraph 6E gives you the right to make a final audit of royalty payments.

Paragraph 7A allows the Licensee to assign the license if they sell their business. But you have a right to approve of the new Licensee. You want this provision for many reasons. For instance, if you do not trust the new Licensee, you may want to change the royalty or accounting provision. If they are holding a competitive patent, you may want some assurances.

Paragraph 7B says that you can transfer this license whenever you want. This would be particularly wise if your income becomes relatively substantial. You would want to consider a corporation or trust.

8A You want the Licensee to hold you harmless of all claims resulting from their operations. With all the suit-happy people in the world, you do not want anyone looking to you to file a lawsuit. This paragraph protects you against both claims in manufacturing and any product liability claims.

8B You ask the Licensee to have a $1,000,000 insurance policy in the event they are sued.

E.   Any termination of this Agreement shall not prejudice the right of Licensor to conduct a final audit of the records of Licensee.

7A.   This agreement shall be transferable by Licensee whether directly or by operation of law only together with Licensee's entire business and only with the prior written consent of Licensor, which shall not be unreasonably withheld. Upon transfer of this agreement, the transferee shall execute a written undertaking in a form provided or approved by Licensor. In the undertaking the transferee shall (i) assume all of the obligations undertaken by Licensee hereunder; (ii) acknowledge that it has satisfied itself that the Licensed Patent Rights and Licensor's right to license same are valid and incontestable; and (iii) covenant not to directly or indirectly contest, challenge or deny the validity of any of the Licensed Patent Rights in any forum or for any purpose.

B.   This Agreement may be assigned by Licensor and shall inure to the benefit of Licensor and its successors and assigns, and all obligation of Licensee shall run in favor of the successors, assigns or other legal representatives of Licensor.

8A.   Licensee agrees to indemnify and hold Licensor harmless against any and all claims, expenses (including reasonable attorneys' fees), costs, charges, taxes and the like arising out of Licensee's operations under this License Agreement, and/or Licensee's manufacture or sale of Licensed Products.

B.   Licensee agrees to maintain products liability insurance in force in the amount not less than $1,000,000 (one million dollars), and to have Licensor listed as additional insured on said policy. Licensee shall provide such evidence of this insurance, as Licensor shall reasonably require.

C.   Licensee (i) acknowledges that it is satisfied that the Licensed Patent Rights and Licensor's right to license same are valid and incontestable; and (ii) will not directly or indirectly contest, challenge or deny the validity of any of the Licensed Patent Rights in any forum or for any purpose.

9A.   No warranty or representation is given or made by Licensor that any goods sold are free from infringement of the patent rights of others.

B.   A waiver of any of the terms or conditions of this Agreement shall not be considered a modification, cancellation or waiver of such or any other term or condition thereafter.

10.   All notices for all purposes of this Agreement shall be given in writing and shall be effective when either (a) served by personal delivery, or (b) deposited postage prepaid in the United States certified mails addressed to the respective parties at their given addresses or at such other addresses as either party may later specify by written notice to the other.

11.   This Agreement shall be interpreted and construed under the laws of the State of _____.

12.   This instrument contains the entire and only understanding between the parties and supersedes all prior agreements between the parties respecting the subject matter, and any representation, promise or condition in connection therewith not incorporated herein shall not be binding upon either party. No modification, renewal, extension or waiver of this Agreement or any of its provisions or any termination shall be binding unless in writing.

IN WITNESS, the parties hereto have caused this Agreement to be executed as of the day and years first above written.

Licensor:

By: _____

      name   title

Licensee:

By: _____

      name   title

---end of agreement---

9A   You may have to do just the opposite and guarantee them that your patent does not infringe another, if indeed this is true. However, you do not need to give them any assurance against the infringement of another patent, due to some aspect of the product's design.

Paragraph 9B states that if one part of the agreement is waived, the rest of it remains intact.

10   It is important that any changes are made in writing.

11   The state you select should be yours. If a legal problem arises, you want them traveling, not you. A variation on this theme would be if your prosecuting attorneys were out of state, you might want to use that state instead.

Paragraph 12 states that there are no other side agreements that are pertinent to the license.

Sign the licenses in duplicate originals. One is for you and the other is for the Licensee.

The preceding license agreement is not necessarily conclusive, but it is thorough enough for most simple licensing applications. After some thought, you should be able to determine the details you want to have in your license agreement.

A CREATIVE APPROACH TO LICENSING (A SWEETHEART AGREEMENT)

An approach that can put you in a more "hands off" position, but provides great incentives for a licensee is what can be called a "sweetheart agreement". A sweetheart agreement would be used for a very special company that can give you solid guarantees on sales. Here are the basics of how it works:

1. The license is exclusive in the licensee's trade, country, industry, etc.
2. You give the licensee a drastically reduced royalty rate. For instance, instead of 3%, reduce it to 1%.
3. The licensee guarantees an agreed-upon monthly income from royalties. Set up a reasonable timeline to meet the schedule.
4. The licensee pays for all patenting, R&D expenses, training, travel, etc.
5. You retain ownership of the patent.
6. In the event of infringement, the licensee pays for prosecution of infringers. It has a lot more to gain than do you as the inventor. The benefit is that you may lose thousands of dollars in royalties, but a licensee may lose millions in sales. With willful infringement being vulnerable to triple damages, this can mean a huge reward for a licensee, which makes for a very good incentive. In such a license agreement, ask for 15%-20% of the infringement reward.

This type of sweetheart agreement with guaranteed payments would invariably ensure that the licensee would aggressively take your product to market. Likewise, it can give you security and allow you to focus your efforts on what you do best--innovate and invent.

A SIMPLIFIED LICENSE AGREEMENT

What follows is a simplified license agreement printed with single spacing. It totals about 1-2/3 pages. This license contains all the elements contained in the preceding "sweetheart" agreement. The agreement is one targeted for business associates you trust. No legal opinion is given herein on its validity, but it is an agreement written by an attorney, subsequently modified and signed.

Royalty Incentives

Think about this. If you receive a 3% royalty and you have to pay your R&D costs, attorney's fees, etc., you would be much better off accepting a lower rate and having your licensee pay those costs instead. Your licensee will most likely have a budget to pay for some of those expenses. With lower royalties, they can be much more competitive in the marketplace and really propel sales to some high volumes. The outcome of this approach is obvious...it is a win-win situation for you both.

Retaining Ownership

A patent is to intellectual property what a deed is to real estate. Remember, you should never assign your patent to anyone if they are paying you royalties on a monthly basis. If they want to buy the patent from you, assign it only after you have received the final purchase payment.

The same is true of real estate. You will assign the deed only after you have received the last payment.

SIMPLIFIED LICENSE AGREEMENT - EXAMPLE

THIS AGREEMENT is made this _____ day of _____, 19___, between _____ (Licensor) and _____, a _____ corporation (Licensee).

Recitals

In these first paragraphs, fill in the blanks as required or better yet, type the information.

A.   Licensor is the owner of certain technology and know-how and intellectual property pertaining to _____ in which Licensor has filed a patent application (No._____) revealing both versions of the invention (the "Invention").

B.   Licensor desires to grant Licensee the exclusive right for the manufacture and marketing of the Invention in the United States and Canada and Licensee desires to license the rights to manufacture (including subcontract via designated sub-contractors) and market the Invention in the United States and Canada (the Territory).

NOW, THEREFORE, in consideration of the premises and of the mutual covenants set forth herein, it is agreed by and between the parties as follows:

1.   *The Intellectual Property Rights.* Licensor defines its intellectual property rights (Rights) as those falling under the above referenced patent application and also includes the trademark, _____™, and any trade dress that results from the manufacture and marketing of the Invention. It may also include the following alternate marks owned by Licensor: _____™, _____™ and _____™.

This agreement includes the licensing of trademarks and trade dress as well. Trademarks and trade dress can outlive patent protection, as there is no expiration of the rights.

2.   *Grant of license.* Licensor represents that he has full and complete authority to license the Rights to manufacture and market the Invention in the Territory and Licensor grants to Licensee the exclusive Rights to manufacture and market the Invention in the Territory. This exclusive license granted by Licensor to Licensee is specifically restricted to the manufacturing and marketing of the Invention in the field of _____ and _____. Licensee understands that Licensor also intends on granting exclusive licenses of the Invention to other entities in at least two other unrelated fields; one of which is in the field of _____ and the other of which is in the field of _____, both of which are specifically not in Licensee's field. Exclusive licenses in the other fields will specifically include clauses excluding of the ability to manufacture and market in the Licensee's field.

The field of the invention is specifically confined to a specific field. For clarification, the other exclusive fields are listed as well.

3.   *Royalty.* In consideration of this Agreement, Licensee agrees to pay Licensor a monthly royalty based upon _____ % of the gross sales revenue derived from the sales of the Invention. For purposes of this Agreement, gross sales revenue will be calculated based on the amount stated on customer invoices issued by Licensee and is payable on the 20th of the month following the close of any previous month. The royalty check will be accompanied by a sales summary.

The royalty percentage in this type of sweetheart agreement should be low. For instance, 1% instead of 3%, or 2% instead of 5%. Remember that this license will have an indefinite future because of the trademarks.

4.   *Maintaining Exclusivity.* The exclusive Rights herein

will remain in force based upon Licensee maintaining minimum sales and minimum royalty payments which are calculated on a quarterly basis. If for any reason Licensee does not meet the minimum quarterly sales volume it has the right to maintain the exclusive license by payment at the end of each quarter of the corresponding minimum royalty. Minimum sales in order to maintain the exclusive license are:

	1st Quarter	2nd Quarter	3rd Quarter	4th Quarter
Year 1:				
Year 2:				
Year 3:				
Year 4:				
Year 5 and thereafter:				

If for any reason Licensee decides it no longer wishes to maintain its exclusive license, then this agreement shall become non-exclusive, this paragraph 4 is then stricken and Licensee's royalty rate will be subject to re-negotiation.

5.   *Records.* Licensee agrees to maintain complete and accurate records of its manufacture and sale of goods subject to royalty and will request the same of any sublicensee. Such records and other operations of Licensee or sublicensee shall be available during ordinary business hours for examination by an authorized employee or representative of Licensor.

6.   *Pricing.* Licensee shall have the right to establish the price at which the Invention will be sold.

7.   *Reimbursement of Costs.* Licensee agrees that in lieu of the favorable royalty rates that it will reimburse Licensor for any related patenting costs, trademark or trade dress registration costs, now or in the future, and any other R&D costs incurred by Licensor on behalf of Licensee.

8.   *Defending the Rights.* Licensee agrees to defend all the Rights owned by Licensor in the event of infringement in the field of Licensee's exclusive license. In the event of an award (which may also include damages) being granted Licensee for its lost sales and profits, Licensee agrees to pay Licensor _____% of the net award.

9.   *Parties and Assignment.* This agreement shall be binding upon and inure to the benefit of and be enforceable by the parties or their successors or assigns. If Licensee wishes to transfer the license with the sale of its business, it must have the prior written consent of Licensor, which shall not be unreasonably withheld. Upon transfer of this agreement, the transferee shall execute a written document declaring it will: (i) assume all of the obligations undertaken by Licensee hereunder; (ii) acknowledge that it has satisfied itself that the Licensor's right to license same are valid and incontestable; and (iii) covenant not to directly or indirectly contest, challenge or deny the validity of any of Licensor's Rights in any forum or for any purpose.

10.   *Insurance.* Licensee agrees to maintain products liability insurance in force in the amount not less than $1,000,000 (one million dollars), and to indemnify Licensor against any and all claims.

11.   *Amendment and Termination.* This agreement may be altered, amended or terminated only in writing and signed by both parties.

In Paragraph 4, the exclusivity is based upon performance. Allow sufficient time for the Licensee to capture the targeted market.

Here's a suggestion: Agree upon the sales volume to attain in five years and have targets of about 20% of this amount in year 1, 40% in year 2, 60% in year 3 and 80% in year 4.

Paragraph 7 says that the Licensee will reimburse you for your costs in exchange for the low royalty rate.

Paragraph 8 says that the Licensee will defend your rights in the event of infringement. This is also in exchange for the low royalty rate.

If a windfall award is granted the Licensee in such a case, your percentage should be about 15%-20% of the net reward.

12.   *Governing Law.* This Agreement shall be interpreted and construed under the laws of the State of _____.

        IN WITNESS WHEREOF, the parties hereto have caused this Agreement to be executed as of the day and years first above written.

Licensor

By: _____
        Licensor's authorized signature

Licensee

By: _____
        Licensee's authorized signature

> *In Paragraph 12, indicate the state in which the license is being generated.*

MODIFYING AGREEMENTS

It is perfectly acceptable to use a general license agreement such as one of the preceding examples and insert names, addresses, products, etc. It is also perfectly acceptable to modify the agreement by crossing out words or inserting additional language. If you do so, here are three guidelines to follow:

1. **Crossing out.** Cross out words with a single, bold horizontal line. Use a ruler, line it up over the words and strike a line directly through the middle of the unwanted words.

2. **Adding words.** A license agreement is usually double-spaced. This makes it easy to add words and/or additional language between the lines. Neatly print the new language between the lines.

3. **Initial any changes.** If you cross out words or add language, *both signors* of the agreement should initial nearby. The changes are invalid without both initials acknowledging them.

WHAT IF A POTENTIAL LICENSOR IS NOT READY TO LICENSE?

There is one particularly good alternative you can pursue. Use a "letter of intent", which is similar to an "option". Letters of intent are not uncommon. Many business people use them for various purposes, so why not as a means of temporarily securing the rights to your invention? A letter of intent allows a marketing company to get a "test drive". The following is a letter of intent from a potential licensee.

Some Licensing Pearls of Wisdom

- *There are no rules of thumb to know how much a royalty should be. Try asking your licensee what he/she thinks is fair. Frequently they will have a larger amount in mind than you!*

- *Never assign a patent for money up front unless it is considered "payment in full". Once assigned, a patent is like a deed conveyed. In other words, don't expect any more payments.*

- *Don't get greedy. If your licensee is taking all the risk, then it should get the largest share of the profit. Greed is the #1 deal-killer for inventors.*

- *Experienced negotiators, licensors and licensees never let attorneys negotiate for them. That is why attorneys carry the nickname, "deal killer". You and your licensees reach a mutual Win/Win agreement, then afterward, run it by your attorney to dot the "i's" and cross the "t's".*

LETTER of INTENT

Dear _____ (Licensor)

We, _____ (Potential Licensee), are prepared to enter into a licensing agreement for the _____ invention with _____ (Licensor) as follows:

Invention: Put in a description of the invention.

Patent: The invention is as described under U.S. Patent Application No. _____.

Exclusivity: In the territory of the U.S. and Canada.

Royalties: _____ percent (__%) of net sales. Net sales are defined as invoice price less freight, discounts and rebates. The royalty will be reduced with higher volume sales, as we will agree upon in the license agreement.

Payment of Costs: All costs for patenting in the U.S. and Canada and all R&D costs incurred by Licensor will be paid by _____ (Potential Licensee).

Timing: The License Agreement will be executed within 90 days of the signing of this Letter of Intent.

Undertakings of Potential Licensee:
- To test market the _____ during the 90 day period. This will entail any equipment conversions required, assessment of the economics to manufacture as well as the evaluation of value added pricing in the market.
- Following the above assessments and determination of market demand, _____ (Potential Licensee) will broaden supply capability and expand sales.
- _____ (Potential Licensee) agrees to pay Licensor an advance against royalties in the amount of $_____ as follows:

$_____ upon signing.
$_____ in 30 days.
$_____ in 60 days.

Undertakings of Licensor:
- To provide a valid U.S. and Canadian patent within _____ years of signing this agreement.
- Work with _____ (Potential Licensee) to develop a marketing plan.
- Work with _____ (Potential Licensee) to develop future improvements.

> In these paragraphs, a friendly agreement is struck between you as the Licensor and your potential Licensee. If you are generating the letter, don't fill in the blanks of a form letter, but create a new one with the pertinent information.

It is our desire for the two parties to enter into a mutually beneficial agreement that will provide both of us profit in the years to come.

Sincerely,

Signed (Your name)

HUMAN NATURE AND LICENSING

Licensing is best accomplished as early as possible and is best done when you have established relationships. Keep in mind that you should enter into licensing relationships based on mutual benefit to both parties. The best way to do this is keep human nature in mind. Here are a few suggestions:

- **Be friendly.** People like doing business with friends. Smart businesspeople know that if they can become friends with the other party at the beginning, they are more likely to have a successful business relationship. You can do this too. Try to discover your mutual interests and spend some time apart from business to get to know one another. It certainly can't hurt.

- **Be positive.** Keep in mind that a license can be threatening to the other party. Maintain a positive approach to your licensing activities, proceed in a positive manner and solve the problems that are presented. Your attitude will encourage the other party to be positive as well.

- **Be understanding.** Not everyone is willing to enter into a licensing agreement or understanding of what it takes to launch new products. A licensee is naturally conservative in guarantees, since much of what they are doing may be unfamiliar.

- **Don't be greedy.** Inexperienced inventors tend to think that their inventions are so incredible that huge royalties are in order. This is rarely the case. The number of license agreements that are killed due to unreasonable royalty demands is staggering!

- **Be happy.** When you have succeeded in signing a license agreement, go out and celebrate. Be happy about it and remember the feeling, because that feeling will help you strive for many more successes.

Remember All Those Who Persisted and Won

History is laden with stories about those who persisted and won in the end. Charles Darrow, Monopoly, Tesla and AC electricity, even George Washington and Benjamin Franklin during the American Revolution, were all winners in the long run.

If you maintain a spirited, persistent effort, you too will eventually get what you want. Think about it...if you make a commitment to learn all there is to learn and to do all the right things, you can't even stop yourself! There's only one thing that can stop you from achieving your dream. Know what it is?

There's another thing to remember too. When someone tells you "no", then tell them "thank you"! Why? Well, this only means one thing...that is...you are that much closer to hearing a "yes!"

> *Licensing is the culmination of your invention activities and what most inventors seek. Once you have achieved one success, you will be motivated to create many more. Continue to invent and license and you will have the best time of your life! ...Bob DeMatteis*

CONCLUSION

Look, I have been inventing for quite awhile and have seen incredible things happen. By reading this book you will have taken the right step in the right direction. As you move forward do not rush--take your time, learn all that you can learn. Your creativity and your commitment to seeing the job through will get you to a certain level. Once you reach that level you might find yourself on unfamiliar ground. I hope this book provides you with a road map to answer some of those questions.

I have been very lucky in my career. I have had many opportunities to learn from failures--this is normal. If you feel something is wrong--or your invention development is stymied, remember:

1. Don't despair.
2. Have you checked out all the alternatives?
3. Always remember what you have learned for future reference.

Should you have any questions regarding this book, you may find it helpful to review our Web site: www.frompatenttoprofit.com. You'll also find a list of seminars and workshops throughout the country that I conduct along with other experts in the field. If you like, you can call us at 1-888-53-PATENT (1-888-537-2836) to get a listing of these workshops.

I sincerely wish you the best in your invention activities!

APPENDIX
INVENTOR RESOURCES

INVENTOR EDUCATION RESOURCES

IPT (Inventions, Patents and Trademarks Co.): Bob DeMatteis is also the creator of the *From Patent to Profit* workshops now available throughout the Western U.S. and expanding nationwide. These workshops are given by Bob or another expert. They are based upon the book, *From Patent to Profit* and give first-time and experienced inventors the ability to learn hands-on the *From Patent to Profit* system. IPT is also an ever-expanding resource for inventor-related books and materials. These materials include: (1) *Resource Guide*, patent filing forms, confidentiality agreements, invention disclosures and license agreement you can copy for your personal use; (2) *Inventor's Journal*, a log book made just for inventors; (3) *From Patent to Profit* audio cassette tape series which includes the *Think-Book*; and more. For more information about the workshops and products, call IPT at 1-888-53-PATENT (1-800-537-2836) or go to their Web site at **www.frompatenttoprofit.com**. Bookmark the site as you will find it to be an ever expanding educational resource for inventors.

NCIIA (National Collegiate Inventors and Innovators Alliance): Sponsored by the Lemelson Foundation, this tremendous resource supports colleges and universities that teach invention, innovation and entrepreneurship. The NCIIA provides grants for the establishment of E-teams (Excellence teams) in order to develop some of the student projects. It is also a resource for curricula, patent advice and services, technology transfer and assistance in locating business incubators and enterprise development organizations, industry experts and sources of capital.

INVENTOR ORGANIZATIONS:

United Inventor Association of the U.S.A. Provides members with the following services: (1) Identifying reputable services; (2) updating members regarding developments in the patent reform process; (3) promotes and advocates small inventors at the national level; (4) facilitates communication and networking amongst the nation's inventor groups. For more information, contact Carol Oldenburg, Administrator, at P.O. Box 23447, Rochester, NY 14692-3447, 716-359-9310.

National Congress of Inventor Organizations: The National Congress of Inventor Organizations is the oldest cooperative inventor organization in the United States. For more information contact the president, Stephen Gnass or Marsi at P.O. Box 93669, Los Angeles, CA 90003, 213-878-6952.

TRADESHOWS:

Invention Convention® The one and only invention related tradeshow on the planet where you can find legitimate licensees and write orders for your new products. It is the single best invention tradeshow where you can learn how to propel your invention efforts forward. For more information, call 1-800-458-5624, or, look them up on the Internet at **www.inventionconvention.com.** If you are new to the world of inventing, you will not want to miss the Invention Convention® held annually in Pasadena, California over Labor Day weekend.

Tradeshow Central: The most extensive tradeshow resource available anywhere is on the Internet. In fact, it is not worth it to mention any others. Use their search engine to locate national, regional and local tradeshows at **www.tscentral.com**.

LICENSING AND MARKETING CONTACTS:

Arthur D. Little Enterprises, Inc.: This famous company develops new ideas and innovations and has a high degree of success. But they only take on those inventions that they are sure will be big winners. If you think your invention fits, send them a summary. For information on submitting proposals to Arthur D. Little Enterprises, contact the Manager, New Business Development, 15 Acorn Park, Cambridge, MA 02140, 617- 498-6685 or send an Email to **coriat.d@adlittle.com.**

Dirt Devil: Primary brand name of Royal Appliance Mfg. Co. They are aggressively searching for new mass-consumer products in the areas of home maintenance, yard maintenance and cleaning. Contact Ken Robbins, agent for Royal at 404-233-0332 for a submission form.

Accessory Brainstorms. Topsy Tail, Hairdini and Wonderbrella are among the products marketed by these experts. Representing fashion, beauty and lifestyle products, Joan Lefkowitz's company sells to Television Shopping Channels, Infomercials, Mail Order Catalogues and retailers. Contact Joan at 5 West 36th Street, Suite 500, New York, NY, 10018, 212-971-7300.

SnS International. Specialize in the home and bath industry, but not necessarily limited to them. Contact Darren Quon at 18850 Ventura Bl. #221, Tarzana, CA 91356, 818-345-4346.

Aztech: Evaluates inventions in the field of products for aging and persons with disabilities. You can call and ask for Jeffrey Kohler at 716-833-7870, ext. 23. You can also visit their Web site at: http://cosmos.ot.buffalo.edu

The Hook Appropriate Technology: Hal Meyer works for inventors to help them find marketers and manufacturers to license their inventions. He earns money based only upon results. He will also list certain technologies wanted at his Web site. Contact The Hook at 52 Bank St. Suite A, New Milford, CT 06776-2706, 1-800-HOOK-VOX, or check out the Internet site at **www.thehooktek.com.**

Vogel Applied Technologies & Brainwave. David Vogel has had many successes in introducing new toy ideas to industry. Contact him at 36 East 12th St., New York, NY 10003, 212-677-3136.

IMG Technologies. High powered, high-volume, sports related licensees and marketers. They have licensed many of the everyday sports innovations we use today. Contact Stuart Jenkins, 3075 E. Thousand Oaks Bl., Thousand Oaks, CA 91362, 805-379-1328 or Ted Meekma at One Erieview Plaza, Suite 100, Cleveland, OH 44114, 216-522-1200.

R.E.P.S. Gift related items you want to get *sold!* Contact Beverly Ulvan, R.E.P.S., Los Angeles Gift Mart, 1933 So. Broadway, Suite 850-A, Los Angeles, CA 90007, 714-786-0263.

Manufacturers' Agents National Association: Commonly referred to as MANA, this is a highly professional organization of manufacturers' representatives in virtually every industry. Since manufacturers' reps make great marketing experts, you can advertise in their monthly publication in search of such experts. They can be contacted at 23016 Mill Creek Road, P.O. Box 3467, Laguna Hills, CA 92654-3467, 714-859-4040.

Gray Electronics, Inc.: Phil Henry, president is looking for electronics products, scanners, etc. for consumer use. Gray Electronics licenses a few good inventions every year. Located in Las Vegas area. Contact: Phil Henry, President, Gray Electronics, Inc. 1843 Somersby Way, Green Valley, NV 89014, 702-456-9660 or go to the internet site at **Phenry.com/gray**.

Solve-It Marketing Co.: For free evaluations and marketing assistance and referrals, contact Harold Westbrook at 4990 Speak Lane, Suite. 280, San Jose, CA 95118, 1-800-771-8348.

West Coast Innovations: Derek J. Gable seeks toy inventions and will help you package them for presentation to major manufacturers. Contact him at 7246 Avenida Altisima, Rancho Palos Verdes, CA 90275, 310-541-6953

Nordic Track: Seeks new inventions in the in-home fitness field. They would like to hear from you; call them at 1-800-967-2113 and ask for your submission packet.

Safety Components International: For safety and security related technologies, contact Lisa Zummo, 7580 E. Gray Rd., Suite 102, Scottsdale, AZ 85260, 602-596-9811.

GeeWhiz Inc. Toy Mfg.: John DeCesare looks for new toy ideas from inventors. Contact him at 169 Hillside Ave., Glen Ridge, NJ 07028, 201-680-1459, or on the Internet at **jjdjjdjjd@aol.com**.

Excel Development Group, Inc.: Places new toys worldwide. Contact Andrew Berton, 1721 Mount Curve Ave., Minneapolis, MN 55403-1017, 612-374-3233, **Exceld@aol.com.**

Tovard Products, Inc.: Seeks toy ideas. Contact Richard Leeb, 1425 SW 20th, Suite 101, Portland, OR 97201, 503-228-3231.

Kraco Enterprises: Looking for aftermarket auto accessories. Contact Brad Kraines, 505 E. Euclid Ave., Compton, CA 90224, 310-639-0666.

Educational Products: Hearlihy & Company is seeking technology and curriculum related products for middle level schools. Contact Scott Papenfus at 714 W. Columbia St., Springfield, OH 45504.

Rectorseal Corporation. Seeks plumbing, HVAC related products, contact Laura Fishman, P.O. Box 14669, 2830 Produce Row, Houston, TX 77221-4699, 1-800-231-3345.

OfficePro, Inc.: For office related products call Mark Kozhin, 104-70 Queens Bl., Suite 300, Forest Hills, NY 11375.

Perrin Mfg. Co.: This company is seeking kitchen and bath, hardware, stationery and automotive aftermarket accessories. Contact Mitchell C. Carson at P.O. Box 1320, City of Industry, CA 91749, **www.perrin.com**.

WestBend Co.: For household appliances, contact Chris Gessner, New Products Dept., 400 Washington St., West Bend, WI 53095.

Better Sleep Co.: Interested in new bathroom accessories. Contact them at 80 Industrial Rd., Berkeley Heights, NJ 07922, 908-464-2200.

Supertyre: For certain specialty aftermarket automotive products, contact Barbara Olson at 225 Broadway, 19th Floor, San Diego, CA 92101, 619-460-6161.

Inno-pak: If you have a packaging related invention that can be used in the bakery, deli, produce and supermarket or fast foods industry, contact Jon Sill at 163 North Sandusky St., Suite 202, Delaware, OH 43015, 614-363-0090.

L.H. Dottie: For electrical and plumbing fasteners and fitting for the residential and commercial trade, you can contact Lane Satnick at 6131 So. Garfield Avenue, Commerce, CA 90040, (213) 725-1000.

Erico Products Inc. (Caddy Fasteners): For electrical fasteners for the commercial/industrial trade, contact New Products Development, 34600 Solon Rd., Cleveland, OH 44139, 216-248-0100.

The Creative Group. They look to help you license toys, juvenile and baby products, hobby, health and beauty and dentistry to industry. Contact them at 400 Main St., Suite 210, Stamford, CN 06901, 203-359-3500, or toll free at 800-678-5306.

WIN: Walmart Innovation Network will take and evaluate submissions. For a complete information packet, contact Walmart Innovation Network, Southwest Missouri State University, Center for Business and Economic Development, 901 South National Avenue, Springfield, MO 65804, (417) 836-5671.

members.aol.com/morlicense/page6.htm John Morehead has 25 years experience. This web page can lead to locating manufacturers that are seeking licensing.

American Seminar Leaders Association: To learn how to effectively use seminars to help launch your new innovations and products, contact June Davidson at 2405 E. Washington Bl., Pasadena, CA 91104, 1-800-735-0511 or 626-791-1211.

Baby Net: Is a place where you can locate 400+ manufacturers of baby, toddler and juvenile products. Contact them at 23521 Foley St. Hayward, CA 94545 or on the Internet at www.thebabynet.com/manufacturers.htm.

QVC: For a kit to learn how to submit your new product to QVC, call 610-701-1000.

The Shopping Network: For information on submitting new products, call 813-572-8585, Ext. 4750.

bigbook.com This is a great search site to look for all types of companies. It always seems to produce excellent results regardless of the type of product you are marketing. It does not focus on invention related products, but it is more thorough than any other business related internet site including the Internet Thomas Register.

TRADE MAGAZINES:

PATNEWS: A daily news service with topics including worldwide Patent Office news, stories about who is suing who, interesting new patents, styles of patent drafting, statistics on issued patents (focus on software), reviews of patent books and computer programs, and biting commentary if Greg happens to be in a lousy mood that morning. To subscribe, send the message "NEWS" to patents@world.std.com. Please include some information on what you do and how you might use this patent news source.

Inventor's Digest: The best inventor publication available anywhere in the world. Contact ID at 310 Franklin St., Suite 24, Boston, MA 02110, 1-800-838-8808.

www. Rjriley.com/news/rjriley-trade-pub.html. On the Internet, look up Ron Riley's site to locate trade magazines in the field of your invention.

www.penton.com/corp/mags/index.html. Another Internet site to locate trade magazines.

Dream Merchant: Contact John Moreland at 2309 Torrance Bl. Suite 104, Torrance, CA 90501, 310-328-1925.

PROTOTYPING AND MANUFACTURING:

Compression: This is probably the leading prototyping company in the world. Yet, they are not too big for small, independent inventors (they were such inventors when they literally created the prototyping business a couple of decades ago). For information on the location nearest you contact their office at 13765 Alton Parkway, Suite B, Irvine, CA 92618, 714-586-5891.

T2Design: Experts in invention prototyping and product design. Contact Paul Berman at 1650 Tenth Street, Santa Monica, CA 90404-3706, 310-581-1926.

America Invents: Ken Tarlow is a well-known prototype expert. Contact him at 21 Golden Hind Passage, Corte Madera, CA 94925, 415-927-1728, fax: 415-927-1768.

Master Tool & Die: Specializing in metal stamping design, development and manufacturing. Contact Dave Ferber, President, at 2921 Miraloma, #1, Anaheim, CA 92806, 714-632-8957.

CADDCO, Inc.: Provides CAD drawings for a variety of purposes and specializes in concept drawings for presentations and prototyping. Can help specify material types as well. Contact Tim Strandberg at 2571 360th Street, Dayton, IA 50530, 515-547-2867. Or, visit their web site at **www.netins.net/showcase/caddco.**

CMTC (California Manufacturing Technology Center): This state agency helps inventors and manufacturers turn their inventions into real products. They have a large resource of smart people to tap. Contact them at 151 N. Sunrise, #1108 Roseville, CA 95661, 916-773-6472 for the office nearest you.

Local colleges and universities: Don't forget that most local colleges and universities have metal, plastic and woodworking shops that can help you develop your ideas into prototypes. Some will charge you and some won't. The quality is generally excellent.

bigbook.com This is a great search site to look for manufacturers (who might even be good marketers) anywhere in the U.S. More thorough than any phone book and probably has more listings than the Thomas Register, albeit not as thorough.

www.thomasregister.com The famous Thomas Register is available on line, although not as complete as the volumes you can find in the library.

PACKAGING:

INTEPgroup: Some of the smartest package designers on the planet, they can boost any invention's sales dramatically. Contact Leo Shemza at 528 Mateo, Los Angeles, CA 90013, 213-589-1555.

Medici Alliance: Internationally renowned packaging and product positioning specialists at your service. You will be impressed. Contact Michael Spinelli-Medici at his San Diego office at 1010 University Avenue, San Diego, CA 92103, 619-291-9292.

New York Design Studio. A high-profile design company can help you perfectly match up your image to your target market. Contact their office at: 516-569-8888.

Local colleges and universities: Many local colleges and universities have art departments that can help you with package design. In particular, you can hire students at some reasonable rates. The quality is generally pretty good, but they are usually no match for seasoned professionals.

PATENT ATTORNEYS AND AGENTS:

Beehler and Pavitt: Highly experienced counsel, contact Bill Pavitt or David A. Belasco at 100 Corporate Pointe, Suite 330, Culver City, CA 90230, 310-215-3183.

Douglas English: Specializing in patents for independent inventors anywhere in the U.S. Also, ask Doug about obtaining "legal insurance". Contact Doug at his virtual office at 1-800-544-5677, or County Square Professional Offices, 674 County Square Dr. Suite 201, Ventura, CA 93003.

George Morgan: An inventor and now Registered Patent Agent can be contacted at 401 Tyler Avenue, Evansville, IN 47715-3243, 812-476-4065.

Norton Townsley: Contact Norton at his office at 100 Corporate Pointe, Suite 330, Culver City, CA 90230, 310-645-7259.

M.I.P.S.: Millord's Intellectual Property Services: Registered Patent Practitioner, Millord Keshishzadeh, J.D., can be contacted at 1925 Century Park East, Suite 500, Los Angeles, CA 90067, 310-203-2240.

Robert Platt Bell & Associates, P.C.: An ex-patent examiner, contact Robert Bell at 917 Duke St., Alexandria, VA 22314-3648, 703-683-8823.

Patent Venture and Law Group: Gene Scott is a Registered Patent Agent. Contact him at 3151 Airway Avenue, Suite K-105, Costa Mesa, CA 92626, 1-800-74-PATENTS or 714-668-1900.

Andrew Pierce: Andrew is an experienced patent attorney who can be contacted at 161 McCracken Drive, Seneca, SC, 29678, 864-972-0603.

U.S. Patent Office: Provides a publication called, "USPTO's list of Attorneys and Agents Registered to Practice before the USPTO". It is available at the many Patent and Trademark Depository Libraries or can be purchased from the Government Printing Office. You can also call the U.S. Patent Office at 1-800-PTO-9199 for the PTDL near you.

PATENT SEARCHING:

IPT: The Best Patent Search on Earth: A limited number of patent searches and invention evaluations are conducted by IPT. They include a domestic and worldwide search at the USPTO by an experienced searcher. However, it is more important to know if your invention--based upon the search report--has commercial value. You don't want to chase a false dream. You can find all this out plus receive guidance on your manufacturing, marketing and licensing direction from accomplished inventors/marketers. For more information, call IPT at 1-888-53-PATENT (1-800-537-2836), or visit their Web site at http://www.frompatenttoprofit.com.

Gregory Aharonian, Source Translation & Optimization: Greg is a master searcher, and particularly in the field of software patents, where there is probably no one better. Contact Source Translation & Optimization at P.O. Box 404, Belmont, MA 02478, 617-489-3727 or visit his Web site at srctran@world.std.com.

U.S. Patent and Trademark Depository Libraries. Located throughout the U.S., you can try a hand at doing your own preliminary patent search. Their experts will help show you how (but they won't do it for you!). For more information on the U.S. Patent and Trademark Depository Library near you call 1-800-PTO-9199.

GOVERNMENT ASSISTANCE:

U.S. Patent and Trademark Depository Libraries: Are helpful for conducting patent and trademark searches. Some allow teleconferences directly with the U.S. Patent Office. They are always helpful and are enjoyable places to visit. They also provide some seminars and workshops for inventors. For more information on the U.S. Patent and Trademark Depository Library near you call 1-800-PTO-9199.

SBDC (Small Business Development Centers): Big Brother can help! The SBDCs are almost always willing to provide strong counsel to inventors/innovators. The SBDC starts you out on the early stages and its big sister, the SBA, will take over from there. They have over 1000 offices throughout the U.S. If you are starting out, this might be one of the most valuable first steps you take! For more information, go to their Internet Web site at http://www.asbdc-us.org/delivery.htm.

Manufacturer's Assistance Program: Sponsored by the California SBDC, this is a powerful tool when seeking out the manufacture of a new product. For information, contact Kay Graham at 530-885-5488.

U.S. Copyright Office, Library of Congress: For copyright information contact the U.S. Copyright Office, Library of Congress, Washington, DC 20559-6000. They also have an internet site at **cweb.loc.gov**. You can download copyright forms at this web site.

Federal Trade Commission: If you want to verify that a company which you have contacted is not under scrutiny of the FTC and Project Mousetrap, call 202-326-2222. To find out the latest news as it is announced, call the FTC 202-326-2710 or visit their Web site at http://www.ftc.gov.

INTERNET SITES:

www.frompatenttoprofit.com This Web site is the leading Web site on the Internet for education in inventing. It is dedicated as a reference site to make sure you get started in the right direction and stay on track afterward. Keep up to date on all the best publications and inventor education aids to help you on your journey to success. Bookmark this Web site to ensure your continued success.

www.gibbsgroup.com This Award Winning Web site created by Internet wizard Andy Gibbs is a must for inventors. Keep up with news (Eye on IP) on the world of inventing and patenting and keep in touch with new inventor resources on the Internet. You can also offer your invention for sale at this Web site.

inventnet.com InventNET is a central point of the inventor's community in cyberspace. One of the most incredible services it has is its List Serve (the Inventor's Meeting Place). Here you can join in an Email discussion group with experts from all over the world. InventNET also has many other services for inventors/innovators. Bookmark this site to ensure your success.

www.thehooktek.com/links This single web page has a huge volume of links to just about every possible invention and patent related site on the planet. Visit Hal Meyer's site and get the newest, most updated links available.

http://patent.womplex.ibm.com IBM's site has patent searches available with full texts. Also has some availability to list inventions available for licensing.

http://web.mit.edu/invent/ This is a super informative at MIT University and a fun site to visit. Includes Invention Dimension with lots of great information on inventors and inventions.

www.uspto.gov U.S. Patent Office web page. A thorough overview of what is going on at the Patent Office. Limited patent searching showing only the abstract and patents back to 1972.

cnidr.org A joint venture between the U.S. Patent Office and Digital computer. You can do the same patent searches as those at the USPTO web site.

www.clari.net/brad/copymyths.html A very good informative site addressing basic copyright laws.

www.bus.gov Want to sell to the government? Here is a one-stop electronic link to government business and how to do it.

www.ftc.gov The Federal Trade Commission has an internet site where you can keep abreast of fraudulent inventor scam companies. Included is information on the recent bust from Project Mousetrap that seized the assets and indicted seven companies, indicted at least fifteen other companies and ten or more individuals.

INTERNET NEWSGROUPS:

alt.inventors If you have a little time, this is a good site to visit where you can post your questions. It has some very interesting and heated discussions at times.

misc.int.property This group is similar to the alt.inventors group but more focused on the legal side of patents, trademarks and copyrights.

INVENTOR ADVOCATE GROUPS:

Alliance for American Innovation, Inc.: This is your bodyguard for protecting small entities and independent inventors patent rights in Washington DC. Contact them at 1100 Connecticut Ave. NW, Suite 1200, Washington, DC 20036, 202-293-1414.

278

FROM PATENT TO PROFIT ℠

STRATEGIC GUIDE ™

	A	B	C	D	E	F
I — INVENTION TIMELINE	Get an idea. Date: ☑	Brainstorm to develop the idea into a potential product. Date: ☐	Determine whether you are going to manufacture the product or if you will need a company to make it for you. Date: ☐	Make a general design prototype if you can. Think about various trademark and service mark possibilities. Date: ☐	With the general design prototype—and with your marketing expert's input—determine the best size, shape, color, etc. Date: ☐	Continue to refine prototype to test best attributes with your sales and manufacturing partners. Date: ☐
II — PATENTING TIMELINE	Learn all you can about patenting. Take seminar series "From Patent to Profit." Date: ☐	Write an invention disclosure. Have it witnessed or notarized. Date: ☐	Conduct and evaluate a patent search on the internet and/or through the U.S. Patent and Trademark Depository Library. Date: ☐	Begin writing provisional patent application. Date: ☐	Interview patent attorneys and agents if you do not already have one. Date: ☐	Continue writing provisional patent application. Date: ☐
III — MANUFACTURING TIMELINE		How can the invention be manufactured? Who can help you determine the best process? Date: ☐	Prepare a list of potential manufacturing or import partners. Interview them by phone, letters or at trade shows, etc., with simple "product summaries." Date: ☐	Have best potential candidates sign confidentiality agreements before meeting in person and revealing details of your invention. Date: ☐	Weigh the producer's enthusiasm and commitment to manufacture. Date: ☐	Based upon strategy, appoint or license the manufacturer. Date: ☐
IV — MARKETING TIMELINE		Ask yourself, "Where can my invention be sold? In what fields?" Date: ☐	Seek potential sales experts and interview them by phone, mail, or trade shows, etc., with simple "product summaries." Date: ☐	Have best potential candidates sign confidentiality agreements before meeting in person and revealing details of your invention. Date: ☐	If candidate says, "I can sell that," get information on a suggested sell price and sales volume. Date: ☐	Based upon strategy, license or hire your sales expert. Date: ☐

Invention:_____

Inventor:_____

When filling in this 2-page chart, work from left to right on each level.

G   H   I   J   K   L   M

G	H	I	J	K	L	M
Complete and confirm prototype testing with your sales expert. Have your manufacturing expert confirm its ability to produce.	Oversee the in-house testing of the working models.	Give input into the tests and any assistance to sales experts in developing and finalizing brochures and so on.	Continue to oversee project and offer assistance as required.	Assist in overseeing first test market if you can. Gather valuable information, watch for red flags.	Based upon test market results, begin thinking about future improvements or companion products and markets.	Confirm with your sales expert which improvements are best. Then, do it all again!
Date: ____ ☐	Date: ____ ☐	Date: ____ ☐	Date: ____ ☐	Date: ____ ☐	Date: ____ ☐	Date: ____ ☐
Continue writing provisional. Include the "preferred embodiments" that have been confirmed during testing.	Remember to include all inventive attributes you can imagine. If new matter and processes were discovered, prepare additional applications.	Before finalizing the provisional patent application(s), ask yourself, "What are the possible design-arounds?"	*File all provisional applications now.* Do not offer for sale or publicly disclose until they are filed.	Register any trademarks, service marks or trade dress you have developed.	Consider patenting overseas by end of first year. Can your licensee pay for this cost?	Before year's end, file the permanent, non-provisional patent application(s). Your attorney prosecutes it.
Date: ____ ☐	Date: ____ ☐	Date: ____ ☐	Date: ____ ☐	Date: ____ ☐	Date: ____ ☐	Date: ____ ☐
Prototype transitions from your crude designs to the manufacturer's real time working models.	Build working models and test in-house.	Solve all problems to the satisfaction of inventor and sales expert.	Testing of working models is completed, producer gears up for production with raw material, shipping materials and so on.	First order(s) shipped to first test market.	Any problems on the first shipment are corrected and manufacturer continues to produce based upon sales.	Manufacturing process is perfected. Expand as required.
Date: ____ ☐	Date: ____ ☐	Date: ____ ☐	Date: ____ ☐	Date: ____ ☐	Date: ____ ☐	Date: ____ ☐
Sales expert starts to develop packaging, specification sheets and price breaks. Sales expert starts thinking about who first customer(s) will be.	Sales expert interacts with manufacturer on the in-house testing of the working models.	Sales expert puts "stamp of approval" on in-house test models. Finalizes brochures, spec sheets, price sheets and so on.	With the provisional applications filed, sales expert officially offers product for sale to the first test market customer(s). This is the first public disclosure.	Sales expert is involved hands-on with the first test market customer to resolve any remaining problems.	With test market problems resolved, sales expert expands sales base—first to a region, then nationwide.	Sales expert prepares to expand sales to new target markets and perhaps *internationally.*
Date: ____ ☐	Date: ____ ☐	Date: ____ ☐	Date: ____ ☐	Date: ____ ☐	Date: ____ ☐	Date: ____ ☐

© 1997, 1998, 1999 Bob DeMatteis Co. and IPT Co.

Bob DeMatteis

Years ago, Bob DeMatteis had an idea he wanted to pursue. He pursued that dream, patented it, and today is a successful inventor-marketer with 14 U.S. patents and 6 pending. Sales of his inventions exceed $25 million a year and are used by national giants such as Sears, Walmart and Kroger. You have most likely used some of Bob's innovations at one time or another. . .when you carry your merchandise in one of the stores' printed plastic bags.

What is interesting is that Bob's inventions and patents do not focus on engineering or scientific advances, but on making products "people friendly". He quickly became an innovative leader in the packaging industry by developing packaging systems in niche markets.

Bob has a passion and a commitment to getting his inventions developed and producing income. He focuses on people's true needs. He enjoys tackling potentially insurmountable problems and always strives to continuously improve. A secret to his success has been the ability to get a new invention marketed quickly and producing profit during the patent pending phase.

Bob had another dream recently. . . that is, teaching others how they too can realize their dreams. He enjoys teaching just as much as patenting and inventing. Bob developed a seminar series called *From Patent to Profit*™. These exciting seminars help inventors, innovators, entrepreneurs, small businesses and those who have ideas they want to develop, patent their ideas and make money at little or no cost. His friendly and enthusiastic manner of training gets rave reviews from seminar participants.

Bob has written four books: *The Art of Innovating; The Art of Patenting; The Art of Licensing and Marketing* and *From Patent to Profit*. These step-by-step information-packed books were written from his years of experience, and for novice inventors they are the most easy-to-read innovation and patenting books available in the U.S. today. Bob is also widely published on the Internet and in magazines such as *Inventor's Digest*.

Bob is a nationally known inventor, author, and educator. He is the founder of the American Innovation Workshops, a certified Seminar Leader of the American Seminar Leaders Association and Advisor to several small company development organizations funded by federal and state governments, such as the SBDC. He is also a contributor and in-demand speaker at dozens of colleges and universities, the Patent and Trademark Depository Libraries and many inventor organizations throughout the United States.

INDEX

IPT Co

Call us toll-free to charge your order: 1-888-53-PATENT
FAX: 530-274-1288

15850 McCourtney Rd. Grass Valley, CA 95949, (530) 477-2750

Ordered by: **Date:** _____   ☐ **Ship to:**

_____   _____

_____   _____

Phone: _____

Item No.	Description	Price each	Quantity	Price
	From Patent to Profit Book	$29.95		
	From Patent to Profit Tape Series	39.95		
	The Art of Patenting Book	9.95		
	The Art of Innovating Book	9.95		
	The Art of Licensing & Marketing Book	9.95		
	Resource Guide	9.95		
	Invention Journal *Colors:* ○ Blue ○ Tan ○ Paprika	12.95		
	From Patent to Profit Video	19.95		
	Home Study Course	74.95		

Method of Payment: Please include credit card number and expiration date with charge orders.

☐ Charge to my (*circle one*):
Discover   Visa
MasterCard
American Express

☐ Check or Money order   X _____
Signature (as shown on credit card)

Expiration Date   mo. ____ / yr. _____

Charges for Shipping & Handling	
Total Price	S.&H.
$0-12.00	$2.50
$12.01-35.00	$4.25
$35.01-70.00	$5.75
$70.01 +	$6.95

Total price of items	
USA Shipping	
Sub Total	
Tax	
☐ PAID **Total**	

IPT Co

Call us toll-free to charge your order: 1-888-53-PATENT
FAX: 530-274-1288

15850 McCourtney Rd. Grass Valley, CA 95949, (530) 477-2750

Ordered by: **Date:** _____   ☐ **Ship to:**

_____   _____

_____   _____

Phone: _____

Item No.	Description	Price each	Quantity	Price
	From Patent to Profit Book	$29.95		
	From Patent to Profit Tape Series	39.95		
	The Art of Patenting Book	9.95		
	The Art of Innovating Book	9.95		
	The Art of Licensing & Marketing Book	9.95		
	Resource Guide	9.95		
	Invention Journal *Colors:* ○ Blue ○ Tan ○ Paprika	12.95		
	From Patent to Profit Video	19.95		
	Home Study Course	74.95		

Method of Payment: Please include credit card number and expiration date with charge orders.

☐ Charge to my (*circle one*):
Discover   Visa
MasterCard
American Express

☐ Check or Money order   X _____
Signature (as shown on credit card)

Expiration Date   mo. ____ / yr. _____

Charges for Shipping & Handling	
Total Price	S.&H.
$0-12.00	$2.50
$12.01-35.00	$4.25
$35.01-70.00	$5.75
$70.01 +	$6.95

Total price of items	
USA Shipping	
Sub Total	
Tax	
☐ PAID **Total**	